Praise for *Brai*

'Pick has an expert understanding of our hidden drives [and] *Brainwashed* is thorough and illuminating, its pages thick with fascinating case studies and meditations about the mind. This thought-provoking book will make you think differently about our paranoid world, your own mind and the maddening distrust between them' *Financial Times*

'A clarion call for better ways of thinking and better politics. Daniel Pick is an intelligent, thoughtful, well-read psychoanalyst who is always worth reading' David Aaronvitch, *The Times*

'An extraordinarily engrossing and wide-ranging analysis of a word and a concept. I fell under its spell immediately' Simon Garfield

'Pick is well-placed to write a fascinating history of thought control … he has produced a superbly researched and highly readable book, which could not be timelier' *Jewish Chronicle*

'A great preoccupation of the twentieth century was the suspicion that our minds were being manipulated through hypnotism, advertising, fake news, brainwashing and the like. Importantly, this suspicion arose in democratic as well as totalitarian societies. Where did it come from and why has it been so hard to shake? Daniel Pick, who is both a psychoanalyst and an historian, has here taken a great step toward answering this question' Professor Eli Zaretsky, author of *Secrets of the Soul: A Social and Cultural History of Psychoanalysis* and Professor of History, New School for Social Research

'Daniel Pick's book is a fascinating exploration of brainwashing, advertising and other mind manipulations. Focusing on the second half of the twentieth century but bringing the story right up to date with a penetrating consideration of recent conspiracy theories, it is absorbing, accessible, scholarly and of profound contemporary importance' Stephen Frosh, Professor of Psychology, Birkbeck, University of London

'Fabulous – both brilliant as history and penetrating about the present' Lisa Appignanesi, Royal Society of Literature

'A guide to the frightening place where the science of the mind and the politics of paranoia come together' Vassili Christodoulou, *How To Academy*

Daniel Pick is a psychoanalyst, historian, writer and broadcaster. A professor emeritus at Birkbeck, University of London, he is also a fellow and training analyst at the British Psychoanalytical Society, and is author of several books on modern cultural history, psychoanalysis, and the history of the human sciences.

wellcome collection

WELLCOME COLLECTION publishes thought-provoking books exploring health and human experience, in partnership with leading independent publisher Profile Books.

WELLCOME COLLECTION is a free museum and library that aims to challenge how we think and feel about health by connecting science, medicine, life and art, through exhibitions, collections, live programming, and more. It is part of Wellcome, a global charitable foundation that supports science to solve urgent health challenges, with a focus on mental health, infectious diseases and climate.

wellcomecollection.org

BRAINWASHED

A NEW HISTORY OF THOUGHT CONTROL

DANIEL PICK

This paperback edition first published in 2023

First published in Great Britain in 2022 by
Profile Books Ltd
29 Cloth Fair
London
ECIA 7JQ
www.profilebooks.com

Published in association with Wellcome Collection

183 Euston Road
London NWI 2BE
www.wellcomecollection.org

1 3 5 7 9 10 8 6 4 2

Typeset in Dante by MacGuru Ltd
Printed and bound in Great Britain by
CPI Group (UK) Ltd, Croydon CRO 4YY

A CIP catalogue record for this book is available from the British Library.

ISBN 978 1 78125 790 6
eISBN 978 1 78283 331 4

To Isobel

CONTENTS

A NOTE TO THE READER

This book was written in another epoch, before Russia invaded Ukraine, claiming that the war was a 'special operation' to 'denazify' its neighbour. On 14 March 2022, a TV editor, Marina Ovsyannikova, interrupted a live news transmission on the Russian station Channel One, bearing a poster that said, 'Stop the war, don't believe the propaganda, here you are being lied to. Russians against war.'

The horrific scenes that dominated the news throughout that month seemed to many observers uncanny – tanks rolling across a European state's borders; cities pulverised; citizens killed in their thousands and displaced in their millions. As this book went to press, NATO was reinforcing Eastern European states with the aim of deterring the Russian leadership from enlarging the conflict. Inside the Kremlin, apparently mired in conspiracy theories, Putin put his nuclear weapons crews on high alert, reviving our collective sense of existential dread. His allies, meanwhile, mooted the possibility of a Korean-style division of Ukraine in future. These dire and potentially apocalyptic military events provide a new context in which to revisit the Cold War era, those decades, after 1945, when new ideas about captive minds, disinformation, propaganda, groupthink and brainwashing gained such prominence.

PREFACE

I have a distant memory from my school days: an interesting lesson, in which a teacher invited us to consider how the media might skew our perceptions. He set our class to work, monitoring the daily news. In one exercise we were required to scan newspapers and magazines, tasked with identifying emotive phrases, noting the slants of editorials, gauging the intended impact of headlines and recognising the hierarchical placement of certain more-or-less 'important' articles on the front or inside pages. We duly cut out snippets, and stuck them into exercise books, with our accompanying critical notes.

Some years later, around the mid-1980s, as a research student, I began wondering about the acres of coverage devoted in the media to a new market measure, the FTSE 100. This is shorthand for the Financial Times Stock Exchange Index of the hundred largest companies by capital value listed on the London Stock Exchange. Reports of the shifting fortunes of that index arrived with the regularity of tides; expert opinion was always on hand about how to construe the outlook, in light of that figure: has the number edged up, slid, plummeted or not budged at all? Are things looking bullish or bearish? Is all well with the world?

Whether you were interested or not, invested or not, I came to realise, this regular flow of information about the FTSE Index was exhibited centre stage in the news, simply part and parcel of the media-driven theatre of modern life.[1] Today, the 'Footsie' still just sits there, as though an incontrovertible barometer of collective health and well-being. That diet of information was and still is regularly fed to us with the same sense of inevitability as are the weather reports. In fact, the two bulletins – the temperature of the air and of the stock market – are frequently announced adjacently. What of all the other stats, I mused, after that first realisation, which might complement, complicate or even substitute the news about the FTSE 100, Nikkei or Dow Jones?

As a university student, first of literature, then of history, I had become steeped in ideas about ideology, social construction, false consciousness, paradigms, mythologies, linguistic turns and discourse analysis. We were taught to be alert to the language we use, the presumptions that we make, the stories we internalise and, as George Lakoff and others put it, the 'metaphors we live by'.[2] The writing of history, we gleaned, was also shaped by a variety of cultural conventions and story-telling techniques. It was a time when the work of Michel Foucault loomed large over our studies in the humanities: so much we had previously taken for granted about the self and society, madness and sanity, normality and perversion, life and death, health and illness, productivity and idleness, crime and punishment was cast into question.

It was in the context of my attempt to grapple with such issues – during an epoch when the benefits of markets in all spheres of life were being heavily promoted, the gross domestic products of nations apprehensively compared, and neoliberal policies developed on both sides of the Atlantic – that I found the media's constant declaration of the singular stock market number increasingly curious, or even suspicious.

What words and models, I wondered, best capture this process of information flow into our lives? Are we educated, accosted, informed, accustomed, acclimatised, habituated, normalised, familiarised, influenced, nudged, conditioned, shaped, manipulated, programmed or maybe even … *brainwashed*, so that we treat the City of London's or Wall Street's dominant position without question, and with all reverence? Inspired by what I'd been taught and read, I found myself thinking harder about those questions and these 'natural' news updates, and how they might relate to a larger package of claims about meaning, value and truth.

But when I expressed this concern to another student, with a different political outlook to mine, he questioned my and others' supposedly 'radical' views, asking if we were the ones who had been conditioned, by books and charismatic teachers. He pointed out that I might be too utopian and / or too cynical in casting doubt on this crucial index; either way, to dispute the automatic newsworthiness of the Footsie, he felt, risked ignoring the importance of business and commerce, and thus of national prosperity and growth; the bread-and-butter concerns (jobs, livelihoods, pensions, etc.) on which we depend.

Lately, I've been reminded of those heated discussions about the conditioning we endure, the influences we succumb to, the measures we use and the ways we then frame them. While I was researching this subject, for example, it was commonplace for critics of the Democrat Obama and the Republican Trump presidencies alike to decry the privileging of Wall Street over Main Street. Commentators denounced Trump's obsessive tweeting of each passing uptick in the value of stocks, warned against the ever more arcane instruments and arrangements of the vast banks and hedge funds (despite the previous near total meltdown of the system), and drew a sharp contrast between the fantastical world of high finance and the 'real economy'. Trump managed to speak to large numbers within an aggrieved, white, 'dispossessed' class of people, who felt ignored by a liberal establishment, even as he catered to the wealthy, offering tax cuts and talking up the Dow, whenever it suited him.[3]

But this kind of debate over the prominence given to such daily news updates – crucial information or mode of conditioning? – is just a skirmish in a much older battle of ideas about religious and secular forms of indoctrination, and the way a vision of reality may envelop us. Over the centuries, many efforts have been made to disenchant communities; to disillusion adherents of religions, as well as to disabuse proponents of, or fellow travellers with, particular ideologies. So much that we may assume as a given fact of nature, or 'plain reality', after all, is the product of a culture and value system. Nietzsche, by offering a genealogy of morals, invited the reader to question, perhaps even transform, their own basic values. Marx talked of religion as the opium of the people, and Freud also speculated about organised faith, under the heading 'the future of an illusion' – which is not to say any of those thinkers had the full measure of religions or were free of illusions themselves. But they were all brilliant analysts, seeking to confront readers with their guiding assumptions or unexamined symptoms.

Marx aspired to awaken the workers from their slumbers and to free them from chains; he claimed that they might have nothing to lose, and he pointed out the potentially deceptive nature of their everyday notions of reality or justice; for instance, the illusion that they entered into a fair trade with employers in 'contracting' their labour in factories, unaware that a surplus was extracted by the capitalist. A system and way of life, Marx and Engels pointed out, might appear solid and then 'melt into air'.

A neurosis too, Freud added, may seem to the sufferer entirely unremarkable; worse, that symptom can be treated as though indispensable for a time, perhaps even a lifetime. He looked at the repressed thoughts and conflicted feelings that might lie behind certain symptoms, for example in cases of hysteria; and he also suggested that everybody is prone to succumb to fantastical wishes and beliefs. Freud once remarked that an aim of psychoanalysis was to help patients to work and to love; on another occasion he expressed the hope that this treatment might assist people to give up hysterical misery and in return accept ordinary, everyday unhappiness. We can tell ourselves all manner of stories about our own minds and the world around us; remain committed, unconsciously, to our neuroses, for fear, rightly or wrongly, of suffering worse fates without them. People may rely unconsciously, he showed, on knotted-up disabling narratives, repetitive mechanisms or what psychoanalysts in more recent times have called 'pathological organisations' and 'psychic retreats' inside the mind. Yet such organisations and retreats, however restrictive and distorting, may harbour us from total chaos.

Moving out of a settled system, or sheltering world of illusions, even delusions, carries risks; perhaps of feeling ashamed, exposed, disorientated or terrified, as the psychoanalyst John Steiner has finely observed.[4] If we are fortunate, we find help from others in navigating difficult impasses and making changes, tolerating the movements that take place in our minds and facing painful disenchantments of one kind or another without getting stuck in a state of apathy, mania or melancholia. To lose former creeds, or idols, can also leave one bereft, as though God has failed, or as though life itself is devoid of meaning. Times of change can be bracing, creative and also bewildering, as imagined solidities melt, and as we try to find new bearings, individually or collectively. We live, the late social theorist Zygmunt Bauman has observed, in an epoch when certain former anchor points have gone – an age, he said, offering us yet one more metaphor, of 'liquid modernity'.[5]

How beliefs mediate people's interpretations of events in the world, and how the environment shapes popular beliefs, has been disputed for centuries. Critique of our former mass political and economic conditioning – critique that had come to my attention, as I have mentioned, during the era of Reagan and Thatcher – is now roaring back into public view, if it ever really went away. For example, compelling new work has appeared by economists which probes the ossified thinking that has too often governed their discipline. They insist we must analyse afresh, and with open minds, basic tenets; look again at what is most valued *and* devalued by policy analysts, law makers and electorates too.[6] Once again the call goes out that we need to be freed from former illusions that once passed as virtually incontestable truths.

Certain assumptions about the world, Kate Raworth remarks in her illuminating 2017 book *Doughnut Economics*, 'slip swiftly into the back of our head, wordlessly whispering the deepest assumptions of economic theory that need never be put into words because they have been inscribed in the mind's eye'. Such images, she suggests, may linger 'like graffiti on the mind'; so much 'intellectual baggage' that comes to be:

> lodged in your visual cortex without you even realising it is there. And – just like graffiti – it is very hard to remove. So if a picture is worth a thousand words then, in economics at least, we should pay a great deal more attention to the pictures that we teach, draw and learn.[7]

In modern society, she shows, selected images, graphs and nuggets of data are illuminated in the media headlights, on a rolling twenty-four-hour news cycle, reflecting and reinforcing a particular way of seeing the world.[8]

A few years after I first began teaching at a college of the University of London, and while I was also training to be a psychoanalyst, a sceptical academic colleague declared to me, 'Ah, so you've been brainwashed to believe in the so-called "talking cure".' He made clear he had never had psychoanalysis, and that he assumed those who did, let alone those who trained in the practice, gave up their critical faculties and bought into the process blindly. Perhaps these risks do exist in any psychotherapy; a procedure supposed to provide an open-minded exploration can be commandeered, in exploitative ways, of course. For example, instead of analysing the unconscious feelings stirred up by the process, the analyst (as Freud had duly warned his colleagues) might misunderstand, or worse, exploit, the patient's transferred passions and apparent 'love'.[9] The patient is in a vulnerable position, and may well idealise, at least for a time, the clinician, the treatment or the theories on which it is based.

A 'talking cure' can exert its own seductive appeal, arouse myriad unconscious ideas and feelings and impose coercive pressures. At worst, such treatment may be co-opted for the analyst's selfish needs, or adapted explicitly in the name of a state, commercial enterprise or political ideology; therapy can morph into a sinister project of conversion and thought control. Freud's method during the twentieth century was appropriated for multiple purposes; the same goes for other modes of therapy and 'psy' disciplines. A peculiar and bowdlerised version of a talking cure had endured even in the Third Reich, and was used in methods of 'group re-education' in the communist world. So, my colleague's fear that a supposed mental health treatment can become a form of 'mental hygiene', an instrument of conditioning, or even might end up as tantamount to brainwashing, has a long and significant history; it is a concern that needs to be taken seriously. And yet despite that warning, I still maintain that psychoanalysis need not be like that; it can be a place of safety and of trust; it has a different, therapeutic potential. The practice can be genuinely exploratory, radically challenging, open-ended; it may well prove supportive, as well as disturbing. Indeed, it may offer a unique place to encounter more of ourselves, away from other demands, providing a means to cast light on our unconscious identifications and idealisations, perhaps even our penchant for zealotry, rather than serve to reinforce them.

Some years after my colleague made that remark, I set myself the task of reading a now largely forgotten literature in the West; a literature that explored the concept of brainwashing, along with others such as 'conditioning', 'groupthink', the 'captive mind', 'hidden persuasion', 're-education', 'mind control' and 'thought reform'. I wanted to understand better what 'brainwashing' really consists in, how the idea arose, and how far it can be of use in understanding the interlocking crises we face in present dark times, when the minimum that is required for creating a viable, sustainable, planetary future for humanity is so much more than the maximum that appears to be deliverable within prevailing economic models and electoral systems. This book is an attempt to think about the past and to see what this language of thought control might tell us as we struggle to respond to the dire state that we are in.

Ideas about brainwashing were explored intensively in the period following the Second World War. Many commentators used this vocabulary in the decades after 1945 because they wanted to open up a new set of questions in political psychology and to issue urgent warnings; to show that modern citizens are at grave risk – through government, commerce, social pressure, cults, modern science, medicine, advertising or secret security services – of warping or losing their minds. *Brainwashed* takes up such ideas and phrases; it shows how they were explored and developed; and it discusses why they still resonate today in a new age of hot and cold wars, caught up in a maelstrom of discourse about fake news, conspiracy, big tech, populism, radicalisation and paranoid political thought.

As I found in researching this topic, brainwashing is a slippery concept, hard to pin down and often contentious. Is the narrative of inevitability implicit in the routine attention paid to the FTSE 100 by assorted anchors, financial analysts, newscasters, hosts and pundits best viewed strictly as brainwashing? Or is that word appropriately reserved for more extreme practices, including those so hideously 'perfected' inside closed societies, cults and compounds? If one wants to be critical of such customary news coverage, then normalising or habituating might perhaps be the more fitting labels. On the other hand, the question of brainwashing is certainly worth considering even in relatively open political systems or institutional settings, in which people can be fed deceptive stories, fantastical promises and false reassurances.

This book not only stakes out positions on brainwashing, but also explores a history of discussions about its provenance, reach and effects. I want to consider this controversial idea and its applications, showing how the problem of brainwashing has been diversely scrutinised or even exploited (one person's brainwasher, another's freedom fighter), and how the notion is often diffuse and difficult to define exactly. My aim is to provide an historical framework for assessing how and why this key word arose, alongside a cluster of associated terms; to investigate how this notion has been used to enhance (or hinder) our capacity to analyse modern societies and psyches; to assess the role played by psychology in contemporary life; and to think about the hazards of thinking itself.

Brainwashed thus places the idea in context and reflects upon its continuing significance, how it might be most usefully located, and where it has previously been most powerfully portrayed. I contend it is worth our investigating how commentary on brainwashing first arose, and how the subject was then shaped, nuanced, challenged and sensationalised. This study invites the reader to look afresh at brainwashing and related conceptions of mind control, influence, pressure and manipulation. It excavates how such ideas have been deployed in the past in many contrasting settings and asks how they might serve to investigate contemporary lived experiences of commerce and culture, society and politics.

'Brainwashing' is a component of a psychological and political language we now seem to assume. It is built into how we might routinely think about minds and societies, and what imperils them. The language we inherit can affect how we view ourselves and other people; perhaps a particular vocabulary proves useful in sharpening understanding. However, it might also work to reorganise or even dull it. Since the dawn of philosophy, groups have met to converse and grapple with the problem of what it means to think logically, or at least what is required to think seriously. In modern times, psychology too has occupied a central role in considering healthy and pathological thought processes, in different phases of life. The psychological professions have played an important part in fashioning how we understand mental conflict and pain, or even how we evaluate a life well or badly lived; they offer many accounts of what it is to be human, perspectives on the way people struggle, for better or worse, with various developmental challenges during what came to be called the 'life cycle'. Through the optic of these 'psy' disciplines, we have inherited numerous theories and thick descriptions about mental health and pathology, hypotheses that may guide how we think about ourselves and feel about others or imagine we once thought and felt long ago. Psychoanalysts, for example, have done a good deal to investigate and consider the minds of babies, and sought moreover to explore the factors that may foster or thwart an infant's capacities to play, think and explore, to love and be loved, to recognise feelings of rage or envy, and to cope with a dread of being hated (or even annihilated). Such clinicians and theorists have written extensively about what factors might enable some people better than others to forgo simplistic views, recognise complexities or allow their own doubts to exist, without being crushed. To tolerate the frustrations of not-knowing, after all, is a prerequisite for learning; or to put it the other way around, if we are to sustain our curiosity, we may well have to bear painful uncertainty.

Historians, philosophers and social scientists, pursuing other methods, have written about the conditions that may make it more-or-less possible for groups and communities to question received assumptions, and to assemble together and freely deliberate, reorganise to meet a new crisis or respond imaginatively to new opportunities. A people may be helped or hampered from even wondering about other ways of organising life, let alone about deciding between different options. Researchers have also charted the development of a host of modern techniques of incarceration, interrogation, propaganda, hidden persuasion, mind control and brainwashing. Each section in the book weaves between such disparate literatures and moves across a variety of modern discussions of 'inner' and 'outer' worlds of human experience. Most especially this study explores a now largely forgotten set of debates, from the Cold War period, about the social, cultural and political forces around us, the agencies and procedures that can hijack and then redirect our own minds. I contend that revisiting the past might assist us in examining new kinds of hidden persuasion and brainwashing in future. In short, this history invites further consideration of the processes that can facilitate or deform our capacities to think for ourselves.

PART 1

BRAINWASHING

Sometimes, a new word emerges that expresses a concept already well understood. A word might bring new ideas to public consciousness, combine notions previously kept apart, describe a thing that nobody had really apprehended before or that everyone knew previously under some other name. Designations may disappear, move to the margins or be redeployed in new contexts, as when we talk of a computer virus or mouse. Old words sometimes become obsolete, or acquire notable new significance and meanings, as we can see, for instance, with a word such as 'queer'. Words may, in some cases, have relatively consistent and stable meanings over long durations; they can also be problematised, reclaimed and re-inflected with each passing year. We make micro-adjustments, as listeners and speakers, attentive to shifting contemporary idioms and slang – noticing, for example, whether the word 'sick', in a certain context, means unwell or amazing.

A word, in other words, may redescribe something already well known, an old wine in a new bottle; or signify an unprecedented phenomenon. It would be inaccurate to think of the internet as just a new expression for an abstract idea that people had already apprehended hundreds of years earlier, even if you might find glimmerings of this proposition in science fiction or technological speculation before our digital age. Yet the concept of poorly paid or repetitive employment existed long before 'McJob' entered the English language (in 1986, to be precise). Words can have multiple meanings, and they may also be weighted with all kinds of distinct nuances, assumptions or moral implications. So, 'McJob' might have quite different resonances when used in, say, a trade union campaign, a stand-up comedy routine, a suicide letter or a snobbish magazine airily describing the lives of the poor. And then again, two people may hear the same word very differently, when uttered by the same speaker.

Whether the word 'brainwashing', first used in English around five years after the end of the Second World War, ushered in a novel way to understand an older reality was itself soon cast into question: pundits argued about whether it was a mere restatement of something that had been fully perceived by previous generations, or a description of an emerging phenomenon that had no prior equivalent in history and public consciousness. Opinions differed about its reality, location and urgency, and its exploitation to generate alarm.

Some commentators suggested that the term captured a distinct and nefarious combination of power and knowledge at work here and now. They warned of a terrifying form of state that had already arrived, at least somewhere abroad. It was, after all, a time when the superpowers were deploying an arsenal of psychological sciences. Others argued that the term merely referred to practices already well rehearsed, and widely understood, long ago. Sceptics also pointed out that the notion might be heavily spun to serve different interests; a rhetorical vehicle for conjuring up a host of imaginary threats, a means of generating panic about fragile minds in modern times.

In September 1950, during the first year of the Korean War, Edward Hunter, an American journalist who had worked in wartime intelligence, and post-war with the CIA, coined (or, more accurately, first popularised) the term brainwashing, and left no doubt for his readers that the problem was important and real.[1] He suggested a profound shift had occurred; new historical conditions existed for governing the mind.[2] In using the term, first in a piece for the *Miami News* and then in other writings and books, he was pointing to what he claimed to be a frightening and rising danger. Hunter described a form of psychological intervention that was being perfected by certain enemy states. This involved a veritable onslaught upon people's minds. Though he recognised some precursors, he would elaborate during the 1950s upon how the brainwashing threat had truly come of age; a deadly *new* amalgam of ideology, technology, medicine and psychological sciences that was now transforming social reality in certain foreign places, but potentially in any state.

Hunter's first article, '"Brain-Washing" Tactics Force Chinese into Ranks of the Communist Party', adapted a commonplace Chinese phrase, 'xǐ nǎo', meaning to wash the brain. That was a euphemism; it was not about cleansing, literally, but rather destroying and substituting. The word's Chinese provenance was highlighted, and this gave more than a clue to the American's most obvious concerns: Mao and his communist revolution.

The warnings from Hunter and his fellow 1950s writers about brainwashing found a willing audience, perhaps primed by earlier dystopian scenarios explored in literature – all those compelling accounts of a supine society, terrorised by omnipotent masters, and/or fed by modern equivalents of ancient 'bread and circuses'. Some writers, such as Aldous Huxley in *Brave New World* (1932), had pictured a future of captivity through anodyne entertainment, sexual so-called liberation and drugs; others, including George Orwell, whose *Nineteen Eighty-Four* was published in 1949, depicted a world where people are broken and held in a state of permanent totalitarian subjection.

By that time much had already been written in the West about both Nazi and Soviet propaganda warfare. During the First and Second World Wars, substantial efforts were made by both sides to target propaganda efforts more efficiently, and, increasingly, to monitor shifts in morale and public opinion. Clinical expertise was sought, and deployed, in the efforts during the 1940s, to analyse and redress the deep psychological and social consequences of Nazism. The Nazis had sought to recast the population; they used the term *Gleichschaltung* (translated variously as coordination, synchronisation or consolidation) to convey the ambition to refashion society across the board.

The aim of the Nazi Party was to shape profoundly not only politics, but also every facet of society, and, ideally, to end all opposition in the minds of the people: in sum, to achieve a total harmonisation. It was never fully realised, but the German people lived for twelve years under the Führer; millions had voted for him, fought for him, agreed with his aims, loved him and accepted his world view, even in the face of impending calamity. During the Second World War, psychological and anthropological researchers, including psychoanalysts, worked for the Allies in the army and intelligence services. They attempted to understand the mass appeal of fascism and the psychological consequences of living under such modern forms of tyranny; they would also help with assessing the testimony of POWs, refining propaganda, mounting 'dirty tricks' operations, seeking to decipher the deeper intent and impact of enemy broadcasts, and, after victory in 1945, assisting the victors' efforts to 'denazify' a defeated German population. That terrible history continued to shadow Cold War debate on brainwashing.

At the same time there were dramatic developments in neuroscience and the elaboration of 'psycho-surgery'. Some pundits heralded the great advances made in mental health treatment for all, thanks to the advent of electric shock therapy and new techniques of brain surgery. By the 1950s and 60s, some surgeons, including prominent figures notably in the United States and Britain, would make grandiose claims that they could cure or tame those who were presumed to be suffering severe and chronic mental disorders by conducting lobotomies. But if medicine and science might claim jurisdiction and have a key role in fixing pathological conditions in brains, from cancerous tumours to schizophrenia, others feared that drugs, shocks and surgery could also facilitate new modes of social control, including the pacification of the troublesome, unhappy, disturbed and eccentric inside a supposedly liberal society.[3] Such debate about the advances and potential dangers in science, medicine and technology also profoundly shaped the language of brainwashing.

Post-war movies updated older conceits in the mode of Frankenstein, featuring white-coated technicians who invade brains even, perhaps entirely rejuvenating and controlling minds and bodies. At the same time, some analyses of totalitarianism focused on the potential role of medicine and psychology in helping the state to ensure compliant or enthusiastic states of mind in a captive population, be it for fascism or communism. Hunter was one of the pundits who set the scene for a vast array of new explorations of mind control, suggesting that the techniques of thought interference exploited by contemporary foes of Western liberal democracy, like the Chinese state, had to be revealed in all their horror, and then fought with all possible means. Brainwashing, he declared, was the current experience – and the terrible plight – of the Chinese population and all those who had the misfortune to fall into the clutches of their 're-educators', foreign prisoners included. Left unchecked the dangers would spread.[4]

The process was akin to a new and total form of psychological enslavement, Hunter and many other Western critics of China warned; it was responsible for the extraordinary sufferings and political illusions, even delusions, of countless men and women who were now at the mercy of the Communist Party. Mao's unleashing of a

Cultural Revolution in the 1960s, where students and others in their hundreds of thousands became Red Guards, gave new momentum to such perceptions of a vast population of brainwashed foot soldiers, fanatical comrades, or even mindless automata.[5]

Given what came to be known about Mao's thought-reform programmes or, later, the Cultural Revolution, such fears of mass indoctrination expressed by Hunter were not completely absurd, but the language that he used to characterise 'brainwashing' was obviously biased, polarised and sensationalistic. Those in power both in China and elsewhere, he suggested dramatically, had a large range of secret tools available to snatch away not only freedom of movement, expression and assembly, but also freedom of thought *entirely*, and to impose an absolute will on captive subjects, en masse. In the most severe cases, he warned in his 1956 book *Brainwashing: The Story of Men Who Defied It*, victims were utterly changed; they could find themselves transformed after being imprisoned and '[p]ut under a terrifying combination of subtle and crude mental and physical pressures and tortures'.[6] All this, he believed, required urgent research; dealing with the crisis brought about by an array of modern mind-control techniques necessitated extreme political vigilance and a battery of practical countermeasures.

Hunter and other commentators writing of brainwashing at around the same time feared that a systematic policy of psychological conversion was being rolled out on a scale the world had not previously witnessed. It was no good simply to equate this phenomenon to prior procedures, they claimed; nor was it right to imagine that the brainwashing happening in China was tantamount to old-fashioned authoritarian diktats, propaganda campaigns or heavy-handed education under the banner of nationalism. Nor was the crisis just a secular version of old and familiar religious forms of indoctrination. At the very least, indoctrination, if such it could still be called, had reached an extraordinary, clinical level of precision, they argued. These writers pointed to how some new combination of surgery, pharmaceuticals, hypnotism, psychological experiments in animal conditioning (most famously associated with the work of the Russian physiologist Pavlov) and group shaming might be used to cement absolute political allegiance to the cause of communism.

'Brainwashing', Hunter insisted, is 'similar in many peculiar ways to a medical treatment'[7] that might well be conducted upon a subject, indeed millions of subjects, without their informed consent. Lurking in the background of this argument about communism's mastery over the mind was the earlier realisation that medicine, and the people who practised it, could be perverted and co-opted by a monstrous state. After all, evidence had just emerged about the crimes of the Nazi doctors, some of whom were put on trial at Nuremberg alongside the major war criminals; men who had experimented mercilessly upon helpless victims in concentration camps, in grotesque violation of the Hippocratic Oath.[8]

Hunter wanted Americans to know that brainwashing threatened them too. He offered readers anxious glimpses of how in this new epoch, medico-psychiatric programmes could be unleashed with alarming rapidity. The methods might be overt or practically invisible. He saw links to the past but also differentiated this emerging period of history sharply from earlier ages, when other varied techniques exerted by political movements, religions, parties or states won hearts and minds. The question for Hunter was whether the prisoner/patient in latter-day regimes such as Stalin's or Mao's could ever resist, and what tools could be offered to make people more wary, critical and resilient.

Hunter recognised the possibility of psychological resistance, and explored more gradations than these simple absolutes. Whatever the rhetoric, his accounts begged more questions than they answered, not only about how best to meet the challenge, but also about how brainwashing could be isolated conceptually from other ideas about education, persuasion and influence. His writings suggest the modern origins of the word; the mixture of fascination and fear the process evoked; the dramatic pictures so often painted, and yet also the blurred edges of that Cold War debate. Was the procedure so total and indelible? Where and how might people hold out? What about partial brainwashing, split convictions, half-hearted conversions and milder forms of pressure and cajoling? His role as a journalist and pundit on brainwashing was also significant, for much of this debate would be conducted not in seminar rooms or in parliaments, but across the airwaves, in popular magazines, newspapers, on TV and in the cinema. People had to evaluate the stories they were being told and assess the authority of the columnists and opinion-makers who told them what to think, where the dangers were coming from, whom to fear or how to resist.

When it came to describing what forms brainwashing actually took, and explaining the precise mechanisms involved in the process, Hunter reached for metaphors and analogies that, far from pinpointing the science, in fact made it seem truly scary, and also tantalisingly vague; for brainwashing, he proposed, somewhat loosely, is 'more akin to witchcraft with its incantations, trances, poisons and potions'.[9] The whole thing 'was a mixture of old voodoo as it were but all with a strange flair of science about it all ... [a] magic brew in a test tube'.[10] Mysteries still abounded; he said the Chinese tried to cover up what they were doing. They didn't want to call it brainwashing, even though they knew, apparently, that was precisely what it was. The first requirement, in Hunter's view, was to identify the methods of brainwashing and then explore what would help people to withstand the assault. To work most effectively, the process, he proposed, depends above all on the subject's ignorance of how it is conducted; so, to educate might also be to arm us.[11] If brainwashing could overpower free will, a well-prepared mind and well-equipped society could – maybe – push back against dangers abroad, or here in its midst. On the other hand, the brainwashers were becoming ever more sophisticated, and perhaps a day would come when resistance was futile; but then again, maybe not ...

Stories from the post-war period provide an indication of how rapidly reading publics were expected to engage with the problem, and how swiftly news reporters also seized on the term. In 1950, *The Times of India* took up the expression, describing how 'China under the Red flag' witnessed such 'brain-washing', and equating it to 'a new version of the mental purge'. In 1955, *The Times* of London reported how special military forces were being prepared to undergo, by way of training, 'realistic "brainwashing" procedures for those who are "captured"'. It also soon found its way into popular culture, as well as into angry fulminations against its dangers.

The topic has never really gone away. Readers, viewers and listeners from the early 1950s onwards could scarcely avoid encounters – in the English-language press and magazines, at the cinema, on radio or TV, in everyday conversation – with the problem, enigma, accusation or perhaps even alibi of brainwashing.[12] The watchword would appear in grand slogans as well as in small print over the following decades. It was a buzz phrase in feature pieces and storylines about just about everything, from prison-house conditions to the newest dance craze, from assembly-line manufacturing to heavy metal concerts, from school reform programmes to marital breakdowns. As the label migrated from one setting to another, it acquired new associations, and served as a foil in all manner of arguments, including debates about the nature of identity, authenticity, creativity and freedom.

Zooming forward to the recent past, it is clear the extent to which 'brainwashing' has entered our everyday lexicon, and how often it may be invoked, casually too, not least as a way of arguing both about our interactions with one another (for instance, online) and our relationships as individuals or groups to a larger structure, overarching agency or controlling institution. Reference to brainwashing may perhaps also reflect our anxieties and puzzlements about the limits of freedom. 'Brainwashing' can be claimed by some as a matter of certainty, and then used by others more interrogatively, a springboard for further explorations of power.

This was illustrated for me by an encounter not long ago with some sixth formers at a state school in London. As part of an exercise, the students had been asked to come up with some associations and then concrete examples in response to the word brainwashed. Some jumped in with accusations about their own school education; that, they said, was brainwashing them just as much as anything else. Quickly, other members of the group challenged that assertion, pointing out that if school was just an exercise in brainwashing, how come they were allowed to discuss it like this? Several looked rather uncomfortable when their teacher felt (or at least appeared to feel) crestfallen by their account, and asked the group gently, 'You think I'm a brainwasher?' They immediately reassured him that despite their view of the school they really appreciated him personally: 'Not you, sir, it's the system brainwashing us,' said one of them helpfully.

Brainwashing, the class eventually agreed, was not a process you could simply equate with him, or with their school. They began to reflect on the pressures the staff, as well as the students, were under, and to tease out where brainwashing proper might really best be identified; a few proceeded to argue about the political state in which they were living.

Those and other young people in London I have talked to about this set of issues (including groups of teenagers who made an interesting collection of video essays on brainwashing and hidden persuasion)[13] have described the forces around them online and off. They have wondered how best to explain their own self-immersion in, say, fashion, video games, music or interminable online chat. I have been struck by their acute sense of the magnetically compelling, yet also hateful, aspects of living practically 24/7 connected to others, through computers. Some spoke of their attraction, as though moths to a flame, to Facebook, Instagram, YouTube, TikTok or other platforms and social networking services; they were aware of the potential for addiction, of their obsession with checking the latest notifications each time the phone pinged, and tracking the number of 'likes' for each posted image.

In feeling troubled by their own behaviour, they were surely representative of millions of others, old and young. They were trying to figure out the degree to which such platforms provide opportunities for freedom, connection, communication and self-realisation; present dangerous traps, brainwashing them; exploit their emotions, in using the human thirst for recognition, affection and approbation; or nurture gleeful, hateful and prurient feelings, to keep users online, and thus constantly return a profit. They asked searching questions about the means, motives, causes and consequences of this daily bargain and the nature of digital capitalism. Those teenagers could often sense or even know full well that they had been virtually hooked, just as previous generations may have come to see themselves as the fodder of the post-war advertising industry.

Online resources have been engineered, they well understood, not only to be convenient and replete with creative tools, but also to be extremely addictive. Thus, software is created to enable the harvesting of data, and geared to exploit the subject's curiosity, colonise time, monetise emotions and play upon all-too-human wishes to be loved. The set-up is constantly honed to be more and more engrossing and hard to leave, even if nobody compels us. It is designed to capture our desire for contact with friends, to see what happens when we dare to throw a thought out there into the world and discover who responds, and in what numbers; or sometimes to license the most sadistic pleasures and exploit the darkest conspiratorial fantasies. Those adolescents spoke eloquently of being beguiled, and yet knew well enough that the attention we all give, and micro-adjustments we make over time, are precisely the product – that influence-prone porous dimension of 'us' – sold by data companies to advertisers.

We are the data that then generates untold fortunes for the vast tech companies. Those school students had no doubt digital life was here for keeps, but that it also needed radical reform.

No one is immune to the many varieties of influence and persuasion communicated relentlessly over months and years. We can debate which age group is most vulnerable now, online and off: the computer-savvy teenager, their parents and grandparents, or perhaps pre-teen children, who are certainly heavily catered for by advertisers (the next generation prepared for the market?). Those school students described their struggles to fashion identities, a sense of self, a set of convictions, beliefs, values of their own, modes of resistance, in a world of great insecurity, amid wall-to-wall messages, advertising injunctions and new forms of public shaming, in place of pre-modern pillories and stocks. No wonder that pressure has mounted for a right to be forgotten, an entitlement to own and/or erase our data online, for an adequate response to hate speech, hounding mobs and fake news, and for a break-up of monopoly companies.

The teenagers I spoke to mostly acknowledged that they had some agency and responsibility, but also articulated the sense of imponderable unseen virtual forces that exert great power over their lives. Even so, they suggested how we may all become active and not just passive players, and participants too. We live in a world where we can all too easily exercise our ability or satisfy our wishes to hear only what we want to hear; to exist in bubbles, where we are provided, if we so choose, only with news congruent with our prejudices and predilections.

Some in those groups envisaged life in this new millennium amid ever greater hybrid possibilities, as AI, biotech and human beings become increasingly fused. They anticipated an environment where chips are inserted into our brains, and where the algorithm knows our desires better than we know them ourselves. In short, the kind of developments well described by historians of the future such as Yuval Noah Harari.[14]

It is hardly surprising that these teenagers had such immediate and intense reactions to the word brainwashing. That term takes on new meanings in their world. It is a concept they have been exposed to in all kinds of ways even though they were born after the period that gave birth to this vocabulary, the Cold War, had already formally ended.

*

Brainwashing became, post-war and after, a ready conceit for adventures, spy stories, tragedies and comedies, kitchen-sink dramas and no end of popular cartoons. In fact, even before the Cold War set in and the word was coined, tales of evil fascist, Stalinist or capitalist global mind-control conspiracies were already staple ingredients of yarns and movies. An American work of pulp fiction of the 1930s, for example, is tellingly entitled 'The Affair of the Brains': it portrays a future interplanetary conflict between a demonic 'Oriental' tyrannical figure, or evil genius, Ku Sui, and a US cowboy-like hero, Hawk Carse, with whom he must fight to the death. In this adventure, Ku Sui kidnaps the most eminent scientists he can find, extracts their brains, puts them in vats, and then by keeping the grey matter alive and interconnected creates a grand cerebral system under this would-be universal dictator's total control.[15]

Comic books and animations have often whizzed their signature characters in and out of political cages and mental states of totalitarian terror; think of Donald Duck, in an anti-Nazi production of 1943, *Der Fuehrer's Face*, waking into a nightmare land of clockwork labour, a society peopled by brutal, coarse ruffians, where he must goosestep, before he wakes again with immense relief home in his own bed, to walk as he pleases and entertain his own thoughts in the Land of Liberty. Or cartoons may alert viewers to capitalist enchantment: witness a Soviet-produced Disney-style anti-Western propaganda cartoon of 1949, *Stranger's Voice*; it warned the good Russian people of the corrosive import of Western jazz, a music, it was alleged, that would corrupt the soul. The communist heartland was represented by a harmonious colony of adorable birds; they must close their ears, to shut out and save themselves from the toxic (American) cacophony.[16]

Later, in the West, thanks to Disney, came the memorable image of Kaa the snake, singing lullingly 'trust in me', while insinuating himself almost irresistibly into Mowgli's mind, in the enchanting 1967 film version of *The Jungle Book*. That very same year, audiences could also enjoy the sight of Tom and Jerry reduced to automata while wearing mind-control helmets, in an episode entitled 'Advance and Be Mechanized'. The barely disguised messaging in such cartoons, both new and old, can itself attract accusations of brainwashing. When a film version of the Dr Seuss story *The Lorax* appeared in 2012, a Fox

News host, Lou Dobbs, warned his viewers about the brainwashing potential of such supposedly left-wing productions, which he suggested were designed to get the public unnecessarily steamed up about climate disaster. A colleague of Dobbs, Eric Bolling, also opined about the clandestine brainwashing message of the 2011 Muppets movie, which vilifies an oil executive, tellingly named 'Tex Richman'.[17]

In 'The Joy of Sect', a 1998 episode of that marvellously inventive cartoon series The Simpsons – made for the Fox Broadcasting Company – Homer attends a free residential seminar offered by a charismatic cult, the Movementarians. He is immediately smitten. Soon he is reciting, parrot-fashion, the group leader's name. The poor sap is indoctrinated completely, and nearly induced to sell the deeds to the family house. He abandons his family and seems perfectly content tilling the soil on the land while a tin-pot guru drives around this private empire in a Rolls-Royce, throwing up dirt in the faces of his ecstatic and grovelling followers. Eventually, he is rescued by his wife, Marge, and the family are reunited and shown back in their town, Springfield, getting on with business as usual; in fact, sitting down to watch … Fox News. We know that the next day Homer, suitably 'freed', will be back to work in the nuclear plant, run by the malevolent tycoon Mr Burns.

The cartoon satirically pokes fun at Fox, inviting the viewer to think, and to pose a more serious question perhaps about brainwashing. Even as that corporation shows you The Simpsons, it pumps out Fox News, notorious to at least half of the nation as a font of wretched propaganda and spin.

Popular music can also be deployed as a way of reflecting on, or even recovering from, brainwashing, something Grace Jones alluded to in her 1983 single 'Living My Life'.[18] Jones has spoken directly about her own efforts to escape the brainwashing conducted upon her: racism, sexism and religious bigotry engulfed her, she said, and while growing up she had been 'brainwashed by all this hellfire and damnation'.[19] Music has often been identified as a possible vehicle for brainwashing too. Repetitive, thumping beats and sheer walls of noise have been used in cruel modern regimes of punishment and torture, a means to torment imprisoned people. This is 'music' that the prisoner can't turn off, sound that totally offends in its sheer volume or its lyrics; vibration exploited as a means to devastate minds, to cause a person's resistance to weaken, even collapse, and thus to assist interrogators and brainwashers.[20] Victims can be entombed in an unbearable din as well as in deafening states of silence.

Music may serve as a means of enchanting, enrapturing or moving a mass audience at a religious meeting, political rally or cultural gathering. And it can equally well be the source of an extraordinary moral panic: scaremongers have warned about the hidden goals of popular bands, or the subliminal messages inside apparently innocuous songs.[21] During the 1960s, right-wing Christian pastors in the United States cautioned that the Beatles were badly confusing young people about their sexuality, and ultimately brainwashing them. The musicians from Liverpool were said to be part of a project of international communist subversion. Yet besides these images of 'the Red Beatles', others noted how Russian young people used their songs to question communism, or even claimed that Beatlemania washed away the foundations of Soviet society.[22] As the accusations flew, the CIA was actively engaged in using music, art and letters to promote the interests and ideals of the West and to sow images of a free society behind the Iron Curtain; the Soviet state also had its own cultural ambassadors, various intellectuals and artists, serving as mouthpieces.[23]

The Beatles were not brainwashers, nor anyone's poodles, but their massive popular influence, and the hysterical response of some of their fans, led certain conservative critics to treat them as such. The group did offer their own wry humour, sardonic quips, experimental musical styles, shifting personas, and lyrics that ventured many intriguing thoughts about conformity, consciousness and revolution. George Harrison's posthumously released 2002 album is entitled *Brainwashed*. Its title song tells of how we are brainwashed by childhood, school, teachers, rules, leaders, kings and queens, God, the Nikkei, the Dow Jones, the FTSE and the Nasdaq.

We will probably never know exactly what prompted Elvis Presley to offer his services to the US government to counter the moral crisis afflicting the next generation. However, his overtures came soon after the Republican vice president, Spiro Agnew, directly attacked the Beatles and the 1960s drug culture which he insisted explicitly brainwashes young people.[24] Presley, like the Fab Four, had himself caused much controversy about his hypnotic effect on the young, as though his musical style, face, hair and gyrating hips were truly responsible for leading young people to some (orgiastic) hell in a handcart. Presley was having none of all that. Just before Christmas 1970, he drove up to the gates of the White House bearing a handwritten letter for Richard Nixon, a letter that explained how the singer had made an 'in-depth study of drug abuse and communist brainwashing techniques', and now wanted to be sworn in by the president as a federal agent at large, so he could use his communication skills to safeguard American youth from all these contemporary dangers.[25]

By the time Presley met Nixon (and was duly rewarded with that role as a special agent, at least on paper), the word brainwashing was twenty years old; it was by then the go-to term for just about everything that ran counter to the conventional mores and stability of post-war Western society: Stalinism, Maoism, neo-Nazism or religious fundamentalism, cults, populism, the counterculture, psychedelia and the general malaise of adolescents. The background thrum of all that discourse continues, as some use it now to discuss climate change denial, Trumpism, Putinism, terrorism or, historically, the interwar appeal of fascism, Nazism and Stalinism. The London students I met might perhaps as easily encounter the idea of brainwashing in religious studies, history, politics and psychology lessons, as in pop art, video games and in literature commissioned by government itself, designed to try to prevent future 'radicalisation'. The concept of brainwashing features in explanations of local calamities and faraway mysteries, such as why crowds weep at the sight of the 'dear leader' in Pyongyang; in psychological accounts of why some women stay for years with their violent partners; in sociological theories about the impact of digital advertising; and in right-wing political dismissals of the climate change campaigner Greta Thunberg, supposedly the brainwashed young victim of her own parents.

In short, brainwash stories of great variety abound; about leaders and followers, small and large crimes, acts of mass killing and self-destruction. We each must assess the different ways brainwashing can be used in arguments, appeals or accusations, and decide what credence to give to claims in the press. Speaking to Martin Chulov, a distinguished writer on the Middle East who reports for the *Guardian*, Osama Bin Laden's mother claimed her shy, bright boy was transformed in sudden and bewildering fashion by sinister teachers. When Osama was in his early twenties, she explained, he grew much more pious and driven. Her son was lost, she insisted, during the time he was studying economics at King Abdulaziz University in Jeddah. It was here, she explained, that he was first 'brainwashed'.[26]

The term has arisen not only in reference to powerful figures like Bin Laden, but also to explain the actions of camp followers in his movement, as well as its rival, Islamic State (IS). But does the term brainwashed sufficiently characterise why so many have flocked to these causes, or make us any the wiser about how best to deal with the threat these movements pose to democracies, how far to punish the followers, and whether to offer psychological treatment, aimed at rehabilitation? The predicament of a young woman, Shamima Begum, recently exemplified this dilemma and prompted heated debate. In February 2015, aged fifteen, Begum left her UK home and her parents, who are of Bangladeshi origin, to travel to Turkey in the company of two other schoolgirls from east London, and from there to Syria to join IS. She eventually found herself marooned in a refugee camp after IS forces were routed by US-backed Kurdish Peshmerga soldiers, and sought to return to the UK.

In 2019, the Conservative British Home Secretary, Sajid Javid, decided that Begum could not be allowed to return to the UK.[27] This block remained in place, despite her young age on leaving the country, the personal hardships she suffered, above all her grief about the deaths of her three infants, and desperate subsequent appeals to be allowed to go home. The decision left her effectively stateless, despite insouciant declarations from the government that she could go back to Bangladesh.[28] What may really have led her to leave the UK, or to embrace this cause, was drowned out in angry headlines, with much talk of her lifelong dangerousness as well as her brainwashing, and a certain confusion about whether the latter gave grounds for clemency anyway.

To the dismay of those seeking her return to Britain, Begum continued to justify some of IS's actions, even as she also suggested she was not quite in her right mind. A typical report in *The Times* quoted her plea: 'I was brainwashed. I knew nothing.'[29] As her case made clear, victims and perpetrators are not always neatly divided; brainwashed or not, she lives on in a desperate twilight zone, although continuing to press her legal case for a right to return. Others more fortunate and less visible than her managed to return to Britain from Syria, albeit often to then face their own grave personal difficulties and much stigma, both within their own former communities and in a wider society. Some returnees found their way to National Health Service mental health therapeutic programmes, despite some critical media pushback, social media objections and even an attempted (unsuccessful) public petition to terminate such services.[30]

The designation 'brainwashed' can serve as a diagnosis, a charge or sometimes even an apology. It can be used controversially in high-profile legal defences to help a defendant argue against accusations of responsibility for mass atrocities.[31] The term featured heavily in media reports about some of the most shocking cases to make the front pages of the 1960s and after. Murderous people, from the Manson gang (or 'family') to the Reverend Jim Jones to Ted Kaczynski, were and still are regularly discussed through this lens. Jones's case was the most horrifying, culminating in the tragic Jonestown mass murder-suicide of 909 people (a third of them children) in Guyana, in 1978.[32] Those who died at the 1993 Waco siege in Texas were also said to have been brainwashed by their charismatic leader. The killing of seventy-six penned-in cult members and their families by the authorities was apparently one of the key events to have enraged Timothy McVeigh, a Gulf War veteran and anti-government extremist, and inspired him to explode a device in Oklahoma City in 1995 that killed 168 people.[33]

Considering the post-war cultural context of brainwashing discussed above, and researching this book, led me to reflect on the history of psychiatry, psychoanalysis and psychology during the twentieth century. More immediately, various communications by patients and colleagues have left their mark on this study, not least by emphasising our shared vulnerability to coercive persuasion.[34] Patients may well seek help through the talking cure, keenly and appreciatively, seeking to break free of repetitive and disabling patterns; yet, however willing to engage, patients may also be deeply worried about losing control. At times, certain patients have suggested to me – or even demanded – that I should think about brainwashing dangers *within psychoanalysis*; asking that we consider, for example, whether the therapy may itself be coercive and secretly persuasive in intent, or a project designed to convert the analysand.

Analysts can always lose touch with the receptive and open state of mind that Freud wanted his followers to maintain when they worked. We risk, no doubt, becoming overt or covert influencers, or moralisers, even without consciously intending to. Patients may want their psychoanalysts to operate, sometimes at least, as coaches, judges, advisers or advocates, and nudge them accordingly. But even when, as analysts, we are working appropriately, in that original Freudian sense, maintaining the role effectively, patients can have grave doubts about the nature of the enterprise, objecting, on the one hand, if the analyst does not 'take sides', and on the other, lamenting their unwanted influence and censorious tone. In an analysis, a patient can feel relieved as well as perturbed to be granting so much access to their own intimate thoughts and feelings. The patient might also feel they have granted a kind of privilege to someone else to help them change their lives, but this very access may also arouse the fear of being possessed, indoctrinated or just overexposed, left vulnerable and excessively porous. A patient might claim, for instance, that their analyst is making them feel guilty, criticising and cajoling or seeking to condition them, when the analyst is inviting their open-minded exploration of a painful issue. We can all bristle and grow defensive when a difficult subject is broached, or when we feel too raw. Many things can get projected by the patient onto the analyst. A patient once complained to me that what I had said to him about what was happening between us during the session was, as he put it, 'cruelly pinning him down'. Although he came to reconsider afterwards whether his family member X and his work enemy Y were as responsible for all his ills as he had claimed, and to question his own first assumption that my interpretation was 'dictating' to him what to do, it was important to him to discover that I was open to exploring the possibility that I might indeed have been pressing him too insistently to take on board my point.

Another patient, who had suffered a very unhappy childhood, spoke at considerable length one day, with a certain relish, about egregious treatments by certain psychoanalysts and psychiatrists in the Cold War United States. He had read about these scandals in journals; and, as he rightly pointed out, those sometimes heavily pressuring approaches were not in fact confined only to then and there.[35] He spelled out that he was talking about conversion therapies, targeted at gay patients, and about bigots and zealots, seeking to make patients straight, to 'cure' them of their sexuality, sometimes through explicit advice, coercive instruction or strong encouragement. My patient pointed to such manipulative and bullying practices, sometimes mobilised by Churches, but also by secular movements, and asked, with a kind of mounting pressure on me, 'Where exactly do you stand?' It was as though it was important to pull the words from me, to force my acknowledgement that I abhorred and condemned this too, or perhaps to seek my active dissociation from these bad practitioners. He 'demanded' to know 'immediately', to have 'a yes or no straight answer'. He knew enough, I believed, by then, of my way of working not to require that I should seek to convince him of my bona fides; indeed had I responded to this demand by instantly affirm-ing my own contrary views, I felt that I would have been playing some kind of required role. Whatever else may have been at stake in that demand, I thought he was conveying not only his critical views of such treatments, but also what it means to be pressured, cornered and controlled; in fact, letting me know what it felt like to be on the receiving end of that experience, which he had so often endured in his own family as a child.

A different patient, a courageous, elderly man named Mr W., who was in his own view quite mentally unwell and both desperate for and wary of my help, raised the question directly of brainwashing by psy-choanalysis. Mr W. had always lived alone and was suspicious about what I, his analyst, might do to him under the guise of assisting him in facing certain problems in his life. He raised the issue of brainwashing, with some considerable trepidation regarding what he half assumed to be my project to adapt him to some secret blueprint of my own.

As he watched me vigilantly (for he was too anxious to use the couch), Mr W. said he needed to try to read my mind. At times he was convinced that he could succeed in doing so, as well as in shaping my thoughts, even as he feared I might be doing the same back to him; he went so far as to liken his head to a transparent glass bowl. One day, he leant towards me and announced that he was worried that the treatment might seriously brainwash him; and it might do this so successfully, he thought, that he would not even realise it was happening at all. He leaned closer still and whispered in a confiding tone (as though fearful of being overheard by a third party): 'How can I be sure that you are not secretly wired up to your organisation's headquarters? You might be receiving instructions about what to say to me through a concealed earpiece.'

This was a concrete expression of his more pervasive fear that I too could be at the mercy of forces I could not control – 'them'. As the session developed, Mr W. explained he was worried that this 'HQ' might, through me, be in the business of brainwashing him. In this version of our relationship, I had already succumbed and been brainwashed myself, and was carrying out 'their' secret instructions. Theirs? His? Mine? He was quite torn about this: he said he wanted to share the thought but was not entirely convinced by his own fear. He was confiding in a more trustworthy version of me his view that I might be a brainwasher, in the thrall of others outside me (or deep inside me). He also had the concern that I might be far too exposed to his own omniscient mind-reading powers over me.

Perhaps Mr W. sought to protect me from his accusations by laying the blame on an omnipotent remote analytic organisation, separate from either of us. He felt the need to reassure me frequently; to check I was not secretly offended – or worse, 'furious', he said – in the face of his grave mistrust. Perhaps all of us (in therapy or not) must bear some anxiety about our own exposure to and dependence on others, and about counterattacks from people on whom we rely, and whose buttons we press. Despite such anxious thoughts, Mr W. continued and made real use of the sessions, hopeful that I could understand how much pain he was in, even as he tended to demonise and conversely to idealise the work we were doing. Later he said, with feeling, that the analysis had enabled him to be less paranoid, to get on better with his own projects, and to help him have more contact, 'on a friendlier basis', as he put it, with family and colleagues.

In 1919, one of Freud's followers, Victor Tausk, wrote an interesting paper about extreme examples of suspicions and fears, and about the role of an 'influencing machine'. This was not just imagined, he said, but hallucinated, by some schizophrenic patients.[36] The 'influencing machine' is of 'mystical nature' and can take different shapes, sizes and kinds; although these severely ill patients mostly only give vague hints of the machine's construction. The machine tends to consist 'of boxes, cranks, levers, wheels, buttons, wires, batteries, and the like … The influencing machine produces, as well as removes, thoughts and feelings in people, by means of waves, rays, or other forces.' In such cases, the machine was often called a 'suggestion-apparatus'. It could also affect motor phenomena in the body, such as erections and seminal emissions, or cause eruptions on the skin, abscesses and other pathological processes that weaken and damage the victim. Tausk added that the interference, as conceived by these patients, 'is accomplished either by means of suggestion or by air-currents, electricity, magnetism, or X-rays'. The influencing machine was taken to be responsible for the patient's illness and incapacity: 'Buttons are pushed, levers set in motion, cranks turned. The connection with the patient is often established by means of invisible wires leading into his bed.'[37]

Tausk found that some believed the machine may be manipulated by an operator, such as the mental asylum's most senior doctor; he noted how these very ill patients had suspicions that their physicians might be in on the act, operators of the dangerous equipment. Had Tausk written of this thirty years later, perhaps the apposite term would have been 'the brainwashing machine'.

After its invention in the 1950s, the term 'brainwashing' gradually filtered into the discourse of both patients and analysts, and grew more prevalent in clinical literature during the 1960s.[38] In an interview with the *New Yorker*, the novelist Philip Roth remarked that psycho-analysis (of which he had had his own mixed experiences in the 1960s) had the potential to become, as he put it, a homegrown US version of Korean War-style brainwashing. His interviewer explained how 'Roth looks back on his own analysis as having been, in many ways, a kind of "brainwashing"'. 'Like the North Korean,' Roth perhaps only half joked, 'the psychiatrist would torture you and torture you with his false interpretations, and when he stopped you were so grateful that you just accepted them.'[39]

I will mostly dispense with using any scare quotes around the expression henceforth. But it is worth remembering that brainwashing is a contentious term, and a powerfully suggestive figure of speech. Admittedly, it is generally treated as a dead, rather than live metaphor, just like, say, 'internet surfer'; one of those words that are mostly used as though they are no longer metaphorical at all. But some commentators have insisted we pay more attention to what we are saying here.

'There is one last example which I find irresistible,' declared a certain Weller Embler, a writer on language, in his scholarly 1959 essay on 'Metaphor in Everyday Speech'. The example was the verb 'to brainwash', which, he observed, 'is a newly-minted metaphor which suggests a clearing of the mind of all previously held beliefs'. Embler urged the reader to consider what this really entailed, and to question how literally we should take the image: 'is it possible to wash away beliefs', he asked, 'in the same way, for example, as it is possible to wash old newspapers of their ink and then to print new words on the fresh newsprint, as though the old had never existed?'

Brainwash, Embler elaborated, is related to another older philosophical metaphor about the mind, the *tabula rasa*, meaning a scraped tablet from which the writing has been erased, or perhaps a blank slate or empty sheet. If, at birth, the mind is a clean tablet upon which is to be written the experience gained through the senses, then it would seem reasonable to suppose that the slate or blackboard could be washed clean at any time. But not so fast, he cautioned: various assumptions may be attached to the word. Suppose, he asked, the mind is not like a fresh tablet at birth, suppose we think of it as like something else. Then what?[40]

Freighted with imagery and preconceptions as it is, the idea of brainwashing may entail or trigger other ideas too, as Embler insisted. Certainly, it can convey a variety of meanings, telling us something about how we view our own minds and others': it is one way for all of us to think about how our psychic lives could be temporarily or sometimes permanently influenced without our consent or agency. Even if we are not simply blank slates or passive sponges on which another external communicator imposes their will, brainwashing stories may draw attention to how our minds are always permeable, and multiple inputs and messages, sometimes entirely unwanted, can shape our thoughts and feelings. Brainwashing is a metaphor but also a practice, with real and horrific flesh-and-blood consequences.

As though to underline that very point a major news story about the Chinese government and its systematic endeavour to 're-educate' the Uighurs loomed large as I was completing this book. Such reports, of which more later, were prominent between 2019 and 2022. They vied with others in the news, helping me keep in mind the topicality of this historical vocabulary and the range of issues it can be related to, from full-blown brainwashing, as in the atrocious treatment of the Uighur population, to a pervasive culture of misinformation, a politics and media rife with lying, deception and 'economies with the truth'. There was the ever more pressing and evident (albeit in some quarters still denied or at least downplayed) climate emergency; the populist authoritarian politics of Bolsonaro in Brazil and Modi in India (to name but two examples); the UK Brexit campaign and its aftermath; and the psychodrama of the Trump–Biden 2020 presidential race in the United States.

Accusations of fake news now circulate constantly; often the phrase is co-opted by leaders who seek to create their own falsely reassuring narrative without reference to widely reported facts. Consider how the Chinese ambassador to London had to provide in the West a sanitised version of the Uighur story, stonewalling journalists, or complaining 'fake news'.[41] Are we now, as some commentators insist, living, in both East and West, in a completely unprecedented 'post-truth' era, when mendacity has lost its opprobrium? Or is this to create a gilded fantasy of a previous 'truth-era'? How do we explain the fact that over 70 million US voters opted to vote again for Trump, despite so much evidence of his lying, and apparently that millions give credence to conspiracy cult QAnon theories?

Though this book cannot resolve such questions, it provides a framework for thinking about the history and politics of such inquiries and fears; it shows how brainwashing is a term we need, but also must treat with a good deal of caution. It is a malleable concept, defined to a great extent by what we consider to be healthy thinking, what we assume about individual freedom, and what kinds of persuasion and causes we deem unacceptable. When people brandish the charge of brainwashing, we need to ask what they envisage, who they are aiming at, or arguing with, and what kind of action they seek in response. I want to set out different vocabularies, theories and stories about the mind that emerged post-war, to explore the problem. The first part of this study focuses on how the most extreme forms of coercive influence were understood by writers in the West, in the early Cold War. However, throughout the book, I invite the reader to compare past and present, and to keep in mind the world we are now in. In sum, I want to move between the post-war debates and the era of Facebook, where billions of people now interact as a matter of course, sharing their feelings, images, stories and profiles, caught up in an endless intersubjective process that is both digitised and monetised, although not always obviously so. One estimate for 2021 suggests the company has close to 3 billion active monthly users. Meta, Facebook's parent company, is one of the largest corporate revenue earners in the world, with advertising income each year running into the tens of billions.

As I conducted research on this topic, I soon realised that no previous project of mine had elicited so much interest from colleagues and friends. You did not need to be a student of the Cold War to become intrigued by the question: what is brainwashing? Can you do it to yourself, or another? Where does it begin and end? When was the idea first formulated? Is it for real? A myth? A fantasy? What features characterise its practices now? Where is brainwashing going in the future? These questions may fascinate us, I suspect, because they also invite consideration of the very opposite: what would be a non- or un-brainwashed self, and what degree of freedom of thought are we capable of? One set of issues is about vertical authority – a state or at least a jailor, exerting control over a captive subject; another is horizontal – how we interact with peers, friends, colleagues and strangers, in new kinds of technology. The corporate system may loom over us, but we are drawn into this ceaseless and indelibly archived interplay with other people, where not only opinion but also so much emotion is on the line. These forums, that we have signed up to in our billions, are where we play with ideas, or are played by others.

This topic prompts us to consider extremes and the many states between a condition of psychic freedom and of alien thought control. For, even if not brainwashed, we are all, surely, at the best of times, suggestible, impressionable and interdependent. None of us is ever discrete, fully self-knowing, self-fashioned, self-made, able to think all by ourselves or fully about ourselves. We are all leant upon, profoundly affected by others, and never in full control of our minds. Facebook knows we practically all want to 'relate', and we all know too that, to put it another way, nobody is free of covert influence, or ever fully transparent to themselves or to others; and we can find ourselves allied unconsciously with others, even without a full-blown brainwash operation.

To speak of drip-drip conditioning in our daily life in the West, to denounce the nexus of weather and financial data that I mentioned earlier as brainwashing, might well seem to you – as it does to me – over the top. News may be outright propaganda and brainwashing; or it might inform, or again persuade, influence, assume, suggest or deny a myriad of things even if it does not brainwash viewers to some incontrovertible singular dogma. Perhaps news serves at times to perpetuate a numbing effect of mainstream norms and expectations upon us. To consider these questions is to begin to ask, what kinds of news and information do we need, to be able to think coherently? Much of our thinking and processing, and decision-making, of course, is not conscious and deliberative anyway. We think 'fast and slow', as Daniel Kahneman has famously shown.[42] But in our ever more commercialised culture, and a digital economy that moves ever faster, thinking for ourselves, in any fashion, perhaps has never been harder.

The extremes of propaganda and brainwashing in totalitarian societies point us back then to consider the middle spaces, those ambiguous states, where we have some free will yet go along in a commercial or political seduction. In some lines of work, of course, people are obliged to be online, the computer an indispensable means to earn a living; but even beyond necessity, a majority seem to have a massive hunger to sign up for far more screen time than is strictly required to get by. We all encounter states of mind or conditions of life where we may have some options but yet eschew them; where we can't bear to face illusions we've already (half) signed up to, and then just continue to go along for the ride; where we deny and disavow our own misgivings, because revising our views feels too costly; where we make promises to be more vigilant against the 'hidden persuaders' and social conditioners (only not just yet); where we acquiesce, or maybe actively luxuriate, in strange bargains with ourselves, that somehow postpone conflict or change; states of mind where we let go, temporarily or permanently, of those sane, vigilant and critical capacities we might have had.

We may do well to reserve the word brainwash primarily, I think, for more extreme kinds of intervention by powerful people, states and agencies, i.e. those holding great means of constraint and control. When the word brainwash came into vogue, it was, as we have seen, most obviously to serve as an accessible way to think about totalitarian ideology (although even Hunter, Cold War journalist that he was, could not resist drawing attention to dangers prevalent in the West as well). We argue over the provenance, scope and location of brainwashing inside still functioning democracies, as well as police states. For more reasons than one, the word, the idea, the scenario that Hunter and others conjured up long ago seems still to disturb many of us now, whatever the polity we live within. For the dangers we face of thought interference are not only to be found in the past or on the other side of some political divide, nor just inside some terrifying but distinct total institution, but here and now in our twenty-first-century world, even if we are fortunate to enjoy conditions of relative freedom. We live in a storm of daily warnings, promises and reassurances about the present and future, amid ongoing arguments about the state of the environment, the climate, the economy, pandemics and the political process; in a time, moreover, of rising paranoid discourse and authoritarian populism, social convulsions, during an ongoing digital revolution, and in the wake of Covid-19, a virus that, in 2020, transformed the economic model of business as usual. Certainly, we are now awash with stories that reflect or stir our anxieties about yet greater loss of freedom as well as mounting insecurity ahead.

'Brainwashing' is always shadowed by the question of what it entails to think for ourselves. The story of the concept, as we will see, is often a vehicle for other social and political debates, as well as a means of exploring the factors that make ordinary reflection and deliberation so difficult. *Brainwashed* charts not only how vulnerable we are to covert persuasion, even when we are not literally held as captives in chains, but also why we might be so mesmerised by, *and* in dread of, total conversion states.

One of my presuppositions in this book concerns methodology and the importance of ideas being considered historically, placed in context. I also contend that psychoanalysis is relevant for this present discussion. It is part of that original context; and it offers tools that we might still usefully employ to consider the issues at stake, and to ask why old debates about breakable captives, in the Cold War, might merit fresh scrutiny in the new millennium. I seek to explore how new vocabularies as well as institutions, processes, products and technologies arose; and to map how a range of ideas emerged to explain what was happening. If this book is a work about modern culture and intellectual history, it is also a study of how people sought to make sense of their changing world, often still reeling from an earlier calamity, endeavouring to grasp the changing political, technological and psychological landscape in front of them, and sift the competing claims made by various experts, eyewitnesses, analysts, storytellers, critics and pundits.

In the following chapters, I will examine several of the important flash points in the history of brainwashing: debates from the 1950s, and after, about thought reform, and the processes of forced confession – involuntary medication, sensory deprivation, solitary confinement and rapid conversion – leitmotifs of the Cold War past. Certain practices of pacification, intimidation and control decried in that literature are in fact widely used in many penitentiary systems and 'supermax' prisons today.

Reports about such extreme and coercive measures that can be inflicted upon people confined, against their will, in prisons and other closed institutions can also offer a way to start to explore the less clear-cut and more subtle forms of manipulation that, arguably, we all may experience in a modern society: hidden persuasion in news, advertising, bad education, mental health treatment, or in varied forms of commercial seduction, political spin or cultural nudge. The kinds of influence to which we may well succumb online are not usually based upon top-down instruction; the platforms, in one sense, facilitate exchange, activity, feedback. We live anyway perhaps inside multiple networks. Much of the influence now exerted upon us comes via our own interactive process, suggestions, invitations and prompts, not through imperial commands. We may be shaped not only by states, dictators and political parties, but through this endless traffic of messages and signs; for we are susceptible to the sway of opinion in peer-to-peer dialogue too. A corporation can use the data about us to feed us ever more 'bespoke' stories, advertisements and news, according to its own (invisible to us) algorithms. Users may have the illusion they are just conversing with friends or sharing their pictures and lives with a selected online community, rather than in fact providing fodder for advertisers and other agencies, who are not part of the overt conversation; or they may know and proceed regardless. Ultimately what may be most interesting – and disturbing – are the many more intricate aspects of our unconscious collusion and persuasion as well; the denial and the unspoken, perhaps unwitting, bargains we make to forsake our own mental capacities, to turn a blind eye to what we know to be true, to what we are doing, and to how we are being propelled, or corralled.

Uncertainties about freedom of thought and our interest in 'brain-washing' may reflect intuitions about the vicissitudes of our own psyches as well as our knowledge of despotic, coercive and beguiling forces that threaten minds from outside. The issue of psychic 'auton-omy' is real, not only because we can be beset by intimidating jailors, shadowy agencies, clandestine movements or the deep state, but also, as Freud suggested, because we can attack our own minds and have a limited tolerance for facing reality, including our own mortality. We are torn, he wrote, between the reality principle and the pleas-ure principle, inclined to make-believe, and to split off unwelcome thoughts and rid ourselves of unpalatable insights into ourselves.

Such human propensities can, of course, also be cynically exploited. 'Brainwashing' speaks to our terror of what can be done in cults and tyrannical states, but also, I think, to our uncertainty about the vagaries of our own minds, the fluctuations of our states of ambivalence, our defences and our fantasies. People may have conflicting wishes, even without obvious brainwashers to hand, to stare certain realities in the face, and might feel compelled to deny, divide, fragment, ignore, discard, fudge and forget.

Although it ranges across the globe, this study is written predominantly about and in the context of the West, no doubt with several other presumptions made in these pages, for instance about the nature of contemporary life, the importance of personhood, the inner world, identity and authenticity. This account acknowledges other ways of seeing the human condition but then draws on a particular model of mind, presupposing, for instance, that we can repress our own unwelcome thoughts. It assumes a distinction between the conscious and unconscious mind, and envisages people, however desirous of harmony, to be nonetheless conflicted creatures throughout the life cycle. Conflicts, for example, might exist between a desire for belonging and a felt need for separation; an acceptance of transience and an aspiration to immortality; awareness of dependence and ambitions of autonomy; a wish to have an impact on others and really 'get through', and a terror of others' potential intrusions, when we are most vulnerable and least able to cope.

PART 2

BREAKING POINT

Ronald Reagan's presidential style always divided public opinion. During the 1980s his poll numbers fluctuated, but he gained broad approval from a majority of American voters, much of the time.[1] He was known by turns as 'the Great Communicator' and 'the Teflon President', because the mess he made never seemed to stick to him. His messages were sunny, self-deprecating, avuncular and sometimes mercurial; he promised to make the nation great again; under his leadership, it would be 'morning in America', he said, an age of strong law and order, lower taxes, free enterprise, national security and proper veneration of military veterans. Gargantuan military spending was to be the order of the day, and on a scale, it was calculated (rightly), that the crumbling Soviet Union could never match.

Reagan was by then renowned as a staunch critic of liberal soft-heartedness and the excessively permissive society. For many, he seemed to satisfy a nostalgic wish to get back to the 1950s. On the Right he remains to this day an admired political figure, an icon of a certain form of masculinity, laced with ideals of independence, muscularity and common sense. Here was the man, conservatives felt, who hastened the end of the Cold War – perhaps even the end of history – and who stood (in the words of former Republican Speaker of the House of Representatives Newt Gingrich) stalwart against 'America-hating totalitarianism' and the 'hard Left'.[2]

Many years before his presidency, Reagan (in keeping already with the tough brand of reactionary politics he came to personify) narrated a hard-line documentary, *The Ultimate Weapon*. This 1962 film argued that military personnel who had not held firm and remained disciplined during their captivity in enemy hands were weak-minded, believe-in-nothing, unpatriotic types. But Reagan was not entirely consistent in delivering such an unforgiving message.

Perhaps he was still sorting out his own views, as a well-known former Democrat sympathiser who turned Republican that very same year.

Reagan's communications about prisoners of war depended on which role he was playing, be it in movies or in his own evolving public life. As Phil Tinline has deftly shown in a 2017 documentary, *The Ultimate Weapon* was certainly at odds with a softer message Reagan had communicated, with feeling, in a now-forgotten Korean War film, *Prisoner of War* (1954).[3] In that movie, Reagan's thinly drawn character, a US military officer named Web Sloane, told viewers that 'every man has his breaking point'.[4] POWs who cracked, succumbed to the pressure, talked, collaborated or even changed allegiance should not be regarded simply as turncoats or weaklings.

The film had its own ideological axes to grind: it was obviously anti-communist, and its 'baddy' characters provided a set of negative Russian and Asian stereotypes. Yet it also took issue with a more ruthless style of punditry. That style was familiar enough during the 1950s (and, also, in a variety of Reagan's later pronouncements); some critics had demanded that POWs bear responsibility for all that they said and did – indeed, for every personal sin of omission or commission – during their years of imprisonment.

In *Prisoner of War* and in some other statements that Reagan made, there seemed to be obvious sympathy for the plight of veteran POWs. (Well over seven thousand Americans were held prisoner during the Korean War, of whom nearly three thousand died.) The film had sent out a clear message and invited public humility, as though to say, 'there but for the grace of God go I'. The picture showed why people, however seemingly tough minded or well disciplined, can be gravely damaged by their cruel captivity, perhaps left with permanent mental scars or even notable long-term changes to their personalities. The US army had initially supported this production but was not pleased by the final version and withdrew co-operation with the producers: for the story seemed to imply that no amount of training, and no stamp of personal character, guaranteed a prisoner would not ultimately break.

Prisoner of War was part of a wave of US responses to the barbarities inflicted by 'enemies of liberty' in modern war; it expressed revulsion against the entire panoply of Korean detention conditions for Western POWs, including brutal, exhausting marches, beatings, inadequate food, freezing cold, insufficient (or completely absent) medical aid, rife disease and poor shelter. Those conditions had precipitated some camp inmates' growing doubts about the war, in some cases (thanks, it was said by the critics, to coercive 're-education') resulting in alienation from their own nation, curiosity about the cause of the communist side, or even, it was feared, more unconscious and mysterious psychological identifications with Mao.[5]

In the film, Sloane is tasked with stealthily entering one of the POW camps, investigating what the North Korean side were doing to men in their custody, identifying contraventions of the Geneva Conventions and reporting these grim discoveries to his military superiors. He finds his compatriots depleted, tormented, crushed, confused and, sometimes, *turned* by their own jailors.

What are we to make of the insistence on 'every man' having his inevitable 'breaking point'? First, to recognise it was a commonplace, if not universally shared, view of that time. Other Cold War reports, films and stories also made the presumption that POWs had this vulnerability to breaking down, and perhaps also to acquiring hard new convictions drastically divergent from former beliefs. Several notable prisoner dramas zeroed in on this chapter in modern history and offered similar general lessons. They spoke, as in the case of *Prisoner of War*, to the human condition. Women were not ignored entirely in this kind of cultural representation and psychological debate, but notable attention, certainly, was paid in 1950s popular culture and academic discourse by men to the state of men, at war with themselves and not just the enemy, inside such camps.

Prisoner of War offered the audience a story to inspire contemplation; a story that suggested we are *all* more-or-less breakable creatures at heart. Who would now really want to argue with that proposition – the notion that people can be brought bit by bit, through pain and suffering, humiliation and terror, to face their own all-too-human limitations and fragility?

Another question, however, is historical: why was the figure of the prisoner, brought to his 'breaking point', such a notable concern of that time? How do we explain the proliferation of clinical accounts, political analyses, novels and films about fractured, crumbling or collapsing military men? Why this focus on people brought to recant former views; to lose (putting it more psychoanalytically) faith in previously cherished good objects; to feel hopeless, confused and utterly abandoned; and then to become vessels for alien thoughts, even thereafter to be induced to profess some foreign ideology?

In this investigation I will return to the Korean War, and also note the United States' lavishly funded secret psychological research projects, developed around the same time, the early 1950s; a covert world of experiments into the mind – what can be done to control, transform or fortify it – that was only much later revealed to the public. Historians and journalists pieced together much of that clandestine story in the last decades of the twentieth century; but it was only after 9/11, in the new century, that the euphemism 'enhanced interrogation' brought it back into prominence, with further research published about mind-control experiments conducted fifty years earlier; experiments in which people were, among other things, confined, medicated, isolated, deprived of sleep, harangued and bombarded with messages and overwhelming sensations. This fear of individual fragility and the larger vulnerabilities it suggested about the nation was matched by a desire to probe those practices and explore potential weaknesses, and more generally to use such insights to advance upon the terrain of psychological warfare.

Hunter, as we saw earlier, promoted the idea that a new threat stalked the earth. He also warned of the psychological fate of inmates cast adrift in enemy territory, and then, perhaps, completely remade. Nonetheless, he rejected what he called a mood of defeatism, proposing instead an urgent set of measures be established to brace Americans and to strengthen all freedom-loving people around the world against brainwashing. He urged the case for a political and psychological fightback, and suggested that resistance had to begin with research, analysis and education about the tools of psychological manipulation at the disposal of the communist state. He wanted to see such measures as reactive – a response to the other side, rather than as practices of experiment and coercion on captives already rife in the West.

Physical and emotional duress, Hunter argued, could be combined by skilled communist jailors; they could develop a softening-up operation conducted in ways that led the prisoner to do much of the job for the captors, destroying the mind from within. Guilt, shame, humiliation, and so on, were to be deliberately engineered by such powers. But ultimately the tormented subject might well start, as he put it, 'smashing up from the inside', unable to withstand such total assaults and tolerate the most lacerating thoughts.[6]

Techniques to destroy minds and bodies had been used on a vast scale in camps within immediate living memory. Modernity and the Holocaust were henceforth inextricably entwined. The Nazis had treated millions of Jews and other inmates as though animals or inanimate objects, stripped of all humanity, mere tattooed numbers, 'vermin' or creatures destined for 'euthanasia', to be massacred in woods and fields, or processed in such 'industrial' plants. No sooner was Hitler established in power than various clinics and hospitals were to become experimental sites of Nazi 'euthanasia' for those deemed degenerate and unworthy of life. And then on an ever vaster scale, as the 'Third Reich' proceeded, concentration camps could be turned into factories of death. They could also be used by certain states across the twentieth century for other purposes – including as part of a project to create 'new men' and 'new women'. The Nazi camps themselves had evolved between the 1930s and 40s from barbaric sites of punishment, intimidation and deterrence for those deemed criminal and for all troublesome opponents of the regime, including many German communists, to the death camps of the 'Final Solution', intended to eradicate the entire Jewish 'race'.

Hunter and others had in mind both Nazism and communism. He argued that the latter, now established so firmly post-war in two vast regions of the world, was in the business of imprisoning enormous numbers of people, physically and mentally; smashing and overwhelming the person, and doing so as but a prelude. For the aim of the communist enemy was not just to break but also to reshape minds, systematically, on behalf of the Party. The 'crack-up', or breaking point, was simply an intermediate stage in an inmate's wretched experience on the conveyer belt to brainwashing. Stalin and Mao's apparatchiks, Hunter explained, wanted to make you 'lap up [your] sorry victuals like a dog', to force you into 'humiliating postures', working you towards the 'crack-up'. Only then could the real ideological work of thought-insertion begin.[7]

Not everyone according to Hunter was inevitably bound to 'crack' in detention, however: some, he insisted, have greater 'mental stamina' than others; even in some cases the power to resist to the end, obstinate through and through. It was as though he was taking issue here with Sloane, or with other writers who expressed any note of what he saw as national defeatism about the presumed total helplessness in 'every man'.[8] The task of resilience-building, he insisted, must be the priority of government: to train soldiers, and also populations at large, to better cope with brainwashing operations in theatres of war and on the home front as well. There was no safe space; the entire world was now being fought over, he implied. 'Free society', he wrote, 'must teach each man and woman that this is everyone's business, for everyone is the target of total war. There is no front and no rear in mind attack.'[9]

It is important to pay attention here to the fanciful and bizarre elements of such analysis as well as the scientifically credible, as we might now see it. The overheated accounts to be found in some journalism, political discussion, cinema or even pulp fiction had material consequences and moral effects; they fostered both a climate of fear and a certain kind of excitement, thus intensifying pressure for new countermeasures to combat the putative danger, or at least providing a moral fig leaf for those who wanted to expand the security and surveillance state in the United States and elsewhere. A great deal of debate has ensued about how minds can be attacked, bodies overwhelmed and brains flooded, even without recourse necessarily to outright physical torture as traditionally understood.

As well as *Prisoner of War*, the 1950s saw diverse works of cinema, fiction, science and reportage address the theme, including the film *The Rack*, another notable Hollywood feature about the Korean War, released two years after *Prisoner of War*. The title references an ancient physical torture, but the film was really concerned with carefully calibrated mental torture conducted upon a severely physically depleted subject, with inmates who might have particular exposure (perhaps running back to a damaged infancy) singled out and targeted.[10] This was a period when book titles on brainwashing appeared, warning of 'The Rape of the Mind'; and concepts such as 'menticide' (the systematic undermining and destruction of the mind) were also suggested by post-war psychiatrists to focus public attention.[11] It was a decade that witnessed many stories about 'puppet masters', 'caged minds' and 'alien invaders', along with multitudes of speeches, films and essays advertising the brainwashing crisis ushered in by the Cold War.

News of poor morale, protests, breakdowns or, worst of all, supposedly total 'thought reform' and conversion among those American POWs in the Korean War caught the attention of powerful figures in Washington and Hollywood, as well as many academics in policy think tanks and universities. Officials and experts turned their attention afresh to prisoner psychology. Commentary abounded, not just reprising older historical concerns with psychiatric conditions in ailing soldiers such as 'nostalgia' (in the nineteenth century), 'shellshock' (in the First World War), 'barbed-wire disease' (in the 1920s, a syndrome supposed to account for captive soldiers' reported hopelessness, memory loss and general fatigue) and 'war neurosis' (in the Second World War), but also charting new paths.[12] The literature was varied, examining the scale, novelty, geography, history, methodology and credibility of the brainwashing threat. Allen Dulles, director of the CIA, duly took note, and recognised an opportunity in his own organisation for fostering technological and psychological research and development.

While some commentators viewed these dangers as nothing new, others warned that the latest generation of troops were especially breakable and labile, and now also exposed to means of attack quite unlike anything seen hitherto in the West, a mode of psychology, an arsenal of techniques, designed to destroy the discrete form of the free-thinking self. These sciences were now supposedly in the process of being perfected in communist Russia and China.

Not everyone went along with the most alarmist warnings about prisoners' brainwashing. The psychiatrist, researcher and writer Robert Jay Lifton, for example, provided more balanced and exploratory papers during the 1950s, and then a landmark book, in 1961, entitled *Thought Reform and the Psychology of Totalism: A Study of 'Brainwashing' in Communist China*. His work took a more careful and circumspect approach. Even in the title, he insisted on writing 'brainwashing' with scare quotes around it. He wanted to signal the hype and the spin, the many inflated, and vague, assumptions that the word carried.[13] Yet, conversely, he cautioned against dismissing the notion of brainwashing as bunk. Studies such as his delved behind populist headlines and fearmongering, but without underplaying the seriousness of the issue, and they too confirmed the importance of continuing scrutiny.

The heated tone of public discussion during the 1950s soon led to critique and sometimes to satires – as we can see in the iconic 1959 novel and 1962 film about brainwashing, *The Manchurian Candidate*. That story seemed as much concerned with the shrill and paranoid anti-communist atmosphere in US politics as the supposed psychological threat emanating from the East. It was hard, no doubt, for readers and viewers to know where *plausible* warnings ended and the fictional horror began: had we really entered a world order where alien creatures could seize and render us helpless and ensure we ended up brain-dead, something akin to the *Invasion of the Body Snatchers* – as another perhaps tongue-in-cheek horror film put it?

This constant circulation of torrid accounts as well as drier research papers meant that 'brainwashing' became part of the zeitgeist: here was a topic as much at home in Ivy League University seminars, broadsheets, radio debates and psychiatric symposia, as in lurid journalistic exposés, tub-thumping speeches by Red-baiting politicians and popular magazines. Although the Korean War was the setting for the initial political alarm, journalists and academic researchers on brainwashing saw the longer historical reach of the problem, and the much wider geographical context as well.

They sought to show how psychological knowledge could be put to work by the great powers to destroy the mind, or to help free it. Psychiatrists and other clinical experts could then be perceived as both part of the problem and potentially part of the solution to brainwashing. Specialists in mental health, including psychoanalysts, were widely regarded post-war on both sides of the Atlantic as important contributors to political debate; they were often lauded as experts with something important to say about domestic policies and foreign affairs. At post-war international forums, including those provided by the World Health Organization, mental health was treated as a crucial matter for all, an urgent concern for global security, not just a question of personal well-being or misfortune. Good mental health was a prerequisite, argued the WHO's first director, the Canadian psychiatrist Brock Chisholm, for sustaining liberal democracy against calamitous political extremes.

Psychiatrists, psychoanalysts and psychologists were thus to avail themselves of new opportunities; they were sought after as consultants in the political sphere, experts in this brave new world of mind and brain; and frequently regarded as dispassionate and scientific observers who could provide cases, experiments, theories, profiles, models and, not least, various important conceptual tools for the study of liberal democratic processes and states of mind, or conversely of fascist, communist or other totalitarian means to transform human beings.

Some mental health experts had played important roles in

intelligence work both during and after the war, for instance in 'denazification' measures, in techniques for training military forces and in refining interrogation procedures. The 'psy' professions were also (by dint of these roles, and others) soon the target of evaluation and a source of apprehension too; cast by critics as dangerous mind-shapers and secret state adjuncts. Such concerns echoed and amplified earlier historical fears that 'mind-doctors' might conspire with others to wrongfully confine the perfectly sane.

Clearly, these psychological sciences, post-war, could be redeployed by both liberal and illiberal states, for purposes quite other than personal therapy, benign social policy or 'pure' research. 'Psy' expertise, warned a growing band of critics, could aid and abet old imperialist endeavours; be used to help crush or postpone new nationalist movements;[14] or be mobilised to reinforce broken political systems. In short, 'psy' science and therapies might serve the state, not the suffering individual; they could work, indeed, for or against revolutionary movements, and in support of or in opposition to ideals such as freedom, democracy and universal human rights.

The abuse of psychiatry in the Soviet Union extended this theme. Incarceration of the politically 'disturbed' became an increasing focus of inquiry and protest by many activists and intellectuals during the 1960s and 70s. This was the most obvious example, a catalyst for a more general and pervasive critique of 'psy' expertise. A stream of clandestine writings about such abuses of clinical knowledge and power were produced in the Soviet Union. Open protests against the abuse of the asylum, and the perversion of psychiatry, also multiplied in the West. Many analyses emerged of how psychiatrists in both systems had been co-opted to lock up dissidents, pacify difficult and marginal people, or to destroy the resistance of rebels.[15]

Robert Jay Lifton's personal interest in the subject of Chinese thought reform had initially been stirred when he worked as a psychiatrist in the US air force at the close of the Korean War. As part of his job he was required to assess POWs' mental states before they were demobbed. Thousands of American and other prisoners, fighting against communism, were filtering back from their military units or from the POW camps: mostly they travelled home slowly by ship, rather than plane, to their country. He accompanied some of them in 1953, on a troop carrier bound for San Francisco.

That vessel (named after a former army man, General John Pope) housed contingents of soldiers now struggling to make sense of what they had experienced in the war and in those grim enclosures as POWs. They were, as Lifton described, often fractious, divided, tense and initially suspicious of him and his medical colleagues.[16] However, over time, on board or later back home, some shared tales with medics, psychiatrists and psychologists about POW camp life. They would offer researchers insights into their views of conditions in the army, on the battlefield or in those communist prisons, and on occasion reveal mixed feelings about coming home.

One man said to Lifton that his worst fear now was 'being babied' by his family; another confessed that all he wanted to do was to disappear from view and go fishing alone, forever.[17] Such men yearned to escape the past, and also, perhaps, to bypass families who they suspected would find it impossible to comprehend what they had suffered and witnessed, or what they had inflicted on others. Over the 1950s Lifton first began to piece together a picture of techniques of thought reform prevalent in Chinese society, as well as in prison camps, during those years.

The issue of brainwashing in Korea thus focused a great deal of research energy as well as public attention on the ordeals suffered by soldiers and prisoners in an age of Cold War. Some of this work insisted the world had entered a quite new phase, while some drew links to older cultural and political phenomena, and pointed back to previous social fears about, say, demonic possession, or debates in nineteenth-century political psychology about mass irrationality.

Long before the word 'brainwashing' entered the lexicon, much had already been written about crazed and possessed 'masses', and about the systematic manipulations that could be effected upon prisoners' state of mind. Prison might destroy the captive's reason, not restore it, as had once been hoped by penal reformers in the nineteenth century. Criminologists had long argued about the role of heredity and milieu in constituting the character of the criminal type, and about whether delinquents were born as such, and if their behaviour could be altered at all. A large psychiatric literature existed on delinquency and moral reform, as well as on the dangers of suggestion, persuasion and hypnosis on vulnerable captive minds. In the wrong hands, hypnosis, it was thought, could lead to crimes of passion or collective acts of murderous violence. There had been much debate too about the mind-bending powers of certain orators and stage hypnotists, and speculations about how modern crowds might be tamed, diverted and mobilised by 'elites', for instance into a new debased form of imperialism and overblown patriotism and jingoism, rather than into class warfare.

Particular mesmerising figures – real or fictional – were to provide lightning conductors for these anxieties about politics and reason. Such concerns snowballed in the Victorian period. Benjamin Disraeli, who became British prime minister twice during the 1860s and 70s, provided one focus of concern; an exemplar, said critics, of the arts of political bewitchment, and a man sometimes credited with special psychological powers. The Victorian historian and sage Thomas Carlyle warned that Disraeli was 'a superlative Hebrew conjurer, spellbinding all the great Lords, great parties, great interests of England'.[18]

The period also saw much discussion of spell-binding musicians and conductors, in real life or in imaginative tales, such as George du Maurier's best-selling novel of the 1890s, *Trilby*, featuring the repugnant but irresistible character Svengali.

These fears about toxic charmers or hypnotic entertainers who might invade, feed off, destroy and remake people's minds soon spread, sometimes intersecting with conspiracy literature, specifically with anti-Semitic representations. A plethora of images was produced of the dangerous psychological power of the Jews (including Disraeli, and the mythic Svengali) over a mass of gentiles. But the issue was certainly not confined to discussion of one supposedly dangerous people or race.[19]

Speculative political analyses multiplied around the *fin de siècle*, warning of the regression of the mind that occurred in any great aggregate; the numberless masses were often described in crowd-psychology treatises as descending into some atavistic, singular, supposedly feminine and devouring mob. Such states of altered consciousness (as well as unconsciousness) in individuals, couples or larger groups were explored in novels and dramas, as well as in psychiatric treatises and criminological accounts, long before all this talk of brainwashing and automaton assassins made the headlines.

The context for this growing anxiety about brainwashing was thus apparent well before the post-war period. Furthermore, show trials in the Soviet Union provided an important catalyst for debate just before the Second World War. These featured prominent victims of Stalin, including some former very high-ranking Soviet Party officials who had fallen from grace. Their fate aroused much consternation and speculation as to how they had been broken down and then made to speak out before facing the inevitable guilty verdicts in court. These dramatic court-room events in Moscow, at their height between 1936 and 1938, revealed how proud people could be brought humiliatingly and, in some eyes, bizarrely to confess to any number of things: former comrades of Stalin publicising the fact they were spies and traitors – a disgrace to their leader, comrades, ideology and motherland.

During the Second World War, Western public attention on 'confession extraction' by Stalin's agents lessened. The focus in the English-speaking world was predominantly upon combatting Nazism rather than communism. However, the alliance of the Free World (as US presidents were now calling it)[20] with the Soviet Union was short-lived, and the dangerous mass psychology of communism soon re-emerged as a regular theme after 1945. Images of monstrous tyrant Stalin, which sometimes in wartime Western coverage had softened (for instance in the more palatable 'Uncle Joe'), reverted to the more sinister version shortly after the victory.

As the Cold War set in, there came a new stream of strange and seemingly will-less confessions, most notably emanating from communist-run Eastern Europe, where the Soviet Union was now exerting control. These inscrutable court-room offerings revived public memories of the admissions by self-sacrificing or psychically destroyed apparatchiks in Moscow before the war. Those reports were now dusted off and revisited. By the late 1940s, observers could link such true-life cases with George Orwell's vision of Winston Smith, or with the story in *Darkness at Noon*, Arthur Koestler's landmark fictionalised account of Soviet confession extraction, published in 1940.

In Budapest, 1949, the most eye-catching and perturbing post-war example of indoctrination during interrogation took place, likewise reviving memories of earlier conversion scandals and incantatory states. A new high-profile prisoner of the communist world was on trial; the 'guilty man' was the leader of the Hungarian Catholic Church, Cardinal József Mindszenty. The prelate revealed to Hungarians his copious crimes against the state: treason, conspiracy, espionage, etc. The trial was not broadcast on film, although some of it was relayed on radio. Reports, disseminated by word of mouth and in print, told of the cardinal's troublingly spaced-out appearance and wooden-toned speech.

Mindszenty's case led to a storm of protests in the West, some of which were spearheaded by the Vatican and the Catholic press. In the dock, Mindszenty appeared to have lost his gravitas, and perhaps also his mind. Suffice to say that he was somehow induced to make extravagant and improbable admissions; he appeared, it was said, to be a man not only confused, but also broken and terrified, or even terrorised, apparently transfixed, and bathed in a deep sense of guilt.

The scale of Western media attention to this story of a man who was broken, lost, yet so open to the minds of others (his jailors), and now so willing to do his tormentors' bidding, should not be underestimated. It garnered much publicity and speculation, even prompting a notable 1955 feature film starring Alec Guinness, *The Prisoner*. Mindszenty's trial had occurred just before that key word 'brainwashing' entered circulation. Commentaries using other related words were already plentiful in the late 1940s, warning about the science of confession through interrogation, and a form of mass conversion that could be occurring in society and most acutely in the prison system. Here was an exemplary case: a once strong-willed Catholic prelate and anti-Nazi stalwart who had been broken and led, it appeared, to a new state of consciousness, directed by others.

Some wondered if his compliance was secured with the aid of Actedron, a drug that stimulates the brain and nerves, potentially interfering drastically with mood and sleep and instigating various side effects. Others speculated about the well-practised skills of the interrogators and jailors who perhaps knew something of the modern psychology of the unconscious and were adept at more subtly triggering and then working over the cardinal's particular constellation of childhood fears and memories. Physical torture in this case was firmly suspected, but nobody could reliably tell exactly what had happened. The case was splashed across the press for months in Europe and the United States. *The New York Times*, *Manchester Guardian* and *Le Monde* were among the papers to devote dozens of articles to the elucidation of this murky tragedy.[21]

Hot on the heels of the cardinal's tale came another case, concerning a travelling American businessman, Robert Vogeler. He too had been arrested and imprisoned in Hungary on charges of spying and sabotage. His court case took place in February 1950, and was soon labelled in the United States as an outrageous show trial of an innocent American visitor.[22] The question, again, was why and how he then not only made his *mea culpa*, but perhaps even internally accepted it. After a period in custody and undergoing interrogation, Vogeler, likewise, confessed to his crimes. He was duly sentenced to fifteen years' imprisonment. The authorities had somehow managed to overwhelm his 'resistances', provoke 'regression' and perhaps even half or fully convince him that he was truly guilty. No ego, this case seemed to suggest, was able to withstand the most desolate and disturbing environmental experiences.

As Vogeler explained after returning to the United States (the beneficiary of hasty diplomacy), within three months of his arrest, alone in his cell, he had completely collapsed. To place a person in isolation, to leave them waiting in anticipation of torments to come, can be torment enough. People may well break down when left long enough to stew. Routine procedure and deadening certainty can lead to despair; and uncertainty too can drive us mad, prompting the mind to play the cruellest tricks on itself. The Vogeler story was just one more illustration of how prisoner psychology and scientific interrogation made great waves in Western political discourse in this period, and another prefiguration of that movie refrain: 'every man has his breaking point'. Vogeler later gave a speech describing the ordeal he had suffered; what it felt like to be stripped, led to a grim cell, 6 feet by 9 feet, there to sit alone on the wooden bed, with a wet floor, in the unbearable cold. He spoke of the horror of the demoralisation he felt at the authorities' refusal to allow him to wash, the psychological and physical impact of the diet he endured of black bread and water three times a day. The worst thing of all, he said, was the steel peephole, which opened every six minutes only to clang shut.[23]

Vogeler added:

> At the time of my trial … I was in no condition to do anything but recite my lines. I had been imbued with such a feeling of desolation that my one desire was to say my piece and have done with it. My voice quavered as I spoke into the microphone that was placed before me. It sounded to me like the voice of another person, and, in a sense of course, it was.[24]

These high-profile cases were far from being the only ones. Each new example, in the Soviet sphere or, soon after, in China, kept the question of how crack-ups and confessions were secured firmly in the Western media eye. Cases were duly added to the brainwash literature; a basis for theories about how best to control, fully know, and break down and/or remake the pliable human subject. The range of possibilities was duly explored – secretly administered 'truth drugs' and 'lie detectors' (both innovations of the 1920s), the offer of traumatic choices (such as the hope dangled before an inmate that they would survive by being an informer or punisher of others), confusing claustrophobic architecture, solitary confinement, deprivation of food, manipulation of light and dark, intrusion of sound or prolonged silence, the warping of time and space, the endless play of the inquisitorial team's alternating kindness, mockery, harshness and cruelty, or the sheer impact of peer pressure, where prisoner groups were required to 're-educate' one another.

Many of these techniques had been explored and discussed in an emerging literature between the 1920s and 1950s. On a small scale, for example, an experiment was conducted in the Spanish Civil War on some prisoners held by the Republican side. It was an adaptation of certain ideas from modern art: just as modernist pictures might challenge the idea of the traditional frame or enclosure, so jail walls and floors might be designed to look out of kilter, with zigzag patterns and psychedelic effects – a built-space that could disorientate minds and then, maybe, loosen tongues.

Such fringe experiments, interwar, came in the wake of earlier, far more important, innovations, affecting much larger numbers: prison design had been radically rethought in many countries during the nineteenth century to suit either utilitarian philosophy or religious creeds (or both); hence the advent of silent and solitary penitentiary systems that could, perhaps, bring the prisoner to a state of complete subjection and compliance as well as repentance.

Post-war, brainwashing was part of a wider conversation, therefore, about the vast range of tools that could be used to extract information and to possess and redirect minds and bodies: architecture, sound, drugs, temperature, precise increments of pain, sudden and bewildering changes of circumstance, and many other variables that made it hard to resist, and that might also reshape the prisoner's inner beliefs. The pharmaceutical revolution of the twentieth century fostered many new aspirations and fears, although it might also have led to exaggerated expectations of scientific 'truth extraction'. British and US intelligence sought to refine such methods and treatments during the Second World War, with mixed results, as for example in the use made of Evipan, the trade name of a particular form of barbiturate, during the interrogation of a notoriously 'amnesiac' prisoner of state held by the British, the former Deputy Führer of the Nazi Party, Rudolf Hess. The army doctors treating Hess were puzzled by what they called his 'hysterical' behaviour, worried by his attempt at suicide, and unsure whether he subsequently faked his claimed memory loss in order to defy his captors, or was suffering deeply neurotic, or perhaps far more serious psychotic, symptoms. Even under the influence of Evipan, known for its sedating and hypnotic effects, Hess left his interrogators and physicians little the wiser. One of the psychiatrists asked the medicated prisoner in 1944 to 'Tell us now what you have forgotten', to which he replied: 'I don't know. Pain! Thirst! … Water! Pain in my body! A fog.'[25] At the Nuremberg trial, Hess's behaviour and statements continued to puzzle the lawyers and even his fellow defendants, and would lead to a great deal of psychiatric speculation.[26]

Lifton, as I have noted, provided one of the most compelling post-war studies of how conditions might be created, above all in totalitarian states, to inculcate beliefs in prisoners. A typical method, he argued, in his exposé of Chinese 'brainwashing', was to wear someone out, intimidate, confuse, terrify and shame, and then provide a new source of identification. The captive subject would 'learn' that they had fundamentally misunderstood their previous life and best future path. A set of techniques was repeatedly used, he argued, to convince people of the unreliability of their prior memories, beliefs and political interpretations, and to induce them to see their story quite differently, thereby to cement new allegiances.

Most conducive to the process, Lifton explained, was creating a closed milieu, cutting off routes to any alternative opinion, promoting a sacred language, exerting the power of life and death, and introducing a culture of confession, purification rituals, loaded language and repetitive slogans – thus first decimating the mind, then possessing and redirecting it. The subject could 'awaken' and take up their place, embrace a new totalised narrative, where the past-present-future all now made sense, the way ahead beautifully clear.

After the breakdown of previous beliefs in a prisoner came the gradual or sudden breakthrough into new and bullet-proof 'understanding'. Or, rather, into a heavily coached and coerced form of personal tale – utterly congruent with the view of the group, the community and, ultimately, the state. It was frequently regarded as essential, at least in some communist states (most obviously China), for such 're-educated' prisoners not only to obey, but to convey this tremendous sense of moral and political awakening *out loud* to others (for instance, their appreciative and encouraging fellow prisoners).

According to Lifton, a new 'totalistic' state of the mind is consistent with the politics of totalitarianism: no hesitation, doubt, contradiction, dissent; no counter-thoughts or ambivalence; just harmonious oneness, the transcendence of all messy everyday feelings, singular direction, utter (and terrifying) congruence. Lifton's account of 'totalism' is still, in my view, an important and relevant account in understanding some cases of what we now call 'radicalisation'. However, it is harder to determine so clearly and to know so fully what any individual subject feels, thinks or believes, consciously or unconsciously, during and after such a process. It is easier to formulate the nature of such psychological projects, to break down the elements of the procedure – isolation, humiliation, shame, repetition, group 'support', and so on – than to be sure of quite where it leaves a 're-educated' person, deep down, in their own inner world.

But what, asked what we might here call the brainwash 'research community' during the 1950s, of the peculiar features of this process? What if the point of bringing a man or woman to a breakdown in precisely calibrated fashion was to ensure not only such disintegration, but total conversion to a new secular form of religion, world communism? Conversion, that is, to a faith implacably at odds with liberal democracy and the market system, the world that we know, above all, in Western capitalism? Lengthy interrogations, blandishments and enticements, constant thumping slogans, and so on, might all be used, mused such Cold War observers, to break and then reconstruct a person for the sake of the Communist Party and its totalitarian creed in the global struggle that was now underway.

The question of state-orchestrated mind-control projects, and the pliability of political subjects to enemy hidden persuasion, thus exercised numerous officials in the Cold War. Many in Western intelligence had followed the Mindszenty story and others like it. Dulles and his colleagues at the CIA knew about previous intelligence efforts, during the Second World War, by the CIA's forerunner, the Office of Strategic Services, for which Dulles and some other CIA staff had also worked; efforts to develop for the 'free world' the science of interrogation, and to dabble in new psychological and medical methods, including those forays into so-called truth drugs and other adaptable chemical products. During the Korean War and after, Dulles received bulletins about these various communist 'advances' in the field of human-behaviour management. The West had to do better, he and his colleagues decided. So, with his blessing, CIA operatives set up secret research programmes to investigate and corner the field; these were given esoteric code names such as 'Bluebird', 'Artichoke' and, by 1953, 'MK-Ultra'.

The CIA, in short, invested heavily in research on the mind and the brain. Once this got going, there was shockingly little central oversight of their clandestine work on human psychology, physiology and neuroscience. Many unwitting human guinea pigs, including psychiatric patients, would suffer the consequences. Such prolific research work in the field of 'altered states', later exposed and investigated by outsiders, was found to be dubious at best, and illegal, outrageous and totally unethical at worst.[27] Conversely, the CIA and the armed services sought to develop new ideas about resilience for servicemen and women abroad, in order for them to be able to endure captivity more effectively, just as Hunter and his peers had proposed.

Such work on the psychology of interrogation and resistance was later described in a notorious CIA secret report, known as the Kubark Manual, published in 1963, now available online.[28] It ran through the gamut of methods of interrogation; it discussed the pros and cons of death threats, sensory deprivation, drugs and other methods of influencing behaviour, while also insisting on the enormous variety of human responses to such methods. This 'science', in other words, could never yield entirely reliable and predictable results in a particular case.

That report brought together some of the work that had been written in the previous decade, a good deal of it sponsored directly by the CIA, to discover what happens, for example, when people are kept awake for days, put into induced comas, loaded with LSD, restricted in small spaces, subjected to stress positions or endless looped messages, or deprived of any obvious sensation at all, just left alone, in terror, in the darkness.[29] As the report coolly observed, '[t]he point is that man's sense of identity depends upon a continuity in his surroundings, habits, appearance, actions, relations with others, etc. Detention permits the interrogator to cut through those links and throw the interrogatee back upon his own unaided internal resources.'[30]

While the CIA's work and that of other intelligence agencies expanded in this field, university and hospital staff in many places were recruited, encouraged and sometimes covertly financed to develop unusual experiments and trials. Looking back at the extent of this ecosystem of research, one historian, Alfred McCoy, compared it (admittedly with a touch of hyperbole) to the top-secret research operation behind the atomic bomb. Here, he said, was the CIA version of 'the Manhattan Project of the mind'.[31]

The extent of such inquiry into mental states and human behaviour in extreme conditions was indeed very considerable; the projects are well described in a pioneering 1979 book, *The Search for the 'Manchurian Candidate': The CIA and Mind Control*, by John Marks. This publication helped inspire numerous other researchers who subsequently fleshed out many of the details. Marks made ample use of Freedom of Information requests to piece together his story, and thus to reveal many schemes that took place under the watch of the long-term director of MK-Ultra, Sidney Gottlieb.[32]

An especially shocking example of participation by a mental health expert requires a mention here: the work of the Scottish-born psychiatrist Dr Ewen Cameron. He conducted so-called 'psychic driving' experiments on patients in the psychiatric facility at McGill University in Canada. Cameron and his team, beneficiaries of some covert intelligence funding, attempted to see what would happen when repetitive messages were played over and over to patients already heavily subdued with drugs. He also sought to erase the memories of schizophrenic patients through electroconvulsive therapy and the use of anti-psychotic medications such as Thorazine. Cameron was willing to conduct experiments in 'psychic driving' on patients without informed consent. The severe and even disastrous consequences for victims would gradually emerge over the years.

Another troubling case was the work of the neuroscientist John Lilly. Post-war, Lilly had undertaken a variety of brain experiments involving the insertion of electrodes into primates and other animals, before his focus turned back to the impact of sensory deprivation on humans. During the 1950s, Lilly, in the United States, and other colleagues, such as Donald Hebb, working primarily in Canada, researched, with ample funding, the effects of total isolation on the brain and the personality. Such forms of research were well conveyed in a 1963 movie, *The Mind Benders*, where we can witness the drama of an obsessive scientist, watched by a senior representative of the intelligence services, going out of his mind after many hours submerged in a tank full of water.[33] Hebb's research students volunteered to sit inside an isolation chamber: eyes covered with goggles, ears subjected to silence or white noise, so the team could see the effects.

What could not be simulated completely was the terror of actual detention by enemy forces. Nonetheless, Hebb also wanted to find out how people changed and grew more suggestible under such circumstances. He hoped to see if they might be susceptible to the implantation of new or different ideas. Lilly, not to be outdone by his colleagues, had created his own purpose-built isolation chamber. His technique involved the total submersion of a subject inside a tank of water, at body temperature. Lilly and Hebb were both appointed to consultancy roles to help establish sensory-deprivation research at the Wright-Patterson Air Force Base, Ohio.

Lilly apparently envisioned a not-so-distant future in which his techniques could be employed to obtain, as he put it, 'push-button control over the totality of motivation and behaviour', leading to 'master-slave controls directly of one brain over another'.[34] Later, however, this once reliable insider and laboratory scientist working for the government changed direction, or as some saw it made a volte-face, a life choice which has since been much explored by scholars. Lilly did not exactly drop out, but altered course, ever more interested in countercultural moods and a range of more arcane social and biological issues. He was not alone in moving from work in the 'military–industrial complex' to rather more obstruse pursuits, including personal researches on the paranormal. Lilly, moreover, came to suggest that isolation, far from being exclusively a means of mind manipulation and control, could also be used to empower and open a greater awareness, a mode of consciousness-raising, autonomy-building or freedom enhancement. Eventually the kind of isolation he and other such scientists researched seemed to find a new context, feeding a novel element into the growing popularity of retreats in the West. Even flotation tanks became part of a set of new practices for securing quiet, contemplation, meditation or general 'well-being', subsumed in a booming therapy and relaxation industry that today is being developed and promoted by companies around the world. In the United States, for example, large sales fairs such as the Float Conference take place, where consumers and industry experts can gather to hear talks about the benefits of the procedure for body and mind, and to explore the latest devices.[35]

Lilly, admittedly, was an exceptional case; an eye-catching story of someone going from the world of such Cold War 'psy warfare' research off into the wonders of the natural world, moving from military to civilian experiments, and enjoying a more offbeat personal life in Big Sur in California. Lilly had, in fact, a long-standing interest in dolphins, their large brains and high intelligence. Early works had considered their potential naval and military value. But publications including *Man and Dolphin* (1961) and *The Mind of the Dolphin* (1967) also helped raise the profile of the dolphin to the status of intelligent and sentient being, worthy of high regard. His story, well charted elsewhere, serves to illustrate the potential cross-over points between 1950s intelligence and the 'counterculture' of the 1960s, or, much later, those fringe intelligence and military inquiries into the paranormal; a secretive world, as the writer Jon Ronson put it, where 'men stare at goats'.[36]

In another such cross-over, LSD was procured for intelligence purposes, and also feted by experimenters as a drug to lead the mind to new worlds of colour, shape and sound. By the 1960s, it had become a vehicle for many people interested in tuning in or dropping out, expanding or investigating mundane quotidian consciousness, and finding an 'altered state'; or as Aldous Huxley famously put it, opening 'the doors of perception'.

But for our purposes, its military and intelligence uses need to be kept in mind: LSD was a chemical that the CIA had a great interest in exploring as a mode of mind control, or an aid to interrogation. Much experimental work on the impact of such drugs on the detainee was conducted in a military context, for example through the US Army Chemical Corps at the Edgewood Arsenal facility in Maryland. Soldiers, psychiatric patients and prisoners in the United States and in outreach projects abroad (including one in Europe in 1961 which was code-named 'Third Chance') were subjected to such experiments, in the 1950s and after. In one calamitous case at Edgewood in 1953, a lethal amount of mescaline was injected into a patient, a tennis player named Harold Blauer, who was undergoing treatment for depression. He was never told that he was part of a military experiment. In another trial, also at Edgewood, it was reported that recipients saw 'horrible green-eyed monsters' or felt 'a constant flow of electricity' throughout the body.[37]

Such drugs, the experimenters discovered, could prove powerful but also remarkably unpredictable, affecting people profoundly differently. If one goal of such research was simply to disable, another was to expose the captive's thoughts to the interrogator. A working assumption at Edgewood during some of the experiments was that LSD would prove most effective when administered to people who were given no prior information at all about what the drug would do to them, or even that they were being medicated. Guinea pig soldiers were thus sometimes misled about the trials, given LSD without their knowledge, and then closely observed. Effects could be extremely disturbing, with the subjects left confused, desperate or frantic.

So, stories of brainwashed Western prisoners in the Korean War need to be seen in context. There were prior and subsequent developments, a host of ideas, theories, experiments and suppositions. An extensive literature, exploring a new kind of battle for control of the mind, emerged in the interwar decades and was extended during the Second World War. It was further amplified and dramatised by mysterious and much-publicised occurrences during the early Cold War.

Instances of confession extraction once again made the news, causing puzzlement and consternation during the war in Korea. In 1952 and 1953, several new cases emerged of guilty, or at least seemingly guilt-ridden, military men from the United States, confirming their crimes (including participation in germ warfare attacks) while in enemy hands. What were the Western public to make of the news of captured US personnel who 'revealed' their own participation in such biological warfare in Korea? Was this brainwashing, or were they broken down and thus encouraged to tell the truth? Accusations spread by the communist side about US use of such armaments circulated from 1951, although the story really gained legs the following year, when imprisoned pilots began to confess. Rumours also emerged about this new warfare method, some telling of autopsies conducted on civilians in communist-controlled Korea; victims who had suffered vomiting and headaches, or, much worse, haemorrhages in the brain and damage to the lungs, the lymph and adrenal glands. Such accounts were reinforced by reports of Western use of anthrax, or other poisonous substances, and of strange objects dropping out of the sky from US planes.

In January 1952, the crew of a US bomber was shot down while flying over the north of Korea. Months later, the pilot, John Quinn, and another officer in the bomber crew, Kenneth Enoch, were produced by the Chinese and North Koreans to go on record and acknowledge their roles in such germ attacks.

The confessing airmen, so it was said by US spokesmen, must have been either consciously feigning their 'crimes', or else had somehow been persuaded erroneously, even influenced unconsciously, to assume that they were responsible. In sum, the government refuted the claims and continued to declare indignantly that the stories made no sense, and that these men must have been abused and over-whelmed, no longer able to tell up from down. The airmen were sowing disinformation under intolerable pressure, claimed angry officials in Washington.

Beijing denied this, insisted on the accuracy of the confessions, and organised a supposedly objective international scientific commit-tee (in fact, comprising broadly sympathetic experts) to investigate. The Chinese authorities published a report to confirm the United States had indeed used such weapons, citing testimony from the cap-tured air crews and others, alongside scientific data (soil samples, evidence of poisoned insects, and so on).[38] Whatever the truth, imagine the further consternation in 1953 when a still more senior US air force officer, Colonel Frank Schwable, also acknowledged his own active participation.

This claim, again, did not seem entirely implausible to anyone neutral, let alone anyone opposed to Western imperialism. After all, in lieu of dropping nuclear bombs (as the US air force had done in Japan in 1945, and as some in the US top brass would at least consider doing when the Korean campaign foundered), it was conceivable to many people even outside the communist world that US forces could have aimed to poison the people and land, ruining agriculture and infecting bodies, so as to bring about mass starvation, not just demor-alisation. Debate surrounding this case of cover-up and/or fake news concerning the Korean War continues to this day among historians.[39] Clearly many critics felt that the devastating policy choices made by the United States in the war that unfolded in Vietnam in the following decade only made the earlier germ warfare claims about Korea seem more plausible with hindsight.[40]

Dr Charles Mayo, a prominent surgeon, medical administrator and commentator on the Korean War, exemplified the indignant response to such claims at the time. He was apparently convinced by the US government's denials and declared these arrested airmen had been broken and brainwashed to say whatever was demanded. Such POWs, he explained, had been left in rags, with untreated wounds, their bodies infested with lice. The men were brutally exposed to the elements, forced to drink infected water and eat terrible food, subjected to threats of execution, bullied and harried constantly, kept awake and regularly beaten. The communists had 'extorted' confessions by 'perverting' Pavlov's work, he said, to 'mould' their minds. Any signs of co-operation by such prisoners, Mayo explained, were rewarded with slight improvements in treatment, thus establishing a circuit of associations inside the brain. Neuroscience, or behavioural psychology, rather than psychoanalysis, he implied, could explain the deep changes affected in their attitudes as well as their public statements.

Mayo asked his readers to understand and sympathise – to see how such captives were brought to the point of desperation and then offered a way out; they might well be simply incapable of resisting, given the state of their brains. The miracle was that some men *could* still resist and not break, could endure this treatment at all, even for a day, and still string their own thoughts together. It was entirely understandable that ordinary people would crack, or be confounded, he insisted; imagine a systematic assault so complete and bewildering that all you cared about was a crust of bread, and that all you desired was an hour of sleep.[41]

You could get most people to say or believe anything, so Mayo continued, given the necessary environmental inputs. Those confessions by the 'guilty' prisoners were thus regularly revisited and set alongside a different story. To the consternation of hawkish politicians and generals, hundreds of American POWs had also signed petitions for peace, expressing their criticism and doubts about war, certainly about *this* war. As the 1950s wore on, bulletins also circulated of disillusionment, cynicism, poor morale in the armed forces; accounts that were very different to those cases of 'cracking' airmen put before kangaroo courts. There were other reports of imprisoned brainwashed men and women: for instance, students and travellers in China who also fell apart and recanted, sometimes swiftly, under interrogation and declared themselves to be, well, whatever the interrogators demanded they should be. One of these students, an American Fulbright scholar in China, Harriet Mills, taken into custody in 1951, was brought to a point where she declared herself an unpaid espionage agent, and confirmed US germ warfare in Korea.[42]

Some of those captives seemed to have been trained, during captivity, to respect, admire or even positively love their jailor teachers. Consider the plight of the person known as Jane Darrow, the Canadian daughter of a Christian missionary, who lived and worked in China as a teacher. Following her arrest, soon after Mao took full command of the state in 1949, she spent four years in captivity. Although perhaps never *entirely* converted, her thinking and emotional life were altered during her years of imprisonment. From life in a family intent upon spreading the Word, encouraging faith, converting people to Christianity, she was schooled to feel a new zeal as a convert to Mao. After her release, she described how she had found herself enthusiastically endorsing the new communist system, voicing an ever more jubilant yes, even as she remained trapped.

Between her first arrival and later 'promotion' to act as a kind of informal instructor to others, Darrow apparently suffered a great deal of shame which was nurtured by fellow inmates, as well as by guards. She was regularly set straight about any lingering idea that she was superior; although whether she began with such a premise was not clear. The task of the group was to ensure her humility, to bring home to her fully her *shameful* membership of an *exploiter class*, an idea that increasingly she came to acknowledge quite openly, and, for a time, to feel despairing about. She grew horrified, so she later told an investigator, by her prior identity – an exemplar of a foreign and privileged imperial world. In time, she was able to dis-identify, up to a point, from that position and instead align her thinking and feeling with the Chinese communist cause.

Darrow, despite her political 'development', was never quite fervent enough to be accepted by the authorities as a fully trusted prison-house teacher herself; being a foreigner cannot have helped.

When she was finally released, she thanked the judge copiously, expressed warmth towards her captors, spoke with gratitude of what she had learned from other inmates – and denounced with conviction all those historical US crimes, including the most recent atrocity, germ warfare.

Such prisoners would thus 'progress' through a custodial system, navigating as best they could amid interrogation, instruction, punishments and rewards. Gradually the new community – its approval and approbation, even its 'love' – might well grow more and more important to inmates, perhaps quite consciously, but also, analysts argued, unconsciously. The prisoner, as post-war commentators on brainwashing explained, 'transferred' to the new figures or to the new group much deeper and more archaic wishes and feelings. This, as Lifton and others would note, was also the classic modus operandi of cults. Darrow, he showed, was gratified by the prison group's extremely enthusiastic acceptance of her statements that she had been leading hitherto an indefensibly 'parasitic life'.[43] Her autobiographical account was thus gradually reworked, out loud, as well as inside her mind, with much support from the others in custody around her. She was cheered on as she made her confessions and expressed bitter self-reproaches for her many past mistakes.

We can only speculate as to what personal feelings or defences may have been disturbed and broken in her, as for any other such confessing subjects who underwent this form of process. We may want to ask what might have made Darrow especially vulnerable to such personal shaming and guilt-tripping. There is much, inevitably, that is unknowable about this experience and the later outcome. I rely here on the vivid description provided by Lifton in 1961. This account serves to suggest how a person can come to be contemptuous of their former self, to believe in the purity of their new-found group membership, to be convinced they now enjoy a deeper liberty than they had before, and to view themselves as more available, thanks to this 'help' in moving towards 'the truth'. Suffice to say that what Darrow and similar inmates might previously have viewed as their cruel and unfair punishment, inside a prison, could morph in the mind into something far more cathartic.

Discourses about brainwashing have been through numerous iterations since that era, from tales of false memory syndrome and reports about the victims of so-called Stockholm Syndrome, to current exploration of young people's 'grooming' and 'radicalisation' to the cause of jihad.[44] The 1970s case of the young heiress Patty Hearst, for example, who was kidnapped by a small, extreme and violent US left-wing group, the Symbionese Liberation Army, echoed such earlier accounts and provided a new kind of label; the case caused a particularly great stir in the media. Hearst apparently came to 'identify with her aggressors' (the kidnappers) and participated with them in a bank robbery in San Francisco. Her conduct and subsequent trial turned Stockholm Syndrome into a household name. This is the condition where hostages develop a strong, positive psychological bond or identification with those who are holding them in captivity. Hearst's defence team argued that none of her criminal actions while in detention had been undertaken freely: she had been abused, drawn into an intimate relationship with one member of the group; she was already a fragile person, suffering a serious psychiatric condition, and was manipulated. In short, she was afflicted by a syndrome that, if not born entirely out of the captivity, and perhaps reflected earlier problems, was exploited by others to control her once she had been abducted. Expert medics who appeared on her behalf seeking clemency included Lifton, and other notable writers on brainwashing.[45]

Over the last fifty years some of the arguments that were once contentious have become more akin to common sense: the argument that an abuser, who creates a menacing, bullying, brutal or highly perverse milieu for a victim, may well affect, even transform, the conscious and the unconscious psychic life of the captive, generating massive confusion, before demanding and gaining inner compliance.[46] There are tales of victims who remain in the kidnapper's jail even when that jail has no bars. Sometimes an abuser may do the most lasting damage by making victims active participants, collusive agents, 'partners in crime'.

Mental health workers today in all likelihood will work under the assumption that what we call the 'internal world', while not just a reflection of the 'external world', can be deeply and permanently affected by traumatic experiences inflicted by others, in very early life, or thereafter at any stage of existence. Abusers can stir up in children as well as in adults complicated feelings, including guilt, shame and mortification. Enforced complicity in actions that contravene the victim or prisoner's own prior belief system can cause a kind of psychic havoc. Later abuses may exploit a person's earlier vulnerabilities, compounding early traumas with others, hence the now commonplace term 're-traumatisation'. Nobody comes out psychologically undamaged from long-term captivity, although some people's capacity to hold on to their minds, even against the greatest of odds, can be a remarkable thing.

Recall Brian Keenan, the Northern Irish writer and long-term hostage in Beirut, who described in an outstanding book the vast range of emotions he went through in four and a half years of captivity. He wrote of the oscillations in his states of mind: times of defiance, courage, compassion, fortitude and camaraderie; and periods of massive and overwhelming psychic disturbance. Between 1986 and 1990 Keenan was held in isolation at some points, and at others in confined spaces with other men, including, most importantly for him, fellow hostage John McCarthy. Keenan provides moving accounts of the love and care of prisoners for each other; of shifting states of terror, fury, desolation, despair; the moments when the mind would fall apart, or perhaps heal a bit; the solace that could sometimes be found in the company of another fellow sufferer.

Who knows how Keenan or McCarthy would have fared had they been entirely alone for all those years; there were occasions, Keenan reports, when his mind seemed to be screaming soundlessly. He gives a sense of what it is to experience the self in its own descent into delirium; but he also conveys the rapid shifts of behaviour and emotions he experienced – fits of the giggles, absorbing daydreams, ingenious games, discussion, rage, argument, even a sense of serenity (however fleeting). He documents well the see-saw between sanity and impending madness, the insight, evasion and confusion, and the terrible occasions when '[w]e [the prisoners] became self-loathing creatures, unable to bear ourselves, and we chose to off-load this burden onto others, someone we admired, perhaps even someone we loved. All of us had to struggle with this inward-turning anger and seek to take control.'[47] To hold on to hope in captivity may be the hardest thing, after years of what Keenan calls an 'evil cradling'.[48]

In more ordinary domestic life, too, a dominant figure may ensnare another, and make that partner betray themselves, think and act like them; for example by committing a crime to win approbation. Much now is made of the psychology and sexual politics of 'gaslighting'. People, in short, can reside in many versions of a micro-tyranny, in couples, or families, as well as in closed communities, or inside a larger society where basic freedoms may exist for the majority. And educators, doctors, jailors, politicians, interrogators, priests and army trainers may profoundly affect the way people feel, behave and think; all the more so if there is no open exit path for the victim.

Some who have suffered at the hands of gangs, or who have lived inside cults that intimidate or seduce them, and require initiation, certainly want to insist that we recognise the reality of brainwashing, and do not focus too much on the mythological components, least of all dismiss it as overblown rhetoric. The guilt of participation may also be the hardest to bear, especially if the perpetrator or jailor manages to stir something more actively cruel, hateful and dehumanising (a thought, or an action) towards fellow victims.

As various writers on the most egregious varieties of thought reform have also been pointing out for decades, not only our feelings and deepest emotions, but even our biochemistry can be damaged by stressful and constricting incarceration and brainwashing.[49] A burgeoning literature on PTSD (post-traumatic stress disorder) intersects with the literature on brainwashing. PTSD, a term elaborated during the 1970s, has been widely applied in both military and civilian contexts. The term is, admittedly, still contested and open to question.[50] It can be a catch-all, and lead both mental health professionals and patients to become over-invested, trying at all costs to align a bewildering and idiosyncratic personal story to the general model, thereby distorting the complexity and variety of each situation. But whatever vocabulary we may choose, it is surely true that people can suffer immense psychic damage, even long after they escape a wicked regime or set of 'evil cradling' experiences.

PTSD is one way, though not the only one, to designate such haunting legacies inside the body and mind – the psychological and physical aftermaths, overwhelming feelings of assault and invasion, states of disorientation and terror – that a person cannot manage to contain and work through in their minds. People can be profoundly afflicted with nightmares, flashbacks, sweats, tremors and more, long after they have been formally rescued from harm's way. So, while we need to scrutinise carefully the rhetorical use of the label 'brainwash', or, indeed, the sometimes casual and ever more elastic recourse in our culture to terms such as 'trauma', it would be a travesty to somehow focus just on the diagnoses, and the vagaries of these labels, and downplay the devastation and cruel suffering that the terminology describes.

Conversation around brainwashing in the early Cold War was often characterised by inflated claims, and sanctimonious assumptions about Western civilised values and moral ascendancy. The unstable combination of evidence-gathering and myth-making reflected the political climate. It was a time, certainly in the United States, of an intense paranoid style in political discourse; a period of grave suspicion not only about communism, but also, on the Right, about liberalism, and on the Left about the brainwashing required by the capitalist state to produce compliant workers and docile voters. Reactionary critics were not in short supply in the United States, lambasting the failings of what they felt to be the weak and excessively liberal administrations of Truman and Eisenhower, Kennedy and Johnson, and decrying modern society, in which supposedly lay a profound loss of moral fibre and a new vulnerability to brainwashing.

The 'callow' Western POWs in Korean detention, men who were now signing petitions for peace, were thus seen by some pundits as a worrying sign of the times. Enter here the US army psychiatrist William Mayer, an inspiration for the aforementioned documentary featuring Reagan, *The Ultimate Weapon*. Mayer apparently had little sympathy for those who wavered, confessed, collaborated or petitioned for peace.[51] Moreover, Mayer detected in this whole sorry saga evidence of a serious national condition: a propensity to 'give-up-itis'. There were too many pathetic young people – warriors in name only – who believed in nothing, he grumbled. In combat and then in custody, so Mayer concluded, they had revealed their 'disease of non-commitment'.[52]

Such arguments were pitched as diagnoses of large groups, not just individual cases. How to explain this shared 'disease'? Some observers in the media, as well as characters playing their part as advocates in the debate on brainwashing in movies such as *The Rack*, suggested the causes lay in disastrous failures of modern parenting. What if boys, especially, were psychologically weakened by absent mothers and cruel authoritarian fathers, and thereafter wide open to new forms of conversion? Or by the loss of their fathers, away on war service, or dead? What if, by contrast, dominating, smothering mothers and other threateningly assertive matriarchal figures were overwhelming young people? Mothers from hell populated the movies; this conceit of maternal brainwashing or maternal failure paving the way to enemy brainwashing was played with in *The Man-churian Candidate*, and was also referenced in many other tales in print and on screen.

The argument (if we can dignify it as such, since it is so clearly misogynistic) was taken up in polemical essays and books: boys were in thrall to a new age of 'momism', confused in their sexuality, and prone to becoming national traitors after their feeble embrace of communist brainwashing. Warnings about the impact of these fearsome and over-influential maternal figures, either too stern and powerful or too soft, sentimental and gentle (but smothering), were set out in various diagnoses of the state of the nation, including in a provocative 1943 book by Philip Wylie, *The Generation of Vipers*. Different versions of this figure of the demanding 'mother in mind' who never lets her son go, or son who never lets his mother go, were presented by Alfred Hitchcock: the comic, neurotic version in *North by Northwest*; the horrific, psychotic version in *Psycho*. This was a theme prevalent in culture, not just in debate about the vulnerable and breakable prisoner-soldier.

The uncomfortable sight of those aircrews confessing to germ warfare would thereafter frequently be understood through the lens of brainwashing. Those far larger numbers of petition-signing POWs, meanwhile, would divide opinion, seen by various critics as evidence of a mass psychological problem. Prisoner psychology in Korea was raked over with great intensity by an army of experts and partisan opinion-makers. These 'defeatist' POWs became entangled with broader concerns – about correct upbringing, abuses of power, the nature of proper education and knowledge-exchange, and the malleability of the generation now coming to maturity after the Second World War. What if 'new' men and women could be made to march in the West too, without exercising any will of their own, to the beat of Mao's drum, just as millions interwar had been persuaded to sacrifice their all in Germany and Russia for Hitler and Stalin? The Korean crisis and the long aftermath of debate on military brainwashing brought then, as we have noted, huge additional prominence to the question of psychological warfare in general; it provided a series of prominent case studies and compelling psychodramas. And it certainly also turned into an important catalyst for inquiries, experiments and subsequent propaganda battles. Experts considered the relative importance of heredity, class, age, environment, religion, education, sexuality, race and national character in steeling the subject against any future possible enemy conversion strategies.

It was as summer turned into autumn then, in 1953, after three years of fighting and the resulting stalemate, with the Korean War armistice signed and peace restored, and after all those earlier tales of confession by captured airmen, that the issue of brainwashing impinged on general, public consciousness. News swiftly spread of twenty-one American POWs who had quite simply refused to come home.

At the declaration of peace, Korea remained divided and neither the North (backed by the Soviet Union and China) nor the South (backed by a coalition under UN auspices and led by the United States) had ended victorious. Large numbers of prisoners had been held by both sides and a prisoner-swap operation now had to be organised. The large contingent of POWs who had been detained in North Korean camps were processed through a reception centre at a place known as Freedom Village, near the tense border that still divides Korea's capitalist and communist states today. And at the same time the many prisoners from the communist side were also readied for release to their homelands.[53]

Repatriation was not automatic: a released prisoner could opt to move to a new country. Thousands who had fought for the North Korean People's Army were thereby able to opt for a new life in South Korea; others ended up in Taiwan.[54] Many factors influenced such decisions. Chinese and North Korean prisoners might at that time be treated in the West as just some faceless horde, but their stories were equally complex and varied. For some, there was no intact home to go back to; for others, family ties remained compelling; and for others again, ideology itself, pro- or anti-communist, might be the crucial factor, with each person sifting a panoply of information (or disinformation).[55] Some POWs (amounting to a few dozen) from the communist side looked beyond South Korea and Taiwan for their own route to freedom or new adventure, and ended up still further afield: Argentina, Brazil and Mexico were to receive a few of these men, while a small number found refuge in India.[56]

During the war, US officials had strongly pushed the case for this individual choice of ultimate destination: they insisted that none should be forced back into bondage.[57] So long as the preferred country agreed and the soldier remained steadfast, arrangements were made. But first, in this drawn-out process, mediated by the UN, the soldiers who sought to relocate were held in a transitional space, a kind of decompression chamber, a place that allowed them some time to adjust and reflect for ninety days, before their decision to go into exile was implemented. It was a means to test if their preferences were consistent and solid; or that at least was the hope.[58]

From the Western point of view, this challenge to any rote assumption of automatic repatriation for POWs was a means to help enemy soldiers escape the hammer and sickle, as well as to gain a propaganda coup. However, to much surprise, a small group of American POWs, numbering twenty-three men at the outset, along with a solitary British soldier and a larger contingent of Korean soldiers, proposed to move in the other direction. They preferred to live, so they declared, in the People's Republic of China – the state founded in 1949 under the leadership of Mao.

Before their final decision was realised, a couple of them, Claude Batchelor and Edward Dickenson, changed their minds and decided to return home after all. When they arrived on US soil they found themselves in disgrace and were dealt with harshly by the army. They were court-martialled, found guilty of various crimes and given substantial custodial sentences.[59] The remainder stayed resolute, at least for the time being. They insisted that they wished to cross the so-called Bamboo Curtain and resettle permanently. This was to the bemusement, apparently, not only of US officials, but also of their Chinese counterparts.[60]

Several of the 'twenty-one' doubled down in front of cameras, insisting on their new enlightened political views, explaining that they did not wish to return to a 'fascist' political landscape in the United States.[61] The men expressed positive views, even a sense of revelation and inspiration, about the egalitarian society that Mao was creating. They gave interviews to explain their decisions and to express commitment to global peace, while criticising the toxic anti-communist McCarthyite atmosphere which prevailed back home.[62]

Meanwhile, in the United States, worried observers, hostile journalists, angry politicians and even members of the men's own families suggested that these ex-POWs may or even must have been *brainwashed*. A vituperative, if supposedly in-depth, analysis of their choices was provided in Virginia Pasley's 1955 book, *21 Stayed*. This noted the soldiers' often poor education, hinted at a lack of intelligence and knowledge, yet also presented the affair as a 'horror story without relief' about a group of hapless 'victims writing their own death warrants' and 'supplying the weapons for their own destruction'. She saw the situation as more than an exercise in 'group tyranny'; it might even be evidence, apparently, of a world that would lead to 'the blanking out of free will and finally of personality itself'.[63]

The mother of one of the men in the group, Clarence Adams, argued they had been doped and subjected to hypnosis by the enemy.[64] The mother of another, Richard Tenneson, informed the media that these long-confined soldiers were victims of torture and must have been forcibly broken. The sustained hardship and psychological disorientation of these captives, she argued, was the prelude to brainwashing.[65] This mode of explanation was echoed by others, and presumably made perfect sense to many Western readers and listeners. How else could these men have made such a choice?

This disastrous Korean conflict, sometimes dubbed 'the forgotten war', was eclipsed by the 1960s catastrophe of the United States' escalating war in Vietnam. Yet one of its never-forgotten legacies, it was said, was '[taking] the lid off the story' of brainwashing.[66]

Some, like Hunter, as we have noted, called for massive new programmes of training, for armies and civilians alike, to build resilience, enhance strength and fortify mental stamina: people needed rigorous preparation to avoid 'cracking up', he insisted, in this new global conflict. Others joined him too, in extolling the virtues of critical thinking, as taught in the best contemporary Western schools and universities. For a total war on the mind, the brainwash experts warned, was in full swing, now and everywhere, and we all had to be carefully schooled to decipher as well as to resist the dangers. For Hunter at least, nobody, at home or abroad, was ever entirely safe. He certainly was granted his wish for a sustained government response to these SOS signals and the need for heavy investment, as we have seen with MK-Ultra and other such programmes.

Let us revisit in a little more detail some of those twenty-one men's narratives, amid all that megaphone diplomacy; and consider the differences between such typical headlines about their condition, and what they may have thought, felt or sought. I will single out three striking examples that may suffice to suggest the gap between generalised formulations, and the varieties of experience.

One of the twenty-one was James Veneris, from Pennsylvania, the son of a Greek communist couple who had migrated from Europe to the United States. Veneris had fought in the Pacific during the Second World War, only to re-enlist in 1950, after falling on hard times. This case is perhaps the least amenable of all to the melodramatic depiction painted thus far. Veneris seemed, as far as one knows, competent to decide, sanguine and, for all one can tell, ultimately reasonably content to accept and embrace the life-changing choice that he had made.

Sent to fight in Korea, he was captured and held prisoner in Camp 3, where fellow inmates knew him simply as 'the Greek'.[67] He was apparently well regarded even by men with very different political affiliations. Lloyd Pate, one of the so-called 'reactionaries' (i.e. the most obdurate anti-communist prisoners in the camps), encountered Veneris, whom he knew to be a 'progressive'; a man who would be willing to offer more than simply name, rank and serial number, to negotiate with the camp authorities and perhaps ultimately to be drawn to their cause. But Veneris, he said, was never a 'rat', and was perhaps the only one of that twenty-one-strong group, in his view, who truly believed in communism. And that, Pate added, was 'because his own parents were communists', thus implying the power of family influences rather than just the lure of alien states.[68] And yet some of Veneris's family were clearly aghast, it would also seem, and far from proud of his choice. His mother told Pasley, author of that critical set of profiles, that poor James had never been a communist; she insisted '[h]e must have come under terrible pressure to come to believe such things'.[69]

Veneris evidently held the view that he had taken this fateful decision of his own accord.[70] After biding his time during the transitional period, he made the train journey to China and settled down there. He studied, acquired some grasp of the language, married Chinese women (twice, in fact; his first wife died of cancer after some years together) and had a family. In a moving documentary directed by Shui-Bo Wang, *They Chose China* (2005), we catch up with Veneris and encounter pictures of him in his old age in the People's Republic, with his children and grandchildren around him. Local people can be seen in the documentary speaking fondly of Veneris, who had passed away the year before the film came out: he was their neighbour, colleague and friend.

Veneris seemed to have done well; he had gained a degree, became a teacher and then a factory worker, a man praised as a loyal, skilled and conscientious comrade, living among the local population. The quiet American had worked for years in steel and paper mills (mostly in a pulp factory), stalwart about his decision, despite requiring protection from the Party to save him from serious trouble during the 1960s when militant young Red Guards suggested he might be a spy.[71] The Chinese leadership praised and possibly saved him: Veneris, they said, was a good freedom fighter.

Veneris survived the ferocious onslaught of the Cultural Revolution and lived long enough to see China's transformation into a dynamic, partially capitalist economy, while still an extremely authoritarian state.[72] He is buried in Shandong province in the east of the country, where he had lived. That 1953 decision proved lasting in his case, although after the thaw in the relationship between the United States and China that led to Nixon and Mao shaking hands in 1972, he was able to make occasional trips back to the United States. As far as I am aware, there were no definitive changes of heart for him.

Others in that self-selecting POW group, however, drastically altered course once again during the later 1950s and 60s and sought repatriation to the United States. Grudgingly allowed back by the US authorities after their years in China, these returnees faced a barrage of criticism and possible arrest, as we can see in the case of another POW, Clarence Adams, one of three African-American soldiers in the original group. His story was primarily bound up, one might well argue, not with Chinese brainwashing, but with race and politics in the United States.

Adams grew up in Memphis, Tennessee. As he later explained, his decision to settle in China was informed by the racism he suffered throughout his life, including during his time in the US army. He believed that white officers regarded him and fellow African-American soldiers as the most easily expendable cannon fodder. Racism was endemic in the army, as throughout civilian society.[73]

Adams was captured in combat and nearly died, like so many other POWs. When he dropped out of a forced march, through exhaustion and injury, he was lucky not to have been shot on the spot. He escaped, ending up desperate on a mountain footpath, menaced by Korean teenagers, when 'an old Korean with a long stringy beard' mysteriously appeared to save him.[74] Shortly afterwards, he fell into the hands of enemy soldiers, whereupon an interpreter declared to him, in words Adams said later he never forgot, '[y]ou are not the exploiters, you are the exploited!'[75]

Inspired by such comradely messages, and by subsequent political teachings in the camp to which he was taken, Adams hoped to find a new freedom never available to him in the United States. I dwell on his case here to show how the Cold War story of brainwashing could be questioned at the time, as well as interpreted in many ways later, and to emphasise such an ex-soldier's understandable choice to escape his homeland. For Adams conveyed at that point that the United States had nothing for him, or at least nothing worth the harassment, pain, restriction and cruelty.

While a prisoner, Adams was impressed that the communist authorities encouraged him to take on responsibilities, including mediating on behalf of other soldiers in securing improvements to camp conditions. He negotiated for alterations to the catering arrangements, for example, so that the POWs might cook their own food in a manner more palatable to them. He even obtained official consent to introduce certain games, to alleviate the men's boredom. Whatever was provided by way of food, medical care and resources, later in the war, cannot be used to sugar-coat the fact of the many hardships and brutalities suffered. Adams made that clear. Others, to be sure, provided less sanguine portraits of those final years spent in the Korean War camps than had he; many were left wrecked by their custodial treatment. Worst, for most of these men, had been the forced marches over long distances, after arrest, before the arrival in camps. Adams wrote in his memoir of his own desperation during those 'death marches', how close he had come to killing himself, and how brutal had been the Korean People's Home Guard, as they pushed their prisoners to walk faster, despite the sub-zero temperatures and lack of food. The prisoners had been guarded by men who had no compunction about shooting those too weak to keep up. Adams survived, despite his injuries and near bodily collapse, only to face the initially extremely bleak conditions of life (and death) in Camp 5. He remarked that he and other soldiers of colour had fared better than many white soldiers because '[m]ost of us were accustomed to getting along on very little'.[76] It was only some months later, in the spring of 1951, when Chinese authorities took over the running of the camp, that conditions improved, he explained, and for the first time the men received a bowl of hot food every day.[77]

Reports suggested that for many POWs prison conditions did indeed improve markedly during the war. Adams noted he had some scope, once his 'progressive' status was clear to the authorities, to secure minor but important adjustments for himself and the prisoners around him. Others praised the assistance he offered to new US arrivals. Another captured man, Jim Crombie, recalled the time he entered Camp 5, sometime after Adams had arrived: 'I have to say in Clarence's defense when I first arrived … he really helped me. He was a short, stocky, very personable guy. He really gave me a hand, asking what he could do to help.'[78]

Adams paid heed to the political lessons provided by camp officials; he was primed, in turn, to give talks to fellow prisoners, to share his evolving views about war and peace, capitalism and communism. Education, or indeed re-education, was regularly on the camp menu, with challenging questions raised and political explanations duly provided. Some of the guards recalled years later that they had been under instruction from their own managers to call the prisoners their 'students'.[79]

Adams had every reason for doubting his prospects in the United States. Racism had been, since childhood, his daily experience. He associated the US South not with the Free World, but rather with violence, hatred and lynching. The Civil War of the 1860s may have led to the end of slavery in the formal sense, but racism was structured into institutional and everyday life at all levels, as Adams sharply pointed out. He remained in the People's Republic for twelve years, clear enough about why he had done so. 'I might not have known what China was really like before going there but I certainly knew what life was like for blacks in America and especially in Memphis … I decided to go to China because I was looking for freedom and a way out of poverty and I wanted to be treated like a human being instead of something sub-human.'[80]

Adams continued to question US propaganda and to recall his own experiences of oppression in the United States, although he also subsequently protested that he was not a communist, had not joined the Party, and in no sense considered himself a traitor to his own country.[81] Yet, in the early 1960s, he broadcast for Hanoi Radio, sending targeted propaganda messages against another war the United States fought in Asia. He addressed himself to Black US soldiers: '[y]ou are supposedly fighting for the freedom of the Vietnamese, but what kind of freedom do you have at home, sitting in the back of the bus, being barred from restaurants, stores and certain neighborhoods, and being denied the right to vote? … Go home and fight for equality in America.'[82]

Like Veneris, Adams adapted as far as he could and made use of the offer of further education after his resettlement. He undertook a variety of jobs, including work for a publishing house, the Peking Foreign Press. He married a Chinese woman, Liu Linfeng ('Lin'), herself a student in Beijing and later a university teacher. They started a family and went on to have two children.

However, Adams had gradually come to see that his situation was precarious, and so he sought a possible new destination. His close contacts in China with other foreigners, including diplomats from abroad, brought him under growing suspicion. As he recalled, while initially he was addressed warmly as 'comrade' ('one of them', as he put it), in subsequent years he was referred to rather more coolly as a 'fighter for peace' (a relegation in status, he explained, from 'comrade'). In the end, he was sometimes just 'Mr Adams' to erstwhile friendly acquaintances. He felt there was a marked falling-off in the nature of his reception by officialdom from those heady early days when, despite the Party's mixed feelings about these foreign 'guests', the twenty-one soldiers were treated as significant men, even dignitaries, offered better pay than average Chinese workers and invited to witness the May Day Parade in Beijing in 1954.[83] He, in turn, increasingly questioned the lack of personal freedom in China and had second thoughts about what country would best meet the needs of his family.

In 1966, Adams and his wife returned, with considerable difficulty, to the United States, travelling via Hong Kong with their two young children. They left just before the Cultural Revolution was fully unleashed. He had been given a possible alternative escape route from China, as Ghanaian diplomat friends offered the family potential asylum, but 'he thought it was just time to go home'.[84] From one kind of coolness, suspicion or even growing threat to his safety in China, Adams now endured another set of problems.

Thanks to the FBI and a hostile political climate, Adams faced interrogation and the prospect of a trial; he was subpoenaed to

answer questions in Congress. He told those hounding him that, as
a Black man, he had done what anyone was entitled to, and gone in
search of better opportunities. His daughter Della Adams recollects
how '[h]e later told me it was a kind of psychological torture, even
worse than the Chinese had ever done. Over and over again, they
would ask the same things. They were trying to get him to confess
that he was a traitor and had sold secrets.'[85] The case was not pursued,
but as a known former 'Red' Adams was put through the mill and
struggled to find work and to remake old friendships.

All the same, the couple battled against these difficulties; they
managed to open a Chinese restaurant in Memphis, on Elvis Presley
Boulevard, and built up a business. Adams remained a volatile, moody
figure. He wrote a notable memoir about his experiences, *An American Dream: The Life of an African American Soldier and POW Who Spent
Twelve Years in Communist China*, which was published in 2007 eight
years after his death, thanks to the editorial efforts of Della Adams
and Lewis H. Carlson, a historian who had already done a great deal
to chronicle the plight of POWs in the Second World War and the
Korean War.[86]

A number of the other former members of the 'twenty-one' also
returned to the United States, or moved elsewhere – one headed to
Poland, another to Czechoslovakia, a third to Belgium – in search of
a better life.[87] Several of the men suffered mental health problems,
further evidence not just of their own personal fragilities, but also
of wider psychological disturbances faced by so many returnees
from combat and custody in the Korean conflict, as later in Vietnam.
Their collective plight and vulnerability to PTSD has been canvassed
in more recent psychiatric literature.[88] Corporal Lowell Skinner, for
instance, who, like the others, had temporarily made a life in China,
marrying and finding work, grew disillusioned. He returned to the
United States in 1963; however, he had grown dependent on alcohol
and spent months in a psychiatric hospital.

Another of those who returned (a good deal earlier than Adams)
was Samuel David Hawkins. He was usually known by his middle
name. David was the youngest of the group who had gone to China,
a deprived, unhappy, white teenage boy from Oklahoma, who had
willingly joined the army as soon as he could. After his release
from the POW camp and his decision about his future, he lived in
various parts of the People's Republic, worked as a lorry driver and

married a Russian woman, Tanya, he had met in Beijing. But after four years in the communist world, he changed his mind about the life he was leading; he found himself once again restless and dissatisfied; oppressed, he said later, by the lack of individual freedom he felt under Chinese communism. His wife would follow him back to the United States.[89]

Hawkins' troubles were different, but no less enduring than that of some other men in the group. His case serves here to suggest how ex-prisoners such as he were far from just passively 'brainwashed'; they made their choices, albeit with limited knowledge of what they were choosing; and then, caught between two worlds, they grappled with the multiple labels that they were offered or had hurled at them – comrade, freedom fighter, turncoat, traitor, brainwashed victims or even, as in Hawkins' case, later, exemplars of Stockholm Syndrome and PTSD.

I had the chance to talk to Hawkins late in his life, and he left a powerful impression. I had been put in touch with him in 2014, when he was living in California. Knowing I was a psychoanalyst as well as a historian, Hawkins addressed me throughout our long-distance conversations as 'Dr Dan'. He joked to me, and my research group, about his continuing need for psychological treatment. He was feisty and witty, quick to spot when we were not following the twists and turns of his story precisely enough regarding his time in Korea, China or back in the United States.[90] Across these interviews, we learned how, for Hawkins, the army provided a welcome escape from a difficult childhood: an absent father (who subsequently died in a fire, while David was a POW), a disciplinarian matriarch, not to mention the shrill sermons he had to hear in a 'fire and brimstone' church – a life of loneliness and considerable bleakness. He was delighted, he told us, to join up and say goodbye to that past, and then, again willing to give it a go, to sign on for a new life in China.[91]

An accomplished storyteller, David Hawkins also spoke grippingly about the experience of re-education in which he had been inadvertently caught up. He was familiar with the experience of being interviewed as a POW by officials on both sides and, after his return from this self-imposed exile in China, by journalists, keen to pin a label on him – although he did not hear much of that other name for this Maoist re-education, he said, until his arrival in the United States, when he was asked if he had been brainwashed.

On occasions, his interviewers had functioned more like interrogators, as when he appeared on US television on the popular show *The Mike Wallace Interview*, shortly after his return from China in 1957.[92] Wallace, a smooth broadcaster, was scathing, demanding that the former soldier account for himself as either a turncoat or a brainwashed person, or both. Asked by Wallace about foreign affairs and what stance the United States should now most appropriately take regarding Mao's China, Hawkins calmly suggested diplomatic relations should be restored, given that this was a rising world power with hundreds of millions of citizens.

But, Wallace bluntly asked Hawkins, how do we know if someone like you may have been brainwashed? The ex-soldier replied equally coolly 'you wouldn't know' – hardly a way to reassure his fellow Americans that he hadn't been brainwashed! Hawkins seemed capable enough of managing the ordeal of that TV cross-examination. He remained rather thoughtful and appeared relatively poised, even when it was put to him that the twenty-one men may really have chosen China to escape justice, having committed certain unspecified crimes in the camps against other Americans. Hawkins again quietly rejected this explanation as false. He was not to be so easily browbeaten. (Mike Wallace meanwhile smoked his way encouragingly through the programme, which was sponsored by a tobacco firm. So as they discussed these dangerous foreign assaults on the mind, the show also sought to influence its watching consumers. But that is to anticipate our discussion regarding the 'hidden persuaders', in Part 5.)

Hawkins, like Adams, found his personal story printed in the press, and in books such as Pasley's *21 Stayed*. What struck me, talking to this man so many decades later, was his painful feeling of injury, and his enduring sense of injustice about the dishonourable discharge he received from the US army. He battled over many years to clear his name, restore his rights and secure a decent army pension. Other labels emerged later, he explained to us, which he seemed more inclined to embrace than 'brainwashed'. These included, as noted, Stockholm Syndrome and PTSD, a diagnosis suggested to him by a helpful therapist. With hindsight, he took the view that 'the choice that I had made to go to China was not really a free choice at all', as though inching his way back to the conditioning, thought-reform or brainwashing diagnosis that he had earlier eschewed.[93]

Hawkins' tone may have been light at points in our conversations, but the content of what he said about his Korean War captivity and subsequent personal difficulties was not. He still recalled vividly his arrest in 1950 by the enemy forces and what he subsequently endured. He recounted that he was about one day's journey from the Yalu River in late November that first year of the war, driving an army truck on the main supply route south. The Chinese blocked one of the main mountain passes, and before he knew it an explosive went off and he found himself lying at the bottom of a dry creek bed. Unable to move normally and realising he had blood on his uniform, he then 'blundered into a Chinese patrol and was taken prisoner'.[94] He told us, almost performed to us in the very drama of his spoken delivery, the intense feelings he had about those key points of transition in his life; from freedom to captivity, from life to near-death, from relative comfort to intense hardship; from the problem of his own survival to the horror of all those other casualties. He could not escape from those memories of dead men who did not make it through the war at all, unlike himself, a long-term survivor. He spoke, for example, of his own awful experience of huddling against a fellow soldier for warmth in the night, only to find upon waking that the man next to him was dead.

Clearly each personal resolution to go to China at the end of hostilities was not as cut and dried, nor monocausal, as some pundits suggested. Hawkins insisted to us that the decision he made in 1953 was neither simply coerced, nor entirely premeditated, and certainly not a reflection of some settled ideological view. His opinions changed with time. His experiences in childhood, in the army, in war, in the camp, in China and then back in his homeland had complex origins and multiple subsequent impacts on him. The decision, he added, to choose China, at the very moment of his release from detention, also owed a good deal to impulse and irritation. He was positively annoyed, he explained, that US officials had arrogantly presumed he would inevitably head back home during that prisoner-swap operation.

Re-education or thought-reform procedures are not equivalent to a uniform factory-production line, churning out products. We should be wary of assuming that those on the receiving end of a programme of interrogation and manipulation are reduced to identikit hollowed-out persons all now entirely the same, as is sometimes presumed, for instance, in depictions of a homogenous re-educated population in North Korea.

There are no will-less homogenous masses of people in any societies, nor in cults or movements, in fact; we are each vulnerable, suggestible and destructible, and can bear only so much; but we are always far more than mere products, never just automata, however compliant, alienated and dissociated or 'mass-like' our actions and thoughts may sometimes become.

All the evidence I've seen on such matters suggests that the captive victim, the potentially brainwashable subject, does not become someone else entirely, never a mere machine-like tool or robot in the manner presented in some reportage and melodramas. Lifton was right to personalise his brainwashing study; to approach it via individual cases, each sharing certain features, but each one also a story unto itself. The historian Monica Kim has more recently provided rich evidence of the lived experiences of the imprisoned men on the other side in the Korean War, of their ordeals of captivity and interrogation, and of the guiding assumptions made about them by their interrogators.[95] People, brainwashed or otherwise, are never truly alike, even if, admittedly, mechanisms of traumatisation and conversion are now well studied by researchers: the sense of entrapment, the induced state of helplessness, the shocks to the body and mind, the removal of other support or explanatory systems, the insertion in the captor's own explanatory grid, the gradual offer of some new saviour, and so on.

Follow that thought experiment further, for a moment, if you are inclined to treat brainwashing simply as some assured science on one side, or scare story on the other, an antiquarian piece of history best confined to the Cold War past. Imagine yourself, in the most extreme situations now, abducted, then trapped in a grim, unknown, deliberately disorientating place; picture yourself terrified, deprived of care or ordinary sensations, locked up in a site (maybe even in a small box), and then, worse, invited to harm another thereby to save yourself or to avoid the torture of a loved one in another room.

How long might you expect to hold out or on to your former sense of identity? If you were still 'yourself', it would not presumably be quite the self you knew beforehand. It is hard to tell in advance, no doubt, whatever your history, faith, training or character, how you might change, under the most extreme duress, and to know where the breaking point might lie.

To acknowledge that our minds are indeed breakable is not to deny that the notion of brainwashing is freighted with a great deal of ideological baggage. Nonetheless, those old concerns – or sometimes dramatised visions – of a process designed deliberately to crush and remake people are still surely salient: they invite consideration of what can be done malevolently to create despair, unbearable anxiety and deepest dread, and perhaps thereafter to raise our awareness of how a person may be drawn into the most twisted and perverse 'love'. Alternatively, would-be re-educators can start with a child, get straight to work early, train or reshape a subject from infancy. An old and famous adage of the Jesuits was 'give me a child until the age of seven and I will give you the man'.

Early interventions can change us profoundly, needless to say; and, at worst, be used to break and remake the nascent personality. Work on infants may indeed prove the most far-reaching and for some surely the most permanently affecting, as one imagines in seeing those terrifying images beamed to the world of child soldiers drilled for service to Islamic State and other militias. To imagine the therapeutic recovery programme required after all that has occurred is surely daunting, especially when the young victims have been made into perpetrators, required to kill and torture others.

Consider that same question in another setting and note what happened to a boy called Okello Moses Rubangangeyo, who grew up in Gulu, northern Uganda, in the 1980s. When he was seven, in 1987, a marauding and crusading movement, the Lord's Resistance Army (LRA), gained strength in that part of Africa. The LRA combined elements of Christianity, local beliefs about spirit possession, charismatic authority, a substantial military organisation and the most sadistic rites of passage imaginable.

Rubangangeyo had every reason to be terrified of Joseph Kony, leader of this movement. Kony directed a force that had waged war against the central government in Uganda and, without mercy, upon the local population. When he was sixteen, in 1996, Rubangangeyo was awakened in his dormitory at school one night and led away, along with other youngsters, by men from that force. He and the others were taunted, tortured, trained and turned into participants: those others, that is to say, who survived the ordeal at all. There was no third way, he later explained: either the abductees learned to do as required by the LRA, or they died. Eventually, Rubangangeyo made his escape and began to refashion his life: in 2014, he met and started to recount his story to a journalist, Adriana Carranca, who subsequently published an account in *Granta* magazine.

Rubangangeyo described to her how he and dozens of others were seized in the night, viciously clubbed, while the rebels who had taken them prisoner mocked and jeered. They had to endure the pain without tears, for crying, they learned, could cost them their lives. 'They put you at gunpoint, and you are not allowed to make any sound,' he said. 'The first twenty strikes you believe you won't survive the pain. But then you stop feeling it.' That was precisely one of the purposes: rendering the victim into a condition of numbness. You either died or survived; the aim was that – numbly – you functioned thereafter and questioned nothing. This strategy, he later believed, after his escape, was systematically pursued to desensitise, depersonalise and 'transition you to the military', as he put it, i.e. to the LRA.[96]

Such abductees were sometimes required to be the executioners of their own family and former neighbours. Rubangangeyo himself, on pain of death, was made to use a small axe to cut off a man's legs. The man before him, in custody, had broken some LRA 'rule' by riding a bicycle. 'I was forced to … I was forced to do it,' he told Carranca with shame, while 'avoiding eye contact'. He spoke to her of his regret that the axe given to him had not been bigger, thereby allowing him to amputate those limbs with fewer blows. Carranca reported her own extreme mixed emotions as she recorded his horrendous life story; she recoiled from the man who was talking to her, even as she sympathised with the devastated boy.

Rubangangeyo was taken by the LRA to South Sudan some months after his abduction. There, Kony appeared, a man in a lightbrown suit, a leader who spoke softly, and declared to the abductees that the LRA had liberated them from the African dictators. He anointed these young people 'the new Acholi', held a Bible, and quoted Matthew 5:30: 'And if your right hand causes you to stumble, cut it off and throw it away. It is better for you to lose one part of your body than for your whole body to go into hell,' so he declared.

Rubangangeyo recalled that Kony seemed a 'very gentle man', even as he wielded absolute power over them. Rubangangeyo also remembered the message Kony offered: 'We are going to kill all the stupid [people] in Uganda … We are uniting our brothers and sisters.'

'Have we abducted anyone among you here?' the leader asked the crowd. 'No, no, no sir!' the terrified boys and girls responded.

Rubangangeyo later told Carranca how they were pretending, but eventually he also suggested – once they were fully habituated to all this, once they had been 'baptised' anew – that they also grew increasingly 'brainwashed', no longer sure what was good and bad, who was wrong and who was right:

> their naked chests, backs and arms marked with a cross, using a mixture of white clay and water. They were anointed with 'holy oil' made of Areca palm nuts, poured on their forehead and parts of their body. During the ceremony they were asked to confess their sins. If they refused, they were told they would die soon. If they confessed, they'd become invisible to 'enemies' and no bullets would ever reach them. 'They were indoctrinating us, brainwashing our minds!' Moses said. 'You start thinking that maybe the polygamy, the killings or even chopping ... might be connected to something spiritual.'

Rubangangeyo eventually seized his chance, as the LRA disintegrated, to find a way back to Gulu, and to gain not only physical but also increasingly some psychological distance from all that had happened: he began to assemble these elements of his story, not merely to live with them, mute inside him, while he sat, silent and numbed. Carranca reports his impressive rehabilitation and how he'd become a caring father. All the same, I wonder what legacies he and other child and teenage soldiers were left with; and what a full recovery from that kind of history might mean, how far it is feasible and faceable. That too must depend on many things.

Here my point is simply that such a story might invite doubt about your or my mental capacities, any more than his, in such adversity to resist or to avoid brainwashing: who can be sure how long they would remain non-compliant or actively defiant, willing instantly to die, or to live and to act on such terms? Who would not lose their mind, even if they preserved their life in the process? A sense of selfhood is never truly iron-clad; self-perception, self-awareness and resilience are, I assume, only ever partial at best.

Perhaps certain people may be better than others, even at surviving rape, or the requirement to rape, mutilation, or the requirement to mutilate, torture, or the act of torturing, with some vestiges of hope, some spark of rebellion, some enduring sense of human goodness, some capacity to go on willing their own escape and eventual rehabilitation. It may be possible with the right kinds of help and resources for survivors to do remarkable psychological work over time; we have common expressions, after all, that reflect that achievement, or at least that hope, such as 'come to terms', 'move on', 'work through' or 'find closure'. But clinicians who work in this field also point out ways that later traumas may compound earlier traumas, leaving complex unconscious legacies in mind and body that are never fully 'recovered from' or 'cured'. The ability to cope with the shame and the guilt, to resist such manipulation, and subsequently to grieve, or even to think for any length of time about the tumble of terrifying thoughts that can come to mind unbidden, is surely variable, as well as limited, in all of us. In the religious belief systems of some African societies, such suffering and horror might be conceived of as a state of possession by spirits, in a manner quite different to forms of explanation assumed in, say, Western psychoanalytic accounts of guilt, trauma or depression. Different societies have all kinds of rites for helping people tell their stories, recover their health, or go through processes of mourning or reintegration. But sometimes a community can also break down entirely, leaving the sufferer entirely adrift. Mourning what we have done or what we have lost, and thinking about our feelings and our experiences, are precious and precarious achievements, not guaranteed mental states. Minds as well as bodies can certainly break, whatever our culture and society, or faith, our explanatory framework or our inner resources.

Human ingenuity at breaking captive people down through mental and physical torture, cruel inductions, the manipulations of guilt, shame, panic and states of abjection, knows no real limits. Torture, we know, has been widely used by liberal democratic states as well as dictatorships since 1945, often as systematic policy too, even without necessarily declaring states of emergency as formal cover. Waterboarding, for example, which has the advantage of leaving no obvious sign on the body, caused an outcry in the 'War on Terror'; this method of torture has a long history, and in fact has been extensively practised by Western and other powers in many other settings.[97]

It would be comforting if one could think of the mass projects of psychic and social destruction sketched out here as just occasional and sporadic fringe occurrences, and entirely outside the purview of the modern functioning nation state, or as the occasional remnants and artefacts of some other lost time, existing in war zones, or in those places we call failed states. Today, just as in the most terrible earlier decades of the twentieth century, when people were also re-educated inside camps, the sheer scale of what is being done to process people through closed re-education facilities and systems is hard to grasp. Perhaps the most chilling state-orchestrated example of all is the fate of the Uighurs, so we need to return at this point to contemporary China. For in recent years a stream of reports and campaigns (spearheaded by organisations such as Amnesty International) has highlighted the plight of this ethnic minority in Xinjiang, in the north-west.[98] The Uighur re-education project dwarfs all other such current global initiatives; it has become, in fact, the largest internment policy for an ethnic-political minority since the Second World War. The policy apparently aims at the systematic transformation of the prisoners' minds *and* their social behaviour.

New light was cast on this programme in 2019, when a cache of secret documents was leaked to the International Consortium of Investigative Journalists by an unspecified individual or group. This material, dating from two years earlier, included a nine-page memo from Zhu Hailun, who was then deputy-secretary of Xinjiang's Communist Party and the region's top security official. It instructed the directors of detention facilities to ensure no escapes; to punish all 'behavioural violations'; to promote repentance and confession; and to '*encourage students to truly transform*', whatever that may have meant. Zhu Hailun made clear that inside these facilities, lives should be regulated, surveyed, reviewed and timetabled daily in every respect. Repentance and confession, his memorandum made plain, were a key requirement in the process: it was crucial that the detained men and women should come to 'understand deeply the illegal, criminal and dangerous nature of their past behaviour'.[99]

When the Chinese ambassador to London made an appearance on the BBC shortly after these revelations became public, he dismissed these charges of brainwashing out of hand: 'fake news', he said. These measures provided by the Chinese state were about *voluntary* vocational training, lifting the Uighurs up, furnishing the people with opportunities, promoting their interests and needs.[100] Beijing claimed that its policy was a proportionate and balanced response to

Islamic extremism and the rise of al-Qaeda, which had affected the Uighur population so adversely.

All societies, the ambassador pointed out, are entitled to defend themselves with every appropriate means. But what is appropriate? Some Chinese officials have claimed that the data leak, so widely reported in the West, was an orchestrated foreign 'smear'. Others have insisted the whole point of the programme in these 'voluntary' facilities is, precisely, to *un-brainwash* the Uighurs, to ensure they are not radicalised by Islamic fundamentalism. Rather than focusing on the scale of arrests, they urged journalists to report the very opposite: the supposed flood of recent releases of these inmates, aka students, from custody.[101] (One indication of the Chinese sensitivity to such foreign accusations: when in December 2019 the German footballer Mesut Özil, a practising Muslim of Turkish descent and at that time an Arsenal player, had the temerity to protest publicly against the treatment of the Uighurs, Chinese state television pulled its live coverage of that weekend's Arsenal game from the nation's screens.)[102]

Yet, whatever officialdom in China declares, many people are not persuaded by these sanguine accounts of what has so recently been happening to the Uighurs. Former inmates tell different stories to the one presented by the Chinese government. Zharqynbek Otan, for example, who was held in one of these facilities for seven months after his arrest in January 2017, and who subsequently fled the country, claimed the goal of this mass detention was to destroy prior bonds and impose in the minds of all inmates a form of ultra-loyalty, in fact 'to brainwash you', he said, 'so you forget your roots and everything about Islam and ethnic identity'.[103]

In some of the cases reported in this chapter, the aim of incarceration is to elicit confessions and then dispense with the person altogether. In others, to create inviolable bonds, produce foot soldiers, or even unquestioning killers and torturers. In instances such as the Uighur camps, the goal is to neutralise opposition and engender the wholesale political re-education of that minority population, to subdue and ultimately manage the future of 'troublesome' people inside a larger state. Reports of compulsory sterilisation of Uighurs have accompanied others of such psychic and physical subjugation. These policies are conducted in the name of the defence of society, i.e. for the greater protection of the majority. Indeed, brainwashing, as with the Uighurs, is perhaps always most likely to be conducted in the dubious name of un-brainwashing and some greater enlightenment.

The central role of camps in the twentieth century has been underlined in many important works of philosophy, social theory, reportage, film, memoir and history. Camps have served to destroy people in their millions, but also to sequestrate, punish and transform. The scale of forced conversion in totalitarian societies gives us pause for thought regarding those less obvious, more morally uncertain examples, where supposedly anti-brainwashing procedures occur, with people in custody, for instance, in the name of decriminalisation, deradicalisation or anti-terrorist measures, in liberal, democratic societies. Some advocates of 'de-programming' otherwise impervious fanatical cult members here in the West also assume the best way to go about the task is to mimic in reverse the approach of the original brainwashers. One tactic is to undertake a violent, cathartic and bullying experience to draw the victim out of their former delusional system, as though freedom must be recovered, in extremis, through some form of counter-tyranny.

There are other ways to look at the process of re-education under Chinese communism. In the 1930s, Mao had already signalled his intent: to take the 'lumpenproletariat', the so-called dregs of society – vagrants, prostitutes, petty criminals, hoodlums, etc. – and enlighten and recast them as part of the revolutionary struggle. If some landlords and counter-revolutionary spies were to be eradicated, others, the downtrodden underclasses, previously seen as incorrigible or hopeless (the old 'dangerous classes' so often also envisioned in Europe during the nineteenth century), were now to be redeemed by Mao as comrades, via new forms of labour camps and classrooms. This was to be a mass project in China to make the wretched of the earth understand their past exploitation and victimhood, and to grasp their own shining future destiny inside a permanent form of revolution. The theory and practice of thought reform was thus, from Mao's point of view, about taking the unenlightened person, including the desperate, exploited outcasts, and reintegrating them with the peasants and workers to produce a productive, determined, cheerful and wholeheartedly united People.[104]

Obviously, that was not how Western critics of brainwashing saw it; re-education and thought control were now precisely the same thing, according to anti-communist US commentators such as Edgar

Schein. 'Brainwashing', he wrote in a 1960 report, published by the Center for International Studies at MIT in Cambridge, Massachusetts (here summing up the previous decade's starkest warnings), is 'a colloquial term which has been used in reference to the systematic efforts by the Chinese communists (and by implication the Soviets) to persuade non-believers to accept communist allegiance, commands and/or doctrines by coercive means'.[105]

Maoist re-education, according to Western liberals, was a gross perversion of an idea that was previously compatible with liberal democracy; the communists had taken a benign idea and made it something else entirely. The efforts of the Allies, after the occupation of Germany, to re-educate Germans, weed out Nazis from influential positions and implant liberal democracy, had now been trumped as well as twisted, they said. Re-education in the East was the antithesis of such liberal ideas, they complained; it was now a project to destroy critical thinking and counter any pluralism. Re-education was the pathway to some singular vision of communist truth.

As Lifton pointed out, Maoist mass re-education in China was indeed at odds with individualistic values and modes of thought. Not everyone in the West, however, shared that sense of revulsion about such Chinese ambitions to transform the 'mass' in society and harmonise the beliefs of the population with the will of the Party: it all depended on your political viewpoint. Mao, after all, had many admirers and defenders in the West too, from the 1930s onwards. Decades after achieving power, as Julia Lovell has shown in an illuminating, wide-ranging history, Maoism still appealed to large numbers of people outside China. Indeed, it was adopted, and partially refashioned, by a remarkable array of groups and movements around the globe.[106] Maoism meant many things to people, according to time and place. It was a contradictory, variegated and evolving ideology, discourse and style of life. Mao had said many things at different stages. But to those in the 1950s who were hostile to communism and alert to brainwashing, the project of *re-education* that was so central to Maoism was certainly deeply ominous and deplorable, even diabolical: for the practitioners it was a means of dictating the truth, sowing terror, and producing a form of compliance, an idealisation of leadership and a total obedience to the Party, as the price of survival.

For many of those who wrote of such matters in the post-war United States, the modern totalitarian state was now corralling ever more people in a zero-sum game. The story was national, regional and global, the fear of an operation that would never stop at any borders; brainwashing not only through coercion and terror, but also through seduction, temptation and desire, as in the case of those 'twenty-one': a psychology designed to instil mass conviction, a culture that inculcated the most fervent enthusiasm. It was more akin perhaps to a revivalist religious meeting, in a territory where all the exit doors are nailed permanently shut; it was also an ideology, some people feared, that could develop underground in the so-called Free World.

In prisons, villages and towns across China, a new and orchestrated form of group psychology was emerging, they warned, built around a mode of extremely coercive *storytelling*, in which there is always the same basic plot, a story in which 'I' takes its place in the homogenous and clamorous 'we'. In fact, as recent scholars have shown, Chinese communism may operate through severe crackdowns and repression, but also through a more complex process for registering public attitudes and recrafting policy to meet dissatisfactions. It is not just about a top-down management style in which hundreds of millions of people adapt to the dictate of the Party. But be that as it may, there were also many other stories of brainwashing emerging elsewhere in the world, of hidden persuasion and moral compromise; tales with more nuance, illustrations of a less polarised kind; reports from writers behind the Iron Curtain; accounts that complicate the history depicted thus far, and which cast a very different, but no less troubling, light on the discussion. These were visions of the captive mind in all its gradations; an array of new metaphors, parables and images of psychic life under pressure that emerged postwar, and which enriched the familiar Orwellian nightmare of total bondage and mental enslavement.

PART 3

THE CAPTIVE MIND

'There is more than one kind of captivity.'[1] So remarked the historian and political commentator Tony Judt in 2010. At the time, he was confined in New York, paralysed from the neck down, and shortly to die from the condition he had suffered for years, amyotrophic lateral sclerosis. But he was writing here about another time and place, and in praise of Czesław Miłosz's *The Captive Mind*, a remarkable prose work published in 1953.

Miłosz was renowned as a poet, his contribution eventually marked by the Nobel Prize in Literature in 1980. After the Second World War, he was admired by some in his native Poland as an avant-garde poet, even if his writings were as yet limited and not well known abroad. He was appointed, in recognition of his personal gifts and reputation, as a cultural attaché, part of the diplomatic service of the Polish government, despite his ambiguous political views. In 1951 he defected. Miłosz was to make his name in that decade as a fierce critic of Stalinism, although he was also a caustic observer of certain aspects of life in the West. His book *The Captive Mind* richly illustrated the basic point that Judt was making; yes, there is more than one kind of captivity, and more than one mode of adaptation, compromise, stubborn persistence and rebellion, in both a totalitarian system and a liberal democracy.

Miłosz provided a much-quoted phrase, 'the captive mind', and, through his long writing career, compelling letters, prose and verse to illustrate the acute psychological dilemmas and life choices faced by many people in Poland. The book on the captive mind considered varieties of personal endurance, collusion, evasion, confrontation and escape, adding important nuances to the understandings of brain-washing we have already explored. It was a work of its time, even if it has implications for other times too regarding the way we may accommodate to power, or compromise our beliefs in a kind of grey zone. It should be said that the compromised figures who appear in Miłosz's study of the captive mind are largely male, white, educated people, individual intellectuals tormented by the conflict between personal freedom and collective allegiance, aesthetic expression and personal survival. His vision can be contrasted with other striking explorations made in the 1950s and 60s, a plethora of new analyses of captivity under Stalinist rule and in Western states too.

Earlier we looked at narratives about military and political prisoners suddenly placed at the mercy of jailors and interrogators; people helpless in custody, before, during and after the Korean War. Miłosz presents us with characters who are not prisoners, strictly speaking, and who can maintain a certain room for manoeuvre. He did not ignore the fate of the millions who were arrested, but he also wrote of those who lived outside such walls; citizens who accommodated political realities, as best they could, and perhaps cheered on the very forces that then constrained them; or those who only gradually realised quite how far they were truly walled-in, constricted and controlled, as well as, perhaps, beguiled, inside the Soviet empire. Here were populations no sooner liberated, as he put it, from the horrors of Nazi Berlin than subjected to those of Stalinist Moscow, obliged to deal each in their own fashion with this fate. As Miłosz showed, different mentalities were possible under the Soviet system, not just some uniform outcome. There is more than one kind of captivity, more than one kind of psychic response to captivity, and more than one kind of psychological analysis of that state as well.

This chapter revisits post-war accounts of totalitarian states and total institutions. It explores ideas about the impact of such regimes on citizens, and reflects upon Miłosz's depictions of people living and dying, complying but sometimes also defying a terrifyingly coercive surveillance society. Taking a lead from his study, the arc of the present discussion moves from the past to the present, and from the East to the West, from the Stalinist state to other arrangements of political life that may also entrap, enmesh and tempt. Miłosz was interested in the negotiations we may undertake with ourselves and others to make a new life possible or more agreeable. *The Captive Mind* offers several angles from which to consider what societies can do to shape thought and behaviour, and to assess how people sometimes adapt adroitly, as well as horribly self-damagingly, to their environments. Miłosz did not downplay the differences between totalitarian and liberal democratic states; however, he complicated various prevalent Cold War assumptions, providing an eloquent rebuttal of the myopic views of Soviet communism he found among some Western left-wing intellectuals, and of the claims, common on the Right, that the whole population in communist countries was being brainwashed, turned into an automaton-like mass.

Miłosz revealed later that, when writing *The Captive Mind*, he had been unsure if those in the West who read it, but who had not lived in such a state as Nazi-occupied Poland or under Stalinist communism, could really fathom what he described. He had struggled, as did many other émigré writers, men and women, who found their way from Eastern Europe to the West, fully to explain to new readerships what life was like under communism, or to present their own predicaments and complex sense of identity.[2] So much, as the writer Eva Hoffman would put it later, in her own remarkable book about this migration, is 'lost in translation'.[3] Hoffman herself would be transplanted at the start of her teens, moving with her Jewish parents, who had managed to survive the war, hidden in Poland, from Cracow to Vancouver and later to the United States, and eventually England.

Miłosz wanted to convey something of the ravaged Polish society that he had lived in and ultimately escaped, and of the dilemmas that that society posed. By the time he left, Poland was firmly under the grip of the Polish Communist Party, itself functioning under the controlling gaze of Moscow. The country was slowly rebuilding after the devastation of the war.

In 1939, Nazi Germany and the Soviet Union had both invaded Poland. The land and the people were split, reflecting a prior agreement between Hitler and Stalin to partition that territory; the deal, which had various secret protocols, was named after the ministers who worked out the details: the Molotov–Ribbentrop Pact. It was signed in Moscow in August that year, mere days before Hitler authorised the invasion of Poland, triggering the onset of the Second World War. In the west of Poland, then, Nazi occupation; a terrifying wreckage of a former society, a garrison and prison-house world, containing still more terrible prisons. These included the Warsaw Ghetto, and the concentration camps, to which the ghettoised population would be forced. The sites in southern Poland, now known simply by the shorthand, Auschwitz, were not only used for slave labour but were also central to the delivery of the 'Final Solution', the genocide of the Jewish population. That policy had been formally authorised, following a decade of ever-intensifying brutal persecution and mass murder, at the Wannsee Conference in January 1942. In 1939, meanwhile, the eastern part of the state of Poland had begun its long encounter with Stalin and with the Gulag, that other world of totalitarianism. This nation thus provided the meeting ground of these two deadly systems in Europe.

While all this was known to many people in the West, they were not necessarily aware of what life was really like for those who lived in Poland through the war years and who then sought to survive in the new regime that emerged after 1945. Hoffman remarked on this mismatch – between the big picture that emerged in the West, totalitarianism, and the day-to-day lived experience, in all its many varieties, for individuals and families. She noted the way Poland and other parts of the Soviet empire were characteristically seen from afar, in stylised, abstract terms:

> For the decades of the Cold War, Eastern Europe was cut off from living contact with the West. Moreover, in the American imagination, Poland, like other countries in the region, was perceived as the totalitarian, evil empire – the new arch-enemy. I think that those images attached themselves to earlier conceptions of Eastern Europe as a savage or primitive realm, and became reified, or petrified, into a kind of mythology that seemed to be in no need of examination or revision.[4]

It is worth dwelling not only on the political landscape of Poland, but also on the word 'totalitarianism' that was used to characterise it. Although Miłosz also used the term, he showed how much could be lost by such general concepts, if we do not consider the many ordinary choices and potential compromises required in everyday life in such a state. The most influential general account of totalitarianism was provided in the work of another émigré to the United States, Hannah Arendt. Her classic study, *The Origins of Totalitarianism*, was published in 1951, two years before *The Captive Mind*.

Arendt looked for common elements rather than the peculiar local conditions in each polity; she wrote about a widespread, dehumanising form of state, and wanted to examine the catastrophic consequences for people's thinking. She explained how in such a state, 'because of their capacity to think, human beings are suspect by definition, and this suspicion cannot be diverted by exemplary behaviour'. The systematic assault on freedom of thought was at the heart of the issue. For to be able to think, she insisted, one must possess the 'capacity to change one's mind'. The totalitarian state was built on propaganda, lies and an atmosphere of perpetual 'mutual suspicion'. This sense of suspicion shaped public exchanges and personal relationships, 'even outside the special purview of the secret police'. In fact, there was nowhere really beyond that purview, she noted, for a form of policing was constantly present in society and the psyche. Policing and terror were not confined to forces of law and order as such.

The term 'totalitarianism' had first made an impact in Europe three decades earlier, in the period after the First World War. The idea was initially welcomed by some commentators, especially pro-fascist philosophers: the total state was regarded by certain intellectuals as a positive and desirable prospect. Champions of fascism and Nazism conveyed their approbation of Mussolini's and Hitler's totalising ambitions, their endeavours to unify and harmonise the state and people, to bring economy, society, culture and law all together as one. A new total state was promised by these leaders and parties, and was to be achieved, they insisted, by eliminating the contradictions, inefficiencies, delays, corruption and hypocrisies of more moderate conservative and monarchical states, or the old 'discredited' liberal societies. 'Totalitarianism' later came to be used in the more critical and now more familiar approach of Orwell, Arendt, Miłosz and others. It was a controversial term, post-war as well, since it assumed the goals of communism (under Stalin) and of Nazism (under Hitler) were broadly comparable, if not even identical. For those who advocated the value of the term 'totalitarianism', the point was to see the underlying similarities between states that are willing and able to use any means to close down entirely all opposition. The modus operandi of such states is terror. To live in such a state is to know the governing power faces no curb and can act with impunity; to be aware that it can make draconian assaults upon an individual person or dissident group, at any time, and characterise its actions as essential preventative measures against 'internal enemies', 'saboteurs', 'traitors', who pose some mortal threat to the people.

However, both Arendt and Miłosz challenged the assumption

that the aim of a totalitarian system is to ensure that each and every person is brainwashed into a condition of total conviction. Instead, the goal is to daze, confuse and intimidate populations, to disorientate and disable thinking, and to achieve a kind of blitzkrieg on truth. So, under totalitarianism you might end up completely _lost_ as to what words like truth now really meant, or even as to whether the distinction between truth and lying really matters. Arendt wrote: 'The ideal subject of totalitarian rule is not the convinced Nazi or the convinced Communist, but people for whom the distinction between fact and fiction (i.e. the reality of experience) and the distinction between true and false (i.e. the standards of thought) no longer exist.'[5] In a passage in _Mein Kampf_, Hitler had speculated on that very possibility; on how a world can be built on lies, a people effectively stupefied, not necessarily fully persuaded. Of course, he blamed the Jews for the lying (itself a fundamental lie on his part). If lies are big enough, he had mused, those lies may endure, and perhaps go unchallenged. Lies may be so colossal, say in official propaganda, that nobody can really believe the lies' authors have the 'impudence', as he put it, to distort the truth so drastically.[6]

Totalitarianism, post-war writers such as Arendt and Miłosz explained, is built around lies, obfuscations and the sowing of deliberate, massive confusion. Totalitarian states had built a huge apparatus to orchestrate bodies and minds, through mass party membership, communication, education, culture and constant police repression. Ultimately the system required a vast and terrifying security state, even if it paid lip service to plebiscites or parliament. The latter, if still there, was just for rubber stamping decisions. Such states used new technological means to repress, and to disseminate their own core messages, including many lies great and small; they subjected their populations daily to centrally controlled 'news', or disinformation, and kept up a constant barrage of symbols, exhortations and denunciations, via radio, film, newspapers, magazines, as well as slogans, songs, pamphlets, pageants, marches, parades, rallies, popular dramas, etc. Perhaps people believed the political messages, or maybe they just gave up on believing, merely seeking to survive by paying the necessary dues. A totalitarian political system, those writers also explained, strips away entirely the protection of 'suspect' minorities, snuffs out freedom of the press and destroys all other liberal and democratic bulwarks (such as different political parties, open elections and a separation of governing powers, with an independent judiciary).

Of course, the totalitarian authorities might claim to be doing the opposite, explained these analysts, looking after all the good people within its realm, allowing discussion, fostering democracy, safeguarding minorities. The states that Arendt and other theorists of totalitarianism described were shown to have much in common, and to stand in dramatic counterpoint to liberal democracies. Following that approach, one might want to compare the operation of Hitler's Germany, Stalin's Russia and Pol Pot's Cambodia, albeit noting differences. It would be less plausible to associate, let alone equate, conditions in such states with those now faced by the vast majority of people in the present-day European Union, even if we can note how some totalitarian impulses, or draconian policy directives, may nonetheless return, like ghosts from the past, and threaten our freedoms.

The idea of the 'totality' occupied a central place in such Cold War accounts. It could apply to a vast society or to a tiny island. The point was the exercise of absolute power, the assault on the barrier between truth and lies, and the presumed entitlement to and attempted exertion of total control over all subjects. After all, as the Canadian sociologist Erving Goffman argued, 'total institutions' with absolute power over their inmates have been created for some people within a liberal society, even as the majority population around them enjoy greater freedoms.

Goffman and others began to think about these examples as micro-totalitarian entities for their inhabitants. They suggested that some prisons, or the worst kind of closed hospital wards, might hold their populations helplessly confined. Some categories of people can be dehumanised by our 'liberal' system, made entirely abject, left in impossible catch-22 situations, and treated as dispensable, inferior, even dregs, by government officials and sections of the press. But for others, even a majority, in such a society, conditions might differ and 'total control' not be an appropriate description at all. Admittedly, there are some governments in states today in the European Union, including Poland and Hungary, that have undermined their own fragile liberal and democratic safeguards, moving manifestly into an authoritarian style, ready to declare and then exploit conditions of 'emergency', and to crush dissent. But dire as recent developments there and in some other parts of Europe are, still we cannot equate them with the full horrors of Nazi Germany and the Soviet empire which Miłosz and Arendt were talking about back in the early 1950s.

Arendt had insisted in _The Origins of Totalitarianism_ that whatever liberties we may now enjoy in a democracy, we always need to remain vigilant, watching out for the emergence or re-emergence of totalitarian propensities. She also pointed out how nineteenth-century imperialism, in which Britain and France were central players, provided crucial foundations and pre-figurations of what later would become a modern totalitarian politics: i.e. a form of governance based upon notions of racial superiority, the exertion of power, a range of modern armaments, the exploitation of rapidly advancing technologies, and the assumed right to enact at the centre whatever violence the state needed at its peripheries, thus to dominate vast territories and disparate peoples, and to make that total claim to jurisdiction. Arendt was interested too in the origins of the very idea of a 'world politics'; she sought to trace the lineage of that notion, from imperialism to totalitarianism.

Arendt, moreover, noted that Nazi Germany and the Soviet Union led citizens to live with the police state inside their heads, and to deal somehow or other with the lies, even if not to swallow them wholesale. Such states might use any number of legal forms as carapace, but ultimately they claimed the right to take anybody away, on suspicion, while choreographing what passed as truth. The state assumed the absolute prerogative, in principle, to interfere in every nook and cranny of civil society; there was no separation of state and society in this creed. Of course, Soviet Russia, Nazi Germany and their conquered territories were, in practice, too complex for this, even at the height of the terror under Hitler or Stalin, and every last action could not be policed. But the assumption was that the state had no legitimate restraints, and was entitled to adjudicate who is unworthy of life; how citizens engage with each other; and what art is shown, books read (or burned), films produced, education provided, dance, music and sport sanctioned.

To openly dissent in a totalitarian state is to place your life on the line; to risk being denounced at once as part of the so-called degenerate and parasitical internal enemy, or an ally of a dangerous foreign power, to be expunged.[7] For the Jews or the Roma people in Nazi Germany and Hitler's occupied territories the option did not exist to fit in with the regime, but for gentiles it mostly did. In theory, the whole population in Germany, aside from the Jews and other 'degenerates', were supposed now to give themselves over entirely to further the shared cause, the vision of the *Volk*, perpetuated by the Nazi Party: a single people, presided over by a single leader. During the 1930s 'working towards the Führer' was cast as the fundamental goal, the aim to which all good Germans should aspire.[8] If you did not know what the leader thought or wanted, you had to 'work towards' him, fulfil his assumed desire, put the pieces together, realise his ultimate mission.

The other ideology that theorists of totalitarianism were most focused upon exploring in the 1950s was Stalinism. This ideology was based on elements already clearly present in the thought of Lenin, who had justified the need for a centralised party leadership to steer the potentially wrong-headed mass in the 'correct' Marxist direction. This was much to the horror of some other revolutionaries, notably Rosa Luxemburg (originally from Poland, but based in Germany), who wanted to allow revolution to have a more spontaneous and uncertain direction, so that the leaders would learn from the people, as revolution unfolded, in open ways, not just shepherd the population and insist where their history should take them.

From Lenin to Stalin came a politics intent upon pursuing a singular plan, while vigilantly silencing all unwelcome dissent. Stalin himself was to grow ever more extreme in that mission, and ever more venerated by the Party as the great leader, the force whose superior mind ultimately governed the lesser ones of his comrades. Here was the supreme arbiter of policy, even as the ideology espoused the equality of all. In practice, there were many contradictions, and Stalinism created a world of favoured and constantly jockeying appointees, the *nomenklatura*, caught up in an endless struggle between purges and routes to promotion. The requirement of Stalin and his circle was total loyalty; the price of dissent, or sometimes just of suspicion about possible dissent, was imprisonment or death.

During the war, in Nazi-occupied Poland, Miłosz had on occasion aided acts of resistance. There were cases of individual people and groups that willingly laid down their lives in skirmishes and acts of sabotage against the occupiers, however hopeless the odds. Some Poles hid Jewish people, relayed clandestine messages and assisted fugitives. Others collaborated passively or actively, offering sustenance, support and labour to the German authorities, blackmailing Jewish families and plundering their property. While some Polish policemen helped German forces in hunting Jews, others participated in underground resistance, or even on occasion collaborated with and resisted the Nazis by turns.[9] Many Poles sought just to stay alive and avoid being noticed, as Miłosz observed, struggling in bleak conditions to hold on and to protect their families. He would write prose, as well as poems, that recognised the indifference, callousness, denials or complicities of many Poles in face of the carnage.

The entire land, he insisted, was bound up thereafter with this history of occupation, of misery, that struggle for survival, amid so much unfathomable cruelty, and so much denial. His earliest memories of life in what became the state of Lithuania, where he was born, and later of Warsaw and the Polish countryside, where he would survive, under the occupation, overshadowed a good deal of his poetry; he provided many musings on what it meant for him and for others to live through that history, and to endure thereafter, when so many hadn't survived, abandoned to their fate. In one of his elegies that appeared in the 1960s, he asked how one could live at that time, responding at once to the question to admit that he could not say. Nonetheless, he sought concise words to evoke the devastation, alluded to all that was taken, and pointed to those such as himself, who, while not reduced to ashes themselves, lived on with remorse:

> We learned so much, this you know well:
> how, gradually, what could not be taken away
> is taken. People, countrysides.
> And the heart does not die when one thinks it should,
> we smile, there is tea and bread on the table.
> And only remorse that we did not love
> the poor ashes in Sachsenhausen
> with absolute love, beyond human power.[10]

Poland, liberated from the Nazis in 1945, was reunited, albeit with the loss of substantial territory, and now under the domination of the Soviet Union and its Red Army. Remaining spaces for civil society, and for artistic or political expression, independent and critical of the leadership, were relentlessly pared back from the second half of the 1940s onwards. Artists were expected to denounce the West and actively champion the aesthetic style of the Party, socialist realism. Soviet-style penal facilities for political opponents continued to operate, a fearsome prospect for those who caused trouble.[11] Society, including the entire artistic 'community', was to be brought together as far as possible, Miłosz explained, under this new communist mission; workers, soldiers and artists all working, ideally, for this one great cause, and celebrating the genius of Lenin, Stalin and the Party.

The Warsaw Pact was formally created in 1955 to institutionalise the alliance between the Soviet Union, East Germany, Poland and the other satellite nations; the Polish army became the second-largest force inside that new international organisation. The Pact required each member state to defend any other attacked by an outside force, and, in this respect, mirrored NATO. The Roman Catholic Church retained a strong presence in Poland, although heavily hemmed in, and at times actively attacked by the Polish government. Soon statues of Stalin sprouted up in villages and towns all over the country. A network of informants and secret police was also swiftly built up, post-war. Such uses of state power – the reality of close observation and, where necessary, coercion of any prominent doubters and waverers – became assumed facts of life, shadowing the movements of those who were 'free', outside of labour camps, to go about their business. All those who wanted to stay alive, including Miłosz's friends and peers, had, at the very least, to watch their step and keep up the appearance of support for the Party wherever a wall might have ears.[12]

Miłosz called Warsaw the 'most agonising spot in the whole of terrorised Europe'; he wrote of a world in which one feared arrest, a land where hardship, death and suffering were everywhere obvious. People grew wary of speaking out, or even of being seen at all. Many had already learned during the war to say nothing and just walk on by, even if they saw a corpse on the street; expressing nothing untoward remained a survival strategy for many thereafter.

The Polish population, this implied, reeled as it moved from the immediate dangers and mortal challenges of wartime to the new society in the years that followed. Some chose to ally themselves fully with the Party, or conversely opted for opposition and even martyrdom. And in between those options, people might make countless gross adjustments or subtle accommodations in regard to the communist authorities. For a time, the political situation in post-war Poland was more fluid, a government coalition of sorts; you could try to just go about your work and your leisure, get enough food on the table, do the minimum, remain unobserved – but the Party's grip was growing ever tighter.

Miłosz sketched a picture of a society where experiences and personal solutions to the conundrum varied, but one thing was entirely shared: nobody could ever be sure where surveillance began or ended. The population, especially the intelligentsia, were either signed up to the Party, or were obliged to cloak their feelings; to watch themselves and others, to police their own conduct all the time. But in the end, for public intellectual figures like Miłosz, silence was not possible. He and others were counted upon actively to endorse party positions whatever they thought privately.

Miłosz invites us to think about the burdens of a particular national and personal history, but also to consider the different ways we can talk ourselves into a kind of stomach-churning allegiance, or semi-allegiance, to new forms of power. Citizens might accommodate any new reality, and thus endorse or at least accept their own subordination to a party line, for many reasons other than brainwashing; from an instinct to survive to a vaguer longing for harmony and happiness, or some inchoate wish to be part of the 'masses'. We are not all broken down and forced to conform. We may be tempted, he suggested, to take a kind of happiness pill, and rationalise our own shifting positions, collusions and betrayals. Moreover, he wrote about how people can attempt to split entirely their public and private selves into compartments when this is what the circumstances necessitate.

Miłosz added a further arresting observation: from the point of view of the political system, it might not really matter anyway. Totalitarianism worked even if some of its subjects operated cynically, hypocritically or ambivalently. To speak what you do not believe and to listen to others doing the same could even become a shared style of life. Miłosz recognised how a totalitarian state, or a total institution, can exert extreme forms of behavioural control over its population; governments can seek to dominate all aspects of personal expression and to interfere as far as possible with dissident thinking. A battery of techniques can be applied: if not to homogenise all opinion, then at least to silence the tongues of opponents. And yet, people may not privately agree, but rather go on telling themselves all manner of stories about what is happening to them, or inside them, as they publicly do what is asked of them.

★

Reading *The Captive Mind*, I found myself recalling a famous proposition articulated by the seventeenth-century mathematician and philosophical writer Blaise Pascal. It dealt with different possible grounds for prayer. We need to discriminate, Pascal showed, between those who pray because they believe, wholeheartedly, in what they are doing, and those who might operate according to a precautionary principle, reckoning it prudent to pray, whatever their doubts. He made an argument in favour of prayer as a sensible gamble, in case God does exist, since who knows for sure? If God does not exist, nothing is lost except the time spent in prayer. If you wager the other way, fail to pray, actively reject prayer, and God does exist, the price is far higher.

What Miłosz draws out is how if one citizen saw another in their acts of (secular) devotion, in Poland, paying homage to Stalin and his acolytes, or lauding the wonders of socialist realism, they may ask themselves silently if this comrade is a true believer, or a person who is going through the motions because it is the safe bet. Let's mention here another philosopher, writing in the nineteenth century, Jeremy Bentham, who sought to design a perfectly rational and efficient prison. He called it the panopticon. One of its crucial features, as Michel Foucault famously showed in his 1975 book *Discipline and Punish*, was that the prisoner should never know for sure if they were being watched from the central control tower. In a state such as that which Miłosz had fled, citizens knew the eyes and ears of the surveying power always were or might be there, even without a literal tower. To survive, you needed to assume that the state (or some informant whose views would be relayed to an agency of the state) could be present. The problem was internalised, so you tried to mind your speech, not speak your mind, become your own censor, and read between lines when others were speaking. You might believe, or you might 'believe', but either way you needed to make a decent show of it. Perhaps you could retain the split between inner and outer protestations, forever, or maybe after a while, practice made perfect, and the mask would become your actual face.

As a young man, before the war, Miłosz had felt a sympathy with the ideals of socialism and had a strong distaste for the authoritarian direction of the 1930s government in Poland. After the war, and before the Stalinist net closed in fully over Eastern Europe, he sought to retain, however precariously, a certain independence. Even though he was not formally a mouthpiece, or even a member, of the Communist Party, his standing led to him being appointed a cultural attaché and given an opportunity to present Polish culture abroad. Losing hope that the Party would reform and bring a greater degree of enlightenment and freedom for the whole people, he faced an agonising political choice: would he follow the requirement, as an artist, and as a spokesman, to espouse socialist realism, the aesthetic creed that he personally despised? It sickened him to do so. He also feared the net was closing in on him personally, as his discomfort and coded reservations had not gone unobserved in Warsaw. He felt he was living on borrowed time, not yet fully a suspect, but clearly not quite trusted either by his own government. He was moved closer to home, withdrawn from Washington to Paris, and he feared that at any time he'd be recalled to his country. So, in 1951, he became a defector.

When he wrote *The Captive Mind*, then, Miłosz was already something of an outsider in both societies, seeking to find a new space for himself. He looked at both systems critically and quizzically. He lived in Western Europe for years, but in 1960 would move again, thanks to an attractive university job offer in Berkeley. But although he had a new kind of security and comfort in California, he was never in fact fully settled. He continued to write, still in many ways as an outsider, never entirely acclimatised, certainly never uncritically attuned to American life, any more than he had previously felt at home in the French literary scene. He remained a Polish writer in exile, acutely conscious of how much is lost in translation.

During his years in France in the 1950s, Miłosz could not fail to be aware of conflicts within the Western European Left, and especially among French intellectuals, about whether and how critically to support communism, and how far, if at all, to condone the variety that had emerged in Russia, or later in China. Some would stay silent in face of growing doubt, and all the evidence about vast numbers of people oppressed, imprisoned and killed; prominent intellectuals would offer rationalisations for supporting Stalinism, or sometimes Maoism, and for avoiding open criticism of the Communist Party. From the comfort of a university lecture room, in the pages of journals, or from the table of a chic café on the Left Bank, notable writers, free enough in their own movements, insisted you had to take a side despite the mass of evidence of Stalin's and Mao's crimes and horrific miscalculations, costing the lives of millions.

Those who spoke out more critically against the Communist Party, such as Albert Camus (a writer and person whom Miłosz admired), were singled out and criticised by others for betraying the Left. Indeed, Camus and Jean-Paul Sartre fell out dramatically over their respective political attitudes in 1952, just at the time when Miłosz was writing his book.[13]

For some erstwhile Western supporters of the Soviet system, the dream evaporated later, perhaps with the crushing of Hungarian dissent in 1956 or with the sight on TV of tanks rolling into Czechoslovakia in the summer of 1968; for others, it came through reading translated Russian and Eastern European novels, memoirs and histories. Some of those accounts were devastating. Testimonies from survivors of the Gulag were mounting up; stories from people who had been subjected to arbitrary arrest, interrogation, long stints of penal servitude, or indeterminate years of internal exile.

Into the Whirlwind is the title of a book (first published outside the Soviet Union in 1967; it would not be issued in full, in Russia, until 1990) by one of those victims of Stalinism, Yevgenia Ginzburg. She had been found guilty in a brief hearing in Moscow in 1937 of participating in a supposed Trotskyist plot: there was no appeal. Ginzburg ended up serving an eighteen-year sentence. For those in the West who wanted to know what had happened to so many victims in Siberia and throughout the penal system across the Soviet sphere, testimonies and reports were emerging in the decades post-war. The mass of data and personal narrative eventually could not be dismissed by those on the Left, except perhaps by the most obdurate deniers, as lies confected in right-wing Western propaganda. This literature and news reporting confronted and often confounded former apologists. There was now proof enough of the monstrous oppression, the dogmatic beliefs, tragic cruelties and the madness of what Stalin and the Party unleashed, for all those who wanted to know, even before Aleksandr Solzhenitsyn's novels began to appear, with much publicity, in English translation in the 1960s. Solzhenitsyn's vast non-fiction work, *The Gulag Archipelago* – assembled between 1958 and 1968, hidden from the KGB, successfully smuggled abroad and then finally brought out by English and French publishing houses in 1973 – caused a further storm in the West.[14]

The Captive Mind was hailed by several influential Western readers in the 1950s as a major work of political psychology, and a blow for freedom in the Cold War. Miłosz was praised by luminaries in the arts, philosophy and sciences, including Heinrich Böll, Karl Jaspers and Albert Einstein. He would find himself compared to Arendt, Arthur Koestler, Bertrand Russell, André Gide, John Dos Passos and Albert Camus, and, later, likened to Solzhenitsyn and Milan Kundera (critics of both East and West, communism and capitalism). It was a list very largely if not exclusively made up of valiant *men*, of letters and science.[15] Miłosz was elevated to a kind of pantheon, celebrated sometimes in ways he did not quite recognise, as a champion of the Cold War West, led by the United States. Miłosz certainly rejected the lure of communist one-party rule and reductive Marxist histories where 'class struggle' was all. He wrote, with grim hostility, about how the Poles had found themselves living under a single and intolerable 'philosophy', 'dialectical materialism'. And yet he also pointed to patterns of conformity he found in the West, rejecting the polarised thinking that he identified in the attitudes of governments on both sides of the Iron Curtain.[16] In a later preface he noted that the book caused some confusion and debate at the time – a sell-out for fervent Leftists, and too socialist in sympathy in the eyes of conservatives.

To reinforce his account of people's intricate psychological acrobatics (performing, while not believing), Miłosz made use of another instructive story, previously told in 1865 by the French writer and diplomat Count Joseph Arthur de Gobineau. It concerns the concept of 'Ketman' (or *kitmān*, in Persian). Gobineau had grotesque theories about 'race' and 'miscegenation', but his value, for Miłosz, did not lie in his racial views but rather his description of a (supposed) medieval society based on the total divorce between public expression and inner belief. According to Gobineau's account, there were no 'true' Muslims in that long-ago Persia, even though everybody in that society might *appear* devout. Rather, people there were familiar with dissimulating, taking it for granted that the observances were needed to fit in and avoid disapproval and risk of punishment.

For Miłosz, this idea was beautifully suggestive of the contemporary Polish predicament. Under Stalin's rule, he argued, there was even less room for personal, political and artistic freedom than had existed in the medieval Persia that Gobineau portrayed.[17] In his exploration of Ketman in Poland, Miłosz went further, however, than simply to note the constant role-playing and the erosion of art and public debate. He suggested that there could be a potential perverse form of enjoyment in this never-ending accommodating charade. Some people might gain a secret gratification from toeing the necessary political line, and doing so effectively, a bit like a tightrope walker, impressed at themselves for avoiding the dangerous drop through their own rhetorical subterfuge. Might one gain silent satisfaction, he asked, in thus disjoining mind from speech, keeping the private recesses of the self under lock and key, safe from scrutiny?

Miłosz added:

> A constant and universal masquerade creates an aura that is hard to bear, yet it grants the performers certain not inconsiderable satisfactions. To say something is white when one thinks it black, to smile inwardly when one is outwardly solemn, to hate when one manifests love, to know when one pretends not to know, and thus to play one's adversary for a fool (even as he is playing you for one) – these actions lead one to prize one's cunning above all else. Success in the game becomes a source of satisfaction.[18]

He recognised how he and his comrades were caught in a society that degraded authentic human relations and, in the end, produced a terrible destitution of the self. This was a vision of a world where people breathed or vomited the corrupted air (I adapt that image from a poem by Zbigniew Herbert, another remarkable Polish writer, who had close links with Miłosz); a world where diplomatic evasion comes to be assumed, and sometimes achieved with aplomb.[19] The question is not only what atrocious regimes can force populations to do, but also what as individuals we may revolt against or stomach, make ourselves perform, and subsequently justify to ourselves and even enjoy: the compartmentalisation, or active mendacity, as the price of just getting by, perhaps even succeeding. Social conditioning, Miłosz suggests, is not just imposed from on high: it is a two-way psychological street, a network of unspoken and tacit trades that exist between people and other people, as well as parties, systems or states. But such splits are not simply conscious or remediable by act of will either.

Many of us, Miłosz suggested, negotiate, acquiesce, genuflect, driven on by a mixture of motives and pressures, trying to endure, or get ahead, despite dispiriting circumstances, in that vast murky field of compromises. One obvious temptation, as he points out, is to deny reality, attempt to remove oneself entirely, switch off, stupefy oneself with drugs and escapist daydreams; or seek, even with a certain appetite for obedience, to submit to the voice of an external authority that insists there is no possible room for any doubt. In this respect, *The Captive Mind* might invite closer comparison with Huxley's *Brave New World*, rather than the main lesson of Orwell's *Nineteen Eighty-Four*. It points to our human propensity to shift moods and attitudes, to dissemble, to retreat into an altered state of consciousness, to flirt with suicide, a wish to be done with the world as it is, or a dazed willingness to endure, and allow the system to roll on regardless.

There may be also a positive attraction, not just a terror, in having another party dictate what a person should think, Miłosz acutely observed, a certain comfort and calm in feeling oneself to be exempted from the worrisome burden of thinking at all. It is possible to desire unconsciously to be mind-less and obedient. This idea had previously been explored by Erich Fromm, a German intellectual and psychoanalyst and for some years an important associate of the Frankfurt School. He had sought to consider, in studies of the psychopathology of Nazism, how people might allow an external leader to become their guiding ego, or perhaps their auxiliary super-ego. Fromm, unlike Miłosz, drew directly upon Freudian theory. His main point was to focus attention upon the desire people might feel to have the burden of perception and interpretation, and the load of internal responsibility for deciding and choosing, lifted away. Fromm suggested that a person with a need in their own mind to submit to an authority figure might seek a cruel surrogate father in political life, a wish that might be fulfilled by a fascistic overseer.

Miłosz had recognised the varieties of authoritarian and totalitarian forms of governance, and the diversity of human experiences within such systems. He suggested that a people need not be completely broken and fully brainwashed, but rather might be just tempted, or desperately inclined, to accept an implicit deal to make life safer and easier. In either system, minds could be distorted, indoctrinated or medicated. Some influential critics of the medicalised treatment of the 'mad' in the West, such as the psychiatrists Ronnie Laing (in Britain) and Franco Basaglia (in Italy), would develop their own critiques of captive minds, pointing out influentially during the

1960s and 70s how warehouse-like hospitals and the vast expansion
in the distribution of pharmaceutical treatments served as a terrible palliative, even as the 'care system' dehumanised and alienated
people. Anti-psychiatry campaigners protested that mental distress
should not just be adjusted by chemical means but linked to social
and familial patterns, or traced back to deeper socio-political sources.

Amid the intensifying political disquiet and increasing economic
upheaval and social decay witnessed in many Western cities during
the 1960s and 70s, arguments about the use of sedating drugs (prescribed for some, or bought on the street by others) assumed growing
significance and came to be linked to critique of capitalism. Proponents of that emerging anti-psychiatry movement, such as Laing,
stated that rather than just treating and quieting the pathology of
individuals, society needed radical transformation, for the madness
also lay there. In short, Valium and a range of other medications to
dampen moods became social and political issues. In accepting such
treatment, embracing the chemical arsenal from anti-depressants to
anti-psychotic drugs, the mental health profession and the people
they treated were arguably accepting their hopeless alienation in the
system; rather than moving beyond their individual suffering to find
creative personal solutions, or to unite to challenge the current dispensation, they remained lonely, out of the way, dazed, said critics, by
chemical coshes, held in liquid straitjackets.[20]

Miłosz was writing that study in advance of the explosive Western
debates of the 1960s and 70s about civil rights and the brute power
of the state. In those decades, numerous new groups sought to 'raise
political consciousness' in the West, to invite fellow citizens to refuse
to fit in with the prevailing system; networks proliferated – not only
of trade unionists and striking workers, but also of students, anti-war
demonstrators, protestors against racial discrimination and neo-
imperialism, feminist activists, anti-psychiatry campaigners. However,
as though prefiguring some of those arguments about the pressure
to conform to an unconscionable political state, Miłosz wrote of a
stupefying drug in his 1953 study. This was the 'Murti-Bing pill'.

Miłosz took the name Murti-Bing from *Insatiability*, a 1930 novel
by a Polish writer, Stanisław Ignacy Witkiewicz, which depicted a
European society in total decay and threatened by a Sino-Mongolian
army and ruthless leader. At a certain point in this tale, pedlars arrive
selling an Eastern remedy, an instantly transformative pill. You can

take it as an anticipation of Valium if you wish, or as a metaphor for other kinds of measures to provide false reassurance, distort perception or accommodate some new political reality, without the citizenry even noticing, intent only on blotting out individual perception and pain. Suddenly the Murti-Bing pill was on offer everywhere, to all. *Insatiability* suggested that under the influence of this pill, a medicated population would no longer experience, as reality, the invasion it had suffered by a hostile army. They would blind themselves to all tragedy, living contentedly in a new dream world, with the illusion of being healthy individuals, beneficiaries of a charmed life, surrounded by the pathologically unfortunate discontented other people who had failed to take the necessary dosage and duly adjust. In Miłosz's account, some of his compatriots, including fellow artists, had become such pill-swallowers, neutralising their doubts and imagining themselves as the enlightened ones, interpreting life and reality accurately through that singular philosophy, dialectical materialism. It was a particular form of accommodation to power and ultimately to the Kremlin.[21]

In other words, Miłosz used this novel to suggest that some of his peers had dulled their brains and buried all doubts about the metaphysical justice of Stalinism in order to enjoy an un-troublingly simple vision. They were commanded to echo the Party's account of the social purpose of art. As he bitterly put it, the pill-swallowers in the circles of writers and artists he knew ceased to experiment with paint in imaginative ways, or trouble themselves with composing 'difficult' music, but simply churned out stirring 'marches and odes', in tune with the odious political times.[22]

He was struck how some people in that society also managed to bury themselves entirely in technical work: scientists, for instance, bunkered down in a lab, engrossed in their tasks, as far as possible trying to be oblivious of all the disturbance that surrounded or even enabled it. Denial and alienation can take many forms, of course. Some people may wish only to work, others to sleep, as means of escape. Parallels with what he had already witnessed during his sojourn in the United States, after 1945, were not lost on him either. His acute observations of life in the communist East invite comparisons as well as discriminations; recognition of the differences that exist between political states, and of the variety of accommodations, addictions, seductions or rationalisations that may occur in our lives.

After all, we can easily get into a kind of wilful blindness; these days the drug might be workaholism, immersion in celebrity culture, compulsive shopping or browsing online. There are various spaces we can enter to make everyday reality recede, for a while, just like for those who live mesmerised in the sunless, air-conditioned 24/7 casinos of Las Vegas, so long as the money lasts to slot into machines or to bet at the roulette table.

Alongside the pill-swallowers, Miłosz also wrote about the widely shared human need for 'even the most illusory certainty'.[23] If some of his contemporaries sought to be entirely convinced, and others preferred a blissed-out state of wilful ignorance, others still, he acknowledged, were trying to attune, adapt and make do, without such complete affirmation or denial, but rather just to act on the precautionary principle, not to rock the boat, and hope that one day the world would turn again for the better. The question as to what ultimately drove some people to deny and disavow – to take the pill – he left to the reader.

In a new preface to the 1981 edition of *The Captive Mind*, Miłosz explained that he was concerned with the willingness of so many citizens to accept totalitarian terror 'for the sake of a hypothetic future'. History also revealed, he suggested, the vulnerability of the 'modern mind' to 'seduction by socio-political doctrines'. Seduction, maybe, but also resignation to a state of mind in which questioning the state could seem futile, dangerous and hopelessly exhausting. The focus was on Eastern Europe, but that book also invited comparison with life in the West. In a market-based economy, after all, you also go about your business, dealing with the reality, and probably accept the terms of trade in practice even if you might disagree in principle, concluding that capitalism is harmful to you. We may be open to such adaptation, to seduction, or to 'gaming the system', but do not necessarily see ourselves as prisoners, zombified victims of mind-numbing forces. What especially interests me here is the situation he depicted in which people are doing just enough to collaborate and conform, while still possessing some personal agency and continuing privately, perhaps, to voice the word 'no', albeit not out loud.

Miłosz made the important point that people make inferences about each other, but they may well elect to keep those inferences to themselves. Sometimes they must do so to survive. Utterances and feelings are not necessarily the same thing, as we all know. There are many situations in conversation where we opt not to press the point and ask someone else what they really mean or how they have compromised; and even if we do, and they answer, we might not be sure it's the truth. In the best of times, let alone the worst, such as Miłosz's own, we do not know for certain what other people are thinking, or at least *all* that they are thinking, either when they are speaking or when they are silent. Every interaction involves decisions, mostly unspoken, sometimes even unconscious, about how much to assume about another person's words, and how far we allow someone else to know what we are secretly thinking, in so far as we are conscious of that, in the privacy of our own minds.

The American psychologist Stanley Milgram added his own perspective on this kind of silent process of figuring out what lies behind other people's speech, through a series of experiments in the late 1970s and early 1980s. This new project came after his famous investigation (in the early 1960s at Yale University) of obedience. In the latter, Milgram had controversially claimed to show how many, perhaps even a majority, might comply blindly with an authority. You did not have to be an Adolf Eichmann, he argued, to be a potentially murderous kind of civil servant or apparatchik, hiding behind the defence of just obeying orders. It was a powerful and stimulating body of work that generated much necessary soul-searching. However, the ethics of Milgram's experiments, which entailed the participation of hapless volunteers, were problematic, as he tricked and possibly also traumatised people to play a part in an unexpected and painful game; perhaps, said later critics, the experiment itself was an exercise in the callousness or cruelty it purported merely to study.

In the much later experimental project Milgram conducted around 1980, he took up ideas about role play and performance; he now sought to investigate the ways we may interpret and fill in the gaps in conversation. He was fascinated by what theatre could tell us about human relations in everyday life, and the implicit assumptions we make about other minds. He may also have been influenced by experiments with AI and human–machine interaction, for example the 'Turing Test'. This was the proposed test famously devised by the polymath Alan Turing, in a 1950 paper. First known as the 'imitation game', the aim was to consider if a machine can simulate behaviour that is impossible for a person to distinguish from ordinary human responses.

We may be held captive, Milgram now suggested, not only by the authority figures and coercive forces that weigh upon us directly; we are also guided by tacit conventions and cues, social mores, and polite guidelines that suffuse conversations between people. He wanted to know to what degree two conversationalists are making unspoken assumptions about each other. Can we be sure, after all, that the character sitting right there opposite us in animated discussion really thinks those thoughts, or even actually scripts those thoughts they are voicing? Might we be held captive by those deeply built-in assumptions?

Milgram designed a new experiment to explore these questions at his university in New York. The test was based on a late-nineteenth-century French play, *Cyrano de Bergerac*; its purpose was to find out whether people could discern if their interlocutor was really speaking for themselves, being authentic, or just parroting lines fed to them by an off-stage prompter via a secret earpiece. The prompter was Professor Milgram, no less, who provided the words while hidden in another room. He found that people mostly try to fill in awkward gaps and make allowances for the contrived rhetoric being recited to them by their interlocutor. In this way they seek to smooth over their awareness (if any) that the person they are talking to could be merely an actor keeping to the allotted lines.[24] Conventions about speech might inhibit as well as guide us, sculp our thoughts, and constrict our actions.

We may well automatically accommodate, make allowances, avoid disturbing strangers, helping the conversation along, fearful of making trouble or sticking our necks out and embarrassing someone, even when we think something is a bit 'off'. For Milgram, this built-in assumption that the person speaking to you is thinking what they say also had potential social uses. Maybe, he speculated, the experiment would help create a society in which troubled mothers could be advised secretly by experts on how to talk to their babies, in real time, through the hidden earpiece; hostage negotiators could receive useful input from a support team even as they talked to kidnappers; police might relay what psychiatrists, listening in, told them to say, and politicians could continue to recycle party lines, as required, via earpieces, or at least teleprompters. Ronald Reagan, the former actor, was in power at the time, and relied upon such technology to help him along when memory faded.

★

Evidently Miłosz was not unique, post-war, in writing of society's endless pressures to conform, the myriad performances, ruses and subterfuges that may be required to survive; nor in exploring how role-play and masks might hide or, worse, become our inner worlds and govern our social relationships. Not long before he wrote his book, a landmark work, *The Second Sex*, had been published, not about role-play under communism, but about the schooling of women from cradle to grave to accept their subordination. Simone de Beauvoir's great 1949 study championed equality, calling for women to exercise their freedom and avoid 'bad faith'. Her account charted women's oppression in patriarchal societies, and showed how they are groomed to accept their supposed inferiority, dress up, play a character, perform roles, be, for men, a 'second sex' – in short, subordinated. The most famous line in the book was: 'One is not born but becomes woman.' (Earlier, Joan Riviere, writer and psychoanalyst, and patient and translator of Freud, had anticipated at least one element of this post-war feminist argument in a notable paper in 1929, suggesting how 'womanliness' might be a kind of masquerade, expected or assumed of women, to spare men from anxiety and feelings of inferiority.)[25]

The 1950s was a decade that brought much new discussion of performances, masks and roles in different political milieu, in social struggles, in the workplace and in domestic situations. The term 'role-play' itself had appeared in the English language (1950, according to the OED). In 1956, the theme was influentially elaborated upon by Erving Goffman in his study *The Presentation of Self in Everyday Life*. Here is Goffman's opening account and elaboration in that book:

> When an individual plays a part he implicitly requests observers to take seriously the impression that is fostered before them. They are asked to believe that the character they see actually possesses the attributes he appears to possess, that the task he performs will have the consequences that are implicitly claimed for it, and that, in general, matters are what they appear to be.

Goffman noted that the performer might be fully taken in by their own act, sincerely convinced that the impression of reality which they 'stage' is true. Both performer and listener may be convinced that they are simply being themselves, and it would take the sociologist or some other external observer to note the stylised nature of what is being presented. But Goffman then adds another possibility, strikingly close to Miłosz's point, a situation where the performer may not be taken in at all by their own routine, may take a more cynical view and then 'enjoy a certain gleeful spiritual aggression', an 'unprofessional pleasure' from this 'masquerade'.[26] That (cynical) capacity to 'delude' the audience might be justified as good for the audience or the community; a doctor, a mechanic or even a politician, playing the role of professional fixer, might be performing to the listener for some apparently or genuinely benign purpose; to save time, spare the other anxiety, get the job done. But there might also be a gratifying – perverse – dividend for the performer, i.e. in being in the know and exulting while the listener is not aware of what is really happening. Goffman believed people can savour such a state of controlling theatre, and the sense of getting away with it, thereby exercising a secret sense of mastery over others.

These scenarios about performance and subterfuge, either systematically and cruelly imposed on captive populations or artfully played with and used by social actors, who are in a more ordinary sense at liberty, seemed to hang in the air of that time. A range of writers and critics in this period drew analogies between theatre and politics, explored the many ways that language might be used 'performatively' and showed how roles might be required, as well as artfully adopted, in social situations, used by citizens to survive, to persuade, to help a person fit in, to bargain or to provide the mask-wearer with silent enjoyment at the other's expense. But a different kind of role play or mask-wearing was also suggested in this period, one that might occur in earliest infancy, when the crucial process of nurture went badly awry.

Psychoanalysts were especially interested in elaborating on these themes, post-war, and moreover in considering not just general social or psychological pressures to become 'a man' or 'a woman', but also to play an (empty) role, in lieu of developing any authentic identity. Clinicians explored how damaging experiences with the primary carer very early in life might result in the infant adopting a kind of impenetrable armour, keeping out dangers, but also trapping the real self in an imprisoning second skin. An inner core might remain; or perhaps in the most serious cases, the assumed persona or mask might be all there was. Of course, none of us is entirely free of masks, or able to function without some sense of a social performance, as Goffman had explained. Even with a benign upbringing or reasonably supportive societal context, all of us may be expected to occupy a plethora of roles, to fulfil our social commitments, or become at times, for our own reasons and needs, and when pressured, more like caricatures of ourselves or echoes of others. Who has not slid imperceptibly into character, perhaps as a child in a family, donning some familiar role as expected: the 'dreamer', 'little angel', 'joker', 'high-achiever', 'troublemaker', 'disappointment', 'doubter', etc.

The 'false self', wrote the paediatrician and psychoanalyst Donald Winnicott, a decade after *The Captive Mind* was published, 'is built up on a basis of compliance'. This false self, he observed, can have a defensive function: the protection of the true self. A child may desperately cling to some inner core, even if – Winnicott surmised – the parent had trouble tuning into the genuine messages emerging from that core self. Here was another approach to the captive state of the mind, and the way people might, from earliest life, have to insulate something precious, and also copy, slip into the guise of another, or even end up hollowed out, nothing other than their psychological masks or designated character.

Winnicott was among a group of psychoanalysts who wrote, during the war years and after, about such early infantile developments, and our internalised, vital relationships. Through that dire period of European history, he and his peers were also active in considering the challenge for any psyche, and any society, of sustaining a way of functioning based upon liberty and democracy. Anna Freud had written a major book in 1936 which bears upon that question too, through her consideration of the ego and its defences. This reflected her deep concern at how, or even whether, a rational and questioning part of the self would survive intact or succumb to other forces in the modern age of extremes. She considered how people might have strong or weak resilience, struggle with fragile egos thanks to a combination of factors, including their constitutions, upbringing, relationships, drives; they might be drawn in turn to the most irrational and destructive political parties; most immediately for her, of course, the Nazis.[27]

These clinicians were mindful that the ego was vulnerable not only to being waylaid by the mind's own id or superego, but also to being recruited by the skills of totalitarian propagandists. Ernst Kris, another analyst, made a sharp-edged distinction in 1941 between the forms of propaganda that he said were characteristic of totalitarian and democratic political systems. In the former, propaganda 'covers the range from persuasion to hypnotism'; while under democratic conditions, the range is 'from persuasion to education'. In the totalitarian case, the propaganda is all about 'domination of the individual'; in the democratic case, at best, it 'aims at the rule of reason within the individual'. So, analysts looked at the operation of particular political systems, valorised democracy and recognised its vulnerability. They also warned of our wavering unconscious identifications, the instability of the self, and the risks of reversion to what another analyst, Erik Erikson, along with Lifton, called 'totalism'.

We internalise elements of others to form our egos, mused such clinicians; the ego is always a complex amalgam, not a unity, comprising diverse identifications, and in part unconscious too. However, some grow stronger and more solid than others, they argued. They worried, for good reason, about how conditions in a family, an institution or a state might function so as to mean there's no option for that emerging ego but to mimic or serve another. What if we have no viable defences that ultimately work, or no secret (treasured) interior space that can survive, through adversity, beneath the desperate, artful and essential mask, or the imperious calls of others? For Winnicott,

> A principle governing human life could be formulated in the following words: only the true self can feel real, but the true self must never be affected by external reality, must never comply. When the false self becomes exploited and treated as real there is a growing sense in the individual of futility and despair.

A society could fall into a state of shared cultural despair, other writers would argue, leading people to abandon all caution, fall in with some crazed party, and seek false 'solutions'.

Miłosz shows us that even, or perhaps especially, in the fraught, extreme circumstances of that era in Nazi and Stalinist Poland, people are variable, so such labels as 'true' and 'false' self should be treated with caution. Political states too are always more complicated than the shorthand terms that we use routinely to divide them, such as 'liberal', 'authoritarian', 'totalitarian', 'imperial', etc. Indeed, the tensions between liberalism and democracy (the former focused on individuals, the latter on majoritarian decisions) may be swept under the carpet by blithe talk that a state is some paragon of 'liberal democracy'.

Just as clinicians continue to debate, or sometimes renounce, general diagnostic labels about people's mental health, wondering if a person is best seen as, say, neurotic, psychotic, borderline, or at the very borderline of that so-called borderline condition, so academics still argue over the contours of political statehood. We need such epithets about persons and states; they offer useful starting points, but also require critical scrutiny. As we begin to fill in more details, we may start to observe what is lost in translation, between the particular case and the general model. Miłosz, as we have seen, firmly contrasts East and West, totalitarianism and liberal societies. But he also looks at each case more questioningly. For each person's and nation's history is not just an exemplar, but also a story that is distinct. Poland, for him, was an oppressed society, but was not just a cypher for 'Eastern Europe' in general. He wanted to explore certain affinities as well as differences between lived experiences. And he invited us to notice how easily a language of politics goes stale, turns into mere phrase-making that freezes our thought.

Cold War rhetoric, the 'totalitarian world' versus 'free world', of course begged many questions. Where should we draw convincing lines, for example in defining a particular state as liberal democratic? What skeletons lay in the cupboard of the so-called land of the free? How do we resolve the contradictions between liberty and security? When might a description of a state as 'free' or 'democratic' seem adequate, and when does it become mere window dressing, a mask for imperialism, or for fascism? And where might we most appropriately set the boundary in our time between an authoritarian and totalitarian system? In the West today, the textbook cases that clearly are not in much dispute as totalitarian entities include North Korea. But opinions vary over the accuracy of 'totalitarian' to satisfactorily describe, say, 1950s apartheid South Africa, or brutal military regimes that have ruled Latin American states, for example Chile during the 1970s and after. And what of Putin's Russia, or Xi Jinping's China? Take the latter: the measures used there today against the Uighur minority, as we have seen, pass the yardstick of 'totalitarian', but what about the captivity of the rest of the population, or even of those who are granted privileged status and Party support, so long as they abide by the explicit and unspoken rules?

For example, on 2 November 2021 an internationally renowned Chinese tennis player, Peng Shuai, posted a long note on Weibo, protesting at how a senior Party official had forced her to have sex with him three years earlier while pretending that theirs was a romantic relationship. Her message went viral, fuel for the growing #MeToo movement in China, but so did news of her subsequent disappearance and mysterious reappearance in various staged images. An interview in December in which she denied that she had ever accused anyone only increased doubts about her freedom and safety, fuelled discussion of totalitarianism and intensified calls abroad to boycott the 2022 Beijing Winter Olympics. Hearing of her retraction of the earlier claims of assault, Chinese dissident Ai Weiwei suggested she was simply required to be a 'soldier' of the Communist Party. 'She is a sports person, which is like being a soldier in the army. Any person in sport is considered as property of the Party.'[28]

One approach would suggest that during the 1990s, China, after a brief thaw and embryonic signs of liberalisation, reverted to type as totalitarian state. However, some commentators reach for other designations, such as authoritarian capitalist one-party system, or point to regional variations, suggesting shades of totalitarianism, or an interim stage, 'approaching totalitarianism'. Still others would suggest that to call China one single 'total' society is itself an illusion.

For prominent voices in the US Republican Party, the preferred term, however, is usually 'totalitarian' for China and 'free' for the United States, although sometimes with slight qualifications, with words such as 'becoming' added in, as though the issue is not entirely settled. Consider a recent opinion piece by the historian Lee Edwards, to be found on the website of the ultra-conservative think tank The Heritage Foundation: in response to the question 'Is China totalitarian?', his answer is yes, or almost. Edwards writes, '[b]y any reasonable measure, the PRC is becoming a totalitarian state whose actions are dictated and determined by Xi Jinping and the Communist Party he heads'.[29] In support, he cites former US national security advisor Zbigniew Brzezinski's six traits to define a totalitarian state: an official ideology, a single political party typically led by a supreme leader, a secret police, party control of mass communications, party control of the military and a centrally directed economy. That state of 'becoming totalitarian', Edwards explains, could be traced through a series of moments in history – from the first phases of the People's Republic through the Cultural Revolution to the later one-party settlement, which accommodates a version of capitalism.

In the aftermath of the 1989 Tiananmen Square Massacre, it became clear that the Party, under Deng Xiaoping's leadership, had decided to crush all movements that advocated for radical political reform and liberalisation, and to silence the right to engage in politics beyond the remit of the Party. Dissenters were brutally beaten, imprisoned, tortured and then often 're-educated' during the nationwide clampdown that followed. Through the 1990s, the Chinese leadership remained intent, however, on its own new experiment, combining one-party rule with measures to promote an increasingly liberalised economy based around the massive global export of cheap goods. The problem, answered with both tanks and with rising living standards, was how to tame any rebellious mood of individualism and political liberalism, or old-style Maoist backlash, that such an economic liberalisation might then unleash.

The significance of the rebellion in 1989, dissidents continue to insist, lay in its defiance of the notion that the Chinese people had no burning desire for freedom of mind and no need for constitutional democracy. The Chinese novelist, dissident and exile Ma Jian claimed that Tiananmen exposed a regime prepared to massacre its own unarmed citizens to maintain power at all costs. He added:

> It is both mistaken and morally repugnant to argue that the deaths were necessary to 're-establish order' and guarantee future growth … [U]nder the slogan of authoritarian capitalism, [the Party] has filled the bellies of the Chinese people while shackling their minds; encouraged a lust for material wealth while stifling the desire to reflect on the past and ask questions about the present.[30]

This repressive set of policies during the 1990s was followed, after 2000, by a vast new digitally enhanced apparatus for state surveillance and control of citizens' social behaviour. Today it is not only the Uighurs who are surveyed to a degree that might have surprised Orwell, Arendt or Miłosz. The state now possesses an unprecedented capacity to monitor the behaviour of its 1.4 billion citizens. China not only utilises a great 'firewall', blocking unwelcome foreign websites and creating wherever possible an alternative, highly orchestrated version of cyber reality compared with that available in the West; it also builds up detailed profiles of its citizens.[31]

Despite the restrictions on internet use, digital technology in China is a vital resource for the individual as well as for the state. Online, customers can browse as they wish, as free individuals, within the prescribed limits. They can make their own choices, not least about what to acquire; click Amazon China or other shopping emporia, such as Alibaba. The buyer, however, must not only consider the seller but also the political state that lurks in the background of the marketplace: purchasing items online, or even just browsing, sends a message not only to advertisers and businesses, but also potentially (or so you must assume) to surveillance authorities.

It is through this capacity for constant state-run observation online that the Chinese leadership has sought to control the explosive problem of individualism and capitalist growth in a one-party state. So, while a person has the freedom to procure an item (or not), they might well also consider, 'what am I saying to "them"?', i.e. to the 'eyes' of state power, through such actions. 'Is what I am doing right or wrong, seen from that vantage point? What will or might the consequence be?' The online footprint of every individual can also be integrated with other material copiously available to the monitoring agencies: evidence gathered via phone calls and texts, video footage, and through informants, that all establish an indelible record. Villages, towns, cities and highways each have their forests of cameras: the population's movements are recorded across much of the terrain, day and night.

The digital revolution, in its current Chinese version, does not just enable the state to conduct speedy checks to expose a subject's credit worthiness, but also to construct an ever more elaborate political 'credit' score. A political 'credit' (determined through a series of algorithms) is enhanced if a person consistently makes the right clicks; good online conduct can open doors to better prospects of many kinds and allow an individual to advance in the system or have a more comfortable life. Getting tickets to travel around the nation or abroad, for example, is easier with a good score. A seriously bad score may, in the end, lead to a knock on your door. No doubt in some cases this is true, but it may be a simplified version as well. The form of the Chinese social credit system that we read about so often in the West may reflect part of the Chinese political reality, but it may also serve self-congratulatory Western narratives, redolent of the Cold War, where 'we' enjoy unrestricted freedom while 'they' suffer 'totalitarianism'.

The systems of course are very different. All the same, behaviour online in the West is also monitored by corporations and we are fed information (or rather mostly advertisements) thanks to algorithms, coaxed to become addicted and to consume ever more so as to fuel capitalist enterprises. Information is harvested and exploited by political parties and governments, and tracked as necessary by intelligence agencies (the NSA in the United States and GCHQ in the UK). We may or may not be aware we give licence to snooping by businesses as we tick those boxes that say 'agree', without reading the small print. Western journalists often draw sharp contrasts between surveillance in China (or still more extremely in North Korea) and the liberty of the West. They also, however, sometimes make more disquieting comparisons between 'their' and 'our' 'panoptical' societies.[32]

The argument about the top-down complete totalitarian control of the people by the Chinese Communist Party, as scholars have argued, also risks a serious over-simplification. For the CCP now exercises power in a more complex and nuanced and often two-way fashion than such an account of total repression and complete mastery would suggest. While the Party does indeed employ a vast network of surveillance and coercive policing, it also uses all means possible to gauge opinion and then, quite frequently, to adjust policy, to see off social discontent, or to meet grievances. A larger argument has also been made, not only about China, but more generally about how contemporary non-democratic regimes may 'mimic' democratic forms of sampling and interaction, thus creating spaces of continuing dialogue and adjustment by the regime in response to citizens' feedback. So, police action and the threat of brutal imprisonment may coexist with other allowable forms of protest and criticism. A politics of crackdown and dialogue, a firm response to those who go too far, along with the state's acute sensitivity to public opinion, may all operate in a delicate balance. The internet serves to survey, but also to observe and accumulate disparate views, and then helps the leadership and the bureaucracies to adjust state policy, where it is deemed possible within the larger goal of the Party, to maintain mass consent.[33]

To think of societies as 'panoptical' also bears some further examination. As we have seen, the panopticon, as presented by Bentham, was a prison in which every prisoner could be seen but would never know when exactly. From the point of view of the authorities, or the state, Bentham argued, this was a rational and efficient way to organise things; the task of surveillance was always to be assumed; it would shape behaviour and mean a minimum of expenditure on guard duties. Through the constant possibility of observation, a seeing eye had to be assumed by the prisoner, and perhaps thereby internalised. During the twentieth century new ways of analysing the impact of bodily and mental captivity, and of conceiving the place of incarceration and surveillance within society, the economy and mass psychology, were also developed.

'The prison–industrial complex' in the US, wrote the journalist Eric Schlosser in 1998, 'is not only a set of interest groups and institutions. It is also a state of mind.'[34] That coinage, first found in the 1970s, emerged to prominence during the 1990s. The phrase echoed another, 'the military–industrial complex', introduced into common parlance by President Eisenhower in his valedictory speech in January 1961. It described the infrastructure and the enormous scale of human labour in the field of defence, intelligence and military research. In both cases, 'complex' is an appropriately ambiguous word, to convey both a material reality and a psychic problem. Preceding the coinage 'prison–industrial complex', we should also recall the concept of the total institution, and the place this occupied, alongside discourse on totalitarianism in post-war political thought. High-security prisons, like the worst psychiatric asylums, became important reference points in Cold War discussions about both the West and the East. For, as critics pointed out, total institutions could also exist, largely unremarked, in a seemingly liberal society.

In the 1950s, Goffman had analysed the total institution, explaining how sites and mechanisms were created so that authorities could hive off a particular population, and there destroy barriers between a person's private and public life. In the total institution, officialdom could tear away a citizen's identity, remove all life-enhancing opportunities and means of personal fulfilment that others (outside in that same society) enjoy. The total institution, Goffman pointed out, intentionally breaks the divide between the inner and the outer, and between any notion of labour and leisure, workplace and home; it exerts blanket control and surveillance of the designated 'inmate'. A context for this kind of analysis by Goffman and others was the institutionalisation of large numbers of people in the post-war West, not just in the 'totalitarian' East, or in the Western past.

The political reasons for concentrating people inside such places, Goffman showed, varied considerably. The total institution could be based upon blueprints that were more-or-less sinister in their intent; some had originated in notions of social care, rather than simple repression, products of a world where families are no longer able or willing to nurse the elderly, or to house the seriously mentally ill. Some total institutions, as pictured by Goffman, were in part educational in aim, or at least had been created to produce efficient, intense and rapid training (including, for example, military barracks). Others, however, were built and administered entirely for the purposes of segregating and dehumanising those regarded by the governing authorities, or its various proxies, as socially dangerous or psychologically deviant.

These institutions provide the site of punishment and aim at full managerial control of internees. Some were there to serve as a mode of deterrence for all; others rather as warehouses, driven by the need to keep a minority confined and out of sight. A common characteristic of total institutions, Goffman argued, is that they create 'inmates'; these are the people whose character is boiled down to their location inside the system, reduced often enough to prison number, mugshot or vital statistics. Indeed, the moment a person is placed in custody inside such an institution, Goffman claimed, they are stripped not only of their freedom to come and go, but also of their prior identities as three-dimensional individuals with a delicate web of relationships. The institution reduces identity to basic functions, and monitors, or sometimes eliminates, contact with the outside community – former workmates, friends, family or any other support systems.[35] The aim, he warned, is to regulate minds and bodies. Liveliness or 'spirit' in inmates is broken, either by deliberate design, or simply as a by-product of the structure and deadening routine.

Inside the total institution, the 'self is systematically, if often unintentionally, mortified', Goffman memorably wrote. He set out this thesis in a 1957 essay, subsequently republished in various texts.[36] In this kind of sealed-off silo, which clearly bears some comparison to a totalitarian polity, the inmate is always subjected to a sharp hierarchy, a world of vertical power. There is no guaranteed field of privacy, no protected area for autonomous personal choice, no option of complete unobserved refuge for the inmate in such a place. Each phase of the inmate's daily activity may be carried out in the enforced company of others (unless the individual is placed in punitive isolation, where they are also potentially held under constant observation); each human being is governed in such a site by some supposedly rational plan 'purportedly designed to fulfil the official aims of the institution'.

The re-education facilities for the Uighurs are one example of a set of institutions aiming at the wholesale control and reconstitution of a particular population. But total institutions are not of course all alike, and nor are they confined to any one part of the world; witness the grim revelations in recent years of religious correctional facilities in the United States, provided with state funding, which house troubled teenagers in sites that cut them off almost entirely from family and friends, for months, and operate draconian systems of reward and punishment, shared slogans, and shunning and silencing for any perceived insubordination.[37] Or consider the inhuman re-education programmes that were organised and meted out by the Canadian state to children from the Inuit peoples of the Arctic regions, forcibly removing them from their communities to be 'remade' or 'assimilated'. Scholars, recently reviewing what has happened to that population, point out how Goffman's argument still has validity. As he had shown, institutional arrangements aim to annihilate the past, denying the inmates access to their former familial and cultural memories.[38]

Goffman's point was that supposedly therapeutic or educational institutions (as well as penal ones), no less than political states, can, at worst, be turned into soul-destroying processing plants that seek to neutralise as well as to reorder the minds of captive inmates. Some Western mental health facilities, as well as prisons, he argued, may aim not only to capture, coerce, intimidate and mortify, but also to mould. An asylum can become a depository, with broken-spirited denizens. It may not matter if you are in the West or the East; if you are confined in a closed ward, you may be subject to the worst kind of re-educative 'nursing', where there is no accountability or supervision, and almost anything at all can be done to the body and mind, regardless of the mode of liberal government operating outside the walls of that closed institution. The fate of IRA prisoners in British detention facilities during the Troubles, subjected to what later came to be known as 'enhanced interrogation', that is to say torture under another name, is also well described in other accounts of the history of brainwashing. Britain was not 'totalitarian', but such facilities aimed to overwhelm entirely the psychic defences of the imprisoned subject.[39]

During the 1960s and after, academics influenced by Goffman, Foucault and others examined the variety of social institutions – from clinics to schools, asylums to prisons – analysing each nexus of power and knowledge, and exploring how regimes of 'truth' and systems of thought operated across the Cold War divide. One notable consequence of such critique, as mentioned, was the anti-psychiatry movement; in various countries in the Western world it made real waves, while in the Soviet Union anguished protests circulated in samizdat publications. *One Flew Over the Cuckoo's Nest*, Ken Kesey's novel (1962), adapted as a film (1975), directed by the Czech émigré Miloš Forman, chimed in with this mood, offering dramatic insight into the terrors and powers that might lurk in a 'therapeutic' psychiatric unit.[40] It was a vivid story that gained a wide audience and resonated with what came to be called the 'counterculture'. Kesey's tale set out in stark form an argument that would be elaborated more formally within the broader anti-psychiatry movement. Along with the work of Goffman and Laing, a major influence on the field of anti-psychiatry was Foucault's history of madness, first published in 1961.[41] It told the story of the discourse of psychiatry and, he said, of the silencing of the 'mad'.

Kesey's novel showed how doctors, nurses and care assistants could operate with impunity in the institution. The story portrayed how mental asylums could become the very reverse of the ideals they claim to uphold, repositories entirely for guarding and breaking, remoulding or simply rendering invisible neglected, difficult or unruly people, and thus sustaining a form of living death. The protagonist Randle Patrick McMurphy (memorably played by Jack Nicholson in the film adaptation) is an Irish-American petty criminal and brawler committed to a psychiatric institution. McMurphy is rebellious, branded by the system a recidivist or incorrigible. He is a Korean War veteran who had already led a breakout from a POW camp. McMurphy had believed he was choosing the softer option by faking insanity and thus avoiding the prison work farm. Ultimately, however, this choice proves disastrous – McMurphy is given a lobotomy and reduced to a vegetative state.

There is a clear message about contemporary oppression and the role of 'psy'. Kesey wanted to suggest how easily those outside the asylum might also be bound by their own straitjackets. Staff in the institution 'treating' McMurphy and company may be active sadists or just bureaucrats and officials, servants of a system, abdicating independent thought, going about their business routinely and indifferently. Such a facility of 'care' in the West could breach every ethical constraint, endeavouring to destroy people, without ending their biological lives. Moreover, the story requires that we note the relationship of past and present conquests; that we consider the politics of such an institution today, and locate it in a history of capture, control and oppression that was integral to the making of the United States. Several of the subordinate staff in the facility are Black; one of the patients, long institutionalised, and who elects to be mute, is Native American. Kesey's story alludes to the past, the reality of slavery, and the murderous process that was required for the settler population to move the frontiers west. It is a history where stolen terrain was treated as though virgin land; a history that witnessed the destruction of a way of life, the violent 'pacification' of resistance, the stifling enclosure of the Native American population.

Kesey offered the story as a warning about the total institution, and invited consideration of complicity, denial, deception and violence in the way a state goes about rendering recalcitrant people safe. Perhaps it is also a kind of parable: inviting the readers to ask themselves, how free are they to make their own paths, think their own thoughts, exercise freedom?

Such fictions saw institutions as microcosms or used them as parables. Many had already been penned, showing what could be done to patients, as well as to prisoners, in the name of reform or therapy. The Victorian period has no shortage of novels, such as Wilkie Collins's *The Woman in White* (1859), exploring wrongful confinement in asylums, highlighting the drama of ordinary people put away for no good reason at all. But the fear took on new shapes in the age of 'brainwashing', a time when electroconvulsive therapy (ECT), lobotomy and modern drugs could serve, in the guise of a new humanitarianism, to silence patients and medicate citizens.[42] Lobotomy was always highly controversial, despite being heavily promoted by some doctors post-war (notably a cavalier American surgeon, Walter Freeman), and became less common beyond the 1960s. It was dwarfed in scale by the uses made of drugs – for instance, Chlorpromazine, a non-invasive alternative treatment for severe mental illness, which came onto the market in 1954.[43]

The 1960s and 70s witnessed a variety of popular critiques of the asylum as precisely sites of 'the captive mind', or symbols of a brainwashed larger society. Writers such as Laing asked, what if the mad are reacting as best they can to a 'mad' world outside, albeit in often disturbed and self-destructive ways? At the same time, some feminist writers revisited a Victorian literature on hysteria, wondering whether these 'disturbed' women were better understood as rebels against patriarchy; 'the mad woman in the attic' conceived here as a subject who refused, in body and soul, or in the unconscious, to live inside an intolerable and stifling world. The clinic, the prison, the asylum – and the 'psy' professions that sustained them – became fields of extensive academic exploration and practical protest. Kate Millett, author of the influential book *Sexual Politics*, was mentally unwell in the 1970s and found herself involuntarily confined and medicated in a US asylum, later describing her experiences in agonising terms, in her own version of that cuckoo's nest:

> How cruel and stupid to punish this as we do with ostracism and fear, to have forged a network of fear, strong as the locks and bars of a back ward. This is the jail we could all end up in. And we know it. And watch our step. For a lifetime. We behave. A fantastic and entire system of social control, by the threat of example as effective over the general population as detention centers in dictatorships, the image of the madhouse floats through every mind for the course of its lifetime.[44]

During the same decade, there was increasingly prominent critique on TV and the newspapers, and in the US Congress, about what the Soviet government was doing to intimidate and pacify political dissidents in its own psychiatric hospitals.[45] In the second half of the twentieth century, much attention was also paid in the West to remarkable true-life stories of psychic and physical survival, stubborn persistence or even creative triumph, against all the odds, in clinics, prisons and camps. Numerous testimonies emerged about the Nazi camp system, including the writings of Primo Levi; and about the Gulag, with the revelations of Solzhenitsyn, Ginzburg and others, showing how the Stalinist system of punishment and exile operated, and what was endured. Levi, it should be added, was only a tempo-rary survivor: four decades after his release and return to Italy from Auschwitz, in 1987, he fell down the stairs of his building in Turin, crushing his skull, leading to much speculation about whether the fall was a suicide or accident. What was not in doubt was that Levi was suffering severe depression at the time.[46]

Exceptional cases, where long-term inmates of camps, prisons or total institutions somehow remain psychologically 'uncaptured', dignified, critical, alert, still somehow themselves, after enduring years, even decades, of existence behind bars, understandably attract our sense of awe. Seemingly miraculous, these stories stand out as exceptions to the ordinary rule – the devastation of the long-term inmate, the irrecoverable harmful legacies. The universally admired real-life case of a mind persisting intact in a terrible custodial system is Nelson Mandela. He was imprisoned in South Africa between 1962 and 1990, held on charges of conspiring to overthrow the apartheid political state, yet he emerged an indomitable figure, still so clearly his own person, a leader willing to negotiate, but not sell out, and then to preside in the new state. His autobiography, *Long Walk to Freedom*, is peppered with acute and strikingly compassionate observations about the jailors and oppressors as well as the inmates and countless other victims of this system. He sought to avoid dehumanising his captors: 'I would see a glimmer of humanity in one of the guards, perhaps just for a second, but it was enough to reassure me and keep me going.' He viewed his guards as subject to their own forms of mind control, and in their own way 'captives', concluding 'that the oppressor must be liberated just as surely as the oppressed'. He went on, '[a] man who takes away another man's freedom is a prisoner of hatred; he is locked behind the bars of prejudice and narrow-minded-ness'. Mandela also observed how '[t]he oppressed and the oppressor alike are robbed of their humanity'.[47] This might be compared with the many observations by the psychiatrist, writer and anti-colonial activist Frantz Fanon, about how the mentalities of the coloniser and the colonised were always locked up together. Brian Keenan, held hostage, tortured and beaten by an Islamist faction in Lebanon, came to similar conclusions, born of his own experience and observation, remarking on the appalling impact of the kidnapping on the mental state of the prisoners, but also the grotesque psychic imprisonment, inside a creed, of his guards.[48]

Sometimes the wish we may have to hold on to the unsullied, 'uncaptivated' and fully uncorrupted hero leaders, who walk from custody, is thwarted, and those previously hailed as resplendently free in spirit follow a different and disillusioning path. Many felt this about Winnie Mandela, a victim herself of long oppression and harassment. We are forced mostly to make sense of mixed legacies, and sometimes betrayals, the good and the bad, perhaps laudable aspirations as well as collusions, compromises, cruelties; in short, stories that preclude in most cases the endurance of singular mythological and transcendent images. When a hero 'falls' we may project our sense of shame and guilt onto the broken idol. We are encouraged to idealise former political prisoners, and then be disappointed when they fail to meet great expectations. Aung San Suu Kyi was named as a true heir to Gandhi's vision of non-violent politics by *Time* magazine in 1999, but her conduct during the second half of the 2010s led to much bitter disappointment and painful reassessment. Her shocking unwillingness, from high office, properly to condemn, let alone halt, her state's systematic persecution of the Rohingya people led many former liberal admirers to withdraw their endorsements. Some called for her to be stripped of the former international honours she had received. Following a further military crackdown in Myanmar in 2021, she found herself once again under arrest.

Much of the 1950s discourse on brainwashing, as we witnessed earlier, was concerned with the fate of prisoners, held alone, or amid fellow victims, broken and then re-educated. But as was so clear from the testimony of American POW Clarence Adams, who endured captivity in the Korean War, those supposed victims of brainwashing answered back, providing rhetorical challenges to Western complacency. Not all supposedly mind-controlled prisoners, such as Adams, who 'fell' for Mao or his communist cause, would accept the stark contrast proposed by the press, politicians and so many Cold War pundits between the free-thinking, free-living citizen in Western liberal soci-eties and the fate of those 'captive minds', the Eastern victims of totalitarianism. It was essential, for Adams and many others, to insist on the daily lived reality of racial oppression in the United States. They did not buy the Cold War rhetoric about freedom and pointed to the racial system still so firmly in place around a century after the Civil War ended.

Such rhetorical challenges to congratulatory stories about the 'Land of Liberty' post-war were part of a long tradition; some echoed the compelling language of Mordecai Wyatt Johnson, the Christian academic and first African-American president of Howard University (1926–60). In a lecture at Harvard in 1922, Johnson had spoken about the broken hopes of the Black population, the 'widespread disinte-gration' of their faith in the capacity of the federal government ever to deliver its promises. He alluded to bitter Black soldiers, returning from war, to find the revival of old racism, and even the resurgence of the Ku Klux Klan.[49] Others, after 1945, sought to rework and draw conclusions in line with nineteenth-century anti-slavery campaigners who derided fantastical claims that the United States was a bastion of human freedom. They might recall the words spoken by former slave, writer and campaigner Frederick Douglass. Posing the question 'What to the Slave Is the Fourth of July?', he declared to the Anti-Slavery Society in Rochester, New York, in 1852:

> Go where you may, search where you will, roam through all the monarchies and despotisms of the old world, travel through South America, search out every abuse, and when you have found the last, lay your facts by the side of the everyday practices of this nation, and you will say with me, that, for revolting bar-barity and shameless hypocrisy, America reigns without a rival.[50]

In fact, post-war, at thriving centres of African-American intel-lectual life, such as Howard University where Johnson presided, there were to be many new lines of inquiry and a plethora of different critiques and calls for radical change, derived from both religious and secular ways of thinking; a host of new explorations of US self-delusion, racism and imperialism. Prisons too, however oppressive, could become for some men and women new centres of learning, protest and writing; places to provide lived examples of struggle.

Just as Douglass had declared that America was the very essence of barbarism, George Jackson, a Black prisoner and an uncompromising and outspoken figure, would take the same view a century later. As he served out an indefinite sentence in California during the 1960s, Jackson would make the claim, based on his experience of racism, that the US population was brainwashed to believe the illusion that all its citizens were free. In his clear, contentious political analyses, sent out in letters from jail, many addressed to his parents, he sought to enlighten all those who retained illusions about the nature of the American state, and called for active resistance as well as a revolution in mind. He rebutted any idea that people of colour had ever experienced liberty in the United States or could ever do so in future, within the prevailing system. The nation's self-presentation was for him based around a colossal lie, and he suspected those living under communist rule enjoyed far greater opportunities and liberties than any Black person possessed in his country.

The 1960s was a time of civil rights protests across the United States, with public opinion dividing not only between those 'for' and 'against' transformations, but also between moderate approaches based on reform, and outright calls for insurrection and revolution. Black leaders, such as Malcolm X, represented one strand of opinion, arguing that the state deliberately kept Black people in conditions of permanent debility – physical, moral and psychological. He too was intent upon exposing the illusion of freedom portrayed in the idea of the United States as a great and wondrous melting pot.

As the novelist and essayist James Baldwin wrote in 1962, 'one did not have to be abnormally sensitive to be worn down to a cutting edge by the incessant and gratuitous humiliation and danger one encountered every working day, all day long'.[51] Whatever political programme might follow, or personal solutions might be found (in Baldwin's case, self-imposed exile in Paris), the first task, many writers and activists agreed, was to analyse the day-to-day reality of conditioning and brainwashing for an entire population. The African-American poet Gwendolyn Brooks wrote ten years later of her political awakening: 'I – who have "gone the gamut" from an almost angry rejection of my dark skin by some of my brainwashed brothers and sisters to a surprised queenhood in the new black sun – am qualified to enter at least the kindergarten of new consciousness now.'[52]

Toni Morrison, herself a graduate from Howard, would later reflect, from a different vantage point, on the unspoken racial dimension within the constructed patriotic sense of American 'togetherness'. She remarked how new immigrants to the United States in the nineteenth and twentieth centuries were invited to share and at the same time to bond in their sense of not being Black:

> But to make an American, you had to have all these people from these different classes, different countries, different languages feel close to one another. So what does an Italian peasant have to say to a German burgher, and what does an Irish peasant have to say to a Latvian? You know, really, they tended to balkanize. But what they could all do is not be black. So it is not coincidental that the second thing every immigrant learns when he gets off the boat is that word, "n-----." In that way, he's establishing oneness, solidarity, and union with the country. That is the marker. That's the one.[53]

As a Black prisoner and self-taught Marxist during the 1960s, George Jackson rejected perceptions that the Russians or Chinese were more captive, in mind, than Americans. He came to admire the teachings of Mao, and to celebrate all that the Party had achieved for the Chinese population. Not only people of colour but also whites were brainwashed in the United States, he argued, to accept the illusion that the system was something quite other than a racialised police state. Jackson had been jailed in 1961 aged twenty, for stealing $70 at gunpoint from a gas station. He was given a sentence of one year to life, and due to various disputed prison incidents and infractions, remained incarcerated until he was killed during an attempted escape in 1971. After encounters with the police and the law as a 'juvenile', and time in a youth 'correctional facility', Jackson spent his decade of adult life undergoing the brutality of prison and regular stints of solitary confinement. The US penitentiary system provided for Jackson and many others that 'total institution' which Goffman had identified, a system that perpetuated a racist society. One must bear in mind that at present in the United States, over 2 million people are incarcerated and around 70,000 experience solitary confinement. African Americans make up around 13 per cent of the US population, yet they constitute over 35 per cent of the nation's prison numbers, with even higher rates for those convicted for life sentences or on 'death row'.[54]

Jackson's prison letters, first published under the title *Soledad Brother*, in 1970, swiftly became a literary sensation and a source of much controversy, given their unflinchingly revolutionary stance. They offered a searing account of the fate of Black inmates, detailing how they were constantly surveyed (often at the end of the barrel of a gun) by the prison authorities. Jackson presented an unforgettable account of the constant menace and violence, the role of gangs, and of how white racist groups of prisoners were aided and abetted by guards. He wrote of how the latter might also encourage white prisoners to throw rubbish and faeces at Black prisoners and turn a blind eye to their knives. The letters described the constant threat of beatings or death, the grim routines, the forbidding, life-sapping physical environment that instantly confronted the new inmate – the horrible smells and noise, the cold, the withheld or contaminated food, in short the assault upon the mind and all the five senses. The whole apparatus of punishment was designed, he explained, to destroy 'logical processes of the mind', to 'disorganize thoughts' and intimidate totally.[55] In spite of his incarceration in such a system, Jackson retained a capacity to resist and produced a singular, stark political analysis of what he considered to be mass American brainwashing.

Inside prison, Jackson took the chance to educate himself and develop his uncompromising political conclusions. He became a member of the Black Panthers, and rewrote his will to leave royalties from his writings to their cause. In the sense that he had some means to read and write, and to send messages outside to friends and family from time to time, the system was not at the very limit of the 'total institution' that we have sketched. Jackson still had scope to use and retain his memory, to make use of his intellect, and to find some resources to pursue his own thinking, albeit in a custodial regime.[56] He debated ideas, and read, for example, stories, essays and poems about the plight of African Americans by Richard Wright. He also drew upon the ideas of the left-wing psychoanalyst Wilhelm Reich, as well as Marx and Engels, Lenin and Mao. From his autodidact studies, he reached those stark conclusions, commensurate with his own penal experience. In Jackson's view, the US state sought total control, and operated through permanent surveillance, repression and violence, which liberal critics had associated with Soviet and

Maoist jurisdictions. He concluded that African Americans had no choice, once appropriately radicalised, except to rise and to fight.

In the 1960s and 70s on both sides of the Atlantic we can witness such sentiments and debates about the 'totality' of the liberal democratic system, not just custodial spaces within it. Some angry protesters and critics, white and Black, saw the armed 'self-defence' of minorities as essential; others believed that armed action against the state was the only way out of a collectively captive and brainwashed mentality. Their aim was to awaken the 'masses', the general populations of Western democracies. Their choices generated heated divisions among much larger bodies of students, workers and activists. Were these 'revolutionaries', enlightened and appropriately disenchanted, de-captivated, or, conversely, instances of people brainwashed, even maddened, by their own closed-mind ultra-left-wing thinking, into following a disastrous and useless violent oppositional political path?

Admirers saw them as free spirits; opponents viewed them at best as full of illusions, at worst as depraved criminals and/or mentally ill. Revolutionary cells, brigades and clandestine networks emerged in various countries within the Western world: for example, in Italy, the Red Brigades; in the United States, the Weather Underground; in Germany, the Baader–Meinhof Gang. These groups rejected what they saw as the fiction of liberal democracy and derided proud claims about the Free World, seeking to learn from the strategies of Lenin, Mao, Ho Chi Minh and Che Guevara, and thereby to create 'guerrilla actions' in Western cities.

Ulrike Meinhof's writings charted her own move towards this violent conclusion, the vital importance of 'propaganda of the deed'. Her dread, already apparent in 1960, was that, as in the 1930s, people were victims of self-serving wishful thinking, assuming that the worst kind of conflict inside Germany about the future of democracy could somehow be avoided, that an ultra-reactionary politics, even fascism, would gradually soften of its own accord, without a direct and militant confrontation. She noted how past inaction had cost millions their lives, and claimed that the political tendencies of the Federal Republic of her own day 'justify every kind of fear'. She treated optimism about benign amelioration as 'the reserve of fools', and insisted that all those who, like her, 'feel the suspicion, the mistrust and the discomfort of the moment' should 'come together to prevent what happened in the past from happening again'. By 1967, she was writing scathingly about political repression and curbs placed on freedom to oppose the system; in the West, she said, it was not deemed a criminal act to drop napalm on women, children and the elderly, but protesting those acts was. The same could be said for terror tactics and torture when deployed by the state, and effectively opposing them. She thus celebrated how sections of the student movement and extra-parliamentary opposition were not 'playing nice' anymore, people were 'no longer concealing their annoyances, or sweeping conflicts under the rug, or explaining [their] nausea as a consequence of a pill, or fighting melancholy with coffee, or stomach aches with mint tea, or depression with champagne, or vapid sobriety with schnapps'. The contradictions of society, she said, were now coming to the surface. 'Fake harmony', she added, with evident relief, has 'gone down the tubes'.[57]

The small but determined organisations like the Baader–Meinhof believed that what was required was a violent set of shocks; exemplary actions were needed to awaken the people from their state of captivation. They hoped that their actions could focus public attention, kick-start a larger uprising, perhaps even a new age of revolution.

Jackson's views about how the penal institution is the heir to slavery have been further analysed and developed, not least through the work of the academic, writer and political activist Angela Davis. Davis's own personal story was caught up with that of Jackson and other prominent Black prisoners during that period. She also had suffered arrest, interrogation and trial. Although eventually found not guilty and released, she endured a sixteen-month sentence.[58] Davis and others built on those earlier critiques, using the term 'prison–industrial complex' to describe the US archipelagos of custody and punishment and their psychosocial effects. She conveyed how this enormous network of institutions and practices had to be understood as the contemporary site of mass repression for Black people, a massive structure and permanent endeavour to sweep up the 'troublesome' population, the dispossessed, disadvantaged and poor.

As a colleague of Davis's reflected, around 2000, in a conversation with her about the forms of analysis, activism and protest she had undertaken, and which sought among other things prison abolition: '[t]he logic of the prison-industrial complex is closer to what you, George Jackson, and others were forecasting back then as mass containment, the effective elimination of large numbers of (poor, black) people from the realm of civil society'. Davis reflected on this remark, insisting that 'penal abolitionism should not now be considered an unrealizable utopian dream, but rather the only possible way to halt the further transnational development of prison industries across the world'.[59] The point was that to really see the condition of prisoners in custody, the fate of people broken and subjugated in that 'complex', was also to identify the true fault lines across an entire society.

In this chapter we have moved from East to West, and from the past much closer to the present. In a sense we have followed that passage with Miłosz, who moved from Poland to California. Miłosz may have penned *The Captive Mind* while in exile, but Poland was everywhere present and painful in his thinking, even if the lessons he told were intended to have wider geographical and political importance. He considered the diverse ways we might fall in love with a crazed ideology or devote our lives to opposing it; on the other hand, live somehow or other half-following rules, keeping our heads down, assenting to power, making trade-offs with ourselves and thereby, he suspected, seeking to drown out guilt for the past and corrupting the better sides of our natures.

Such ideas might well interest and trouble us now, in very different political contexts than his own. The Polish system that Miłosz had left sank quickly into conditions that corrupted and destroyed basic freedoms, threatened life, and compromised independent thinking and artistry. Communication in post-war Poland, so Miłosz said, was based on a shared understanding that each person was participating in a 'constant mass play'.[60] The difference there, rather than here in the West, he thought, was that making the wrong move, even into liberal opinion and democratic expression, might well kill you. For each 'comrade', maintaining the role play was crucial, and in this live drama, under the eye of the Party, false steps could be deadly.

As well as the horrors of Stalinism, Miłosz was also interested in unpicking the contradictions inherent in this notional divide between mass conformity in the East and individual freedom in the West. His book was not just a series of revelations of his fellow Poles' abjection under communism, designed for Western liberal self-validation. He made clear in his writing that it was not only under that one political system – Stalinism – that people swallowed 'truths' or accepted 'inevitabilities' they knew to be inadequate, distorting and inimical to an authentic life. *The Captive Mind* shifted the ground from the

Manichean visions that often prevailed, suggesting, as Judt put it, 'there is more than one kind of captivity'.

By the 1980s, as the Soviet hold on Eastern Europe gradually weakened, several writers revisited and re-evaluated Miłosz's book. Among those who had rejected the work initially, in the 1950s, only to revise their views later, was Susan Sontag. Speaking in 1982, in the context of the spectacular rise of Solidarity (a trade union and political movement in Poland, led by Lech Wałęsa, which confronted the sclerotic Soviet-backed government), she explained why she and her friends had previously had so little time for Miłosz's book: '[w]e had identified the enemy as Fascism. We heard the demonic language of fascism. We believed in, or at least applied, a double standard to the angelic language of Communism.'[61]

But Miłosz was not interested solely in the brainwashing potential of closed milieus – although any state that determines entry and exit visas, any institution that can lock up the gates, to keep people in and observers out, or of course any compound, camp or cult with barbed-wire perimeters and watchtowers, has an advantage in doing so. He also wanted his Western readership to consider the scope for manipulation and the orchestration of opinion, as well as for mindlessness, conformity, compliance and captivity in liberal democracies. This was not to equate the societies, but to explore certain human propensities that might interact with pressures that came from outside. These ideas have been further developed by others in the West, seeking to undercut the language or simplistic paradigms of Cold War tub-thumpers who decried what was happening in the East and congratulated the West for being the true home of freedom, the acme of civilisation.

Even before his defection, in the years he lived on the East Coast in the late 1940s, Miłosz revealed in his private correspondence that he found US culture and society seriously perturbing. He had attended cocktail parties during his Washington stint as a cultural attaché for Poland and confessed he found the small talk insufferable, the scenes of unbothered enjoyment among well-to-do socialites somewhat surreal, and the level of cultural understanding, to say the least, patchy. The world was freer, and yet the air of smug assurance and sometimes stupidity were shocking, he felt. For Miłosz, this New World seemed replete with its own (admittedly very different) psychological manacles and blinkers.

In letters to friends, he voiced doubts about the reality of freedom in the United States, wondering, for instance, why the concept could not be expanded and sustained more positively. There, he admitted, people enjoyed a certain liberty from the state, a capacity to roam, to meet and indeed to consume so many things, at will, and yet he found so much highly questionable and distasteful; all that talk of being the land of liberty, and yet so little provision for meaningful, positive social aims, or collective entitlements, say, to healthcare or higher learning. These should be available for the entire society, not just the fortunate classes and elites.[62]

Miłosz's recoil from the United States had an aesthetic as well as a political dimension. Reeling from the platitudes he heard in Poland where America was deemed by some ardent communists as merely 'the land of Coca-Cola', on the East Coast he found himself alienated by cinema audiences who displayed infantile reactions and poor taste, for example by bursting out laughing at tragic scenes. In one of his letters, he diagnosed '[t]he spiritual poverty of millions of this country'; it was a condition he found 'horrifying'. 'The only living people', he declared airily, 'are the blacks and the Indians.' He was appalled that so many lives revolved around watching or listening to what he regarded as complete dross; popular culture and radio chat were evidently not for him. For a 'normal person', he insisted, 'being subjected to a two-minute dose of [radio] would make them sick'.[63]

According to Miłosz, such media were offering ersatz entertainment, mass excitement, distraction and political cant. This was a period when the great powers all used radio as part of the Cold War propaganda struggle for hearts and minds. In the 1950s, the radio station Voice of America, funded by the US government, ramped up its production, or as critics saw it, sold America to the whole world. Meanwhile, CIA-funded stations such as Radio Free Europe and Radio Liberty were established to reach Eastern European states and the Soviet Union. The British Broadcasting Corporation (BBC) – albeit with its wider, patrician mission, and its arms-length distance from government – was broadcast overseas daily from London, in the name of facts, balance, cool analysis and notions of liberal democracy. Radio Moscow – under the more direct orchestration of its political masters – produced its own weekly diet of ideologically loaded content for listeners.[64]

Miłosz even went so far as to argue in his private communications, at least, that the art of brainwashing had reached a kind of perfection in the United States, precisely because it was less obviously and crudely conducted than in Stalin's empire: '[t]he means by which public opinion was moulded in countries such as Poland were child's play compared to the art-form the Americans had developed, and the methods used by [the US] security services'.[65] Miłosz saw Soviet-style endeavours to hack people's minds as rather antiquated compared to the Americans' own 'exceptionally subtle methods'.[66] Freedom was to be wished for, he suggested, but rarely secured. At the very least, the outcomes of this much-vaunted freedom seemed to him dismal; if this was true 'freedom', more was the pity.

Miłosz perhaps half recognised that he might be thought a snob for his strictures on post-war US culture; but he could not resist railing against a society that was peopled, he said, by 'unfortunate American puppets': a population characterised by a 'depressing inner stupor' and a value system where the supreme good was often reduced 'to money alone'.[67]

During the 1960s, as Miłosz looked on from his new academic position at Berkeley, growing numbers of Americans were inveighing against their society, voicing their demands for a decisive change of direction in government, or, more militantly, for an end to capitalism, the illusions of the free market, the unbridled nature of corporate power. They were outraged by official denials about the escalation of the Vietnam War and US neo-imperialism. So not everyone was successfully 'brainwashed', or stupefied, whatever Miłosz believed; there was an enormous public backlash. Critics who sought to call out the 'brainwashing' were plentiful, especially among the young; they demanded full exposure of the mendacious and often fantastical, as well as grossly ill-informed military policy, and the naive anthropological belief that the United States' 'offer' to liberate all people would be received with unmitigated joy in Vietnam, or indeed by millions of peasants, factory workers, rural and urban dwellers in Africa, Asia or Latin America.

Outspoken American writers, scientists, doctors, entertainers, musicians and sporting stars also denounced US warfare in South East Asia, and the manner in which the government was in thrall, they felt, to misguided and pernicious assumptions. A rebellious generation of students reviled a mainstream political class that they complained sought to take the American public for dupes. Muhammad Ali, heavyweight champion of the world, made waves in his blunt rejection of the 'white man's war' in Vietnam, and accordingly faced censure, the loss of his title from the World Boxing Association, and the threat of long-term imprisonment, in an endeavour to silence him. Prominent figures ranging from the expert on childhood and parenting Dr Benjamin Spock, to the writer Arthur Miller, to the singer and actor Eartha Kitt, also called out government lies, delusions, hypocrisies and spin.[68]

It would be inappropriate to liken the scale of persecution for dissidents and protestors under Stalin or Mao to the punishments meted out to critical intellectuals in the United States or other Western liberal democracies in the post-war decades, even if imprisonment or, in theory, execution for spying were possible there too. (In one case – that of Ethel and Julius Rosenberg – this punishment was carried out in the Cold War United States. They were found guilty of revealing atomic secrets to the Russians and were executed by the electric chair in the state of New York, in 1953.) All the same, we should not minimise the scale of surveillance, harassment and sometimes active oppression of the most militant and challenging left-wing and other radical political opponents of US policy in 1950s and 60s America, including some who were white, privileged and well established.

As the historian Gary Gerstle writes of the 1950s: '[w]ith a great shudder, American institutions were ridding themselves of alleged subversives, and a big chill enveloped American society, freezing most radical dissenters, Communist or not, in their tracks'.[69] Serious, certainly revolutionary, dissent against the existing order was policed, albeit in different ways, in both of the two world systems, communism and capitalism. In this second American Red Scare (the first had followed the Russian Revolution in 1917) anyone who challenged capitalism from the communist position was open, in principle, to state investigation. The Left, in these years, Gerstle argues, was decimated as an organised force. Where membership of the Community Party in Poland was a passport for many to survive and find promotion, it was a passport to trouble and investigation in the United States; the climate of McCarthyism and the ministrations of J. Edgar Hoover and company at the FBI ensured as much.

Yet, even so, some spaces for spoken, written and artistic principled opposition remained in the post-war United States, unlike in China or the Soviet Union at that time. Even in the shrill and intolerant 1950s the work of a critical writer such as Arthur Miller was available to audiences and readers. He could script a play like *The Crucible* (ostensibly about the Salem witch trials but clearly speaking to the McCarthyite 'hunt' for communists) and see it performed, in 1953, the very same year that *The Captive Mind* was first published. Miłosz, by contrast, had to flee to write his polemical book. Miller's thinly disguised denunciation of the hysterical, and sometimes career-ending, anti-communism bedevilling the United States was caustic, but it did not result in the author being sent to a labour camp.

However, the FBI's now well-documented assaults on freedom were real and intimidating, and often decimated livelihoods. FBI files on US citizens and the capacious political use of the label 'un-American' were pervasive, and many careers, collaborations and personal relationships were ruined; people lost jobs, and often their health. Miller himself was subpoenaed to appear before the House Un-American Activities Committee (HUAC) in 1956, to be quizzed on his communist leanings. He refused to name other suspected communists. Eventually the verdict arrived; Miller faced fines and the confiscation of his passport, for contempt of court, but then appealed and the judgement was reversed. His life was interfered with, although not – as was the case for others – destroyed.

It cannot be ignored, then, that much self-censorship and political care was required of US critics if they wished to prosper without attracting the attention of agencies within the state. Post-war, Southern congressmen were able to use HUAC to reinvigorate the claim that a combined Black *and* red conspiracy was imperilling the Southern way of life, and, moreover, that this threat to Southern security was equivalent to a mortal danger to national security. They took advantage of the re-emergence of the Soviet Union as the great US foe to tie anti-communism to race politics, and to bolster their own resistance to greater civil rights. Politicians such as John Rankin of Mississippi, always fearful that Black radicals, alien agitators, liberals and Jews would conspire, used HUAC to insist that all such groups required careful vigilance by the authorities. In linking race to communism, he was knocking on an open door at HUAC, where others were also highly alert to 'dangerous' links between the Communist Party, the civil rights movement and organisations such as the National Negro Congress. Indeed, the latter had been listed as 'subversive' by the US attorney general during the Truman presidency.[70]

The African-American population had to deal with entrenched racist structures, as well as 'micro-aggressions' (to borrow the useful term that a Black psychiatrist, Chester M. Pierce, provided during the 1970s).[71] Even though various reforms were made in the 1960s, and policies turned into legislation that sought the end of formal educational segregation, racism endured at multiple levels, as it does now. Jackson's representations of the custodial world and the racial dimensions of policing remain as relevant as they did at the time. His aim was to suggest the prison-house world also existed outside of the penitentiaries; he would select the word 'brainwashing' in some of his letters, to bring home to the reader the captive state of the American mind.

Miłosz's book pointed directly East, but also obliquely West; or at least, it invited debate about how, in a polarised political world, people may project fantasies into certain objects (even caricatured versions of other nations), engage in denial, swallow pills or become caught up in Ketman-like psychological convolutions in order to make ends meet. Miłosz's book remains a useful mirror that can be held up to explore captive minds in that Cold War past, and in the present.

In September 2018, a notorious anonymous article appeared under the title 'I Am Part of the Resistance Inside the Trump Administration', published in *The New York Times* and penned (it was assumed) by a senior staffer who was unwilling to go on record. He was later revealed to be Miles Taylor, a former Homeland Security official. The article painted a picture of disarray, and of the constant manoeuvring and dissembling of the president's staff. It illuminated the persistent doublespeak, if not doublethink, required of them at the White House; a workplace rife with cynicism, dexterity and bitter rivalry. It suggested how those more morally troubled members of the retinue felt they had to operate in code, finesse Trump's messages, moderate policies, deflect the leader from one course or another, massaging his ego, even when aware, presumably, of the perversity, or even absurdity, of so many of his pronouncements, and the venal nature of his goals.

What was the alternative? To swallow the Murti-Bing pill? In fact, a third alternative existed: to resign or get fired, and then reflect painfully on how on earth they had got sucked into these politics or the orbit of such a man. Yet many of the officials went about their business professionally and apparently unruffled by it all, even if personally unconvinced of the cause. No doubt, alongside the so-called resisters and tortured souls within that administration (those using Ketman) were others who, with less anguish or ambivalence, did as required, believing, not just 'believing', helping as needed, including arranging (when necessary) uniformly cheering and smiling crowds behind the presidential speaker at political rallies. Many cheered passionately. But on some occasions, as has been widely reported, glum or doubtful, let alone protesting, figures in the line of the cameras were moved out of the way by Trump's staffers. The aim was to ensure that the facial expressions of those gathered around him were suitably joyful, respectful and expectant, for the benefit of the TV audiences. (This is simply a glaring and crude example of the image-management practices that are commonplace, regardless of the party.)[72]

Miłosz anticipated the argument often made today by critical theorists: that far from requiring absolute inner conviction in a bureaucracy, or a citizenry, an ideology may operate effectively when we simply do as required, grumble privately, but in practice accept that there is no alternative.[73] We may well find ourselves doing what we deem 'necessary', even as we comply. In other words, millions who may well deplore the operation of a system in theory turn a blind eye, and therefore provide tacit acceptance for dire policies.[74]

In his article in praise of *The Captive Mind*, Judt recalled how, although many certainly did dissent, the voting public in Britain and the United States had been strongly encouraged to support massively destructive foreign policies thanks (in good part) to political deceit under the direction of Tony Blair and George W. Bush. In the British case, a notorious example of how government policy could be based on a false prospectus to the public was the decision to invade Iraq. The policy, or at least the public presentation of the policy, partly hinged on a 2003 briefing document issued to journalists by the government: this detailed an account of Saddam Hussein's likely possession of weapons of mass destruction with far greater certainty than the evidence supported. The document came to be known in popular parlance as the 'dodgy dossier'.

The administrations in the United States and the UK, fumed Judt, created a 'hysterical drive to war'. The leaderships of those administrations required their ministers, officials and ultimately the people at large to fall in line with their policies; as though these bellicose or messianic convictions rested on a balanced view of the evidence; as though their own judgement calls, resting on 'faith', or even delusion, were backed up by incontrovertible intelligence, and any prolonged debate was disloyal.

In their support came cheerleaders and apologists who defended this muscular approach of liberal interventionism as the best hope for the future. Some intellectuals, as well as politicians, Judt noted, equivocated, bit their tongues or buried their scruples; thus they 'typically aligned themselves behind [the leadership] while doubtless maintaining private reservations'. When the mistake became clear, they 'blamed it upon the administration's incompetence ... With Ketman-like qualifications they proudly asserted, in effect, "we were right to be wrong", explaining away their acquiescence.' We in the West, Judt lamented, appease 'the market' as we once sacrificed to the gods; he sought to pinpoint our Western versions of Ketman and Murti-Bing pills, our willingness to live in thrall to an ideology that requires in effect – even in the absence of totalitarian brainwashing – that we forgo the imagining of, let alone the endeavour, to realise viable major alternatives.

Neoliberalism has prevailed for decades throughout much of the world and has brought about privatisation, deregulation, lowered taxes, unfettered capitalism, globalisation, and so on. It has brooked little contradiction, whatever the cost in lives, livelihoods and human misery, and the calamitous impact on the climate and the environment. Judt remarked, with an eye to this ideology, the remarkable scale of 'intellectuals' voluntary servitude before the new pan-orthodoxy', adding that '[o]ne hundred years after his birth, fifty-seven years after the publication of his seminal essay, Miłosz's indictment of the servile intellectual rings truer than ever: "his chief characteristic is his fear of thinking for himself"'.[75]

Recognition that life choices are not always morally clear cut, and that people often live in a murky territory, full of negotiated compromises, half recognitions, partial reckonings and self-deceptions, is part of what Miłosz requires us to face, along with the existential struggle to be authentic and in good faith. The West may have seen totalitarian communism as having 'brainwashed' populations, but 'brainwashing' may also mislead, a label that suggests something too one-way, too unilateral to capture the full array of experiences even in those tyrannical Stalinist years. In the real world, however constraining, we need to consider the complexity of the adjustments that occur in people, the different ways a society affects the individual, and how diversely we may opt to navigate, both publicly and privately, that social order.

To read Miłosz's reflections upon what people in Poland after the war slipped into, fell for or were willing to bear, and what they felt obliged to perform, invites comparison with the way we may now play our cards. In writing this book, and revisiting that literature on totalitarian and capitalist modes of persuasion and influence, I have found myself thinking harder about the constant accommodations or rationalisations we make now so as to conform in practice, even if dissenting privately. For instance, I might say to myself, I'd rather not use Amazon *ever*, given what I know about how it operates, and what it represents in the world. I'm against offering my custom to Amazon in theory, but they've still had my money, at times. I accept the arguments, I read about all that is terribly wrong with this company – the outrageous low-tax arrangements, scale, crushing of rivals, work practices, use of surveillance and generation of obscene wealth for a few, above all for its ultimate owner, a business entrepreneur and tycoon, who then exercises great leverage in the media, and enjoys glitteringly publicised joy rides into space. And yet, when too busy, for convenience, I put the problem aside and participate, knowingly seduced, as it were, diluting or bracketing my belief for now, negotiating with my conscience.

  I perhaps might half-heartedly justify this to myself by vowing that, if only I had world enough and time, I would never consort with this labour-exploiting corporation that pays such shockingly miniscule taxes. Here is a business from whose values, in principle, I prefer to dissent completely, by way of boycott. It is not that I have no choice, even with that enterprise's gargantuan expansion, but that to counter such impulses, it just seems too wearying to give up this option entirely. Perhaps I can just shop here occasionally, I might say to myself, when I am especially pressed. Clearly, I've been 'bought'. Little denials or disavowals may let me get on with my day, yet leave an uneasy feeling of complicity: the sense that something that ostensibly offers me more freedom, more choice, is somehow drawing me into a collusive process, half against my own wishes. The technology makes the transaction – both literal and psychological – extremely smooth. It only takes seconds. We may be forced to be captive, or we may opt to participate in the self-justifying ways that Miłosz also described.

Before coronavirus hit the news in 2020, many of us were already in theory fierce critics of the airline industry in the larger context of globalisation. We understood and feared the climate emergency, recognised the link between our Western way of life and the problem and accepted – in principle – that each of us should do what we can as individuals (albeit recognising effective action had to be international as well, and organised through the work of political states). We even felt agonised about it, and yet the majority did not take a strong, principled position. We flew all the same, as it were *despite ourselves*, preferring not to keep in mind our carbon footprints, or to imagine a little bit of recycling or compensatory tree-planting would do the trick. We felt the problem was too big, or too remote, and we were mostly willing to be complicit – even benefiting from low prices, thanks to the lack of proper taxation on aviation fuel. No doubt some people don't feel conflicted. Others, however, including myself, clearly did, and do. But something then can get lost in translation. Not because, in some utilitarian calculation, we necessarily believe our own choice of flying (to a business meeting, or a holiday) would really be justified – truly indispensable – but because we have other, more messy, self-deceiving and/or selfish explanations, or internal compromises. Gradually, perhaps, when galvanised, we may swing around to a more consistent position; but in many cases, only long after the cognitive move was first made to see the reality of the emergency and the radical contradictions that exist between how we are living and what is required of us, individually and collectively.

What I have sought to examine in this part of the book is not so much, or at least not only, the way a subject complies, conforms or does things out of pure fear of authority, or in recognition of the state's power, but how in more ordinary circumstances, at liberty, we may consent to psychological accords, perform 'deals' in an elaborate negotiation with external agencies *and* internal voices as well. We might be completely unconscious of the contradictions between our overt values and beliefs and our actual conduct, or we may be aware (or half aware, a little guiltily) of the way we have kept the contradictions apart, telling ourselves that this separation is temporary, a 'solution' for now, something I'll think about later when I'm less stressed; make me virtuous, one might say, as of old, but not yet …

A Polish friend tells me that the original title of Miłosz's book could be translated as the 'enslaved' or 'compelled' mind, even if 'captive' serves well enough. Miłosz was also talking about the servile mind, the compromised mind, the sceptical mind, the cynical mind, and more. A key lesson to draw from him, I think, is that people are not necessarily entirely brainwashed, even when they appear to be so; they still exercise certain preferences, and know about certain splits. This speaks to both a weakness and a strength: we conform but we can also rebel. We can go through the motions while knowing, at least in ourselves, that our utterances bear no relationship to our real inner beliefs.

Judt set out his final critique of neoliberal policies in an excoriating book, *Ill Fares the Land*, published posthumously. It asks these questions: '[w]hy do we experience such difficulty even *imagining* a different sort of society? Why is it beyond us to conceive of a different set of arrangements to our common advantage? Are we doomed to lurch indefinitely between a dysfunctional "free market" and the much-advertised horrors of "socialism"?'[76]

The stories we reach for when thinking about brainwashing are instructive: Orwell's *Nineteen Eighty-Four* gave us 'doublethink', 'memory hole', 'thoughtcrime', 'Room 101', 'telescreen' and 'Big Brother'. *The Captive Mind*, far less well known, offered us instead fables about 'Ketman' and the 'Murti-Bing pill'. We have the household word 'Orwellian', but not 'Miłoszian'; and perhaps that is the term now most urgently required.

PART 4

GROUPTHINK

In 1952, a striking article entitled 'Groupthink' was published in a US business magazine. Accounts of dangerous crowds running riot, making a mockery of reason and logic, can be traced back through millennia; but this article and others that followed soon after identified something new and dangerous afoot in the post-war United States. Here is how that essay began: 'A very curious thing has been taking place in this country – and almost without our knowing it. In a country where "individualism" – independence and self-reliance – was the watchword for three centuries, the view is now coming to be accepted that the individual himself has no meaning – except, that is, as a member of a group.' This was not a meditation on the human condition, nor a study of totalitarian brainwashing, but an essay on contemporary trends in Western society, and a warning about unintended consequences of business organisations.

Post-war literature on groupthink merits scrutiny here, alongside the fear of brainwashing. Group dynamics became a notable topic of research in management theory, a foil for popular films, a premise in history, and an object of inquiry in experimental psychology and psychoanalysis too. Evidence derived from surveys, tests and polls built up; such results then informed broader discussions about the perils of conformity, convergence and obedience. This chapter sets out a number of those most arresting findings and diagnoses, along with putative remedies for groupthink. I want to revisit that vocabulary, consider diverse post-war experiments in and speculations about group psychology, suggest how writings on this topic connected to the representations of human captivity and conversion we've already considered, and finally to indicate some of the political projects that capitalised upon these ideas much later in the twentieth century.

The first thing to note is how this term, groupthink, was proposed in the early years of the Cold War, around the same time as reports about brainwashing, menticide, thought reform, re-education, the captive mind, the hidden persuaders, etc. The second is how the word was deployed in arguments about the relative risks faced by two competing economic systems in a polarised, political world. Commentaries on groupthink mulled over the prospects of future stagnation and prompted discussion about how to encourage renewal to strengthen the West in its global struggle with the Soviet Union. Some suggested Western decline, if not impending disaster, and foresaw the death of innovation in a modern capitalist society where droves of businessmen in their identical business suits were commuting from the suburbs to impersonal enterprises, and all supposedly behaving and thinking alike; others pushed back at this alarmist story.

The writer who set some of these hares running, and first introduced the phrases 'groupthink' and (in a 1956 book) 'the organization man', was William H. Whyte.[1] He was an East Coast journalist who had previously been a corporate man himself, an executive at the Vicks chemical company. Whyte retained a niche for some years in the business world (via the magazine *Fortune*) and was in the employ of a large media organisation (Time Inc.). Once his book sales permitted, however, he became a freelance writer. Whyte was aware his generalised diagnoses of groupthink did not cover everybody. But his critical interventions were substantial and heartfelt. He offered extensive illustrations of what he assumed to be the mindsets and habits of many of his compatriots – people who found their way, as had he, into the executive ranks. Many men, like Whyte, would thus steadily move up the ladder, going from school to university, preceded or followed by military service in the Second World War, into the corporate world. Whyte's work sold well and became a catalyst for other debates about conformist pressures to be found in the academy, the armed forces, corporations and the media.

Whyte feared that corporations were creating a new kind of secular priesthood; he pointed to a collection of rituals, devotions and habits. A basic ethos was inculcated across disparate careers and professions; and the name of the game, he lamented, was just fitting in. Thus, there was much in common, he thought, between the mentality of a dutiful doctor, working in a clinic or hospital, a novice scientist at a government laboratory, an apprentice engineer in the huge drafting room at a company like Lockheed, and a young attorney in what he called a Wall Street law factory. Each had their niche job and technical know-how, but at a deeper level they were like peas from the same pod. A kind of unconscious and strangely comfortable synchronisation in values and lifestyles was taking place, he suggested, with schools and then the university sector churning out more and more affable, complacent, technically minded people; a generation who wanted to work for a corporate body and fold themselves into the communal effort of their firm or business. The United States, seen through this lens, was fast becoming a standardised realm of business graduates, engineers and technocrats, who shared in the same anodyne, middle-of-the road unargued assumptions. And ultimately, he warned, this insipid era of groupthink might constrain the West's capacity to win the Cold War.

Whyte had every reason to note the prevalence and growing power of large corporations. In his light-touch 1952 article and his more substantial book, he developed a striking analysis. What Whyte dreaded was the possibility that homogenous beliefs could ultimately spread through much of the population, ironing out wrinkles of character and personality in individuals. He was concerned, moreover, that company employees, who were in theory free to withdraw their labour and head off in search of new frontiers, were subtly regimented to stay in a single office, firm or bureaucracy for life; they might well find the financial rewards and security irresistible, and the level of corporate remuneration, and all the associated benefits and care, too tempting.

Many executives and their families, said Whyte, as he sketched out these trends, might opt to stay put in one place forever; or else move around the country only at the behest of their organisation or industry. Loyalty, greatly prized, and largely uncontested, he feared, was becoming a governing managerial principle. As a result, young graduates were effectively conditioned to assume that their future was really to be dependable cogs within colossal machines, such as, say, Ford or General Electric, or some branch of federal government, rather than encouraged to break the mould, set off on their own and hatch small businesses, or what later came to be called 'start-ups'. Whyte wanted an economy that rewarded the workforce for sticking their necks out, fighting consensus, travelling to unknown pastures and braving failure, as well as courting unusual success; in short, fulfilling a version of the American dream. The phrase 'thinking outside of the box' was not yet part of the vernacular of the 1950s, but it spoke to the same kind of aspiration as Whyte's.

Such portrayals of groupthink were partly novel but also drew on older tropes. We might recall earlier, intense discussions about the soul-destroying effects of the mass assembly production line on workers, or how, in Europe as well as the United States, fifty or a hundred years before Whyte's account, there had been no shortage of ruminations on the anonymous 'man in the crowd', bourgeois ennui, and the intolerance of the consensual majority population for maverick people, geniuses and eccentric artists. One forerunner of those discussions about American people's compliant attitudes was the French diplomat, traveller and writer Alexis de Tocqueville, whose half-admiring, half-trepidatious account of life in the New World, *Democracy in America* (1835–40), offered sharp observations on the tyranny of the majority and the dangers of bland convergence and unthinking, mass agreement. The great Victorian liberal philosopher John Stuart Mill also anticipated some of Whyte's fears about the risks of conformity, a society where public opinion could be reduced to unthinking assumptions, with critical scrutiny of commonplaces treated as though an optional extra. The French novelist Gustave Flaubert provided his own 'Dictionary of Received Ideas', compiled in the 1870s; a collection of examples of groupthink, long before that particular word had been introduced.

So, one antecedent of post-war debates on groupthink concerned the risks of people latching onto the views of some 'herd' or 'tribe', becoming alike, mutually absorbing fads and fashions, and regurgitating society's mores without any real individual judgement at all. Another concerned the power of corporations to dominate states and peoples. The architects of the US Constitution had sought to create a system that ensured no tyrannical power (such as the monarchy) or monster corporation (such as the East India Company) ever held sway again. Americans were taught how the Boston Tea Party in 1773 was a response to the Tea Act, which had protected the interests of the East India Company at the expense of American patriots. As John Dickinson, an important influence on the American Revolution, had warned, soldiers of the East India Company, having already pillaged vast wealth in India, were now 'casting their eyes on America as a new theater whereon to exercise their talents of rapine, oppression and cruelty'.[2]

Such polemics anticipated something of the complaints that became familiar in the twentieth century, targeted at unaccountable corporations and rapacious multinationals whose power might ultimately threaten nations. The East India Company, complained its bitter opponents in the eighteenth century, had far-reaching tentacles; it could finance armies of lawyers and lobbyists; and, if it required, could bend the political state to its will and buy the votes of British parliamentarians, as needed.[3] Whyte thought that in his own time US corporations might become simply too big, and assume the power to shape the thinking and even the feelings of the people who staffed them. These entities generated, he complained, a pervasive requirement of 'belongingness'. *The Organization Man*, which became a best-seller, noted the irony that the anti-communist global alliance, led by the United States, might undermine the liberty and creativity that it extolled. The West may have pitted itself resolutely in favour of individual rights, against the kind of psychological uniformity supposedly to be found in those eastern communist countries; and yet through its businesses, Whyte claimed, it might also be conditioning its own workforce and the younger generation.

Advice manuals, magazine quizzes and features in that era often seemed to steer the public towards certain implicit values, cementing conformity, spelling out clearly appropriate ideals of citizenship and family life. For example, the conservative physician and psychologist Dr George Crane provided obvious moralistic advice. Crane's questionnaires were disseminated across the country in high-circulation magazines; they invited readers to test the state of their careers, courtships, marriages, etc.; to help them understand where they fell short, or were succeeding, according to his criteria. He introduced tests in the late 1930s and then extended them after the war. According to his questionnaires, American men were doing well if they could confirm their steadiness, reliable job prospects, courtesy, chivalry, dress sense and praise of their wives' cooking and housework. Women could gain a high score by confirming that they went to bed promptly when their husbands did, avoided slang and profanity, darned socks, sewed buttons and laughed at their spouses' jokes. 'Mr' and 'Mrs' would be graded with 'merit' and 'demerit' scores according to their answers.[4] Crane spoke for a particular strand of conservative, God-fearing opinion. He provided syndicated columns and even set up a supposedly scientific marriage bureau in the 1950s to introduce eligible partners. Whyte, by contrast, challenged the very idea of a safe, predictable pathway for Americans as the necessary basis for a successful managerial career. *The Organization Man* illustrated how much had gone awry and how people were treated as part of some spurious, harmonious whole. However, Whyte's book was short on any systematic analysis of how glass ceilings (to borrow a later phrase, coined by the management consultant Marilyn Loden in 1978)[5] constrained women, and how racism shaped the prospects of people of colour.

As his title suggests, Whyte assumed a world where all senior positions within business were men's preserve. Many women worked in paid employment, as he was aware, and not all, evidently, were suburban housewives, even if he paid that stratum of society a good deal of attention. High-ranking jobs in the corporate sector in the United States, as in the UK, were, indeed, boys' clubs. It helped hugely (or might even be deemed essential, depending on the club or organisation) for the applicant to be a 'WASP' (White Anglo-Saxon Protestant).[6]

Whyte recognised how a company man might well be expected, or even required, to have a wife who would fit in well with the codes of the company, host dinner parties, be an agreeable companion at social functions. A well-rewarded raft of managers, he observed, would tend to promote people who were like themselves; it was a self-perpetuating system, in which they would feel no need and be offered no incentive to question.

Whyte also implied that victory over Nazism, while obviously crucial and rightly a source of jubilation, had played into a climate of anti-authoritarianism in his country that could, in extremis, have unintended negative consequences; for instance leading to a situation where men were excessively worried that they would be immediately typecast as loud-mouthed, bullying and overbearing if they stepped out of line. Instead, they might become docile, team-spirited, unchallenging company staff. Reading his book, you could be forgiven for imagining that an entire generation were succumbing to groupthink, meeting and bonding with one another, affably agreeing, all to be seen chatting on the front lawns of their faux ranch houses when they got home in the evenings, grumbling superficially about the treadmill or rat race, which (as Whyte also caustically noted) mostly they had no intention of quitting. They had given themselves over, he said, to an ideology of collectivisation. And yet this was all so at odds with the Protestant ethic that had been crucial for the rise of capitalism. Indeed, he thought a major shift was occurring away from all that past emphasis on individual salvation and personal toil. For the key thing now demanded of all such employees was 'fealty'.

A further problem worried Whyte. Not only were large companies treating the group, not the individual, as the key unit of worth; they were also naively reverential of science, or rather of pseudo-scientific formulae, at the expense of flair, and thus were not cultivating the best prospects for future dynamism. So, Whyte's 'organization man' had to confine himself inside the company's ontological and episte-mological grid, and to accept the same managerial so-called scientific problem-solving toolkit as one another. Whyte called therefore for a change of direction in teaching, business and government, and urged that US culture should portray and celebrate unconventional people; he wanted greater recognition of human differences, less reference to the supposedly typical, like-minded citizen.

His aim was to reform and perhaps even turbocharge corpora-tions in future (although, he might also have endorsed the phrase 'small is beautiful', which would later become part of an influential critique of capitalism and the corporation). His argument did not align directly with the outlook of either of the mainstream political parties in the 1950s United States, and some of his polemics seemed to take issue with much of the dominant political rhetoric of his own time, where, in congratulatory fashion, a totalitarian enemy was pitted against a picture of a right-minded, united people – an imagi-nary 'us' who belong, get on, live similar lives and all think broadly alike. An ideal of freedom was offered, but, thought Whyte, the reality so often was in fact unthinking compliance.

President Truman had strongly conveyed the message that Amer-icans enjoyed the *togetherness* of being a land of individuals, a people who genuinely celebrated freedom and fairness and sought to defend it to the hilt. He urged people to bury their differences and unite behind what he called '100 per cent Americanism'; the trouble was, of course, that in reality there were so many versions of that.[7] In the 1950s, Eisenhower, his successor, also often seasoned his speeches with rhetorical calls to unity, stressing this shared purpose and allegiance, as much providing exhortations as descriptions of how and what the entire nation had in common and truly believed. He would some-times urge directly that his fellow Americans look beyond political differences to see they were in conflict not with each other but with a deadly totalitarian foe; and he appealed to their deeper sense of a singular American community. Painters such as Norman Rockwell played into the narrative, depicting in sentimental terms a firmly rooted world of typical, fellow Americans. These depictions led in turn to pejorative labels such as 'Rockwellian' or 'Rockwellesque'.

In his critique of national groupthink, Whyte was documenting, at most, the mores of a particular segment of a social class in selected sites of the United States, but his ideas were influential, and remain interesting still. I want to set his account alongside other explorations of conformity that drew very different conclusions; and to note some of the remedies proposed at that time in order to deal with it, including the abolition rather than revival of capitalism. I dwell upon 'groupthink' and 'the organization man' at some length because they are further pieces of our historical jigsaw; elements of that larger vocabulary about mental adjustment, thought control and behavioural conditioning that crystallised in the post-war period and continued to inform political and managerial discourse long thereafter.

Whyte offered an eye-catching depiction of traits and types that were recognisable back then to many of his readers. His work was part of a genre of books that sought to help corporate workforces become more innovative, distinct and ultimately profitable. Whyte and other such critics identified something that was certainly real – the way people might be affected psychologically as well as socially by the workplace, and required to make constant minor modifications in order to fit. Candidates for posts who were otherwise qualified but somehow deemed to be 'not quite our type' might be weeded out; others chosen in job interviews because they were already seen as a naturally good match, according to pre-set assumptions, thus reducing or even negating an open society or true meritocracy.[8]

Whyte recognised that each business, large or small, was more varied than his vision implied, but did not want his readers to get so focused on details as to lose the overall picture. He made a clear argument about where society and the economy could be heading if corrective action was not urgently taken. But he was also concerned with delving beyond this, to consider, for instance, different subcultures in organisations, or even within departments of a corporation:

e.g. 'accounts' compared with the 'creative' or 'design' offices. What he could not be sure about was whether the organisational cultures he sketched might ultimately adapt, rather than simply expect their workers to adapt. Indeed, many in the business world sought to respond to the challenges such critics had posed, seeking to reverse the bland and stodgy working arrangements or incentives to groupthink that Whyte had made famous in his account of 'the organization man'.

Many attempts were made to counter the risks that Whyte identified. Indeed, if we fast forward half a century after such 1950s warnings about convergent and consensual corporate cultures, we can see the most innovative companies at the forefront of the digital revolution, such as Pixar, or later Apple, led by Steve Jobs, striving to design working environments to encourage at least some of their own more privileged staff to break conventions and to constantly innovate. While many of the workforce in big tech are, of course, required to do standard, homogenous jobs, others are supposed to free their own thinking, taking advantage of campus-like environments.

In some cases, indeed, the office architecture of the new high-tech giants was designed intentionally to prevent the risk of staff isolation and to counter employee conformity. Behemoths of Silicon Valley varied in ethos and style but many would radically extend the concept of 'open-plan' office design that had begun already in the 1960s as means to help staff interact and to think creatively together more regularly. The 'campuses' of these computer giants enable employees to hang out, go roller skating or play ping-pong, and see the in-house doctor, while still at work. It seems to be about care, freedom, the valorisation of the unconventional and original, even as these organisations also exert new forms of monitoring and of control.[9] The dystopian aspects of this new form of 'care' and this regime of constant exposure, social pressure and panoptical digital scrutiny (of staff, as well as consumers) in the great corporate empires have been satirised by various writers in recent years, including memorably by Dave Eggers in his 2013 novel *The Circle*.[10]

In fact, even as Whyte's thesis about groupthink was first advanced, other writers and business executives were already proposing remedies and antidotes, and ways to shake up employees and get them to meet and interact far more at the proverbial water cooler. Thus, long before all the architectural and technological innovations of the later parts of the century, new practices of 'brainstorming' were being promoted, post-war, to galvanise businesses and bureaucracies. Brainstorming was another idea that, like groupthink, would become a notable influence, as well as a cliché. It was first popularised, if not actually dreamt up, by a pioneering American advertising executive, Alex Faickney Osborn. A striking chapter of his 1948 book _Your Creative Power_ was entitled 'How to organize a squad to create ideas'. Here he seemed quite carried away by the military metaphor – inviting the reader to consider 'using the _brain_ to _storm_ a creative problem', and doing so 'in _commando_ fashion, with each stormer attacking the same objective'.[11]

Brainstorming, in Osborn's vision, was a means to encourage companies to create groups that would produce the very opposite of groupthink: arrangements could be made to get the entire workforce actively involved in _productive_ mental labour – thinking together, not just obeying instructions or passively receiving the company codes. One person might seed an idea and so precipitate unforeseen responses in another, which would grow in the mind of a third, before being transmitted again, like a fast-moving game of ball, with diverse proposals freely ricocheting around. It was important, Osborn said, to get rid of hierarchy at such meetings, and allow people to explore any side alleys of thought they wished.

Perhaps there was some glimmering of applied psychoanalytic theory in this enthusiastic account; certainly the hope that unconscious processes could be recognised, tolerated and ultimately harnessed in business. Osborn advised that the group's creativity had to be carefully nurtured: critical responses, or even yawns and frowns, which might suppress the free thinking of other staff in meetings, were to be actively discouraged. Premature expressions of dissatisfaction and impatient gestures suggesting a mood of negativity had to be admonished so as not to squash fledgling ideas, however half-baked they looked at first to the majority or to the senior staff. Brainstorming was all about unleashing human potential and freeing associations. He sought to encourage other companies to make use of his innovations by organising times and spaces for this loosened-up form of interaction, licensing all concerned to liberate even their most apparently crazy thoughts – since who could be sure if what some deemed crazy might not turn out to be an inspiration? In such approaches, or at least in the idealised version of such approaches, everyone's imagination and thinking was to be valued.

Brainstorming was to be celebrated as a tool for use in the classroom, the boardroom and on the shop floor. It could be adapted in new settings, Osborn proposed; used to coax people to work with one another co-operatively, rather than merely to outdo each other in competitive or zero-sum contests for favour, bonuses or the top jobs. It was heralded as the antidote to authoritarian, top-down modes of teaching as well, a challenge to boring lecture-style courses where students were merely supposed to absorb.

In search of models of brainstorming Osborn was impressed by some past examples of commercial and academic interdisciplinarity. By the time that he was writing, leading US universities had developed a range of deliberately interdisciplinary think tanks and research institutes where the kind of brainstorming Osborn extolled was an obvious element. Above all, however, wartime examples of military or intelligence-based co-operation exemplified the process that Osborn sought to encourage. Perhaps that explains his penchant for military metaphors. During the war vast projects were developed to create new forms of armaments. A large, critical mass of experts was brought together.[12] People with varied skills were tasked, in a way that Osborn admired, with solving technical and theoretical problems in science far greater than that which any individual person, or even any single discipline, could master alone. The brainstorming that went into the creation of the atomic bomb, the Manhattan Project (and subsequent nuclear warfare development by both the United States and the USSR), was the supreme and also most morally disquieting example of the process at work. It involved, crucially, the pooling of the talents of a group of theoretical physicists, but also mathematicians, engineers, chemists, metallurgists, electronics specialists and many others.

Such post-war business discussions were sometimes linked to metaphors of war and conquest, and located as part of an international race in which one side would ultimately win and the other would lose. Like Whyte, Osborn argued that business managers needed to think about the big national picture, rather than exclusively corporate advancement, personal greed or the pursuit of profits for profits' sake. He emphasised the benefits that a thriving business sector could offer to assist in the collective American endeavour, and to help defeat the ideological opponents of the West. Osborn praised the imaginative vision of US automobile giants such as Chrysler in lighting up the future for all. Whyte stressed the importance of selling America to Americans and to the world, thereby refuting Soviet lies that American capitalism was a form of authoritarianism and a manifestation of cultural barbarism.[13] Such authors wanted dynamic businesses to present a new vision to the American people and to export that vision of American success to other nations around the globe. In fact, in Europe and in other continents, American corporate values, and particular brands associated with the United States, were ever more pervasive.[14]

The idea of brainstorming was treated by Osborn as the precise opposite of centralised dictatorial Soviet thought control. He floated the idea that his country's diplomats and politicians, as well as army generals, should henceforth prioritise brainstorming.[15] The kind of group activity he had in mind was all about team members strengthening each other's cognitive abilities and emotional range, encouraging colleagues to grow a little *wilder* and hence less conformist. What was needed, he said, was to unchain the human *imagination*. In keeping with the capitalist-vs-communist context, Osborn's account was not just about such advantageous Western business camaraderie; he also proposed using the group's internal rivalries to benefit the corporation. In yet another competitive metaphor, he compared the commercial effort to a race where the winner benefits from the whole team's 'pace-making'.[16]

The idea of brainstorming received a mixed press; its value, warned some later critics, could easily be overdone, and it could become in itself an example of a tired groupthink formulation. Any assumption that brainstorming is always what's needed to think the unimaginable and to forge ahead could become a new form of managerial conformism. Sometimes, after all, as other managerial experts would insist, it was best to allow loners to labour and dream, without assuming the desirability of this constant imperative for everybody to engage with colleagues. Experimenters at Yale University in 1958 set up a test, with undergraduates divided into dozen-strong teams required to solve certain puzzles.[17] They were found to do worse in groups than a control sample of students figuring out these problems alone. The value of the group might be greater or lesser depending on the composition and mood of those assembled, they concluded, as well as the nature of the problem at stake. No management technique should simply be turned into a new and unquestioned communal refrain.[18]

Some of these post-war debates about groupthink and brain-storming have gained a new kind of saliency in the present-day digital economy. Indeed, in the face of the Covid-19 pandemic many workers found themselves faced with new challenges of homework-ing, entirely online. Millions had to grapple with the question of how best to balance solitude and group engagement, withdrawal from others and the pressure of imposed brainstorming too. A sense of irony about the injunction to network as much as possible may not be lost on workers stuck in isolation at home. Arguments about the chaining effect of the computer today, or the limitless flow of email, also have echoes of older debates about the bind of all that paperwork in offices (open plan or otherwise). An online state of alienation in the lonely crowd thus might well seem like a sequel to 1950s visions of groupthink. The internet may bring people together and enable global brainstorming on Zoom, Skype, WhatsApp or attractively named teaching platforms such as Teams or Collaborate. These are game changers and can feel uncanny: facilitating group engagement, and yet also enervating, isolating, tantalising. Online renditions of teach-ing and learning, playing, shopping, consuming entertainment or just simply chatting, may well feel like a pale approximation of their real-life counterparts and of a working community. On the other hand, faced as we have been with regular shutdowns and lockdowns, and the need to change our travelling habits anyway to counter climate change, such technology is ever more vital, a means for millions to stay in touch, talk, hear, engage and, indeed, brainstorm.

Although Whyte first wrote of groupthink in a light, debonair style in *Fortune*, he made clear the issue was urgent and that ultimately the fate of nations hinged on addressing his concerns. *The Organiza-tion Man*, by contrast with the earlier magazine piece, was a longer, more erudite study. In the latter, Whyte cited Weber and Durkheim, along with Dewey, William James and Freud. But the scholarship and research did not blur the stark warning Whyte wanted to offer his country: a compelling vision of an age dominated by like-minded men in their uniform suits, a system facilitated by big business, which encouraged groupthink and thus damaged minds, societies, indeed entire modern capitalist economies of which the businesses were the central part.

The lucky, affluent class, Whyte thought, were habituated to the implicit deal. They lived in 'Little Boxes', as a hit song had it in 1963, yet might feel superficially satisfied. That tune, sung by Pete Seeger, also popularised groupthink, as it told of the young going to university, marrying, becoming business executives, playing golf and drinking Martinis. They were far too at ease in their little boxes, the song implied, comfortable but in a psychologically impoverished state. The point was that people might end up in this condition, with no searching questioning; meek and accepting of their predictable compartments, even without re-education camps, to ensure agreement.

Whyte hoped that to offset groupthink the government would make greater investment in the humanities, so as to help sharpen minds. He thought the liberal arts, requiring a student's immersion in great classics, logical arguments and animated debates, could offer some protection, or at least a useful basis for the kind of critical thinking the country now so sorely needed. On the other hand, he had doubts about what he saw as the abstract modes of thinking and the largely consensus-seeking models favoured by doyens of the social sciences. Too many academics had bought into the same managerial ethos, believing that adjustment and accord were necessarily the highest social goods. Moreover, sociological descriptions of normal and average views could turn too easily into prescriptions; surveys can mutate into guidelines for what people ought to think, as they look over the data.

In support of his thesis about this endless adjustment towards consensus, Whyte cited a recent poll that revealed that many of his fellow citizens regarded the task of high school to be (merely) twofold: to create jobs and to teach young people to 'get along better with other people', as though being employed and being congruent with others (that is to say, suitably affable) were the highest achievements. The universities were in his view often little better: they could lead students to easy forms of convergence, or to reciting fashionable 'mumbo jumbo', aping each other or their teachers. Whyte's contention was that too many of his compatriots felt ashamed of standing alone, discouraged from challenging authority, including that of their university professors, or just too protective of their prospects to take any chances. He wanted his readership to recognise how easily we all switch off from thinking for ourselves or airing our criticisms, and prefer instead to be part of a crowd. You could not hide the fact that millions of lives were spent watching TV, or consuming the same movies, and that working days were spent by vast numbers inside huge factories or office blocks; a world where some – well-remuner-ated managers and executives, and perhaps even their entire staff – were encouraged to adjust, and then weld themselves, or maybe wed themselves, to a homogenous corporate 'philosophy'.

Whyte was right to argue that the pressure to conform can be subtle as well as gross, indirect as well as flagrant, accidental as well as intentional. Even to monitor staff attitudes and then relay the findings back to that workforce may be an exercise in persuasion, or an invi-tation to behavioural compliance. The process of sharing 'findings', in other words, could also have harmonising effects on the human sources of that data: polls and reports might lead people to fine-tune themselves to the norm, in a business, a community or across a national population. Take the 1929 'Middletown' study, the work of wife-and-husband team, sociologists Helen Merrell Lynd and Robert Staughton Lynd. Their book was based on their explorations of life in a particular city, Muncie, Indiana. The authors acknowledged that no place simply plucked off the map could be typical of everywhere, and yet they also treated this site and the attitudes they measured and studied there as representative of a large range of American com-munities. Muncie became 'Middletown', and a source of growing interest, even fascination, not only to the researchers but also to the wider population. Readers were fed reports about the attitudes of the people who lived there, the extent of their faith, the degree of their deference (or irreverence), their views of the past, the present and the future, and, in microcosm, their responses to material goods, down to relative preference for cotton or silk stockings.

That study by the Lynds, and later follow-ups, did much to foster a shared understanding of a quintessentially American way of life, or of a typical national state of mind. Where previously readers might have looked to storytellers for portraits of themselves and their fellow citizens, they now found new mirrors through polling and social science profiles. Citizens in the United States and many other coun-tries too would find themselves awash, post-war, with information about what surveyed portions of the population really think, feel or believe. And that information can affect in turn how people think about themselves, and how self-conscious they grow about their own attitudes and manner of relating to others.

Historians today quite often single out the Lynds' account of

Middletown, alongside the regular data provided by George Gallup's polling company, founded in 1935, and post-war reports by biologist turned sexologist Alfred Kinsey, as significant agents of social change. Papers and magazines relayed new discoveries about behaviour and beliefs: what made the headlines were often claims about what was now typical or characteristic. So, a national reading public might be at risk of attuning ever more to one another, fixated on the same questions and problems, comparing their own views and actions with others, and wondering how far their personal experiences in the bedroom, the bathroom, the kitchen and the workplace were ordinary and healthy, and, if not, might try to conform. To read such surveys, critics argued, was to internalise certain pressures to adjust.

A trickle of such surveys in the 1920s turned into a regular stream, then, later, a torrent of reports and summations about the state of the nation. This constant buzz of commentary about social polling data might also prove influential, or at least an unavoidable form of news that you had to engage with. So, you could learn from anthropologists, psychologists, sociologists or pollsters, what it meant, or what it ought to mean, to grow up somewhere like Indiana; and you could contrast growing up in a particular part of the West with growing up somewhere else, across the world for example, by reading articles in the media about what anthropologists had discovered of social mores in faraway places such as Samoa. An important question arose, about what this flow of news about social observations and interpersonal comparisons might do to the people observed, to how they think, bring up their children, court one another or view their careers. Selective descriptions might be used to recognise difference and diversity, or serve at other times as forms of prescription, inviting continuing self-surveillance and adjustment.

As Gary Younge remarks in an article about the Lynds' foundational work, this 'typical America' was largely deemed to be white and native-born, and mostly shorn of its internal 'foreigners'.[19] Sarah Igo develops this point in her study *The Averaged American*. She shows how large numbers of US citizens were schooled to expect statistical surveys and observational reports to appear and to reflect their reality, clarifying the limits of human diversity and the nature of similarities.[20] Sections of the population also came to understand that their opinions might well be sampled, their feedback solicited by all kinds of agencies – commercial, academic, political – on a regular basis. And their feedback was then fed back to them in the polling literature. This continuing interaction between at least some of the electorate and the pollsters was well established in the United States by the 1930s and 40s; a decade or two later it was also a feature of life in Britain and France, and many other countries too.

We saw in Part 3 Miłosz's descriptions of the secret bargains people made with themselves to survive under Stalin. Rather than inquiring into psychology under extreme conditions, Whyte was interested (as in fact Miłosz had also been on arriving as a cultural attaché from Poland to the United States) in the way people might be very comfortable with the daily fodder they were fed in the West, acclimatised quite nicely and smoothly to some group mentality, adjusting inside their family, leisure activities, education and work. Those who benefited from the system might come to assume there was no need for nor any possibility of radical change. Whyte's account might thus be read alongside Miłosz's depictions of life under communism and in the West: both these writers suggested how a particular way of life might appear exit-less, but for some, the fact it was, or at least seemed so, was not a problem. For a corporate executive, that sense of inevitability about the here and now might lead to the rhetorical question, 'what's not to like?'. As though the company and the state now offered all that could be imagined, or desired …

For all that Whyte focused on 'the organization man', women in the 1950s arguably faced even greater pressure to conform – from spouses or other family, and from schools, peers, magazines, films, adverts and business organisations. Beginning in early infancy, as feminist writers were pointing out, girls were acculturated to wear pink, be given dolls, taught about motherhood, and steered towards a caring career such as nursing, where boys might be offered toy guns, and encouraged to lead. Readers today may well be more alert than their forebears to how Whyte's own title subsumed the figure of the 'woman' inside the broader category of 'man'.

Post-war, many women would explore the groupthink that sustained gender inequality, a two-tier system. They identified and challenged the expectations and prohibitions in Western societies that meant that girls were supposed to be content as 'the second sex' and to embody the 'feminine mystique'. Critics of sexual *and* racial stereotypes in the 1950s and 60s exposed many social codes that served to sustain material inequality, to channel the way people think and to curb what they may aspire to. The civil rights movement took up and extended much of the 1950s thinking about conformism and normalisation that we've considered, seeking practical measures and legislative redress, and at the same time exploring socialisation through family, the legal system, education, religion, culture, sport and work. Even as popular culture could reinforce stereotypes about what it meant to be white or Black, a man or a woman, some movies, cartoons, magazines or songs could also subvert such expectations and cast a quizzical lens on those norms, showing how women and people of colour were re-conditioned en masse to domestic, second-ary and decorative roles. Black people continued to face enormous pressures to assume their ultimate systemic subordination, even as civil rights were won.

It was Betty Friedan, in her best-seller *The Feminine Mystique*, who put the issue of women's collective thought reform and brainwashing prominently on the map for many Americans and overseas readers. Her 1963 study analysed how women at large were ushered into their homemaking roles, and groomed to be sexualised, winsome figures in the interests of men, at heavy costs to their psychic as well as eco-nomic well-being. Friedan made direct comparison between women and those bands of 'brainwashed' POWs from the Korean War. Her argument was that all women, not simply some unfortunate minor-ity, experienced heavily coercive expectations to function inside this constricting system, in effect within an invisible prison. Notwithstand-ing differences of race, ethnicity, class, religion, region, age, and so on, she argued that women were an undeniable social category, lumped together as a supposedly inferior sex, and effectively programmed to think (or rather to not think) *alike*; to assume their own destiny as being first and foremost companions to men and guardians of children, and to be persuaded to not be 'difficult', and saturated by a culture that invited acceptance of inferiority and ideas about ladies' gracefulness and stereotypical forms of charm. (Friedan would later be criticised for failing to recognise that class and race, not just sex, are crucial factors in social relations and psychic experience, and that several forms of oppression can intersect, so that Black women and white women were not necessarily simply sisters-in-arms, fighting on the same terrain.)

Feminist accounts from the 1960s, such as Friedan's, are evidently at play in a satirical novel by Ira Levin which was turned into the

1975 film *The Stepford Wives*, directed by Bryan Forbes. Beneath bourgeois norms, the movie reveals a hidden, surgical assault by men upon women's brains; mind control and brainwashing, in all its raw violence, to make women into uncomplaining, doll-like eye candy. *The Feminine Mystique* pointed to the terrible toll on women's mental health of living in suburban 'prisons'; *The Stepford Wives* dramatised this further, reflecting a growing sense of scandal over lobotomies that had been carried out in the 1950s and 60s on those with certain conditions deemed hopelessly and incurably mentally ill. The film suggested above all that a misogynistic system had been devised to turn once lively, free-thinking people into mannequins, worked over in body and mind. It also anticipated the remarkable growth of the cosmetic surgery industry. Women, primarily, would be invited in ever larger numbers, as the century wore on and the twenty-first century began, to resculpt bodies from head to toe, and have a 'makeover'. The decision was often presented as simply an individual consumer choice, or a mode of personal empowerment; while critics pointed instead to the desperate alienation and depression that was also instigated by idealised images, all those heavily prescriptive beauty standards, myths and forms of fashion tyranny.[21]

We see the women in the *Stepford* movie, after their covert, non-consensual brain treatment, as interchangeable members of a homogenous group, like living Barbie doll creatures, robotically moving their trolleys around the supermarket aisles. (A 1978 cult zombie film, *Dawn of the Dead*, would later extend this theme, in its own satirical exploration of consumerism: the shopping mall becomes the setting for a terrifying conflict between the zombies and the desperate, embattled last few human survivors.) Far from being innately secondary to men, women, as Friedan had so powerfully argued, were systematically undermined, handicapped and made to feel inadequate in a system that shored up the egos of one sex by denigrating the other. Weakness was actively projected, by men, onto women.

Debates on social conformity and groupthink were also thrown into sharp relief by perturbing psychological experiments, as well as by popular narratives and films depicting people leaving the rat race, refusing to continue as corporate employees or dutiful homemakers and taking up new paths. There were many new counterculture movements and discourses by the 1960s that invited people to 'drop out', seek out new forms of commune or community, or dive into a more adventurous, personal life, in active rejection of the supposedly predictable, mind-numbing, capitalist and office-based world that Whyte and others described as a mounting problem of post-war society.

Psychoanalysts tended to take a different approach, less focused on the particular post-war conjuncture, and more inclined to suggest certain universal psychological predicaments and conflicts, not least between desire and group-based morality; conflicts that constituted the human condition. Freud, at least, often suggested as much, although some of his followers took his speculations on group affiliations in new directions during and after the Second World War. They built upon his landmark 1921 study *Group Psychology and the Analysis of the Ego*. Some developed forms of therapy for groups adapted from Freud's basic ideas and model of clinical work with individual patients. Pioneers of this approach, such as Wilfred Bion, considered afresh Freud's thoughts about the formations of fantasy that exist inside the mind. These clinicians wanted to see what emerged when a number of patients are gathered together in a structured setting, and then left to respond, as they see fit, without instruction from a leader. The concept of the 'leaderless group' emerged.[22] Unlike Freud's more speculative studies, Bion's exploration of group phenomena was based on his own clinical evidence. It also had more obviously direct, managerial applications. He first got involved in this form of group work as an army doctor and psychiatrist faced with the problem of treating soldiers with psychiatric symptoms in a military hospital in the English Midlands during the Second World War. His own military experience and interest in such collective behaviour, however, derived from the battlefields of the First World War, where he had been a tank commander. Later, he published several bulletins and a co-written account about his methods of working with soldiers, and then continued with other therapeutic groups long afterwards. This tradition of group work was also developed by others during the 1940s and 50s, for instance by S. H. Foulkes.

These analysts gathered evidence, demonstrating what Freud had already implied: fantasies can shadow the life of groups; splits, projections and denials may operate within a gathering of people, as well as in the mind of an individual. Aims in group therapy vary, but they might be to help the constituent members become more aware of such fantasies and prevailing assumptions, to find some containment, tolerate challenge, gain insight into the unconscious processes that can be silently at work in the mind, or an aggregate of minds at some assembled gathering. In such meetings, individuals might come to note their own active or passive part in the way the group develops, to ask more searching questions about their own minds and roles, or to test previously inchoate presuppositions about other people.

Bion and other innovators around this time sought to recognise groupthink but also to facilitate more creative thinking in groups, and to invite greater self-reflexive attention. They wanted to identify and show how and why it often becomes difficult or even impossible for creative thinking to happen. Groups can provide us with the crucial foundations for thinking, they argued, yet may also become curiously sealed off, complacent, or operate in active negation of the task that has brought them together in the first place. At the most extreme end lay mass psychosis, but there were also potentially mass neuroses that might be revealed and analysed in this way, through the experiential group. For example, Bion considered how a company of people can energetically repress unwelcome information, perhaps ostracise or subtly shame an individual member for some unspoken reason, and exert pressures that weigh heavily upon everyone, even without anyone describing those pressures directly.

Combinations of professional people who are committed, in principle, to think about such issues, for instance in university departments or psychoanalytic societies, can be equally affected by such group processes. An anecdote I heard from a former candidate, who was in psychoanalytic training in the early 1960s, illustrates this point. She presented a clinical case to a seminar run by Bion, finished her account in customary fashion, and was then met with prolonged silence. It seemed a rather stony silence to her. Feeling anxious, she quickly offered to present further material, and started rifling through her notes to see what else she could provide. Here Bion intervened, and said, 'yes, I think that is what you are supposed to feel you have to do'. He had picked up the way the group's shared silence seemed to be operating, stirring a feeling in her, as though putting her under an implicit obligation to be the active one, while the others sat back passively and watched. After his intervention, the presenter managed to resist the temptation to supply more data, and eventually her colleagues started to think aloud about what they'd heard.

Bion once described a therapeutic group whose members seemed determined repeatedly to offer one another inane advice and bland encouragement, even though all concerned knew such responses to be useless. On another occasion, he noted how a group he had convened ignored him pointedly for three or four weeks, as though he was 'an oracle in decay', or a man 'in bad odour', until a patient began to display what the group regarded as symptoms of madness, making statements that appeared to be the product of hallucinations. As their anxiety rapidly rose, Bion found himself readmitted to the group and restored to a commanding position in what had now become, he thought, a 'miniature theocracy':

> I was the good leader, master of the situation, fully capable of dealing with a crisis of this nature – in short, so outstandingly the right man for the job that it would have been presumption for any other member of the group to attempt to take any helpful initiative. The speed with which consternation was changed into blind complacency had to be seen to be believed.[23]

After the alarming situation arose, Bion postulated that for the group he had become, in effect, 'the centre of a cult in its full power', a kind of guru. He did intervene, both in seminars and in therapeutic groups, but often he would hold himself back, allow the group to develop. That was not to say that he switched off, but the group did not quite know what he was thinking. They would make of his silence, as of his words and his bodily presence, what they wished. Bion and other colleagues who developed the tradition of group therapy sought to be alert to the powerful play of emotions circling within such a community, and in themselves. This kind of participant-observer role for the convenor, or therapist, drew on the psychoanalytic method, and perhaps also owed something to the insider-outsider position of the anthropologist. The psychoanalysts, in short, were interested in the fantasised figures and groups that shadow the mind of the individual, and the shared role of dreams, illusions and dreads in the life of such a community. As the poet Walt Whitman had put it long before Freud said a similar thing about the ego and the group: 'I contain multitudes.'

Group therapists following the psychoanalytic approach would try to avoid being too obtrusive; they might need to speak to hold things together, if the anxiety or aggression grew too severe, but often would seek to remain quiet for a considerable time, carefully listening and observing, allowing the process to emerge and providing a containing function with certain agreed protocols (for example, regarding meeting times and confidentiality), and, as far as possible, eschewing the directive, managerial role. Every now and then they might comment and interpret, as would a psychoanalyst with a patient in the consulting room. Whether some, such as Bion, might also revel in the guru position attributed to them is a further question. The aim, however, is to disenchant, rather than re-enchant. The therapist might note what the group is doing (or failing to do), and seek to clarify how it is proceeding (for instance, in a cult-like fashion). Or perhaps the therapist might mention some other 'elephant in the room'. Interpretation is a difficult craft; the therapist or analyst trying to judge as best as they can when it is timely to take up issues with a patient, or in this case with a group; and then to gauge how far, if at all, that interpretation proves useful, and, moreover, what is done with that intervention once it is made. They try to be attentive to the kinds of feelings or assumptions that are projected onto them by the patient or group. Does the group respond to an intervention, and if so, how, or does it completely ignore the remark, perhaps even gang up against the therapist in order to make them feel left out? The possibilities are endless.

Bion's 1961 book *Experiences in Groups* explores this idea of how so much can go on unwittingly or unconsciously. He thought there were often unconscious 'basic assumptions' shared implicitly within a body of people. Although each example was unique, Bion suggested that there are certain recurring formations. In the 'leader/saviour' version, the members gravitate around rigid beliefs and seem desperate for guidance. Sometimes the members seem to form a single uncontested mass, defined in relation to an assumed individual hero and rescuer, and/or unite solidly against some other demonised group. He looked at how groups may fight, take flight or huddle in a state of abject dependence. Groups can also become entirely engrossed in what he called pairing, where the participants concentrate upon one or more dyadic formations of individuals, perhaps fascinated by a real – or imaginary – amorous couple. Assumed ideas, fantasies, or sometimes overt conversations about a pair's sexual relationship, for example, may generate a great deal of excitement or worry in a group. In the 'fight/flight' situation, the members may treat the cluster they are in as under mortal threat; as though the assembly is extremely precarious, perhaps far more so than realistically applies. The group may grow terribly anxious about its breakable, invadable state, yet seem unable to share this anxiety openly with one another (hence to alleviate it). Its members may also feel somehow naturally superior, wise, arrogant and entitled as a group, compared with some 'out-group'.

Bion offered intriguing descriptions of the evolution of sessions, moment by moment; he vividly conveyed how the atmosphere could change suddenly, with greater or lesser degrees of a sense of hope, or sometimes descent into paranoia. He also suggested how, with a greater sense of safety and trust, different modes of thoughtful communication became possible, and the group might begin to take more responsibility for its own development.

A field of organisational consultancy work also developed post-war, in parallel with, or sometimes directly inspired by, this pioneering tradition of therapy. New opportunities for consultancy took clinicians into industry, business and education, for example through the applied services provided by organisations such as the Tavistock Institute of Human Relations. Clinical and experiential literature on groups, and such applied psychoanalytic work in workplaces, was complemented by new materials furnished by social scientists, as well as by new accounts of mass gatherings, crusades and millenarian movements over the centuries provided by historians. Some considered afresh the operation of mass psychology in the most recent historical past. One notable point of departure for that was Wilhelm Reich's 1933 study *The Mass Psychology of Fascism*.[24] Erich Fromm, as noted, had also written powerfully in a book in 1941 about a deep-seated 'fear of freedom', profound feelings of loneliness and atomisation, and the mass longing to escape from personal responsibility – psychic phenomena that he thought widely prevalent in the modern age, most disastrously so in Germany from which he had fled. Different balances could be struck in individuals, groups or societies. Fromm wrote later about what might constitute the basis for what he called a 'sane society'.

Thus, post-war ideas about group psychology and the practice of group analysis emerged alongside other historical and sociological explorations of mass phenomena. The spotlight on groupthink could also, as we have already suggested, be turned back upon the academy and upon the clinical professions themselves. For instance, some academic researchers and psychoanalysts provided insights into the nature of unconscious bonding by colleagues and students inside the training organisations of psychoanalysis itself; they invited more debate about the kinds of conformist adaptation that it might require of those who seek to train and work in the field. For an institution might house a nest of other micro-institutions, for instance cliques, or established subgroups, with certain leading figures exerting a charismatic hold.

Robert Jay Lifton, the psychiatrist who explored brainwashing and interviewed ex-POWs on their way home from the Korean War, recognised how groupthink and thought reform of various kinds might occur within the post-war US psychoanalytic organisation in which he undertook training. His concern at the power of the institution to delimit the freedom of trainees was a factor in his own decision to give up the training and change career path.[25] Other critics would explore the way analytic groups and societies operated, intent upon considering to what degree the analysts (or their organisations) might pilot, even dragoon, the analysands, or more delicately influence them. Through the training of each generation of analysts, a multiplicity of coded pointers might operate, about where best to comply to or challenge authority inside the subgroup or the larger community.[26] Such pointers might be reinforced further through forms of professional patronage and institutional promotion (or marginalisation).

Psychoanalysis did not follow a single path, and controversies about interpretation, or more extremely about practices of groupthink, conversion, normalisation, etc., were fiercely debated within the professional organisations, as were also the nature of the appropriate limits and ethical boundaries. Notable European psychoanalysts (most famously Jacques Lacan) levelled the charge that the profession – particularly in the United States – had lost its way by becoming a mode of treatment that promoted adaptation to a given society; others pointed to the conformism that seemed to arise in Lacan's own groups in Paris; the powerful grip and intense charismatic authority that Lacan himself exerted as the 'absolute master' over the seminars he convened; the structures he created, dissolved and then recomposed.

New words were also coined by psychoanalysts to describe how people may, from infancy onwards, become *too* adapted to their primary group – the family – rather than maladapted, in the sense of being overly wild or transgressive. For example, Christopher Bollas (inspired in part by Donald Winnicott's account of the false self) later wrote of a particular bad psychic outcome that he calls the 'normotic' character. Another analyst, Joyce McDougall, made a similar point, preferring instead the term 'normopath'.[27]

In psychological development, McDougall suggested, each of us has to find some balance between conformity and resistance to that conformity. The infant's narcissism has to be punctured; each must learn they are not the centre of the world; we all have to share resources and carers, and not act with complete disregard for others. We cannot be left, or so one hopes, entirely free as children or adults to do our own individualistic thing. Indeed, our partial realisation and adaptation to the needs of others – primary carers, siblings, community – is psychically crucial, she argued; we have to feel our way as infants, children, adolescents and adults, and, yes, we must acclimatise, up to a point, even to make a playgroup work.

Bollas and McDougall were interested, however, in exploring the pathologies that arise when this kind of acquiescence and adaptation is far more extreme: where the requirement for rote adaptation and unthinking normalisation is the overwhelming message received and internalised by the child. A baby or toddler that is excessively agreeable, too pacific, over-sweetly compliant, causing 'no bother', such psychoanalysts suggested, gives grounds for clinical concern. Individuals may also become, as common parlance has it, 'chameleons', able to adapt 'beautifully' and seamlessly to any milieu, and the question might then be what or whom does this perfect transformability serve, in the chameleon's internal world. Case material and theories piled up about how we may become what someone else or a group installed within our own minds requires us to be; and about how certain people might suffer from 'imposter syndrome', or identify rigidly with others, unable to change mode at all.

Such propensities, as psychoanalysts continued to warn one another, could seriously hamper their own profession's development. Some spoke out about the tendency for 'schools' of analysts to close in on themselves and become bastions rather than open spaces for discussion with others. Fearing such defensive groupthink, and anxiously noting circling critics of the talking cure, the American psychoanalyst Ralph Greenson warned in 1969 that there was too much 'placidity, contentment and self-satisfaction'. He harked back to Freud's adventurous spirit and urged that his colleagues provide, in future, better 'breeding grounds' for new ideas in psychoanalysis.[28]

So, to recap, much was written in the decades after 1945 by journalists, academics, psychologists, therapists and entertainers about the nature of groupthink. New ideas and arguments, as well as innovative experiments in social psychology and in psychoanalysis, tested older, abstract suppositions about crowd or mass psychology. Experimental set-ups were devised to explore how people deal with specific tasks, to reveal how different kinds of therapeutic frameworks and organisational structures might help or hinder realistic attitudes, problem-solving or the maintenance of self-esteem.

During the 1930s, the social psychologist Kurt Lewin developed procedures in a bid to test attitudes and capacities of individuals under different kinds of governing authority. He famously investigated how boys aged around eleven went about solving certain challenges that they were set, in groups; to see how they worked and played creatively (or otherwise) in clubs (which he arranged, and then observed). Lewin wanted to know if his young experimental subjects' intellectual capacities differed in a laissez-faire system (that is, one involving little central direction), a democratic arrangement (in which co-operation, participation and inclusion were valued), and an authoritarian organisation (where the adults involved barked orders and gave no satisfactory explanations for their decisions to the children). He was open, I think, to considering whatever arose, although he and his research group were no doubt gratified to find that their tests supported the case for tolerance and greater democracy. Conversely, they exposed the deleterious pedagogic and intellectual consequences of a dictatorial method. Lewin had fled the Nazi regime and arrived in the United States as a refugee. He died shortly after the end of the war but his attempt to create a kind of group laboratory for people-watching in the United States long outlived him.[29]

Other experiments that proved influential showed how ideas about superiority and inferiority, and 'in-groups' and 'out-groups', operate; and how ingrained prejudices shape opinion about others and the self. Experiments were designed in the United States by two Black psychologists and important advocates of racial equality, desegregation and civil rights, Mamie and Kenneth Clark, to investigate children's self-perceptions and internalisations of racism. Their famous 1940s 'doll tests' suggested how children (whatever their skin colour) between the ages of three and seven were already prone to see white dolls as more valuable, attractive and smart than black dolls. The Clarks' experiments were persuasive: they demonstrated how vicious stereotypes and implicit value systems shape the mind of the child, and in many cases, how such stereotypes might foster an 'inferiority complex'.[30]

Adolescent identity and group formations were also the subject of intense scrutiny after 1945. First uses of the word 'teenager' can be found in dictionary entries from before the First World War; however, as a common term, it came of age during the 1940s and 50s. It also acquired new significance in the field of marketing, given the rising spending power of young people. Much interest was focused on 'troubled teenagers' in that boom era, an age also of growing psychologisation of everyday ills. This was a period where new kinds of discourse emerged about the psychology of adolescents, and their fraught occupation of the liminal spaces between infancy and adulthood. Notable movies such as Nicholas Ray's *Rebel Without a Cause* (1955), starring James Dean, or François Truffaut's *Les Quatres Cents Coups* (1959), starring Jean-Pierre Léaud, took up such issues, inviting debate about young people's diverse experiences, personal struggles and peer relationships outside of the family. Such stories, exploring serious emotional difficulties in their subjects, were designed to challenge simplistic and shrill denunciations of juvenile delinquency (a post-war buzz phrase) and invite greater psychological curiosity.

Ideas about conformity and rebellion in the teenager mushroomed; a burgeoning psychological literature aimed increasingly to provide sensitive guidance to post-war parents as well as their offspring. During the Second World War in Britain, the psychoanalyst Donald Winnicott had already paved the way, providing BBC radio talks aimed at helping mothers and fathers understand and nurture their infants, as well as value themselves, constantly encouraging a more psychologically minded parental approach. In France, in the 1970s, the psychoanalyst Françoise Dolto offered her own talks on radio, responding to listeners' concerns about their parenting and their children's welfare. In each case, the use of radio reflected an aspiration to reach out and make psychoanalytic ideas more accessible and vernacular. Winnicott was especially influential, encouraging mothers to do what came most naturally to them, if they were not too anxious or too manipulated by others. They needed to find their own ways, he suggested, rather than succumbing to conformist pressure from so-called experts.

Such clinically informed public broadcasting and popular-advice literature sought to challenge rote or regimented views from the past, and to recognise the range of emotions experienced by babies, children and their primary carers. A powerful revolt was to be encouraged by this cast of pundits and experts against the kinds of rigid and disciplinarian feeding patterns, which had hitherto been commonplace, where mothers were supposed to respond to their babies according to some pre-set drill. In the 1930s, for instance, Frederic Truby King, a New Zealand physician, had been influential not only in advocating for breastfeeding over bottle-feeding, but also in insisting on the importance of adhering to a strict and punctual feeding regime for the baby.[31] After 1945, new guides and advice literature written by clinicians appeared, encouraging mothers to allow themselves to be more spontaneous, 'in touch', and to do what felt right, or at least to do so in light of the findings of psychoanalysis and experimental literature. In a similar vein came a series of challenges to the disciplinarian regimes to be found in so many schools, private and state-run, in Britain, and the traumatic legacies of institutionalisation, brutalisation or prematurely broken attachments. They explored, in short, the long-term damage that schooling can do, precursors to the recent spate of works on conditions such as 'Boarding School Syndrome'.

In Britain after the Second World War, child psychotherapy established itself as a distinct association and profession, with growing public influence. In Eastern as well as in Western Europe, psychology, psychiatry and psychotherapy all played many important roles. Communist governments kept a close eye on anti-conformist attitudes and the 'degenerate' lure of Western culture on youth, especially with the explosion of 'decadent' pop music in the 1960s. Suffice to say that the problem of 'the teenage years', and the power of peer groups, was to be explored widely, and from multiple political and moral points of view, East and West, in the second half of the twentieth century. Both sociologists and clinicians noted that adolescents marked out new group allegiances in their own ways, and struggled with their own first loves and hatreds via 'subcultures', gangs, fashion, popular music, drugs and politics. They might seek to escape family or state orthodoxies, in flight from the dead weight of communism or the iniquities and stresses of capitalism.

In Britain, during the 1960s and 70s, we can see how concerns about fostering individualism, while recognising the shared or even universal psychological challenges we all face in growing up, were articulated in a helpful and thoughtful, if also decidedly 'of its time', series of guides. These books, produced by psychoanalysts and child therapists at the Tavistock Clinic, sought to help parents, as the titles put it, 'understand your one-year-old', 'your two-year-old', etc. The guides explained that the baby, the child, the teenager had to be understood as unique, changing with each passing season. Their minds are irreducible to any other, but also caught up in the same fundamental challenges of negotiating inner worlds, as well as widening social relationships.

One of the books in this series was written to enlighten mothers and fathers about their teenagers, to see how such young people might be resisting and conforming to many different group pressures, and yet how each individual was also bound to be going through a process distinctly their own. At that stage of life, adolescents were, the authors explained, grappling with profound 'identity' issues. They were constantly negotiating new moves in relation to one another; they were also navigating 'the permissive society', learning about the problem of moving on from the primary group – the family – and coping with conflicting wishes, for instance about rebellion and conformity, in relation to sex, school, religion, work or the possibility of continuing qualifications in higher education. Youngsters were inclined, they warned, to take up portentous tones, to idealise revolutionaries, to demand that the world be changed overnight, to fit in with their new 'radical' group spirit, or else to swing the other way into rigid, conservative reactions against their own transgressive wishes and inner aggression.

The Tavistock guide attempted to illuminate the complex psychosocial predicaments of the teenager; to understand the depth of the emotional challenges the youngster had to manage. The issue of 'belongingness', the authors found, was likely to be salient and difficult. Indeed, the drama of psychic separation was inevitably going to be acute, if the teenager was to move on psychologically from the shadow of parents and siblings, and find a place in the world other than as a dependent child. This was a key developmental task of adolescence, a trajectory for every fledgling adult that could not be taken for granted. It was a pathway to be travelled by all, and at a time when the body was in a state of alarming transformation; a body with raging hormones that evoked ambivalent feelings; an emergent adult sexual body that might well precede any kind of mature psychosocial identity, and capacity for new intimate, bodily relationships with others. During these years, antisocial behaviour, the authors explained, was common, as was precocious flight into sex.[32]

Contemporary society, the Tavistock clinicians warned, had a great deal to answer for in its shameless exploitation of children and teenagers for naked commercial ends, and especially for creating an endless parade of seductive advertising and sexual titillation on screen and in print. The danger to youth, they added, was probably not so much from undue inflammation of sexual desires (that was inevitable), as from the continually implied or stated propaganda about how a person ought to feel and to act. They described how a boy might be made to think that unless he is sexually 'with it' then 'he isn't really alive – [but] … left out, left behind in the race to grab something out of life'. Such an account may well still ring true in the age of the internet, when explicit content, or rather a gigantic industry of pornography, is likely to be encountered and navigated, one way or another, by teenagers, and often by much younger children. In the teenage imagination, the Tavistock writers also explained, so much seems to be in constant flux, but sometimes a particular goal could also seem, to them, a matter of life or death: '[t]o have a boyfriend or a girlfriend, and a bank balance, these are two keys to life!'[33]

Teenage conformity or conformist anti-conformity (the heavy pressure to rebel) was thus carefully dissected, offering new slants on the question of individuality, freedom and groupthink. But older people, even if notionally free to make their own decisions, were of course not free of conformist pressures either, so said other psychologists. Solomon Asch, for example, reported influentially his own disturbing findings in yet another set of interesting experiments during the 1950s. These suggested that a sizeable proportion of adults were extremely reluctant to trust their own perceptions and judgements, even the direct evidence of their own eyes, when the majority take a contrary view. (It should be said that many of his participants were students, so perhaps teenagers, or barely older than that, but his drift was clear: conformist pressures may operate in all of us, irrespective of age.)

Asch conducted notable investigations into group-based conformity, which would in turn influence other social psychologists such as Stanley Milgram, who, as we have seen, conducted celebrated experiments on obedience. Asch's findings – like Milgram's later – were felt by many to be startling and sobering. The participants in one of Asch's experiments were told they were all equally placed in the same boat as volunteers, but unbeknownst to one of them, the others in the group were in fact acting and had been primed in advance to agree on the *wrong* answer to the question that Asch asked. He was interested to know if the volunteer would stick with their view or, under internal pressure to agree with the others, say the opposite to what they initially thought.

The group were shown a card with a line on it, and then a second card with three lines of clearly different lengths. They were then asked which line on card 2 matched the line on card 1. Asked to voice the answer out loud, the genuine volunteer (asked last) was far more likely to give the wrong answer – i.e. to agree with the group. Without group interference in individual judgement, Asch found the error rate was less than 1 per cent; under the influence of the rest, however, the error rate jumped up to around 35 per cent. Some people held to their personal views unabashed, but a sizeable number simply switched sides to fit in. As he mused in his 1955 report on this work in *Scientific American*, some of these 'extremely yielding persons' concluded, 'I am wrong, they are right.' Others ceded their own view so as 'not to spoil your results'. Many who went along actually suspected the majority might be 'sheep', or victims of an optical illusion, but all the same sided with their answers rather than trust their own judgement.[34]

But if a group in a room could sway a person, even override their perception, understanding and reasoning powers, what of the role of the nation at large in shifting opinion and forming characters? One response to that question was provided by the historian Richard Hofstadter.

*

In 1948, Hofstadter published a controversial book that explored how guiding national beliefs could determine profoundly the consciousness of the people who lived there. His study, entitled *The American Political Tradition and the Men Who Made It*, suggested how dominant myths had come to prevail and to enjoy a remarkable consistency over the centuries. Indeed, he argued that a powerful vision of American purpose, even destiny, had exerted an increasingly regulating and constricting influence on the population, and especially on those who held social influence and political power. The idea of a national mission was inculcated, relayed widely across generations, and then assumed to have organically arisen in the people.

Although that ideology stressed the freedom to think and express yourself as you wished, the conception of freedom entailed a more basic and limited set of assumptions. The United States, he explained, came to be viewed by millions of its inhabitants, and much of its business class, as 'the land of the free'. That vision was assumed, whatever the unequal realities or indeed mockeries of that freedom in practice. This concept was understood in obviously loaded and restricted ways, and as though there was no alternative to a particular widely stabilised definition – or at least no alternative notion that was of any lasting good. That vision – the imagined community, as we might now say, using the term developed by a notable writer on nationalism, Benedict Anderson – had come to be commonplace in both modern political rhetoric and modern social mentality, as though the United States simply *was*, rather than aspired (in part) to be, that land of the free. Hofstadter argued that this ideal of freedom also assumed a powerful commercial and financial aspect: for a society to be free, businesses must be liberated from so-called shackles, and perhaps even the whole world subjected to shared rules that facilitate maximum trade – ideally 'free trade', without tariffs or other barriers.

In the post-war United States, once again we need caveats before simply endorsing such an analysis; there was no national social, political or even corporate unanimity on the benefits of global free trade. The debate over 'America first' and economic protectionism versus global free trade is both older and certainly more enduring. All the same, Hofstadter was right to claim that, after 1945, many big-business executives as well as politicians and diplomats acted as cheerleaders for a rules-based international system of law, and promoted free enterprise and free trade as the natural human condition and as fundamental, universal freedoms. And he was surely also right to assume that millions of people shared those assumptions, that vision where unfettered commerce and corporate laissez-faire were the keys to a people's and a nation's economic and psychological health. The well-functioning nation was regarded by many as equivalent to a vibrant, unblocked body, or a fluent, free-circulating, well-functioning mind. Policies at home or abroad reflecting this point of view assumed the sanctity of 'the private sector', and granted maximum scope of action to the individual, thus treating this conception of freedom and maximum 'openness' as desirable *without any question*. In sum, Hofstadter's book about American values suggested that this free-enterprise belief system, or vision of the so-called open society, was a dominant American ideology, although, as we have seen, fear of the overweening corporation was also deeply embedded in the nation's history.

There have always in fact been divided views in the United States, as more generally throughout the West, about the meaning, scope, limitations and challenges of achieving liberty. The story of the nation as a society grounded in a love of freedom of thought was itself inevitably a contested narrative, one that was always confronted with the monstrous central facts of the destruction of Native American societies, the conquest of land and the constitutive role of slavery in the nation's founding and development. Long after the formal abolition of slavery, a sutured version of reality prevailed that assumed Americans were now and always had been, as a people, essentially free.

This vision of shared freedom for all US citizens had to grapple with the never-healed wounds of the Civil War, and to somehow deal with the fact that the United States, the great anti-imperial bastion, was itself an imperial power in the world, born out of massive violence. The American ideology that Hofstadter described was never universally assumed by its own population. All the same, Hofstadter was convincing when he insisted that this was an influential and dominant representation, in which the American nation had always assumed a God-given purpose of extending individual and commercial freedom inside and beyond its own borders. He noted that such a vision slid from one conception of freedom to another: as though the right to assembly, expression, property and bearing arms were all of a piece, and psychological, religious, legal, economic and political freedoms are quintessentially American.

Hofstadter wanted to show how the United States was to accept and proselytise on behalf of a particular and constricted idea of freedom.[35] At worst, this vision became a compliant mode of group-think, all about unfettered rights to pursue private businesses. Most Americans after the Second World War, he warned, as he looked on in dismay, seemed to have become increasingly passive and spectator-like figures, not really challenging anything; people, he feared, were increasingly reluctant or ill-equipped to think for themselves, even if they were not entirely brainwashed. They did not apparently see any need to question their own beliefs, even if they enjoyed agency to change themselves and their environment *in theory*.[36]

The majority in the workforce now lived, Hofstadter suggested, with the naive assumption that they enjoyed personal autonomy, able to avail themselves simply by dint of being American, in a land of endless opportunity, without ever really going back to first principles or studying the actual living conditions of so many of their com-patriots. He suggested how basic assumptions were shared between citizens, not to mention between presidents and secretaries of state; even as they differed on particular policies, certain continuities existed from the birth of the Republic to the present-day administration and president. Hofstadter felt that even Roosevelt's New Deal in the 1930s operated within this long-standing Americanised and ultimately indi-vidualistic version of what freedom means. He showed how much was transmitted uncontested over the decades to consolidate the dominant political story of who 'we' truly are, and what 'we' revile. He would no doubt have been as astonished as anyone had he lived to witness a self-declared democratic socialist, Bernie Sanders, emerging as a serious, albeit ultimately unsuccessful, contender for the Demo-cratic presidential candidacy in 2016 and 2020.

What Hofstadter wanted to explore were the common ingredi-ents that bound so many people together and prevented them from seeing beyond the horizon of certain myths. He understood that for them (to borrow a word from the Italian anti-fascist writer Antonio Gramsci), certain 'hegemonic' assumptions shaped how they per-ceived the nature of their lives, their realistic choices and their own aspirations for liberty. Miłosz also remarked on that point: how so many Americans seemed disinclined to demand of their government positive versions of freedom (a right to a decent job, higher education or universal healthcare) as opposed to negative freedoms (the right as individuals, or as owners of property, to be free from undue regulation, taxation, responsibility for others, etc.).

Something akin to groupthink was to be explored a few years later by Herbert Marcuse in a more politically trenchant analysis that appeared in the 1960s. Marcuse would gain an enormous following, as a critic of capitalism. In this case, the point was not, as with Whyte and his 'organization man', to redeem a more vibrant form of market-based system, or to strengthen corporate culture by advocating anti-conformist reforms of modern businesses, but rather to challenge the entire order of things. What was shared across such analyses was that focus on the power of group conformity in a modern society. Marcuse sought to map out the psychological and political experiences that were so commonplace in advanced industrial economies. In his book *One-Dimensional Man* (1964) he suggested how mass conformity might arise, where a nation's value system was mostly just accepted, without need for debate, even though it only satisfied illusory human wants. He was alert to how capitalism might suppress sexuality, but also to how it might actually do the reverse, in using the liberation of sexual energy to distract from political liberation and ultimately promote conservative ends. Rebellion and challenge, he proposed, were so often tamed and subsumed; art too, with all its revolutionary potential, could be defanged, before you knew it, rendered harmless inside capitalism.

A set of toxic values and false needs were reinforced daily through the media and advertising. He argued that a majority in such societies were by then sufficiently well fed, clothed and housed, converted into docile voters and consumers, all ensconced, falsely content with a comfortable status quo.

Marcuse maintained that in place of politics (or, rather, as a form of unspoken politics), many citizens of developed Western industrial society – regardless of class – become narcissistically invested in their own immediate personal fortunes; preoccupied with keeping up with the neighbours or getting ahead, buying more material goods, knowing the latest fashion, obsessing over gossip, getting their 'share', ultimately thinking of little beyond their own circumscribed lives and family prospects. Sold a dream of individualism, they were caught up, he implied, in groupthink. What troubled Marcuse was how this culture and society corrupted critical intelligence and made real solidarity or opportunities for root-and-branch changes in the basic organisation of society much weaker. He presented a picture in which the existing *form* of the state might ultimately appear to most people as the only conceivable one. In short, as he put it on the opening page of his book, welcome to the 'comfortable, smooth, reasonable, democratic unfreedom [that] prevails in advanced industrial civilization'.[37]

Critics of varying political hues also analysed pervasive form of modern loneliness, the loss of deeper solidarities, of communities, and what was often perceived to be a crisis in family life, as people looked outwards – to the public sphere, the media, etc. Take David Riesman's influential 1950 study, *The Lonely Crowd*. This book also identified the prevalence in modern society of a group psychology based around increasingly strong needs for mutual reassurance and the smoothing-out of conflicts prematurely. Citizens seemed ever more anxiously needy, Riesman thought, to be told by others that everything really and truly is going fine. Often that was – and is – what they are told to expect, or aspire to, as in the standard cheery American greeting 'have a nice day', a reflex exhortation however miserable the circumstances. Riesman was interested in a kind of superficial complacency, and in identifying the gains and losses, the pleasures and pains for the subject in adjusting to a community's unspoken requirements, and in identifying the rote gestures with which we comply. Moreover, *The Lonely Crowd* identified a prevalent 'other-directed' character type. This type was sensitive to the slightest criticism, guided by shallow and immediate communal pressures and allegiances, rather than the deeper 'internal' voices that derived from infancy and childhood experiences of being parented. Many were now too caught up in the surface, busy and alienating social world around them, he argued, and had lost touch with their own emotional and familial depths, or any sense of real, sustaining community. And precisely because of those deprivations, or losses of early attachments, many people had lost their real roots, and were growing ever more 'heavy on harmony'; they seemed to have few occasions for personal assertion or existential escape, or in developing a deeper, more authentic, psychic interior.

Such analyses thus invited discussion of selfhood: what it means to acquire personality, what is essential to our human condition, how far each subject is shaped or even constituted in the first place by language and society. In France during the 1960s, within a different theoretical framework, combining certain ideas from Marxism and Lacanian thought, the political philosopher Louis Althusser was producing his own influential analyses of what he called 'ideological state apparatuses'. He was intent upon showing how these operated beyond the obvious brute power of the state (police, army, etc.) to fashion the subject and sustain a particular social order. The apparatus included schools and universities; he wanted to show how we are brought into being, called (or 'interpolated') as subjects. Althusser sought to analyse how we are summoned, and how our very subject positions come to be installed within.[38] You cannot avoid it entirely, just as you may not be able to avoid turning your head when someone shouts out suddenly 'hey you!'. Interpolation, however, mostly happens invisibly; you do not realise you are being summoned at all. Theorists such as Althusser and Marcuse had something in common, even though their models and styles of writing were so notably different: an insistence that our identities, as people and as citizens of a nation, should never be taken for granted, treated as somehow 'givens'. So much that we take to be natural is acquired. To read Althusser is to wonder how 'I' came to be in the first place: to feel more unsure of 'myself' as someone who always existed, a person, somehow always there prior to my being called, inscribed in a language, an order, a system.

Marcuse influenced large numbers of readers in the 1960s 'counterculture' and after, inviting them to find a more three-dimensional life and recognise how compliance and orthodoxy were drummed into people through social arrangements of every kind. He wrote that modern societies, such as the United States, encouraged this continuing synchronisation, so that people come, as he put it, to 'love and hate what others love and hate'. In our working lives too we may easily accept the governing order of things, rather than test or protest presuppositions. Trade unions were not exempt from his political scorn; they often defended arrangements that were corrupt in practice, or unquestioningly assumed the current dispensation – even the military–industrial complex in which so many workers had jobs. Capital and labour then become complicit with each other in groupthink; they could end up equally committed to promoting the interests of profitable business or, for instance, the vast national defence system, and appear incapable of thinking and protesting more fundamentally about this frame of reference. The union boss and the company boss, as Marcuse described, might unite in their common lobbying of the government for a larger number of missile contracts (a bigger slice of that defence budget), without any more fundamental interrogation of the entire framework.[39]

Marcuse, even more than Fromm and Adorno, was to become an influential intellectual figure, indeed, for many, in the United States and elsewhere, a must-read author and political icon. All three were part of a network of critical philosophers and researchers, sympathetic to the Left. This school of thought first developed in Germany. It was based originally around an Institute for Social Research in Frankfurt, founded in 1923. The grouping would come to be widely known as the Frankfurt School. A common element was the endeavour to analyse contemporary social developments, and to explore mundane routines and violent passions driving contemporary politics. Members of this school sought to create new tools of critical analysis, to combine elements of Marxism, psychoanalysis and social science research, and to understand what drew so many to fascism and Nazism. These researchers wanted to understand, as best they could, the sources of contemporary mass attitudes, a form of irrationality, or warped rationality, and to consider the nature of the drives, relationships and influences at work. They wondered about unconscious shared beliefs and fantasies in social movements; the forces that threatened to engulf reason, or perhaps to channel instrumentalised reason, notions of efficiency and purity, or even science, for the most destructive and crazed ends. As Jews and/or as Leftist intellectuals, they had to flee Nazi Germany in the 1930s to save their own lives. In the United States they took some care, given the political climate, not to be easily branded as Marxists, let alone active revolutionary agitators, but continued their studies of the social, political and psychological determinants of fascism in Europe, and also of social conformity and the 'authoritarian personality' type, who might exist even in a prospering liberal democracy such as the United States.[40]

Theodor Adorno was especially interested in what Freud had had to say about unconscious factors that held groups together in shared identifications or unspoken pacts. Freud's writings about identification, projection and the superego provided important ideas in his own body of work. Adorno and his close colleagues in the Frankfurt School were mindful of the political extremes, above all the fascist extremes, but also of anodyne public opinions in the often uncontested liberal 'centre'. They went in search of the underlying beliefs that shaped those surface expressions of popular opinion and choice. Culture, they argued, was itself an industry that fashioned society, often towards conformity, as could be seen in Hollywood and its studio system.

Adorno was the main guiding intellect behind and co-author of a major study, *The Authoritarian Personality*. The book, first published in 1950, was based on social science research about attitudes to be found among American citizens. This work sought to get behind people's political declarations, and to understand their implicit assumptions and views of the self, the group and society. Adorno also observed how we might identify with a political figure who condensed and displaced a number of incongruous or even antithetical ingredients. A dictator, for example, might both represent for people the acme of power and the figure who promises to tear down a structure of power, a big man and little man, a cruel tribune of law, and the mocking transgressor of the law. Authoritarian personalities, Adorno discovered, often seemed to seek a kind of psychic singularity, even as the actual leader they idealised was a composite fantasy. They felt frightened by ambiguities and complexities, and desirous of rigid rules, covetous of severe punishments for others, and ravenous for an authority to dictate what to do.[41] Adorno and his colleagues sought to pinpoint the underlying tacit beliefs and group-based mindsets, and to show how emotional attitudes are often unconscious in the subject, and how implicit relationships, in the mind, shape more overt political identifications and beliefs. People who lack irony, are intolerant of doubt or prone to project all unwanted elements of the self or the group onto some scapegoated minority would find a leader and party to represent them and to valorise sadistic wishes and some internal requirement for cleanliness, hygiene or absolute 'law and order'.

Adorno and his close ally Max Horkheimer explored political psychopathology and group psychological propensities from many angles. They were interested in, and critical of, the mass appeal of the cinema and the cult of celebrity in the United States. They saw the propensity of vast audiences to 'fall in love' with movie stars or of huge readerships to gawp at tittle-tattle in magazines. They viewed such tendencies as symptoms of modern alienation and ultimately of political exploitation, and were wary of the assumption that increasing social permissiveness in liberal societies would necessarily herald greater political liberation, or usher in more critical intelligence and cultural enlightenment. Rather, such trends could leave people vulnerable to yet more ersatz versions of family, or populist surrogates for that paternal figure.

From the 1930s onwards Adorno had written powerfully and controversially about popular tastes in music; so much modern entertainment, even when revisiting classical themes, or centred on classical music, seemed to him to have become debased and vulgarised. People would go to hear some virtuoso or celebrated conductor presiding over an orchestra, playing some bit of the great repertoire, but really, he thought, they might attend in secret celebration of the fact they were part of a group; as though they marvelled that they could be there at all, and enjoyed experiencing themselves in the act of consuming culture, privileged members of such an audience. As he put it witheringly:

> The consumer is really worshipping the money that he himself has paid for the ticket to the Toscanini concert. He has literally 'made' the success which he reifies and accepts as an objective criterion, without recognizing himself in it. But he has not 'made' it by liking the concert, but rather by buying the ticket.[42]

Critics of their analyses would challenge their patrician and dismissive, or frankly snobbish, accounts of what popular culture could deliver. They accused these high-brow intellectuals of losing track of the contradictions, complexities and emotional richness to be found in mass entertainment.

Adorno and Horkheimer, however, insisted that mass culture could certainly generate supine attitudes, or achieve powerful, more-or-less drugging effects. In a celebrated and controversial chapter (four) of their 1947 work *Dialectic of the Enlightenment*, they condemned a system that churned out such banality; they were concerned by, even rather frowned at, people's enjoyment of popular cinema; for instance, the performances of an actor like Mickey Rooney or of cartoons like Donald Duck. 'By artfully sanctioning the demand for trash, the system inaugurates total harmony,' they said. They noted the conformism of such work: in fact, both consumers and producers, they felt, 'content[ed] themselves with the reproduction of sameness'. 'The defrauded masses today cling to the myth of success still more ardently than the successful ... They insist unwaveringly on the ideology by which they are chained. The pernicious love of the common people for the harm done to them outstrips even the cunning of the authorities.'

Grown-ups were schooled by the media; children were schooled by, of course, schools. So radical intellectuals sought to experiment with schooling too, to theorise its groupthink functions, and to seek to create in place of that apparatus a different approach. A critique of traditional schooling had generated several experimental alternative establishments during the interwar period; these were anti-authoritarian antidotes to the conventional model, including, for example, the co-educational progressive experimental boarding school created in 1926 at Dartington Hall, in the countryside of Devon. Now, again, critiques and experiments emerged, with reformers mindful of the capacity of schools to 'brainwash' and 'condition'. These critiques gained new traction amid the wider swirl of 1960s protest movements.

One strand of this critique especially popular in the 1970s was spearheaded in the United States by another charismatic intellectual, Ivan Illich. He was interested in countering such modes of conformism at the very earliest stages of schooling, and insisted a whole new prescription was needed to restore creativity, respect difference, foster genuine thinking and support individual freedom in society. His proposal was to create a radical project to 'de-school' society, or rather to free children and adults from the illusion that most learning happens in schools, and that learning requires so much cajoling, ranking and manipulation. Illich protested against the way nurseries, schools and colleges established a series of conformist rites of passage. He regarded the US university system as the very nadir of this initiatory system, in place of open education: a conveyor belt that is dull, protracted, expensive and ultimately invites the student to buy into a national myth.

Illich wrote about the huge benefits that might follow for children and adults alike, from the replacement of formal education by new forms of conviviality and lifelong informal learning. Known already for his exposés of modernisation and for his attacks on the corrupting impact of big institutions on creativity, Illich energetically argued for new kinds of 'learning webs'. He also railed against the dead weight of all those people deemed professionals and experts. We needed quite different educators and institutions in future, he argued: indeed, we desperately required more spontaneous formats, and more relaxed and anarchic convenors, to inspire children, students – everyone, in fact – into less deadening competition and more creative thinking and caring approaches. He believed we had to go back to first principles to think about how to think, and to play with how to play; we needed different ways to learn about how to learn; to be more curious about what it means to be curious, achieve things, explore, think and rest. There was something utopian, of course, in his vision, just as there had been in Marx a century earlier when he envisaged a society where, beyond the Revolution, you could entirely transcend narrow specialisation: hunt in the morning, fish in the afternoon, rear cattle in the evening, criticise after dinner, without ever becoming hunter, fisherman, herdsman or critic. However, as with the other varied commentators I have charted in these pages on groupthink, Illich too offered valuable insights; indeed much of this work from the post-war decades about social conformity and the stultification of human creativity and learning still merits, I believe, our reading today.

Admittedly, Illich offered his own questionably upbeat vision of a transcendent future, free of tension and conflict. But he wanted to weaken the modern obsession with diplomas and degrees, stratification and hierarchy, for it just led people to confuse what really mattered; enough with all of these marks and grades, he said in his influential work *Deschooling Society* in the early 1970s. In a stream of publications, he offered such hopeful as well as bracing analyses and warnings of all that is wrong not only with schooling but also with modern medicine, healthcare, policing and welfare. In 1977, he followed up on the de-schooling proposals with an attack on what he called *Disabling Professions*. This, he argued, was the latest version of the terrible organisation-man type of existence that had risen to dominance. Illich took such ideas in a new direction, criticising the way working lives are engineered, a world of mundane pen-pushers and nine-to-five workers who may never really be encouraged to ask the most searching questions or to break ranks with their peers. As Whyte had already warned: '[w]e are not talking about mere instinctive conformity – it is, after all, a perennial failing of mankind. What we are talking about is a rationalized conformity.' Where Whyte and Illich would have agreed was on the need to create new opportunities – everywhere – to free up the mind.

*

We have seen then in this chapter how arguments developed about patterns of group acquiescence and the powers people might also have to be less amenable, or biddable, and to resist. A multiplicity of stories, experiments and analyses about submission and opposition to groupthink arose, from tales of mass brainwashing, to calls for de-schooling. Critique of groupthink in business was matched by explorations of individuality and socialisation through infancy, guides to the tribulations of adolescence, and sympathetic explanations of the dangers of peer pressure. We have noted how groupthink proved a striking if malleable term for people to think with, a buzz phrase with lasting power; it was deployed in diverse kinds of political debate. In 1971, the journal *Psychology Today* elaborated, glossing the word as follows: 'concurrence-seeking', a state that may be 'so dominant in a cohesive in-group that it tends to override realistic appraisal of alternative courses of action'.

But the debate on groupthink was never quite settled, and commentators piled in on both sides with examples of groups that 'dumbed down' people and of groups that could become genuine work alliances, or adventurous, rebellious and even mutinous, thus in defiance of hierarchy and power. Famous novels and movies of the 1950s sometimes used stark settings, as in *Lord of the Flies* (set on an island), *The Caine Mutiny* (far out at sea) and *12 Angry Men* (a room where a jury are isolated to decide a man's fate), to bring such questions about group formations to mass readerships and audiences. They were ways of highlighting the capacity of congregated people to become apathetic, obedient, despairing, casually cruel, or even murderous, with little if any individual thinking occurring; at least until a rebel appears and challenges a fast-congealing orthodoxy. We need groups to achieve social change and to help us to know who we are; and yet shadowy groups, it also appeared, act as part of the reactionary resistance to change, as though internal choruses, harsh judges or shaming communities, looking on askance, inside of our minds.

The critics we have considered seem to concur that groupthink is at its height when all concerned come to believe there is simply no alternative to a given way of operating, and share the same uncontested basic assumptions. Indeed, this condition, it was warned, could equally or even more alarmingly impair decision-making by those in Downing Street, or at the White House.[43] In October 2021, a major report on the government's handling of the pandemic reached for the term as it sought to explain the series of disastrous policies pursued that resulted in very high death rates that year from Covid-19 in the UK, relative to other comparable advanced industrial economies. The cross-party parliamentary committee, tasked with investigating this public health disaster, explicitly used the term groupthink to describe a key factor in all that went wrong in the government presided over by the hapless Boris Johnson.⁴

The word groupthink was often used as the starting point or endnote for investigations of fraught political dramas in the Cold War, where supposedly independent free-thinking elected represent-atives and high-ranking officials proved unwilling, or incapable, of thinking afresh and then standing up for themselves. Instead, they would parrot orthodox views, rehearse dusty guidelines, echo the will of a dominant faction, or resort to stereotypical assumptions about the psychology of the West's opponents (for instance 'the Russians', or 'the Chinese'). In various 1970s sociological and political post-mortems on the Cuban Missile Crisis of 1962, groupthink also featured heavily, with a number of explorations of the mindset of President Kennedy and his brother (the attorney general) as they dealt with conflicting pressures and the hawkish thinking of some of the top military figures who were in the room at the time. Group-think, some argued afterwards, in celebration of JFK's stance, could so easily have prevailed, leading to a calamitous war between the United States and the USSR. Others thought the Kennedys and later Lyndon Johnson were prisoners of groupthink all the same, timidly tied to prevailing centrist, liberal orthodoxies, when far more radical actions were needed, for instance to call a halt to the escalating war in Vietnam, or to take bolder action to challenge the entrenched racial system that operated in the United States.

Conformity among decision-makers in an administration, argued the sociologist Irving Janis, in a notable 1972 book (*Victims of Group-think: A Psychological Study of Foreign-Policy Decisions and Fiascos*), can have disastrous effects on governance, and may well threaten a soci-ety's survival. Groupthink, he showed, distorts decision-making and warps human relationships, leading to the most impoverished and unimaginative, or indeed catastrophic, policy responses in the choppy waters of international diplomacy, and, in fact, in all kinds of crisis-driven management situations. There are simply too many occasions in the real world where stereotypes won't do.[45] If politics is the art of the possible, it is important that those who enter that field have some suppleness of mind and capacity to think on their feet.

Such warnings about the future of the United States, and of the West, contrasted with many other more upbeat accounts of that period; about improving national strength, health and affluence. Electorates in Western countries such as the UK, by the end of the 1950s, had never before 'had it so good', Conservative prime minister Harold MacMillan famously claimed. Much was also said in favour, for instance, of 'company towns' that offered their workers security, and far more than a wage. Some leading firms had developed over decades, or even a whole century, a formula whereby they would provide their staff with a life package that far exceeded a simple employee–employer relationship. Company towns were once remarkable sights to behold and aroused much interest as well as praise. The ethos of such businesses was explicitly designed to shape the employees' thought-world; in short, to be anti-revolutionary, as Frank Trentmann notes in his panoramic history of consumerism, *Empire of Things*. A variety of large 'forward-looking' businesses in twentieth-century America and Europe would thus lay on housing, health, clinics, sport and education, a programme of support for the individual and the family that came to be regarded as 'the price of a loyal, disciplined workforce'.[46]

Hubs for groupthink? Perhaps. But many found much to like and value in that nurturing business operation, in which basic care of the self and the family were assured, and the company did not just treat its employees as brawn or brains. Here was an instance perhaps of the benefits of group membership, or of corporate life, for many favoured workers. The trend towards harmonious, industrial relations and a more extended version of care for workers, in some places at least, was promoted by business owners. Were such deals a way of 'buying off' workforces and taming industrial dissent, or a remarkable gain, a mode of welfare capitalism, with workers exerting their power to bank greater rewards, a forward march of labour? Historians since have looked at how a form of paternalism and traditional conservative values often went together with new kinds of innovative business arrangement and provision of care. The company town and welfare care model in industry has a long history. It was clearly discernible in a cluster of experiments in model villages, towns and co-operatives in the nineteenth century, and in larger industrial organisations by the eve of the twentieth century in Europe.[47] Paternalistic firms, from Cadburys to Siemens, exemplified a form of capitalist welfarism.[48]

In 1940, an American researcher reported how, in Indiana, a company provided a cornucopia of opportunities for intense team-based collaboration, social engagement and communal leisure pursuits; its managers declared candidly that this was a way of ensuring the workers had neither the time nor the energy to be 'subversives'.[49] Critics on the Left challenged any such mood of assurance and docile contentment in this new corporate world. Liberals too, such as Whyte, noted the human price paid in a system of jobs for life, and in a society built around entirely secure, stable vast business enterprises.

To be an employee in a company town in the United States around the middle of the twentieth century – the period when Whyte was a journalist mapping examples of groupthink – could mean the provision of medical facilities; it could also include schooling for children, holiday adventures, day trips at weekends, prizes, picnics and more. Post-war Japanese industry, under American tutelage, would also foster models of team-based working and living, as exemplified in company towns, whose very names were occasionally renamed, hence 'Toyota City' (1959). Some anthropologists and other researchers assumed the Japanese were intrinsically prone to such collective endeavour, and to groupthink.[50]

The dangers of excessive welfare provision, whether provided by the state to all, or by corporations to their own staff, were discussed increasingly on the Right in both the United States and Europe after 1945. The 'welfare state', in places such as Britain, was said by its critics to deaden the mind and disincentivise people, as it offered too much security; so too the hide-bound paternalistic company. Such developments might result in fatal complacency, it was thought, antithetical to future dynamism and growth. This system went together, opponents thus counselled, with a mindset intent upon 'conflict avoidance', all too prone to groupthink. Too much care, and all the overblown bureaucracy needed in order to provide that care, could be damaging; it might ossify beliefs, stifle minds and hold back the entrepreneurial spirit; in short, insulate societies from bracing, maximal competition. Nostalgia and groupthink went together. In Britain, for example, as the century wore on, critical 'audits' of the nation were offered by some historians and political commentators. They suggested that a kind of collective or groupthink illusion had prevailed for decades, so that neither governments nor electorates realised (or wanted to know) how heavily the economy and society were damaged, mired in what came to be known as the politics of 'post-war consensus', and a financial system that was ultimately untenable. People had it too good, and had grown lazy and complacent in the process, they thought. Audits of war and peace alike suggested too much woolly thinking and too many consensual and erroneous assumptions.[51] Fantasy and nostalgia can thus be seen as a form of groupthink, or perhaps even an emotional 'group-feel' condition, afflicting a patrician British elite as much as anyone else; this, it was said, must urgently change.

The 1960s saw challenges to the status quo from many quarters on the Right and on the Left: the civil rights movement and the women's liberation movement changed the political landscape. Challenges to corporate hegemony by trade unions and uprisings across Europe by students and workers were to have many powerful effects. The 1970s brought a number of major shocks to Western economies, giving further momentum to critique of consensus politics, regarded as tepid, muddled and out of date. Such propensities to find the middle ground were dismissed contemptuously as Butskellism, a word that combined the names of moderate Tory and Labour grandees.[52] The compromises made by successive governments with 'union barons' were increasingly heavily criticised from the Right. Combative opponents of such compromises, for instance inside the British Conservative Party, denounced the consensus-seekers as people unwilling or unable to make essential, hard choices; they wanted to challenge the widespread convergent assumptions, or illusions, of the post-war decades that had remained, for them, too long unchecked.

In the end the most effective challenge to that 1970s crisis of economics and politics came from the Right, with supportive intellectuals and front-line politicians arguing for far greater scope for 'free enterprise', an 'open society', an end to 'red tape'; this, they claimed, would end the 'nanny state', the age of deadly groupthink. Led in Britain by Thatcher and in the United States by Reagan, these iconoclasts argued that what was needed was a real and decisive shake-up, and increasingly the handover of power from the state to individuals, to private industrialists and bankers – or, more often in practice, to a world of finance, credit, tax avoidance and outsourcing abroad. They made the case for the unleashing of competition and free markets, likening such processes to nature itself, red in tooth and claw (such Victorian, 'Darwinian' metaphors had never fully gone away). This would come, it was promised, with a far healthier form of mass psychology, acceptance that the future was, in some respects, always unknowable and not to be prescribed by an overweening state: people should not be insulated from choices by controlling government authorities, or by corporations with offers of jobs for life. Thatcher presented herself as a strong leader, able to 'face the facts'. The party she fashioned would be more confrontational and hawkish. It would aggressively challenge the power of trade unions, promise to bring in reforms that would require people to 'stand on their own feet' and end craven unthinking compliance; this added a powerful psychological gloss to increasingly radical Thatcherite economic prescriptions under the banner of 'freedom' as the 1980s wore on.

Reagan and Thatcher drew on a long tradition. Their political revolution had its roots in the work of economists Friedrich Hayek and Milton Friedman, the critique of social planned economies by Ludwig von Mises, the 'open society' of philosopher Karl Popper, and others. Their work was always profoundly shadowed by the extremes of European politics – Nazism in Germany, Stalinism in Russia. They wanted to steer modern societies as far as possible from all that. They also agreed that capitalism advanced through 'creative destruction', as Joseph Schumpeter had suggested. Hayek, author of *The Road to Serfdom*, insisted that the future was bound to be uncertain, and that too much state interference and centralised planning over people's lives was deeply ominous. Hayek's book intimated how easily a mixed economy model and welfare assumptions might constitute steps on the path to a modern tyrannical state. Popper argued in his influential book of the 1940s, *The Open Society and its Enemies*, that Plato had already opened the route towards totalitarian thought, because in *The Republic* he had made the case for censorship of toxic ideas in the name of collective well-being. The open society and open mind were directly comparable; open systems were a requisite for political and psychological health.[53]

Hayek, Popper and some of their colleagues were extremely critical of anything that interfered with individual liberty; they extended the great liberal arguments of the nineteenth century, but now situated such an account in relation to the history of fascism, Stalinism and totalitarianism. These thinkers sought new economic prescriptions and some of them, Hayek most obviously, sought to row back the post-war welfare state, wherever possible, in the name of greater individualism, lower public spending, maximisation of privatisation, and the enshrinement of the 'free market' cast as the antithesis of the monstrous Nazi and Stalinist states.

In fact, many commentators, with varying radical political points of view, on the Left and on the Right, seized on the idea of groupthink to argue that mindless, seemingly innocuous established *consensus* was the greatest danger to the future of liberal democracies, as the century wore to a close. It was a commonplace rhetorical move to imply that groupthink (or other words to the same effect) was relevant, and that this phenomenon was in dire need of overturning now.

Thus when, during the 1980s, Thatcher, by then at the helm of government, made famous the phrase 'there is no alternative', she implied that beliefs from yesterday simply *had to change*, and, moreover, that the path forward – greater individualism, private choice and market-based solutions – was self-evidently clear. Many people believed her, and urged her to go still further. The basic premise continued to hold sway for decades in her own party, and even in the leadership of the Labour Party. Thatcher took it 'as read' that any intelligent, clear-thinking person would be bound to share her fundamental analysis and prescriptions; these apparently brooked no possible logical contradiction; the real argument of politics, economics and history was supposedly now over – other than in some managerial details. Groupthink would be no more. Private enterprise was so obviously better than 'stagnating' nationalised state-run industries, she declared. Conviction politics was proposed as the antidote to weak forms of groupthink.

The individual (free-thinking) consumer, the 'Iron Lady' would argue, was likely to be wiser and more intelligent than the (group-thinking) state in spending all their 'hard-earned' money. The taxpayer, like the consumer, was often invoked as both a discerning critical and righteously angry figure, no longer prepared to see their resources 'wasted' by the profligate, unproductive and creaking old civil service, or those millions of state-employed workers, many of whom were unionised, who claimed to benefit the people at large. Thatcher's endeavours were always divisive but proved popular for a time with large sections of the British electorate. (Her willingness to take the country to war in 1982, to defend the Falkland Islands from Argentina, boosted her poll numbers hugely.) There was much about the political scene, the bureaucracy, the trade unions and the state before she took power that was questionable, or indeed clearly and desperately in need of change. As even some renowned radical historians and left-wing social theorists suggested, 'Thatcherism' was a powerful and persuasive ideology, albeit possessed of its own contradictions, between a wish for a small state, and a concern to ensure powerful defences and law and order. The Marxist historian Eric Hobsbawm believed the stagnating British economy needed 'a kick in the pants', which Thatcher certainly provided.[54]

The collapse of communism in the Soviet Union and its satellite states at the end of the 1980s came as a huge shock to most people, who had assumed the system would endure, albeit feebly, for decades more; it surprised even Western mandarins who hated the communist realm, and pursued policies designed to weaken it. That final collapse came after a decade of heavy losses for the Red Army in Afghanistan (thanks to a Western-backed insurgency against the Soviet occupiers), and in the wake of the calamity of Chernobyl in 1986, when a nuclear reactor exploded due to covered-up design flaws, lunatic, self-serving management and the groupthink of bureaucrats and many, if not all, of the technicians and scientists. Once the Soviet empire was broken, it seemed to many neoliberals and neo-conservatives as though a new golden age had arrived. The message went out from the 'beacon' capitalist economies: open people everywhere to competition, celebrate the individual, get on your bike, participate in the market, buy your shares, own your house (if you could), and spread the Western order by force if necessary. Previously hard-won 'safety nets' were scorned; old values, conventions and laws branded as 'stultifying', whether in the East or the West, thrown on the bonfires, wherever possible, and enshrined in the policies of the International Monetary Fund.

Ironically Thatcher rejected consensus politics, claiming it invited degeneration, yet famously framed her politics as a matter above all else of loyalty to her, acceptance of that new consensus, the doctrine of TINA – There Is No Alternative. Admittedly, she was obliged at times to change tack, but the basic assumption was that her colleagues were either '*one of us*', or the target of withering contempt, 'wets', unworthy of attention, let alone future patronage.

Naomi Klein has well described in her book *The Shock Doctrine* how radical neoliberal policies were rushed in, during and after the 1980s, on the back of natural disasters, or sometimes long-confected accidents-in-the-making, thanks to lack of prior investment. A notorious example was the policy response to the New Orleans floods of 2005.[55] She describes how a form of 'disaster capitalism', inspired by thinkers such as Friedman, gained ground; policy makers, backed by wealthy lobby groups and think tanks, would swoop into afflicted zones of a country to dismantle past systems and unravel past reforms; thus to destroy public schooling in New Orleans and remake the local economy along different lines. The elderly Friedman's 'radical idea', Klein explained, was that instead of spending a portion of money on the existing public system, the government would give people vouchers to spend at charter schools run by private entities. It would supposedly all be to the good and generate a new spirit of individualism and enterprise, leading to higher standards, freeing the education infrastructure from the supposed groupthink mentality and excessively conformist aims that public provision assumed. These ideas were seized on by right-wing think tanks and the Bush administration, and a rapid-fire policy response was developed, turning the city's educational provision into an experimental laboratory. It was the valedictory note from Friedman, an economist who had enjoyed a very long career as a scourge of what he complained was a previously dominant post-war consensus.

The accusation 'groupthink' was deployed as easy insult back then, just as another term of abuse is commonplace today on the Far Right, and especially in conspiracy theory circles: 'sheeple'.[56]

Those critics post-war, such as Whyte, who had first popularised and dissected groupthink, were surely on to something crucially important, and yet, as we have seen in the present study, a challenging word and interesting critique could itself all too easily become a form of rhetorical pressure. The anti-groupthink of today that becomes the groupthink of tomorrow – catch-all diagnoses, hackneyed slogans and corrupted ideas, serving ulterior purposes. There are books today, for instance, suggesting that scientific concern about the climate emergency is itself simply a reflection of groupthink. The very accusation groupthink may be used to foster complacency and do-nothing politics, or to shame people into accepting the 'tonic' effects of supposedly inevitable reforms that undermine hard-won rights and social advances.

*

In sum, the story of the invention and rhetorical uses of groupthink is clearly worth revisiting – historically, politically and psychologically. Post-war arguments over the fate of the individual and the collective moved into larger debates about the future of modern societies, and about how democracy on one side, capitalism and corporate governance on the other, might need to be curbed, overthrown or renewed. This term, like 'brainwash', acquired a notable life of its own during and after the 1950s. It provided a starting point for explorations of many things – from the educational system to the corporate boardroom, from childhood alienation and gang culture to the prevalence of racism and sexism, from the mindset of individual voters to the leadership skills required in nuclear stand-offs between the superpowers. It was another vernacular expression that served to explore or sometimes entrench ideologies. We can see how neoliberals invoked the idea to decry the orthodoxies that prevailed beforehand.

To put it another way, this and other key terms from the Cold War highlighted here were exciting to many people because they could be used to show how uncontested values and working practices may be donned as though they are simply nature, or self-evident truth. These banners could be used then, as now, I am suggesting, for progressive or reactionary purposes: invoking the idea of groupthink was a way to prompt the listener to wonder whether they might personally fit that picture and thus need to change themselves into more authentic, free-thinking people. As we will see in the following chapter, anti-groupthink slogans and symbols were also easily co-opted by the advertising industry, as it invited the customer to 'think different'. Being different was just as saleable ultimately as the heavily marketised concern to 'keep up with the Joneses'. Groupthink might be used as an insult, or to generate unease, and facilitate the question (a good question) – how free are you *really* to think your own thoughts, even in so-called lands of the free? What is your scope for thinking *and* acting, other than the way you do, within your own community, company or institution?

In the fractious and divisive conditions that pertain in so many countries, including the United States and the UK, in the aftermath of the financial crash of 2008, or in the tumultuous uncertainty of the Covid-19 pandemic (and politics) that emerged in 2020, such 1950s fears about the dangers of middle-ground *consensus* of views may seem strange, even quite antiquated, perhaps. And yet, that earlier critique about people blandly, thoughtlessly 'buying in' still chimes well with concerns we have now about globalised surveillance-based capitalism, a new order of hidden persuaders, and the social media news bubbles and feedback loops that operate. The question is not only does Siri or Alexa do our bidding, or do we serve the technology, and ultimately the advertising industry that harvests the data we feed into our devices; it is also: how are we swayed by our peers? The waves of influence may seem to be directed from 'the top', but can also crash on us sideways, from every direction as well. Facebook, for example, can be both a vast open noticeboard for popular messages, chat, expression, and also an organising matrix that is hard to escape.

As the American philosopher of science Thomas Kuhn argued in the early 1960s, we are not even necessarily aware that we operate our various experiments in life (or in the case of scientists, in labs) within 'paradigms'. Certain ways of seeing, conventions of knowing, methods of posing and answering questions about our own lives, appear to make complete sense in a given community, while others simply don't feature at all, left invisible or entirely unthinkable. Moreover, as psychologists have amply explained, all of us – in infancy, while growing up and when enjoying so-called adult maturity – learn, absorb and respond to dozens of cues, sensitive to continual steers and prompts; from our families, friends, colleagues, teachers and employers, and, of course, also from advertisers.

PART 5

THE HIDDEN PERSUADERS

In 1942, the political economist Joseph Schumpeter warned that rational argument is mostly eclipsed, in modern life, by a barrage of advertising, a political reality whereby, as he put it, 'direct attacks upon the subconscious' are at work.

It is instructive to look at advertising, Schumpeter showed, because it illustrates a broader problem: how political messages exploit emotions and unconscious thoughts in ways that are often not visible to the public. He then added (sounding here a little like Freud) that these crafted messages might 'crystallize pleasant associations of an entirely extra-rational [kind] [and] very frequently of a sexual nature'. The success of advertising demonstrated, in his view, that much of our decision-making in politics is irrational and shaped by unconscious wishes and fears. It is an illusion to assume that masses of people vote, any more than they purchase, in a carefully delibera-tive manner; Schumpeter believed it crucial to understand how then the process is managed:

> Party and machine politicians are simply the response to the fact that the electoral mass is incapable of action other than a stampede, and they constitute an attempt to regulate political competition exactly similar to the corresponding practices of a trade association. The psycho-technics of party management and party advertising, slogans and marching tunes, are not acces-sories. They are of the essence of politics.[1]

Modern societies, warned Schumpeter, are dominated by such 'psycho-technics'. Democracy, he submitted, is not all it is cracked up to be. The electorate might not even know about the policies that will be implemented, thanks to their votes, or understand the real intentions of the parties or representatives to whom they give their support. The voters in one sense hold sway, but he thought that they do not determine the stuff that really matters in government: the important business is organised behind the scenes. The system, in short, is heavily manipulated. It is run by a political class, with no small help from advertisers, who assist by creating emotive messages, vague platitudes, nebulous visions, that people sign up to.

In the 1950s and 60s, several prominent critical commentators, looking at developments in contemporary capitalist societies, while still mulling over the calamity of interwar fascism and Nazism, would take up such concerns and focus on this *hidden* dimension in modern advertising. They also wanted to show how culture, politics and selling were ever more entwined. The advertising industry, they complained, promoted consumerist values, distorted rational thinking and affected the way other sectors of the economy and society functioned. This choreographing of life through advertising culture might be leading, they thought, towards a stage-managed simulacrum of democracy.

In short, these critics pointed out how this kind of craft was designed to pander to people's feelings and their most restless desires; and how advertising could prove so massively distorting to the way we live and think now, and to the social fabric that sustains us. Moreover, advertising seemed to be part and parcel of an economy built upon deliberate waste and obsolescence. They anticipated later fears that modern economies were ultimately unsustainable, damaging to human nature and to the world.

A longer story no doubt could have been told in these pages, about mass influence, conditioning and hidden persuasion, in democracies, autocracies, republics, tyrannies and empires; a chronicle stretching over the *longue durée*, and featuring examples of the underhand selling of wares, the predicament of gullible purchasers and the destructive effects of unbridled consumption, across different phases of history. Ancient storytellers recounted disasters that came in the tracks of bellicose propaganda; calamities triggered by interpersonal misunderstandings, costly misjudgements, made on the basis of sinewy rhetoric. Folklore provides stories of people who imbibe toxic gifts that then cause them to slumber, that paralyse their capacity for appropriate action or thinking. Seemingly innocuous offers from ambiguous hosts to their guests to consume a particular substance, we know, can take people down a terrible, life-changing path. We talk of food for thought, but there is also much said, in legend and litera-ture, about food and drink that corrupts thought, and poisons that masquerade as remedies. Perhaps, if we had pursued such a route, we might even have begun this chronicle with interpretations of the story of Adam, Eve and the serpent. In fact, the story of the Fall was revisited (under the intentionally provocative heading, 'Persuasion Started with Eve') by one of the most controversial figures in post-war advertising, Ernest Dichter.[2]

We will not be tempted further down that path, however; nor dwell long upon Victorian and Edwardian stories about the intoxicat-ing rise of modern advertising. In his popular fiction, H. G. Wells, for instance, had already addressed, as the historian Anat Rosen-berg recently put it, how 'adverts had that seemingly magical power to transport readers to worlds otherwise unknown'.[3] H. G. Wells described that sense of transportation effectively in his 1909 novel *Tono-Bungay*; he chronicled the rise and fall of a quack brand of medicine, using it as a means to explore the frenzied nature of con-temporary society, a world where people are caught in the grip of merchandising, promotion and hype.

Rather, here, we will address ideas about advertising and post-war Western subjects; consumers who were seen in the context of new forms of psychological warfare, mass conversions and brainwashing. Critics now frequently warned how we are all vulnerable to ad land. Schumpeter was but one of several notable commentators to set the scene, showing how advertising is integrated into the economy, society and political life.

Advertising firms reached new heights of public prominence in the 1950s and 60s. These businesses made cultural waves, drawing people in and, as the critics complained, making a mockery of the idea that voters really decide for themselves through untainted information. Rather than capitalism as the midwife to a more disen-chanted and rationalistic kind of society, what was happening, they feared, was the installation of a system that was ever more seductive, clandestine and deceptive.

Researchers studied the changing methods and effects of the advertisers; the ways in which people can be derailed, and drawn, this way or that, into a domain where material things are infused with fantasies. Some writers also considered the larger systems and structures of which the advertising industry was now an integral part.

They wrote with a notable sense of urgency, as though desperate to counter the otherwise irrepressible expansion of 'Madison Avenue' (i.e. the Manhattan location of so many advertising HQs, the place that has become a kind of shorthand for the whole industry). The public, it seemed, had to be woken from this state of subjection, helped out of their complacency, or torpor, through detailed analysis of the underhand processes; people needed to be armed intellectually, given a crash course in order to understand the panoply of new methods that were being amassed to undermine their capacities, to learn the array of psychological ploys now routinely adopted to hold them in thrall.

This and the following, final chapter are in part historical, part contemporary analysis, and part reflection upon the litany of warnings (some plausible, others overblown) provided by that chorus of pundits, polemicists, critics and advocates, regarding the power of advertising in modern life. I want to consider here those ideas and arguments, which gained such prominence in the 1950s and 60s, and that provide foundations for so much of our current discourse and shared anxieties about the state of the world and the future of liberal democracy. The post-war literature highlighted the risks we can face of flight into manic unreality, a state of escapism, or of tipping from realistic vigilance about dark forces of persuasion into a more despairing and/or paranoid mode of thought. A lesson we need to take from classic works about advertising in the period after 1945 is surely that the road ahead – in the online marketplace – *could* be still worse than it is in the present. Not that it must inevitably be worse; the future is open and contestable, potentially changeable from its seemingly relentless course. Whatever the power of the hidden persuaders, we still have existential choices to make. But to say that dramatic reforms, even revolutionary steps, are possible is not to underplay the massive difficulties of effecting progressive changes; nor is it to deny the fact that none of us can be sure quite what the future will hold.

Like many worried observers of the online economy today, that first post-war generation of critical analysts were not always sure to what extent corporate capitalism and the advertising culture that sells this vision of capitalism could be resisted or overturned. They showed how far the craft of hidden persuasion, and the exploitation of human emotions and addictions, had developed, and sought to explain how an increasingly seamless system now worked. They wanted to expose how ideas drawn from behaviourism, mathematics, statistics, psychoanalysis, group psychology, anthropology, neuroscience and even surrealist art were being channelled into the great maw of the advertising industry. One direction possible in such analyses was to urge more protest and challenge, or even to advocate direct actions of non-compliance with the extant market by people acting in concert. Another option, perhaps, either admiringly or with a sad shake of the head, was to insist that capitalism constituted an unstoppable steamroller.

Either way, the post-war advertising industry, as some of these critics counselled (in my view convincingly), was not just in the business of selling products, but often showcasing a whole way of life built around increasing consumption. It so often traded, they complained, in glamourised images, sentimentalism and phony equations of happiness and material acquisition. Advertisers were also often commissioned to foster the brand of a political party, even to shift the images evoked by a nation; to cultivate a sense of belonging, or to recast the connotations of some foreign marketplace we might want to visit or trade with. Commercial campaigns might be used to engender admiration and confidence in certain products, or classes of products, associated with the nation: American jeans, French perfume, German engineering, Italian design, Swedish furniture, and so on. Of course, there had, usually, to be some material basis on which to brand a people, an industry, a product, for the promotion to work effectively; after all, you needed actual sunshine and sand if you were to sell millions the idea of a holiday of a lifetime, via mass travel to beaches abroad.

Several things pinpointed in that post-war literature are apparent to most consumers today, regardless of whether they have read any of those old exposés: capitalist societies are saturated with commercials; these are drummed into our minds, and relayed incessantly into workplaces, homes and streetscapes. They tend to work on our emotions, not just our reason. Advertising has moved with the times, responding to, and reshaping, the digital revolution. That does not mean that we are simply consumers, nor are we exclusively sponges for targeted works of persuasion; nor does it imply that all advertising is equally numbing, objectionable or morally toxic. Discriminations are required between different styles of campaigning, selling, notifying, promoting, etc.

The first commercial messages on radio are usually traced back to 1920; on television to 1941 – in both cases the first use was to be found in the United States. But on both sides of the Atlantic, the 1950s were a big turning point, the decade when large numbers felt the full impact of 'the box' as a means of disseminating news, entertainment and publicity. TV was able to transmit little films – commercials – to Western populations with rising spending power, for the accumulation of goods and services way beyond the requirements of mere subsistence.

Messages broadcast into the homes of mass audiences about what to buy, and advice on how to live well, or whom to vote for, might be transmitted nationwide, or conversely targeted at people within niche social groups, age brackets or regions. It may seem unnecessary to spell all this out, for such features of daily life are, at least in a society such as my own, an assumed fact of existence today, both online and off.

Advertising skills were used then, as now, to refine and distribute civic as well as commercial advice. Sometimes adverts tell an intriguing story in miniature, or impart a useful lesson, for instance about what it means to be a good parent or child, only subtly adding as an apparent afterthought: this product will help. By the end of the 1950s, as exposés of advertising intensified, such commercial messaging in the mass media was ever more closely woven into the fabric of life in many societies.

And yet, while critical exposés of the communist world made no bones about labelling national strategies of communication as propaganda, much commentary about advertising in the West shied away from that term. Advertising in capitalist societies was, after all, far more disparate and diffuse than that to be found in the Soviet Union; it could serve benign or malign social ends, and it emanated mostly from a galaxy of private businesses, rather than directly from the state.

Young people today may feel they live in a very different world to the one in which their parents or grandparents grew up, where they enjoyed good prospects, perhaps, of long-term jobs and predictable hours, and, most likely, sat down each evening across the land to watch the same shows. Each nation's history of TV expansion and programme consumption is different in small or large degrees; but in Britain, to take one example, the venerable BBC faced, from 1955, a terrestrial commercial rival, ITV. By the 1960s the latter attracted about half of the total audience.[4] On that service, programmes were not paid for by compulsory licence fee or general taxation; rather they were regularly interrupted by ads.

In many Western states, the 1950s and 60s brought new forms of legal protection for buyers. The idea was to give the consumer greater confidence so that they could watch, and purchase, with safety, knowing the state's monitoring agencies or at least consumer organisations might save them from the worst excesses. Films continued to be classified, TV output scrutinised, advertising regulated, laws for consumer protection substantially bolstered. So, there was a tug of war between those wanting unfettered freedom to sell, and those in the business of policing mis-selling. If you could not have all the glittering goods that you witnessed in the great churn of movies, you could at least identify with the stars, the jet set or even the secret agents such as James Bond (whose movie career, soon a franchise, began at the start of the 1960s), who appeared to have it all, enjoying their savoir faire, cars, gadgets, travel and sex appeal. And should you seek to emulate all that luxury living, book that fancy hotel, take a flight or purchase a dazzling car, based on the promotions that you'd seen, you might hope that consumer bodies would be there, if you were lucky, to save you from being 'ripped off' (a phrase first popularised at the end of the 1960s).

For those who wanted to do their own research into the quality, price and durability of merchandise, from kettles to lipsticks to trucks, consumer organisations and watchdogs were there, in some countries at least, to provide a source of *reliable* and objective information, in contrast to the 'castles in the air', which bad operators might wish to sell them. In Britain, *Which?* made its first appearance in 1957: this magazine aimed to help consumers (perhaps principally from the middle class) make informed choices, as it were to stage a fightback against those tempting calls to part with their money or to obtain some must-have item on tick. A network of Citizens Advice Bureaus, formally created in the UK in 1939, and offering confidential advice on legal, housing, financial, consumer and other issues, would become a familiar resource on many high streets, in the decades after the war.

In other countries too, consumers were reminded to understand their vulnerabilities, as well as entitlements and motivations, or even to grasp the way they were now being solicited by businesses as an army of, precisely, *consumers*. Each purchaser, so the extensive advice literature explained, had considerable power, not only to complain, demand refunds, or to feed critical suggestions back to companies, but also to act together, as one, through new kinds of pressure groups to fight for the shopper. The public was thus reminded that it was far more porous and suggestible than it may have previously realised, and more potent than it might think.

The consumer protection movement had its origins in the 1900s, and a framework of legal safeguards, advice manuals and organisations had spread internationally since then, but the 1950s and 60s saw the widespread roll-out of new consumer groupings and further legal protections. So, when the Consumer Federation of America was created in 1968, it was putting the seal on developments in public protection that had been afoot, in many places, for a considerable time.[5] Thus advertising, in the post-war era, was not in fact simply a free-for-all. Just as the Wild West of nineteenth-century commercial salesmanship had been gradually tamed (so that, for instance, dangerous 'medicines' could not simply be flogged with complete impunity by quacks, who claimed to be doctors, to all comers), post-war citizens of Western societies came to be offered, and perhaps even to expect, certain *standards* of advertising and codes of accountability, at least on the main terrestrial TV channels, radio, cinema or in the mainstream press.

However, it is always a moot point who sets the standards, and whether it's a winning or losing battle to enforce them. Commentators on radio in the 1930s in the United States (precursors of later inflammatory right-wing 'shock jocks') had been free enough, after all, to peddle anti-Semitism, praise the Nazi pursuit of full employment and racial purity, invite fellow Americans to recognise the achievements of Mussolini, and question the 'anarchy' of democracy. An example was Charles Edward Coughlin (known to millions as 'Father Coughlin', or 'the Radio Priest'), who broadcast weekly in the decade before the Second World War, and gained vast audiences, disseminating increasingly brazen anti-Semitic messages. He even defended *Kristallnacht* ('The Night of Broken Glass', when German paramilitaries and civilians murdered close to a hundred people, and ransacked thousands of Jewish homes, business and other buildings in 1938), as understandable retaliation against the 'provocative' Jews.

In politics, as in commerce, setting standards of conduct and probity could easily seem like a losing game. Certainly, to revisit now the content of TV shows and accompanying advertisements of forty or sixty years ago in the UK is to encounter a culture, and evidently a regulatory system, awash with stereotypes about race, class, sexuality, gender, disability and age.

Advertisers needed not only to follow regulatory guidelines but also to assess the ethos of the company they were representing, opined David Ogilvy, perhaps the most revered of all ad executives post-war. The advertising agency should never get in the way of the crucial message; it was not about selling the agencies, but rather about mounting a brilliant and credible campaign on behalf of a client, he said.[6] Ogilvy had a certain respect for the faculties of the consumer. He was always looking for the edge, the unique selling point that could be turned into the pithiest stories or slogans, without descending into blather and hype the consumer would easily see through.

Ogilvy's agency was vociferously out there in the marketplace, making its presence felt during those booming decades; using artwork, commercial experience and detailed consumer research to underpin campaigns, showing how human behaviour could be coaxed, or even recast. His and other expanding agencies would trumpet (or maybe just include more discreetly, to show greater suavity) their company name, promote the status of their managers and the brilliance of their designers, artists and technical, back-room staff. Thus, advertising sold itself, increasingly, and often openly, in the public domain, certainly within the business world, as a powerhouse that was worth every penny of those fees. The post-war decades were, indeed, frothy times in ad land.

While Britain had its fair share of experts, the United States provided the greatest land of opportunity. A swelling workforce of copywriters, art directors, consumer psychologists, market researchers, public relations specialists, communication strategists, statisticians, data analysts, image consultants and commercial artists would contribute to the advance of the industry. Soon computer engineers and spin doctors (although the latter would not have known themselves yet by that term, in fact coined in the 1980s) would become significant figures too.

The sheer reach of advertising should not be underestimated. The industry spread its influence into the academy, culture and politics; this was so not just in the sense of advertising the wares of universities, movies, political parties and candidates, but through assumptions about the importance of market share, constant promotions, responsiveness to consumer reactions, clear branding, and so on. Advertising also would bring growing public interest in how the various players in the advertising industry were performing relative to one another. Advertising told many stories, but the story of advertising itself was also increasingly prominent, part of economic life and daily news; and the greatest campaigns were also awarded a range of publicised industry prizes.[7]

Many academic researchers therefore turned their attention to studying the advertising industry. New courses emerged in the 1960s and after, at more innovative universities, on film, mass media and the history of marketing. Luminaries, such as the Canadian philosopher Marshall McLuhan, became internationally famous as much for their intriguing epithets and snappy book titles as for the content of their writing about the mass media. It was good, he realised – if books were to sell – to have quirky titles to catch attention: *The Mechanical Bride*, *The Gutenberg Galaxy*, *The Global Village* and 'the medium is the message' are all among the arresting phrases coined by him in the 1950s and 60s.

Students might be alarmed, or relieved, to be provided with such critical lenses, but alternatively they could also use their reading about mass media phenomena to join in themselves on the great and growing bandwagon of advertising, marketing and PR. Thus, no shortage of Oxbridge and Ivy League graduates, who might previously have opted for other kinds of high-status careers, e.g. the civil service or law, came to weigh up the relative prospects of the City of London, Wall Street, Hollywood, TV, or alternatively perhaps a niche at an advertising agency, one of the public relations firms or opinion polling organisations. Advertising culture, with all that sense of dynamism, rivalry, creative fizz and power, was bound up with the American century, and with Western liberal values.

One of the most famous innovators in this new dream (and nightmare) factory of post-war ad land was the psychologist Ernest Dichter. He pioneered, and promoted, a particular approach under the shorthand of Motivational Research (hereafter MR). He claimed that this was a major advance on what went before. Indeed, it might just as easily serve the public good (in contriving the most effective information initiatives) as cater to the interests of private businesses or political parties. MR, Dichter explained, was a set of psychological techniques designed to glean people's attitudes, *in depth*. Dichter hailed originally from Vienna but moved in the 1930s to the United States, where he enjoyed a most successful business career. His surname in German also means poet, but in the New World he was far from that, and represented a new kind of commercial 'strategist of desire', as he put it. The Viennese connection was marketable for him, thanks to the city's association with the founding of psychoanalysis, as it had been some years previously for Freud's nephew and pioneer of the public relations industry, Edward Bernays (about whom more later), whose family had moved from Europe to the United States when he was young.

Dichter designed projects to discover and then take advantage of psychological knowledge, feeding his work to the agencies or to corporations, who then developed, sometimes in partnership with him, the campaigns. He offered his own rather self-congratulatory commentary on this work in various books, articles and media appearances, drawing attention to how businesses in the United States and beyond called on his services.[8] The future of the advertising business, he explained, was all about discovering people's real preoccupations, wishes and fantasy lives, taking proper account of their moods, sensations, revulsions and passions. He promised to deliver profitably that strategy of desire; and he sold MR as hard as he could, while seeking also to explain some of it publicly. So, MR was at one level commercially sensitive, but also a kind of open secret, even something to celebrate.

He founded an institute in New York State in 1946. It provided a base from which to pursue his commercial research and produce reports for clients.[9] He promised to disclose and study thoughts and emotions stirred by products and services, and then to make recommendations for new approaches to selling; he could advise on the big picture and on the details. Catchphrases, sounds, colours and backgrounds – in short, the whole advertising package – had to be assembled carefully. Dichter made great use of interviews and focus groups, establishing an approach commonplace today. He was not alone in doing so but he was especially energetic in amassing such

research and then exploiting it effectively. He would use a loosely
Freudian theory of the mind as he interpreted the data. Perhaps it
was not a unique selling point, but certainly it was one he was able
to market effectively. Hence the disparaging but also perhaps half-
admiring references made about him and his method by his peers and
critics: Dichter as a commercial shrink, a psychological guru, Freud
for the supermarket age; MR as a form of 'mass psychoanalysis'.[10]
Dichter's premise was that much of our mental life is hidden from
ourselves, and not just from other people.

Few would argue now with the basic claim made by Dichter, as
well as by Ogilvy, that advertising can affect us emotionally, sometimes unconsciously, and that it may be used for benign, innocuous or
sinister ends. These days the government in the UK, as in many other
countries, routinely uses adverts to try to change attitudes that might
be harmful to public health. Some of this is orchestrated through the
Behavioural Insights Team, also known as the Nudge Unit. Communications strategies, for better or worse, have been crafted to affect
how we choose to distance from other people, or view vaccination
programmes, to beat back the spikes in Covid-19 transmission rates.
Although, of course, such oversight can backfire, and offer fuel to
the blaze of conspiracy theories about vaccination programmes, etc.

Governments often use techniques that are not unlike MR,
perhaps to save us from our own follies, as in the 'clunk click, every
trip' seat belt campaigns in Britain from 1970 onwards. These days
most of us perhaps take that kind of advertising 'for our own good'
for granted. We may applaud effective campaigns, seemingly simple,
but often the product of much labour, designed to assist us to choose
to avoid drinking and driving, pick up litter, forgo dangerous drugs,
wear masks, or use condoms and practise 'safe sex' (a phrase first
popularised in face of HIV/AIDS). The advertising business can be
channelled for public health purposes just as easily as it can be used
to invite us to party, throw out last year's wardrobe or fly to the other
side of the world; either way it draws on a battery of techniques,
some long established, others evolving with each passing year.

Advocates of the ad industry claimed, post-war, that far from
taking away power from the people, commercials could in fact endow
consumers with greater personal sovereignty than ever before.[11]
Indignant supporters of advertising increasingly strongly demanded
by the late 1950s that Madison Avenue should step up and launch an

upbeat campaign to defend the whole enterprise on grounds of social utility, and to celebrate those untold arts of selling; stress the positive ethical values of the best companies, and underline their contribution to the public good. They sought to reinstate this virtuous picture, in the face of sometimes very bad press about ad land's economies with the truth, nebulous promises or outright lying. The American Advertising Federation (AAF) created an education arm to provide materials in schools and colleges to reverse dire narratives from critics about their work, and to insist on the value, even nobility, of this field. The AAF showcased their crucial achievements in sustaining and expanding an information-hungry society and in supporting a modern economy.[12] Advertising, it was thus promised, could feed the soul, strengthen the body; educate, edify and nourish, in many ways.

As an example, let us look at the story of the humble prune. In its very banality, the prune campaign illustrates Dichter's behind-the-scenes influence on companies and on whole markets, as well as the upbeat claims once made about MR and how it could help us live better and longer, while expanding a market.

Why did prunes matter, and why were they ripe for the post-war MR treatment? At the time, California had a huge share of the global prune market (and in fact still enjoys a strong position).[13] But it had an image problem. Dichter was first called in by the California Prune Board in 1952, and quickly realised from the customer surveys he conducted that he had a challenging task on his hands.[14]

The problem was that even if the product might be good for people, or at least not especially harmful, so long as not taken to excess, there were extreme popular subconscious resistances to the prune.[15] The product, he found, 'was *ridden* with meanings, all unfortunate'.[16] It needed a more joyful, if not actually sexy, make-over. Prunes, he found, brought to many people's minds such images (or rather prejudices) as 'old maids'; they also evoked, apparently, a world of dreary 1950s boarding houses; and most of all constipation, and thus faeces. He was not squeamish about explaining the bodily aversions and disturbances generated by products in the minds of consumers.

Dichter's research led him to note the following: the product suggested dried-up skin, dank pools, sinister swamps and even certain shudder-inducing memories of being controlled in childhood, recollections of commands like 'eat up, or else!', i.e. associations with being small and at the mercy of controlling parents or haranguing teachers. Prunes seemed to be associated for some with being in the highchair, or stuck, helpless, on the potty. And the fruits might even, apparently, arouse unwanted images of a frightening witch. It sounded rather redolent of *The Wizard of Oz*. Prunes were a year-round tinned or packaged good, and thus seemed *unseasonal*. Worse, they connoted the prestige-free, the undifferentiated, and even, apparently, 'socially undesirable … queer, ungiving people'.[17] So if a container of prunes appeared in the customer's sight at the supermarket, or if a shop assistant at the deli dared to suggest them, the unspoken response, Dichter 'discovered', might well be, 'No, I don't want the laxative you are trying to thrust upon me.'[18]

Dichter's work on behalf of this product was a salutary example of what could be done, and of the limits of selling and advertising; one classic ad from 1958, entitled 'Let's Have a Prune Party', was designed to tug directly at the heartstrings of mothers. The prune is placed in the scene of a little party involving four lively and radiant white children.[19] A couple of smart, well-dressed small girls flank two spick-and-span little boys; they are at a table wearing festive hats; the girls pulling open crackers, the boys eating cakes, topped with … prunes. The ad shows they are truly good, wholesome and easily palatable; the accompanying text proclaims, 'Just yummy, Mummy!' She is addressed by the message, with the suggestion, 'win their hearts with prune tarts'. For good measure it is pointed out that this product is 'fairly bursting with energy, iron, vitamins and minerals'.[20]

Dichter and his fellow professionals went even further, however. They sought to recast the product as a 'wonder fruit', a delightful *and* good-for-you sun-drenched *sweet*. Instead of floating in repugnant brown fluid, inside an open can, the product was thereafter to be featured outside of the tin, witnessed in settings outdoors, directly associated with images of whiteness, linked to youth and hedonism; for example, shown amid radiant women wearing vibrant colours, or in the hands of young girls wearing little at all; just there with the prune, consumed out in the sun. They would be pictured at the very moment of eating, acting a kind of rapture at the product's deliciousness, depicted now holding the food right up to their mouths.

Dichter wanted to make the prune more interesting, bright, ripe and attractive – appealing in itself and, especially, attractive to *her*. The prune should appear in scenes of people figure skating or playing tennis, he advised. And instead of suggesting it was created through the extraction of moisture, it would be better, he proposed, to focus publicity upon how the product was made through the concentrated capture of sunlight. Prunes should be viewed as loaded with 'light' and 'energy' – *value added* – not some withered sack, *all about minuses*. The prune was in fact 'bursting' with solar power. Print, radio ads and TV commercials were deployed in concerted attempts to banish associations in the public mind to the sad, the wrinkled, the dry and the dead.[21]

The task, for MR, clearly, was to get people involved in a different kind of *story* about such 'difficult' commodities. However transient the scene, however fleeting the image, daydreams could be encouraged, a tempting invitation created. Ads might suggest where the product could take you: it would be designed to offer some promise of movement, of body and mind, a hint that this product might lead the purchaser onwards, to some better, more intense or more exquisite, experience.

What can be seen in the 1950s critical literature about such campaigns is not just a restatement of earlier warnings about mass psychology, alienation or exploitation, but a discourse about the mind-manipulation risks we face routinely, within a form of modern, corporate capitalism, a world that harnesses concerted forms of media, and the power of the human sciences and arts in crafted campaigns. Specific, and seemingly innocuous, examples, such as prunes, pointed to a larger truth: how much money and expertise can lie behind the selling of everyday items, or rather the promotion of unrealisable desires; how we are invited to dream, to associate more wildly, in short to lose our discernment and succumb to unconscious forces, or buy into certain lifestyle stories. Prunes were harmless, but what of the dangers when it came to things such as cigarettes, alcohol, cars, gambling; and what of the lures of personal debt, as you tried to keep up on big-ticket items? And thus, although the language of both the defenders and opponents of ad land could be lightly satirical, then as now, it could also take on more alarming hues, with comparisons to post-war social conditioning, or even totalitarian brainwashing.

As debate about brainwashing, menticide and groupthink had bubbled away in culture and political thought, so too had warnings about the impact of psychologically sophisticated advertising in ordinary life. Indeed, a variety of intellectuals on the Left, such as

Adorno, who had written critically of Nazi propaganda, were also increasingly focusing upon the nature of commercial persuasion in modern capitalist societies. Even Truman (two-term US president from 1945) protested how advertising could destroy a liberal society *from within*. He was outraged, for example, at how private utility corporations mobilised messages, indeed, he said, indignantly, *propaganda*, to distort mass opinion and undermine government policies.

Such messaging was part of a larger phenomenon. From its inception in the 1940s the Advertising Council in the United States had been instrumental in developing broad campaigns by business leaders to challenge curbs upon corporate freedom, and resist any more serious and effective measures to create a less capitalist-driven form of social democracy. The Council went on to oppose what they regarded as unwarranted extensions of pre-war New Deal policies, in the years after the war. While this organisation supported the Democratic administration's anti-communist foreign policy, and generally agreed to all national security measures, it attacked domestic programmes aimed at restraining free enterprise. It orchestrated so-called public service advertising campaigns during the 1950s, costing millions of dollars, that stressed how the United States was at its best when it created a climate that maximised corporate freedom; apparently a flourishing society required maximum corporate profitability, lower taxes, constant competition. These developments, it was said, would ultimately foster a dynamic, classless, benignly consensual society. The Council disseminated this kind of story through books, articles, pamphlets, movies, billboard posters, radio, TV, comic books, message cards on trains, buses and trolleys, even matchbook covers. It was highly supportive of the Republican Eisenhower's campaign and victory over the Democrats in November 1952.[22]

In a speech to the Electric Consumers Conference in May of that same year, the outgoing Democratic president Truman angrily complained about the amount of money spent by businesses on advertising, or rather on what he regarded as cynical misinformation to thwart his party's urgent political initiatives. He fulminated against those who were 'deliberately and in cold blood setting out to poison the minds of the people. They make no bones about it. Their own manuals say that their purpose is to influence the mass mind in this country by playing on people's emotions.' And this, he complained, is 'nothing less than an attack on the fundamental principles of our democratic country'. As opposed to letting citizens make up their minds, according to evidence, 'this private power company propaganda is deliberately designed to conceal the facts, and to manipulate people's opinions by appealing to their emotions and not to their reason'. Truman even ventured a comparison between the techniques of ruthless companies (and their lobbyists and advertising experts), and the anti-democratic ideologies that the United States stood resolutely against. 'They have taken a leaf right out of the books of Karl Marx and Adolf Hitler,' he thundered. 'They are following the Soviet and the Fascist lines.'[23]

To take another telling, if more obscure, example, consider the report issued by the Medical Officer of Health for Twickenham (London), 1956, headed in glaring capital letters, 'ANY DAY MAY BE BRAIN-WASH DAY'. It contained its own strong cautionary notes about advertising's capacity to distort people's minds and pointed to the interface of business and politics. Like Truman, the doctor referred on the one hand to Cold War brainwashing and terrifying interrogation techniques, and on the other to 'creepy-peepy' researchers who are acting in unconscionable ways to advance the interests of commerce: 'Millions of dollars', the medical officer warned, 'are spent on schemes deliberately and delicately designed to play on the customer's hidden weaknesses, his anxiety, his loneliness, cupidity, and fears.'[24]

Hidden communications strategies were now so state of the art, such commentators warned, as to seriously undermine consumers' and voters' capacity for personal decision-making. The political and economic terrain was far from constant: new industries were developing, cultural attitudes evolving, markets expanding; and advertisers were required all the time to respond to the trends, and maintain and stoke demand.

After the war, conditions of labour, patterns of consumption and relationships between the advertisers and consumers were changing fast. For millions, of course, going to work continued to mean toiling in older established sectors, and for companies that produced raw or finished materials, such as coal or steel. Employment in these advanced industrial economies might well require a person to clock in to a factory that churned out material objects, such as airplanes, cars or cigarettes, or it might still mean toiling on the land. All the same, the scale of office work and new service industries, including so-called 'creative industries', such as media and advertising, were dramatically on the rise in this period. And as societies recovered from the war years, and as economic growth rates continued to rise in the 1950s and after,[25] millions more citizens of the United States and other Western countries found themselves with extra spending money in their pockets, and with an appetite for TV, film, magazines and more. Whatever their basic education, or guile, consumers might be outpaced, and certainly could be vulnerable, as they were now regularly warned, to the messages crafted each day by the 'Madmen' in Madison Avenue and around the world.

True, sales messages did not always work as planned, and nor were such messages all alike. Advertising experts were not in unison, still less were they omniscient or omnipotent. But they did have an enormous *presence*, capturing massive audiences, unleashing a whirl-wind of signs, and releasing an avalanche of stories about how to live a modern, fulfilling life, and what the social and political param-eters were. The advertisers were able to have an influence, as they were quick to insist, even where the viewer's or listener's attention was scant or divided; they might even claim that when prospective purchasers were half-attending, or ignoring the commercials, the message could be exceptionally effective, since information could flow into the mind, or the brain, as it were, without our conscious registering, or at least without full recall.

Long before Facebook and Amazon existed, and we learned of the rise and fall of Cambridge Analytica, critics of advertising were warning the public of where things were heading; how companies and political parties were gaining access to their intimate information, and at the same time modelling and gaming their likely behaviour. These analysts sought to alert the public to how people were tar-geted, and to expose, for their benefit, the ability of corporations to use computer technology, psychology, game theory and other means to help craft their own strategies, and to deploy words, music and pictures most effectively to reach them as voters as well as purchasers, and thus to sway minds.

The writer who most eloquently exposed the dangers of advertising was Vance Packard. His books, such as *The Hidden Persuaders* (1957), *The Naked Society* (1964) and *The People Shapers* (1977), sought to reveal how little the public understood about the sophisticated techniques routinely deployed to invade private life, survey minds, manipulate relationships and influence mass behaviour. He was an acute observer of Madison Avenue and the MR techniques of Dichter. With his withering criticisms and mordant wit, Packard showed how cigarettes, or indeed prunes, were spun into fantasies. He warned that liberty was constantly undermined, even as it was sold as the bedrock of Western societies.

The Hidden Persuaders made an enormous splash and rode high in the best-seller lists. In the book, Packard anticipated many of our later concerns. He showed how advertising might lead people to identify with a product, company or brand without even realising; he exposed how political parties might shepherd the masses, and how covert communications might effectively corrupt democratic elections. Packard's study foresaw how companies might grow ever more adroit at locating and redirecting the most malleable, marginal groups, and expressed indignation at how a well-resourced industry of 'depth probers', as he put it, was on the march, and entering into our very selves. He focused on Dichter as well as several other stand-out examples to illustrate his case. Later commentators built on his critique to analyse more systematically, and with less of this *ad hominem* style of attack, how Madison Avenue was caught up in a larger ideology, selling capitalism, not simply products.

Packard explained the increasing exposure of Americans to hidden persuasion through advancing media technologies. TV alarmed him, as the cinema and radio had troubled earlier critics such as Bernays, and as the internet dismays Packard's successors. Whereas just under 10 per cent of American households owned a television in 1950, nearly 80 per cent did by the time Packard published his book in 1957; by 1960, there were somewhere in the region of 45 million sets, covering around 90 per cent of households across the land.[26]

Packard saw that although you could – in theory – turn the whole thing off, the TV was likely to be left on for much of the time in the home; and he realised how difficult it would be, in practice, to move your eyes away from the constant flow of images. School-age children were especially vulnerable, he felt, and it was important to note how they were subject to this chronic process, as he put it, of 'conditioning youngsters to be loyal enthusiasts of a product'.[27]

In the twenty years following its first appearance, the book sold enormously well, was translated into a dozen languages and remained a frequent subject of debate.[28] Part of the appeal, no doubt, was that *The Hidden Persuaders* promised to fortify readers, to help them resist or outplay the influencers and mind-benders. Better knowledge of advertising techniques, Packard hoped, was the first line of defence; his work invited, indeed urged, the public to get wise to the power of what he accurately insisted was a 'multimillion-dollar industry'.

Dichter merited a good deal of attention in Packard's account. The marketing expert was in his view unabashed about maximising this 'conditioning' approach (even while half-denying it). He was exploiting insights from psychoanalysis that ought, Packard clearly thought, to be devoted to honest research and personal therapy. Techniques mobilised to free up the patient could also be used unethically to loosen up the purchasers, he explained. Clinicians might invite patients to free-associate on couches, for the individual sufferer's ultimate benefit. But Dichter and company were not there for that purpose. Rather they were intent on deploying ideas from the talking cure, relaxing their focus groups, seeking the confidence of these sample publics, inviting free associations, and then using them as the basis to craft messages to lure the flock to the market.

MR experts would apparently listen carefully to everything said, and make interpretations, not to the patient or group, but rather to the corporate client; to note and then exploit the unbuttoned, uncensored, personal thoughts (about the horror of prunes or the erotic associations of a sports car, for instance), and see how all this could be subsequently used. Packard thought that this applied form of clinical knowledge was endangering the public and sullying those scientific professions. These days the same criticism could no doubt be levelled by critics at various behavioural economists, cyber experts, psychologists and neuroscientists who move between the academy, the clinic, the lab, the advertising world, business and government.

Does advertising reflect or transform, understand or pervert human nature? Does it go with the grain of widely shared emotions and desires, or in effect inculcate something new and disturbing? Was Madison Avenue in Packard's own day tuning into the wishes of millions and/or ramping up new kinds of pressure on (especially) women to obsess over the spotless state of their kitchens and bathrooms, stirring guilt, creating obligations, raising the bar on people's anxieties, hopes, rivalries and expectations? *The Hidden Persuaders* suggested the answer was all of these things: the advertising industry, thanks to techniques such as MR, sought to register accurately public interests, feelings of hunger, loneliness or insecurity, but also to encourage new commitments, instil novel cravings and fears, and provoke greater ambitions, in order to bring us into markets. Surely Packard's argument contains an important truth, although many other factors combine to shape social attitudes and individual beliefs; advertising clearly can reflect and help change our inner stories about the worth and purpose of our own lives and evaluations of others.

The issue for Packard was not just whether this or that advertising campaign was directly a semi-fiction or lie. Those who worked in the industry might also be conditioned themselves, he suggested, to become unquestioning contemporary manipulators. He warned how business managers and public relations experts, for example, could easily grow overexcited, lose their own moral compass, forgo their critical judgement or sense of decency, half-brainwashed themselves, mired in the rat race. Those in the trade too often seemed to accept 'the lore of psychiatry and the social sciences', Packard complained, 'indoctrinating themselves' to pursue these approaches, 'to increase their skill at "engineering" our consent to their propositions'.[29] This was to explore a still more disconcerting possibility; of a process that in the end few really wanted, and everybody was affected by, even those who managed the system.

Packard wanted to revive the old Roman warning, *caveat emptor*, buyer beware, and to expose how advertising might mesmerise and disable, if we are not careful, both the professionals and the punters at large. He ended his book with this observation: 'The most serious offense many of the depth manipulators commit, it seems to me, is that they try to invade the privacy of our minds. It is this right to privacy in our minds – privacy to be either rational or irrational – that I believe we must strive to protect.'[30]

The backlash soon followed. Defenders of the advertising industry complained that his book was injudicious; not an academic and balanced account of the span of the work to be found in the field. Nor did it really say enough, they objected, about the varied ethical stances of CEOs, boards, managers and workers in particular companies; rather it was a polemic that singled out the worst examples and spun them to make a good story. His account was deemed partial, gullible, misconceived, populist or even entirely hysterical. Indeed, as soon as its popularity was clear, ad land's supporters used magazines

such as *Printers' Ink* and *Advertising Age* to challenge his concerns as
intellectual (or anti-intellectual) posturing, or to complain the book
was itself a work of self-publicity – against the industry.

Many in the industry would also find themselves *inspired* by
reading *The Hidden Persuaders*. After all, it showed, if nothing else,
quite how much advertising really could achieve. It is also striking
that the critical popular literature and increasingly familiar form of
punditry (where successful authors, such as Packard, were featured in
magazines and sought after as experts in media discussion or even on
the Hill) could be levelled against this kind of development, in which
their own influence on publics seemed like the very symptoms of the
disease they described. This was clearly a world where ideas were
transmitted constantly, by media-savvy people shapers, best-selling
experts, gurus, columnists, lobbyists, style-setters. They represented
an expanding, polemical multimedia commentariat, an assortment
of 'stars' and 'influencers', well paid to use new media opportunities
adroitly, to glide in that era, from the talk-show studios to Senate
hearings, from feature-piece offers to book deals and launches, always
willing to be pugnacious, direct, contrarian, eye-catching and opinion-
ated. Packard, like Whyte and other authors and journalists, whose
successful book-length exposés of modern society and modern psychology made them famous, gained large audiences and readerships
and became sought-after experts thereafter. They acquired influence
alongside or sometimes instead of other kinds of authorities who
shaped public discourse (including elected law makers, the heads of
corporations, union bosses, clergy, scientists, doctors, the university
professoriate, wealthy philanthropists, etc.).

Clearly some critics who sought to puncture Packard's bubble
and discredit his work had a skin in the game, tied to the businesses
that *The Hidden Persuaders* attacked. Dichter meanwhile continued
unfazed in developing and defending MR. He pointed out that advertising was an old and venerable practice; he liked to observe that
messages we can recognise as adverts of some kind had existed for
many centuries; and, furthermore, that the arts of persuasion are as
old as mankind. He swatted away as best he could fault-finders such
as Packard. They were adversaries but both were, in their own way,
hot properties in the market of media commentary.

A strong critique of the ethics of the advertising industry, also
treated insouciantly by Dichter, was to be found in the activism and

literature provided by Betty Friedan and many other women.[31] They were intent upon raising public consciousness about the controlling and coercive view of the sexes that was relayed daily through commercial messages. Friedan wrote influentially in 1963 about how vast sums were spent each year to 'blanket the land' with propaganda, honed by social scientists, to control the bodies and manipulate the psyches of women.[32] By the 1970s many women's groups, including NOW (the US-based National Organization for Women, which Friedan had helped to found), undertook a range of actions to disrupt the advertising industry and target particular ads that degraded, exploited or insulted women.

Equivalent protests in the UK and elsewhere took place; famously the 'Miss World' event in London was disrupted by feminists bearing flour bombs in 1970. Some advertisers duly took note in the following decades; they tried to head off the risk to their businesses by recrafting the campaigns, noting the scale of indignation at commercials that implied a women's task was to be attractive to men, provide domestic labour, be a homemaker, etc. In response to such protests, one of the largest advertising agencies, Batten, Barton, Durstine & Osborn, headquartered in New York, had swiftly begun conducting focus groups among women to try to explore the scale, depth and particular sources of this rising tide of feminist activism and public anger.[33]

Dichter would have approved of that effort to recalibrate messages. The business had to change with the times, and the use of focus groups was his métier. His relaxed response to the various objectors he encountered was, in effect: what's new about advertising, and, anyway, what's so bad? Advertising is essential in a modern economy, he insisted. This stance was already starkly apparent in his contribution to an NBC radio broadcast in 1957 entitled 'The Art of Persuasion'. For that event Packard and Dichter had been brought together, head-to-head. They were asked to debate the ethics of the profession.[34] No sooner had the show begun than it was interrupted by a commercial (the transcript I've seen of this discussion does not reveal what product this was for), as though to make Packard's point – an experience of such interfering messages, the kind that you could not easily avoid, unless you immediately switched off the set. In that very same year, as we saw earlier, an interview took place on TV with David Hawkins, the American POW who chose to live in China.

He was grilled about his own brainwashing. The programme, interrupted by ads, was sponsored by a tobacco company, Philip Morris.

Dichter cheerfully pitched in as soon as they were back from the break, asking the chair, Clifton Fadiman, about the reason for his donning a particular suit, before underlining: 'Most of us suffer from the delusion that we are rational individuals, therefore there must be a rational reason, a good plausible reason why you are wearing a gray suit today.'[35] The discussion zigzagged all over the place; from suits to prunes and their commercial makeover, whereupon Fadiman gamely piped in: 'You are making me hungry for prunes.' In a similarly playful mood, Dichter complimented Packard directly on a nicely chosen phrase he had noted in his adversary's just published book, 'psycho-seduction'. He then defended the business, drawing an analogy between advertisers and parents; the latter are always required to understand, and then tempt, even condition, their children, through rewards, as well as threats, so why blame the advertising professionals?

Dichter's response to Packard's attack on his ethics was essentially to shrug his shoulders, and retort that the activities he pursued were neither new nor sinister, nor worse than others that were equally commonplace; and, if anything, the work that he and his group conducted, he now counter-proposed, should be better appreciated by the public. For such work facilitated ordinary people's capacity for exercising free choice, enjoying a 'full life' and expressing 'creativeness'.[36] He implied, I think, that if those in the business of selling dreams, such as himself, were celebrated, and well remunerated, to convince a segment of a market of this or that arguable truth, so what?

What did readers and listeners make of such counsel about the role of the hidden persuaders, and how far did they take heed of the plugging and pumping, promoting and publicising of goods and of politics? After all, it is one thing to describe high-profile arguments, another to know how they are then received. Some surveys of social attitudes from the 1960s in the United States suggest growing levels of public suspicion of a hidden army of people shapers, at home or abroad. Foreign governments, who might spy, meddle, disrupt, were an object of suspicion, of course; above all the Soviet Union, but also its allies, such as Cuba. Another source of growing mistrust, the ability of corporations to gather limitless data and penetrate the minds of a given population; a third anxiety, the hidden dimensions of supposedly liberal democratic states (be it through the security state, the military–industrial complex, or what later came to be called 'the deep state').

There were and still are many reasons for rising public disquiet about 'psycho-technics', hidden persuasion, corruption and mass manipulation by the state and the private sphere. Mistrust in opinion polling about such indices of public faith in the system would be worth polling too, since many people would come to assume that the pollsters, no less than the statisticians, can lie or conspire. Admittedly, even the notion that we can reliably measure public levels of trust in an industry, an ideology or a state gives serious academic commentators who study such matters cause for … mistrust.[37] Nonetheless, such surveys and polls are still often undertaken to explore public misgivings regarding advertising, business and the machinations of governments.[38]

There is some evidence that majority views about the trustworthiness of government and its associated bureaucracy, in the United States at least, have changed substantially for the worse over the last sixty years. Although the origins of mistrust of the federal system are much older, the post-war period witnessed growing suspicion of Washington and of the secret state. The percentage of US citizens saying that they could confidently have faith in each other, *and in their government*, entered a downward spiral, it seems, during (and since) the 1960s. Some social scientists who have analysed polling data claim to have found close to a thirty-point decline in public confidence in the three decades after 1964, the year after President Kennedy was killed.[39] The percentage of people, in other words, that had confidence in any ruling US administration's ability to 'do the right thing', most of the time, these reports tell us, was higher in the 1950s, and, despite some fluctuations, broadly heads downwards thereafter.

One snapshot, suggestive of the American public's concerns about advertising, surveillance and the widespread manipulation of citizens, is provided in Packard's archives, containing what was clearly once a bulging mailbag of reader responses. The letters of his numerous correspondents, many of them just cold-callers who had read his key work, *The Hidden Persuaders*, as soon as it appeared, are stored in his papers. Such messages give a flavour of those public concerns, and suggest how divided consumers felt about the scale of the problems he raised. Some talked of the risk that critics like him were overstating the dangers of advertising and mass deception; others, the possibility that the situation was worse than he claimed. Readers provided their own cautionary points about the manipulation of the people through a new mode of political psychology. Others insisted on caveats and questioned any one-size-fits-all theory of advertising's unconscious impact on populations.

A woman in Henderson, Kentucky, wrote to question his general picture of people like her, housewives as half-knowing dupes, vulnerable saps, unwittingly at the mercy of all this storm of publicity. She went on to say that in her own view she was not some passive receptacle, just soaking up messages. Packard should pay more attention, she and other correspondents urged, to environmental conditions, the fact that people might be *exhausted*, beset by daily labour, bills, housework and childcare, rather than just supine, manipulated stooges.

It was not altogether clear if she was explaining in different terms her receptivity to advertising (exhaustion, toil, hardship) or challenging his assumption that such campaigns would necessarily affect her at all. But Packard, she argued, seemed to picture a neurotic housewife, in an affluent family, living in placid suburbia. This could not be assumed, she thought; the book did not address those in quite different circumstances, nor register the sense of depletion and hardship endured by so many Americans. It was material reality, more than the tricks of Manhattan-based advertising geniuses, she implied, that might account for the glazed, tired look in many shoppers' eyes.

It was important to see people as 'individuals with souls', individuals who lived complex lives, often in adversity, perhaps in tough neighbourhoods, remote from Packard's personal experiences.[40] Another reader, this time a man, wrote that Packard lived comfortably in a well-off community and mistakenly imagined everybody else was in a similar position. This, the correspondent said, is 'nonsense', for what about the many in the United States who are hungry, needy, living from hand to mouth and in debt?[41]

A former pharmaceutical salesman, based in Kennebunkport, Maine, wrote to make a different point – a plea on behalf of those obliged constantly to sell products to fellow Americans, and who were no less manipulated, he felt, than everyone else. Packard no doubt would have agreed. The correspondent went on: 'I would like to get this story of the brainwashing of salesmen before the public and think that you would know exactly the best way to tell this story.' Senior management in the pharmaceutical company in which the man worked were apparently 'trying to deprive their own sales teams of all individual personality and initiative and at the same time high pressure the doctor into using their products'. It had reached the stage, so this writer suggested dramatically, where big pharmaceutical companies were employing 'Gestapo-like methods'; he wanted Packard to understand the pressures placed on company staff, not simply on consumers out shopping.[42]

Packard had no shortage of adoring readers, as well as sceptical critics. Much of the feedback showed a readership appreciative of his achievement. As one of his admirers declared to him warmly, linking his work with other illustrious post-war studies: 'If I had my way "The Lonely Crowd", "The Organization Man" and "The Hidden Persuaders" would be made required reading for every American mother.' Indeed, mothers should 'think about these books for the sake of their children, if they won't for their own'.[43] Packard also had to deal with his share of conspiracy theorists and cranks. One wrote of the dangers of changing water levels in different parts of the earth as a source of influence over the mind; another insisted the United States was about to succumb to barbarians, as had the Roman empire.

Thus, readers responded to his disclosures and offered advice about ways to pursue his analysis of covert commercial influence, or wider conspiracies. Some were particularly concerned about the effects of technology, notably the onslaught of stories and sales pitches appearing on screen. Packard's writings were laden with references to the dangers we face on the airwaves, but some readers clamoured for yet more analysis of the mass media, and the elaboration of practical plans to combat the disabling effects of so much screen time in a social domain inundated with ads. Packard explained, in graphic language, how words, sounds and images, absorbed from TV, might become permanently 'etched' on young brains, and how all this advertising would have, as he put it, 'conditioning effects'.[44] Clearly many readers agreed, but they also wanted to know what most urgently should be done.

Some of the correspondents shared Packard's sense that the advertisers and marketers were getting stronger each year, triggering certain receptors in the brain, affecting the nervous system, transporting the entire body, not just the mind. The experts of ad land perhaps knew ever more each decade, post-war, how to reach certain parts and to toy with senses, or even memories of senses.

Feminists such as Friedan, as we have seen, offered their own proposals, but others worried the onslaught of messages might be unstoppable, or require a wholesale reorganisation of all mass media. If TV could be so addictive and so capable of affecting your unconscious thought and feeling, what then? Jane Mayer from New York City wrote to Packard after reading *The Hidden Persuaders*, urging him to redouble his efforts to investigate the obvious dangers of all this screen time. He must in future, she urged, convey even more fully and clearly 'the insidious and dangerous workings of our TV system'. She then asked him how 'those of us not yet TV robots' might unite to fight back, or at least to establish a new educational station in the United States, even in the knowledge that such ventures could not compete with the great 'mammoths', as she put it, of the business. Packard wrote back carefully, alluding, not without pride, to his gratifyingly heavy post from his readers, and thanking her a bit woodenly for her message, as though he did not really know what to do with her more militant call to civic action and just wanted to get back to his work.[45]

Not to be forgotten here were those readers who, on the contrary, were enthusiastic for advertising, sought openings in companies or asked the author's advice about how such insights might be redeployed for more altruistic purposes.[46] A lecturer from the school of dental surgery in Liverpool, R. H. Birch, wrote to Packard to ask how such techniques as he had described might help support a large-scale dental health campaign in England.[47]

Packard's work highlighted the techniques of MR that might also be used to plumb the depths of our emotions, to divert our painful pining, inflame our jealousy, shame, greed, longing, lust, competition and all the many 'unthinking habits', as he called them. His point was that we needed to face up to the fact that most of the time we are pitifully *unaware* of what we take in, and what we project onto the people around us, or what they, in turn, evoke in us. The starkest example of the dangers, Packard claimed, could be seen in the new phenomenon of 'subliminal messaging'. Adverts, he warned, might go *entirely* past our consciousness; communications, flashing by, too fast even to knowingly register. A new generation of 'psy' experts, it seemed, could breach or bypass, in a quite unprecedented and irresistible fashion, the subject's ego.

Packard addressed the putative dangers of this technique, for example sudden, imperceptible 'buy ice cream' messages projected between frames in a movie reel at the cinema. During his interview with Packard and Dichter, Fadiman upped the stakes considerably when he mentioned this point: 'Suppose, for example, that a very popular movie was being shown to 50 million people but in between each of the thousands of stills of which your motion pictures are concerned there was a little message saying: "Blow up Washington". Now obviously your eyes do not read that, but theoretically according to Mr Packard your unconscious … takes it in, and theoretically the motivations of people might be changed: that is, a lunatic fringe might be encouraged to take what would be very unfortunate and disastrous action.'[48]

The prospects of subliminal persuasion in advertising were promoted hard in the 1950s by one of the so-called MR 'depth men', James Vicary. He made his name by claiming he could harness science to get to the parts of the consumer's psyche that other ads could not reach. Vicary was, like Dichter, an unapologetic salesman for his own work, arguing that images could be transmitted in movie theatres so swiftly that the viewer or listener would not consciously notice them; secondly, that this could then reliably be made to persuade the subject to purchase a product in the interval, such as Coca-Cola or popcorn. The message asking if you were hungry, followed by the invitation to 'eat popcorn', was an enticement, maybe even an *imperative*. The audience, according to this scenario, would feel an inexplicable *craving*. Vicary made strong claims that advertising was about to undergo a revolution, thanks to such inserts. He boasted of the experiments he had conducted but was then in fact unable adequately to replicate them. His work was later dismissed by others as a hoax.

However, after he made the initial claims, subliminal messaging was decried as a frightening new stage in this modern descent into mass enchantment. Here, indeed, it seemed, was brainwashing proper, a completely scientific form of covert influence that evaded conscious appraisal. Some journalists seized on the notion and had a field day. They predicted the final death of all rational decision-making, and a new age of commercial mind control. *Newsday* described Vicary's technique as 'the most alarming invention since the atom bomb'.[49]

Aldous Huxley, celebrated author of *Brave New World*, alluded to the final abolition of free will.[50]

As the historian Dominic Streatfeild has remarked, this alarm was over the top. Had those experiments proved as effective as promised or feared, it would soon have become 'impossible not to buy Coca-Cola or Camel cigarettes or to vote Republican'.[51] In fact, since its invention cinema had aroused such heated concerns about subliminal mass enchantment. But although Vicary's work was discredited, the idea was suggestive, and a portent of worse forms of persuasion yet to come. Packard emphasised what he called this 'post-war phenomenon', quoting articles in newspapers that also referred to the dangers of 'subthreshold effects'.[52] He warned of the terrible abuse of psychological expertise, and cited an article that had appeared in the *Journal of Marketing* with the title 'How Psychiatric Methods Can Be Applied to Market Research'. Debate continues today about the role of the 'secret sales pitch', whereby the target audience or readership simply fail to see or hear a part of the message, even as it has an impact. Research has been undertaken on the potential use of optical illusions, and the possible infiltration of some imperceptible or at least hazy background images in otherwise more obviously readable photographs.

A notable example of or perhaps ironic commentary upon this approach was a Benson & Hedges tobacco advertisement in 1976, which appeared in *Time* magazine. A young couple were shown in an amorous clinch: if you looked closely, you could make out the shape of a penis, airbrushed onto the woman's naked spine. This phallic shape is not obvious, maybe even invisible to some viewers at first. Once it is pointed out, however, there it is, under the hand of the man, as he holds on to her back. The embrace might suggest she is taking the lead, advancing on him, and expecting more; the look of the man's face as he holds the woman is arguably intended by the designer to be ambiguous; it is for the viewer to determine whether it suggests a confident, or even triumphant, state of mind, or an anxious and startled look. Is he supposed to be worrying he is not quite up to it? Above the image, the caption reads: 'If you got crushed in the clinch with your soft pack, try our hardpack.' The secret or not-so-secret sales pitch plays on men's fears of impotence, offering them understanding, or even an antidote, as well as a possible sexual fantasy. On the other hand, the message and the image might also be construed as an implicit joke to be shared between the wry advertiser and the observant (and potent) viewer, positioned here clearly as a man.[53]

Despite dramatic warnings about subliminal messaging, the greater dangers lay in the general lack of informed consent to so much of the marketing – and increasingly data gathering – to which the public have been subjected, and the emotionally labile experience of the half-knowing consumer falling for the object. It is when we are only half-attentive to adverts, registering the image, but then inclined to forget, downplay or discount them, that many work best. The influence can remain, reawakened later, when the consumer sees an item, or merely thinks about what they want on the shopping list; this is the moment at which a generic product such as cough sweets or trainers becomes a desire for a particular make. You can see how this works today with fast food; the way you might be drawn, as though impromptu, by the thought not of nourishment, but specifically, say, a Big Mac or KFC. In short, it is not just the salt and the fat, nor even purely the price, that makes fast food appetising, but the campaigning conducted day in and day out to help us decide when we are hungry (or when we are not) to seek the next fix.[54]

Advertising, in other words, is mostly not about entirely hidden and subliminal brainwashing, but the cumulative effects of repetitive visuals, jingles and catchphrases that we register consciously, up to a point. These are impressions, often enough, that we cannot ever get entirely out of our heads. Advertising campaigns usually require regular reinforcement; a single advertisement is played over and over; images, slogans and tunes run and run.

Much advertising is effective, not because it entrances us but rather because of this repetitive effect, and because it can key into our generally ambivalent attitude to reality; it offers the knowing attractions of make-believe, a daydream or a getaway. Commercials often play upon our penchant for indulging in fantasy, even half-knowingly. Early critics talked of hypnotic states that occur in people as they move around a supermarket; but in large part the work of persuading is more partial if still effective. The point is to engage us in a conversation, to tap into our wishes, our motives, our perceptions of our own needs, and to respond to what people are longing to find, or desperate to leave behind. As Packard had put it, 'What the probers are looking for, of course, are the *whys* of our behavior ... why we are afraid of banks, why we love those big fat cars, why we really buy homes, why the kind of car we drive reveals the brand of gasoline we will buy ... why junior loves cereal that pops, snaps, and crackles.'[55]

Citizens are bombarded with messages that can prove hard to forget completely; messages that require them to be consumed by the task of being principally consumers, in a vast virtual assemblage of other consumers. The point for critics of advertising in that post-war period then was to show this invasion of our individual, interior psychic spaces, and of shared, social spaces. Packard was at his most effective in pointing out how much behind-the-scenes work goes on to get through our barriers, and yet also to perpetuate the illusion that consumers are free, discerning individuals; people are at once spun and yet persuaded that they can decide fully realistically, in a functioning market economy and liberal democracy.

Packard's mistrust of the psychological elements in advertising was well founded; his work a vital contribution to the compendium of ideas about modern thought control that provide the basis for the present book. His files, now archived at his former university (Penn State), were packed with the materials he researched, about all these corporate, political and scientific assaults on thinking capacities, or on the public's right to be left alone. They contain his critical cuttings, and reflections on drugs, psychiatry, surveillance and assorted forms of 'people shaping' which he explored later in his writing career.

On the one hand, such critical dissections of ad land techniques in the 1950s and 60s sought to provide effective analysis to better equip consumers to live as full, political subjects, making their own free choices, and to show that both sexes could be waylaid, and then influenced. On the other hand, that literature, Packard's contributions included, risked assuming, in a reactionary fashion, that women were somehow intrinsically more likely to be suggestible and emotional, less intellectually muscular, more in need of ultimate protection, than men, from the seductions of the modern marketeers. This work could be read in different ways, for instance as a portrait of a previously largely yielding, passive and naive society, comprising men and women, alike helpless before this advertising juggernaut, or it could reinforce presumptions about 'the second sex' that feminists were challenging. More nuanced work was required to temper the broad-brush accounts immortalised by Packard. Academics would soon respond to his exposé, showing that it was more complex than had first been suggested; that people were not simply 'catatonic dough' in the hands of Madison Avenue, as one of Packard's positive early reviewers had said.[56] For instance, researchers pointed out that many factors might intervene between the message and the recipient; there were constraints, in other words, on what such mass media influencers could achieve simply by sending out messages to all.

Like Packard's own feisty correspondents, and readers, these critical researchers emphasised that we do not all receive images or experience the process of advertising alike. We have our own life stories, and our private repertoires of memories and sufferings, imaginings, dreams, and crucially our own varying powers of resistance. The advert is not some elixir that puts us completely to sleep or renders us comatose, abolishing free will. A groundbreaking 1955 book had appeared, in fact, even before Packard's famous text: *Personal Influence*, by Elihu Katz and Paul Lazarsfeld. That study pointed out how people are not just sponges for the flow of mass communications; personal circumstances, the local milieu, social relations and the broader cultural context, they insisted, profoundly affect how any given consumer or citizen receives and responds to such messaging.[57] It invited more debate as to how or even if a child absorbs the adverts on screen, and to what degree receptivity is affected by what is going on in a family, the nature of sibling relationships, parental attitudes and an array of other factors.

As the Benson & Hedges advertisement illustrates, advertisers, with or without Dichter's assistance, often took note of Freud's ideas, intrigued by his explorations of our divided states, desires and insecurities: they were aware we all have multiple points of view, conscious *and* unconscious. For an advert to work does not require such extreme conditioning, let alone brainwashing. Some campaigns treated people as children; others promised to have a grown-up conversation, and to play upon the warnings about psychic conflicts, and the use of the hard sell. As Freud described so compellingly and as some advertisers could also see, people are involved in many psychic struggles; conflicts between what he pictured as different agencies in the mind. The ego, Freud had suggested, tries to mediate between forces originating in our id and our superego, and to meet, up to a point, the demands imposed by reality. In one of his many vivid analogies, he compared it to a rider trying to direct a wild horse that is inclined to bolt unpredictably from beneath. Even the ego, he added, is partly unconscious, so we may not in fact be aware of how it is also busy compromising and repressing our thoughts.

Dreams, Freud proposed, are wish fulfilments, among other things. The interpretation of dreams, he posited, in perhaps his most important book (published in 1900), could become the royal road to the unconscious. He did not foresee the extent to which commercial interests would seek to capitalise on his work. *The Interpretation of Dreams* (which he sometimes referred to simply as his 'dream book') was fundamental for psychoanalysis, and an inspiration to many in the arts, sciences and political arena, and of course on Madison Avenue.[58]

It is worth noting that Freud had misgivings about America, in general, and about American psychoanalysis. His calls for the retention of what he called lay analysis (where the therapy is conducted by practitioners who are not also medics) were not to be heeded for a long period in the New World. Freud had made just one trip to the United States, in 1909. Although he saw psychoanalysis as a new science (and had been steeped in science himself), he was uneasy about the medicalisation of his discipline, and about its vulgarisation and commercialisation. His visit and attendant publicity had inspired many Americans to think about the benefits (and dangers) of psychoanalysis, and to explore its potential applications not only in therapy but also in academic work, social policy, politics and business. Institutes were founded to pursue Freud's methods and train student practitioners. The impact of psychoanalytic thought in the United States grew substantially, interwar. By the 1940s and 50s, some of its vocabulary had become part of the vernacular for millions of people; the practice of seeking analysis, lying on a couch and free-associating in an open-ended therapy was well understood, an assumed reference point in popular culture, post-war. The psychoanalytic 'talking cure' would, however, always face sustained challenges from other theories and forms of treatment; all the more so by the final two decades of the twentieth century, when 'cognitive behavioural therapy' on the one hand, and drugs such as Fluoxetine on the other (mostly sold under the trade name 'Prozac'), were increasingly widely prescribed. But for much of the last century Freudian thought and practice exerted a profound influence on the way large numbers of people in the West, and certainly in the United States, would understand their own minds.

Edward Bernays, Freud's nephew, was another path-setter, an entrepreneur who sought to make use of psychoanalytic ideas in the commercial world. Like Dichter later, Bernays had a highly successful career in the United States.[59] His family had emigrated there from Vienna in the 1890s; Edward graduated from Cornell in 1912 and by the 1920s was making his mark as a public relations counsel, as well as a commentator on modern politics and business culture at large. He was a precursor both to Packard (the worrier and critic) and Dichter (MR's promoter-in-chief). Bernays began to hire out his services to corporate clients during the interwar period, i.e. before Dichter would establish his institute and approach. Bernays set the scene, insisting to businesses that they take some heed of psychology, and sometimes directly of Freudian psychology; it did him no harm that he could claim privileged direct knowledge of the great Viennese professor, or, by extension, of his complex ideas.

Freud's work was a far cry from that of Bernays or Dichter; little is known of what he made of his nephew's project. Bernays may have sold psychoanalysis to business, but he also evidently had a powerful social and political mission. That mission was to support the United States, uphold what he saw as its basic, decent, liberal values, and to provide alarming analyses about the power of fascist and Nazi propaganda experts in Europe to tap the unconscious. Indeed, as the Nazi Party rose to power, he warned of the demonic skill of sinister mass communicators such as Goebbels, who understood very well how to use rhetorical techniques to woo and excite crowds, exacerbate hatred, and unleash murderous wishes. A war on civilised values, Bernays argued in the 1920s and 30s, could easily spread; democracies could founder and fall, even in those nations where such systems seemed securely established. He was concerned with how minds could be perverted, poisoned, confused or invaded, *anywhere*.

Bernays assumed that although we all have a mix of emotions, including hate, people are not born as fascists or Nazis. Rather the ideology can be implanted, nurtured and communicated, and with alarming speed, especially where the soil is propitious (in conditions of misery, poverty, unemployment, uncertainty, chaos, etc.). The United States should never be complacent about populism and demagoguery, he insisted: liberal democracy had to be shored up and propaganda used effectively – the arts of emotional communication are required to defend liberty, to counter militarism, authoritarianism and racial hate.

As Bernays saw it, all modern states, as well as all forward-looking companies, had to cotton on fully to the dangers, as well as the opportunities, of modern psychology, and to grasp the advances that had been made in understanding the sinister aspects of human nature. Both Freud and Bernays, in their different ways, explored the vicissitudes of group psychology, and the potential volatility, even madness, that might lurk in all of us, especially when under greatest pressure and strain. 'Those who manipulate this unseen mechanism of society', Bernays wrote, 'constitute an invisible government which is the true ruling power of our country.' Or again: 'We are governed, our minds are moulded, our tastes formed, and our ideas suggested, largely by men we have never heard of … It is they who pull the wires that control the public mind, who harness old social forces and contrive new ways to bind and guide the world.'[60]

Strikingly, the history of thought on advertising was often caught up in larger debates about the nature of the mind and the future prospects of democracy. The question was how to deal with a world in which mass enchantments were always on offer, and potentially orchestrated by extremely sophisticated agencies, drawing upon the human sciences. So, from narrower considerations about how a particular campaign for a product was built to stimulate the public's imagination, critics would turn to questions about the unconscious and how it played out in the mass psychology of electorates. They wanted to consider the unclear line people might tread between realistic views of the material world, and these dimensions of fantastical thought and longing that shape behaviour and choice.

Rather than subliminal messaging and states of automatism, the real issue was more ordinary and everyday: we are all shaped by unconscious fantasies, as well as inclined to enter into daydreams; our conscious reckonings are always shadowed by thoughts unknown. Marketers and advertisers can skilfully plug into all that. A commonplace example Packard cited was the practice of dealers placing the sleekest and fastest model up front in the window. The aim, he explained, was to try to entice men into showrooms by presenting open-top and powerful limousines *first*. Once inside, the buyer would probably have to at least partly – maybe even grudgingly – face up to the requirements of reality; the number of people or quantity of baggage they had to ferry around, for example. They might well then opt finally (most times) for the more practical as well as more affordable family car to be found further indoors. But the crucial point was to gain their attention in the first place, catch their desire, through the 'dream' in the window or on the screen. A prospective purchaser's yearning gaze is hooked. We may well be more likely to 'come in' and become a customer, if so 'invited', Packard showed, even if we do not opt to buy the initial 'dream' object (that gleaming two-seater sports car).

At that time the pitch for such an escapist car might be primarily made by the marketing men to other men (presumed to be the most likely drivers or at least the holders of the family purse strings for such large items). But many shop windows, of course, were aimed at women; advertising of everything from cars to furnishings to holiday trips was recalibrated, geared increasingly towards women's burgeoning spending power, and thus designed to enter into their equally fraught relationships with consumerism, health, family, work, fantasy, romance, sex and escape. Campaigns for cigarettes, for instance, were heavily targeted at women, providing reassurance that consumption of tobacco was truly good: 'Reach for a Lucky instead of a sweet', advised those reassuring TV physicians to a female clientele. Adverts featuring doctors were commonplace, interwar and post-war, telling the consumer that product was harmless, or even beneficial to health, as well as a marker of effortless style.

The idea that advertising techniques operate entirely beyond our awareness is contentious. Most people grow adept at realising that they are being pitched a story, not just 'the facts', aware as they watch, or listen, that sellers have a vested interest, and that elements of fantasy and reality are woven together in marketing messages. In fact, when adverts work *too* hard, deny the playful elements, they may prove off-putting, like a pathetic and ineffectual suitor desperate to prevail. It became obvious long ago, then, to many if not all consumers, that advertising revels in symbols and constructs, kindles fantasies, or sometimes invites ironic reflections on those very fantasies that we see in the literal or virtual windows. We can probably read the fact that commercials for cars are offering a kind of pipe dream about the driver and passenger's total escape, the hope of an open and limitless road, even a route to some paradise, and yet the message may work.

Between Bernays' warnings and applications of psychology to commerce and politics in the 1920s and 30s, and those 1950s polemics by Packard and others, much would change: advertising seemed ever more seamless and total, and complex in strategy, as time went on. Glossy magazines and papers, billboards, cold-calls, mail-outs, radio, cinema and TV were deployed one by one, or sometimes in integrated and sustained *campaigns*, so that by the 1970s and 80s companies and political parties in the United States and Britain, not just corporations, were required to spend fortunes on a whole phalanx of professional people from ad land. In the first national election that I voted in, Saatchi & Saatchi played a notable role and became globally famous through their work on behalf of the Conservative Party. Stark images of disconsolate people in queues under the heading 'Labour isn't working' were plastered in public spaces and credited as highly effective works of persuasion, including with many working-class voters. Although the precise impact of such posters on the campaign has long been debated, the 1979 election witnessed, as one commentator put it, a 'quantum leap in the marketing of Margaret Thatcher and the Conservative Party'.[61]

But the gap between the 1980s and the 2020s is bigger still. It has grown harder than it was in the 1950s or even the 1980s, with the fracturing of class solidarities and more automatic allegiances to political parties, to be sure quite how to encompass and interpret what is actually happening to all of us, to know how a trend builds, what can swell a particular movement, what 'news' is hype, or how the people shapers get to us all. What are we to make of the direction and orchestration of politics and of commerce in this new forest of algorithms, this realm where children grow up scrolling and swiping on tablets and phones, where busy people nonetheless spend so much time on Facebook, Snapchat, Instagram, Twitter, TikTok, etc., and where consumers influence each other in myriad ways? What would Packard make of all this?

Nowadays people grow up learning, more-or-less well, how to navigate a way through the endless emporium, to choose, resist, like or dislike, cope with the constant invitations and interruptions of the eye by adverts; we must make our own pathways, and sometimes of course fall down rabbit holes, or bat away pop-ups, designed by the successors of those 1950s advertising corporations. We may hope to evade the obvious hurdles and potholes, but the advertisers are on to us too, ensuring our experience is ever more tailored, or that we somewhere believe in the wisdom of (purchasing) crowds. We no longer just flip through glossy magazines, but rather a potentially endless array of sponsored stories, trip advisers and peer recommendations online.

The depths may still be probed by the experts, the heirs to Dichter, but the effect, as so many people now complain, is of a sense of endless time spent on screens, skimming across ever more surfaces, flitting from item to item, caught up in a kind of depthless arena of buying and selling, grazing through factoids, punditry and surveys, sampling bits and pieces of information; and yet many of us feel above all uncertain about where we are now heading.

Predictions at the American Advertising Federation in 1958 that Packard's bombshell publication and shrill warnings would prove short-lived, and that his basic thesis about the hidden persuaders would soon crash, burn and be forgotten, were not borne out.[62] Indeed, many of his depictions still seem relevant, or even gross underestimations of what has befallen us in a twenty-first-century capitalist world where neuromarketing companies seek to use EEGs (electroencephalograms) to study the brain's electrical frequencies in order to refine commercial online experiences ever further. Many techniques and devices serve now to tighten the bond between the consumer and the product (or the online message), or at least to try to create the perfect fit, the smoothest connection and transaction as possible. You can pay now by waving your phone – no need for physical money at all. One expert put it like this, as he considered the new cutting edges of the advertising business: neuromarketing can help the advertiser read 'the brain's secret whispering'.[63] To access that whispering is perhaps the aim of the research; but also, the means for companies to whisper back to us.

The technology has changed drastically, the ambition of companies to monitor and manipulate the mind, and even the brain, has not gone away; the means are now far more elaborate than those that the critics identified back in the 1950s. So too is the constant pitching for the benefits of yet more advertising pitching. 'If pitches are to succeed, they need to reach the subconscious level of the brain, the place where consumers develop initial interest in products, inclinations to buy them and brand loyalty', so claimed Dr A. K. Pradeep only a few years ago.

With a doctorate in engineering, Pradeep founded and became

chief executive of Neurofocus, a neuromarketing firm based in Berkeley, California. Its website advertises the company as the market leader in bringing neuroscience expertise to advertising, branding, product development, packaging and entertainment, and explains how it can call on the skills of experts with training from MIT, Berkeley and Harvard (among others).[64] Pradeep adds, with evident pride, that the firm uses EEGs and eye-tracking devices to explore customer attitudes to sales messages, websites and movie trailers, and how '[w]e basically compute the deep subconscious response to stimuli'.[65]

How far this is possible, where the research may be leading, and the potential safeguards required are issues of obvious and urgent concern. Modern analysts of advertising warn of a new conjuncture, where, in real time, all our movements online may come to be integrated with our back histories; an evolving situation where the system can constantly feed us offers, not only of products, but also of culture, news, networks, etc., congruent with our own ever-evolving and indelible profiles.

So far in this chapter, we've seen how the Cold War conversation about brainwashing came to be redirected in critical reflections and studies of advertising – or, more broadly, how citizens of a 'free world' are also sold a certain vision of life on behalf of capitalism. Indeed, some critics, long before all these recent worries about the attention economy, set out concerns about how the industry might be selling people ultimately not so much a market of things to buy, but rather a far more encompassing visualisation of what it truly means to be a flourishing person, creating simulacra of choice and freedom, while also controlling so many of the levers that determine those choices and the expression of seeming autonomy. The advertisers, it appeared, were not just encouraging an expansion of consumption, but reshaping the very psychic life of the citizens who did the consuming. Some of that discourse was hyperbole, and yet it cannot just be dismissed as fantasy or fiction.

The questions raised by that post-war generation still resonate as we head into a new kind of Cold War (or worse) between the United States and China. How much in either society are people free to think, and shape the future discerningly? What should I do if my every breath, my every waking thought, my sleep, could somehow be read by technology, and then crafted into adverts and political news designed to reach me? What does it mean if 'I' am the product when I am browsing? To see where some of the thinking about advertising went, between Packard in the 1950s and the recent literature on surveillance capitalism and the deep state, let's consider next the argument developed by the French sociologist and philosopher Jean Baudrillard during the 1960s. He provides a notable example of this continuing effort to update the story decade by decade, and to analyse the impact and full reach of advertising in determining what we assume to be our reality, or our sense of normality.

Baudrillard offered an ambitious, distanced analysis of the advertising industry. In a book published in Paris in that especially turbulent year of mass protests, 1968, he argued that contemporary consumers were effectively being asked to live inside what he called an 'ideology of democracy', as well as consumerism. This was an arena where freedom meant an occasional invitation to vote for this party or that, along with a daily injunction to participate in the market, and to look away from anything that discomforts (such as prisons, homelessness, war, empire, inequality).

As part of this 'reality', Baudrillard said, we are constantly informed that the acquisition of stuff will bring satisfaction; we are sold the assumption that this acquisitive pattern equates to social progress. Each of us, he suggested, is not only tempted by, but constantly *pressed* with, these demands, even obligations to join in. This onslaught is persuasive, yet operates mostly even without our noticing: as though, to achieve our missions in life, we could *only* accept endless immersion in a constructed, marketised world. It is as though we must live in this scene, be inscribed as players in that theatre of goods, assuming products must be not only possessed but also then swiftly discarded; as though each of us is schooled to this subject position, as acquisitive individuals, in a frantic and interminable cycle.

Baudrillard proposed that ultimately the advertising industry had come to sell us a psychological story of human fulfilment, as though procuring, say, the latest Citroën model, or wearing Dior, was the acme of imaginable, personal achievement.[66] The whole thing now had to be deconstructed intellectually before it could be resisted. Advertising, at present, fuels an economy based around this endless circuit of disposal, renewal, obsolescence and repurchasing. This future, according to Baudrillard, was not inevitable. His critique reflected something of the spirit of that year of revolt, with perhaps just a touch of that slogan beloved by students in 1968, 'be realistic, demand the impossible'.

People needed to realise advertising never can satisfy desire, he insisted. Indeed, it is essential to this kind of economy, and to the mode of advertising that supports it, that desire never should be quenched anyway. Ultimately the whole industry is part of a larger ensemble of forces, a staple ingredient in the economy, culture and society that works at multiple levels to shape our desire for ... more desire.

Baudrillard used an idea that had also been explored by psychoanalysts such as Lacan, that we are all too prone to confuse need, demand and (impossible) desire. In advertising's imaginary realm, each discrete non-essential purchase will do the trick, yet it is part of an infinite series stretching ahead; we are incited to pursue and attend to the next year's products, egged on by that regiment of human strategists, stylists, fashion experts, etc., only for the carousel of the latest things to disappoint. It is part of the structure of the world as we know it; the system showers down messages about products that can meet the consumer's wishes, only for fashions to change, with each passing 'season'; that is the nature of the arrangement, the lever of 'growth'. We need to realise that desire is never sated, and certainly not by interminable purchasing. The alternative to that need not be some drab, monochrome Stalinist or Maoist world, although often these too were sold to us in this way, and as though we were all in a global struggle, with only two choices before us, capitalism or those modes of communism.

Baudrillard was notably interested in the roles of waste and obsolescence inside this capitalist system, and wanted to think about the despoiling of material resources to sustain it. Detritus, he emphasised, is not supposed to be minimised in such consumer societies; rather the packaging provides meaning in its own right – for instance, associations with plenitude, surfeit, goodness and bountifulness, or the promise of treasures hidden within. The waste is all too easily left unremarked, but this, he said, was a mistake. It may be an important trope of success and of luxuriance: 'Is not the fact that the glass packaging can be thrown away', Baudrillard mused, 'the mark of the golden age?'

We are surrounded by inanimate and animate models of success and failure in life, often associated with youth, freshness and promiscuous disposability of things and people. Baudrillard wanted to alert us to how 'success' may be linked by an entire industry to this extravagant cycle of acquiring and then destroying value, searching for ever more novelty – be it for newly discovered scents in ingeniously crafted containers, packets and boxes, to the expectation of moving constantly along a 'ladder' in a series of 'upwardly mobile' rentals, or trying to find some ideal home, with ever newer furniture too. That perfectly achieved and desirable place provides the private, individual bourgeois conception of a life well lived in the most enviable, private, glossy habitat. Such visions of the good life, projected all around us in modern societies, had grown ever more disjoined, he suggested, from real social solidarities, as well as from needs. And affluence, for some of us in this increasingly frenetic material and confected imaginary world, was occurring amid so much poverty, misery and degradation, all those noises off, in the urban peripheries, or in the so-called developing or third world. We could suffer, as some psychologists and critical economists had also long warned, from this condition of affluenza.

Such an analysis by Baudrillard reflected and contributed to the emergence of an ecological critique, certainly an environmentalist sensitivity, regarding the sustainable and the unsustainable future. It also introduced, or rather reintroduced, the insistent thought (even as that account emphasised structures and systems) that people, if they so wish, might opt to walk away, not spend their lives in this fashion, or rather with fashion. This way of seeing and living is endemic, and yet also requires participation for the system to work. He wanted to show how this 'spectacular squandering', as he put it over half a century ago, is stitched into the economic system at many different levels. To illustrate his point, he drew attention to the 1960s marketing of one-use-only disposable knickers (80 per cent viscose, 20 per cent non-woven acrylic), and suspected that the hope of the marketers was that the very wastefulness of this product would be part of the lustre that consumers would buy. Or rather operate as a small echo of the sublimely preposterous notion (the supreme symbol of desirability for many, he thought): a 'magnificent dress worn by the star for one evening only'.[67]

Baudrillard and other radical intellectuals of that time insisted that we are prone, even condemned, to function in this 'useless and unnecessary universe', as ideological prisoners in a vast virtual shopping mall. The shop-till-you-drop requirement and the matching mania of disposing of the old in favour of the new, he explained, offer an illusory version of freedom. It was crucial to think and fight our way out of this box. 'The possession of objects frees us only as acquisitive individuals, devoted to that mission (and little else).' Our dominant social order refers us back to the 'infinite freedom to possess more objects, the only progression possible is up the ladder of objects; but this is a ladder that leads nowhere, being itself responsible for nourishing the inaccessible abstraction of the model'.[68] His argument there is reminiscent perhaps of those 'impossible' drawings immortalised by the Dutch artist M. C. Escher. One of Escher's most celebrated pictures, *Ascending and Descending* (1960), shows lines of people moving about on those mysterious staircases. Escher was interested in existentialism, as well as in surrealism; he liked drawing out in pictures a personal dilemma for people; his work was concerned with themes such as responsibility, choice and alienation, as much as with formal questions of vision. His picture shows people actively moving about for themselves; even as they may be trapped in a certain space, they are active, not passive, figures in that landscape.

If we are to step off the ladder, envision a different social architecture, choose an unknown future, rather than the continuation of a governing past, we need to consider both the structural features that entrap us and our existential choices. We need, indeed, to take seriously the convergence of surveillance, the cyber-based economy, the manipulation of politics, and all the rest; and keep alive the prospects of protest and major reform, of change to how reality is orchestrated, including online, by those corporations who, over the years since its creation, have shaped and monetarised the internet. We live now, of course, with certain conditions, a framework, just as Packard had feared, conducive to the fashioning of citizens, but as the best critiques of advertising have previously suggested, a current paradigm can also potentially shift, and new fault lines emerge.

Consider the example of Simulmatics. It can be interpreted in varying ways, and linked to different arguments about politics, campaigning and advertising. It might be taken as an illustration of the relentlessness of the psycho-technics that Schumpeter had once described; a key staging post to our present. Or it could be viewed as a salutary example of journalistic challenge to, and public backlash against, that version of reality. 'Simulmatics' was a company established in 1959, with premises on the corner of Madison Avenue, promising great things in the field of electioneering, thanks to their 'election simulator' machines.[69] The company name combined 'simulation' and 'automatic'; clients were offered expertise in artificial intelligence and a new basis on which to craft effective political messages. A revolution was at hand, or so it seemed.

Simulmatics provided services to the 1960 presidential campaign of John F. Kennedy. The Democrats knew that the election would be a fierce and difficult contest; they would need all the skilled professional help they could get. The party had lost the previous two contests to Eisenhower. Kennedy was a controversial choice as a candidate, even if he had, for many people, a certain star appeal. Nixon, his opponent, also dramatically divided opinion. Polls suggested the contest would be close; there was no guarantee American voters would swing the electoral pendulum back to the other side after eight years of living with 'Ike', as President Eisenhower was chummily known.

Eisenhower's decisive victories had given the Democrats pause for thought; his carefully boiled-down so-called 'Corn Flakes Campaign' of 1952 presaged the changing world of media-driven and, increasingly, TV-based politics. His advisers back then had encouraged him to keep messages as simple as possible, play up the patriotic angle, cast major doubt on the values of his opponent, and present himself as not only a legendary military leader and a personally likeable man, but also as a safe and trusted product you might safely buy. His opponent Adlai Stevenson complained that Eisenhower was sold as though he were more like a cereal than a serious political figure. He lost, then stood against Eisenhower again in 1956, with the same outcome. Stevenson's disdain for television persisted, even as the medium grew in importance.

Eisenhower's team realised much sooner than his opponent's that the media, above all TV, would prove crucial; and, moreover, they saw that it might be a mistake to distract voters with too much small print. Hence, they provided appealing images, folksy messages and catchy jingles that focused the electorate's attention on the qualities of the man far more than on policies; they offered simple refrains such as 'I Like Ike' (or second time around, 'I Still Like Ike'). Long speeches were out. Ike was a figure sold as the man the public already trusted and could trust again. His commercials were fun, even amusing – one had elephants marching along to a musical version of 'I Like Ike'. He had the wind in his sails; the economy was generally doing quite well. Even if voters did not necessarily believe the Red-baiting attacks that rained down from the Right on the left-of-centre Stevenson, Eisenhower had an air of authority, solidity, plausibility. His job in the campaigns was to sustain this aura, play up the personable, ordinary, strong and reassuring persona, and supply inane generalities such as 'It's time for a change'.

The latter phrase was sufficiently 'meaningless ad copy', as the historian Jill Lepore puts it in her excellent account of the rise and fall of the Simulmatics Corporation. It was 'written by the guy who came up with M&M's "Melts in your mouth, not in your hand"'.[70] Celebrities, choirs and cheerful birthday messages for the president were also provided along the way, adding wherever possible to the feel-good atmosphere and general sense of Republican momentum. In fact, the two campaigns for Eisenhower were important turning points in the national or even global transformation of politics to a sound-bite culture, carefully choreographed PR and fast-paced media spectacle. The Kennedy–Nixon election in 1960 made that transformation more fully apparent.

Kennedy's advisers studied the Democrats' previous failures. Many ingredients combined to produce JFK's eventual extremely narrow success over Nixon, but, as Lepore argues, we should not ignore the role of Simulmatics. As the research director at Simulmatics would explain, in the *Public Opinion Quarterly*, in 1961: 'The development of electronic computers and mathematical game theory has greatly stimulated the simulation of human behavior as a means of exploring the implications of theory and extending the analysis of great masses of data provided by surveys and similar sources.'[71]

The co-author of that account was Ithiel de Sola Pool, chair of the research board of Simulmatics and an MIT political scientist. The company's approach was to amass and code data on computers from past election returns and opinion surveys, and then to identify and analyse dozens of voter types and demographic clusters. They sought to model likely reactions to campaign developments, and thus pinpoint what was most needed to produce a result. Kennedy's statements, they proposed, might be tweaked to reflect such precise advice. New technical and psychological support services would then road-test policies, refine the optics, finesse the mood music – i.e. seek to enhance a candidate's rhetoric, and adjust behaviour, style and political commitments to create impressions that affect the thinking of groups of undecided voters as the campaign was underway.

Admittedly, this was all still pretty hit-and-miss, and nobody can be sure quite how many votes the approach affected. It was also an extension of something much older: politicians' use of all means possible to maximise their emotional appeal to voters. The arrival of Simulmatics onto the scene at the end of the 1950s was a crucial development, prefiguring more elaborate forms of data analysis, advertising and targeted messaging. Simulmatics, for example, encouraged Kennedy to go all out to attract the African-American and Jewish vote, by deliberately making an issue of his Catholicism, rather than seeking to hide it away. By insisting that religion should be no bar to any candidate's perceived fitness for office, Kennedy sought not only to neutralise criticism but also to go on the political offensive. He had to do something, as he was being severely attacked as unsuitable for the highest office – a man who might in future do the bidding of the Pope, it was said, and not the American people.[72]

Kennedy's camp endeavoured to counter such charges by taking them head on, connecting the issue of such inflammatory anti-Catholic rhetoric to other forms of oppression, thus making a bridge between JFK and his family on one side and people of colour and other minorities on the other. The message would also play well with younger and/or more liberal voters. The point was to attack *all* such prejudice as un-American, thus, to change the framework of the national conversation on personal belief, religion and racial politics. Critics of Kennedy on the Left objected that so much of this was fake, and that the policies did not go nearly far enough, but all the same this was a striking rhetorical move.

It turned out that in the key places that the Democrats hoped to win, Kennedy had more to gain than to lose by insisting openly on this point, which also helped to offset his previously lacklustre record on civil rights. The very attacks Kennedy would invite from the Republicans could thus be marshalled and turned around: drawing down fire, as it were. Jack Kennedy's style, glamorous wife, and especially his assured performance in a TV debate against a somewhat sweaty, tired and shadowy-looking Nixon, were also important to the Democrats' triumph. On election night, Americans watched the outcome on television. It was to date the fastest-reported result in US history. Kennedy's success in the electoral college system was substantial: 303

to 219. But his popular vote – 49.7 per cent to 49.6 per cent – was the closest result of the century.

In the aftermath of the election, commentators emerged expressing considerable alarm about the arrival of Simulmatics. A debate ensued in various media about what limits might rightly be set, who appropriately controlled such data, and what safeguards might legitimately be introduced in future to protect people from being studied and turned in this way.

Although from our standpoint the computer technology was still basic, a far cry from current methods, some newspapers took the threat of a new high-tech assault on the voter extremely seriously. Lepore describes how the story was picked up around the country, with dire warnings appearing, for example, in the *New York Herald Tribune* of this new 'secret weapon'; a newspaper in Oregon complained that the Kennedy campaign had reduced 'the voters – you, me, Mrs Jones next door, and Professor Smith at the university … to little holes in punch cards'. That journalist insisted hyperbolically that by comparison with this technological and political development, 'the tyrannies of Hitler, Stalin and their forebears look like the inept fumbling of a village bully'.[73]

Kennedy's press secretary played down or denied the significance of Simulmatics in the election. However, speculation about its role and potential was rife. Storytellers were inspired to imagine the dystopian end point, a hybrid future where the worst of the past (think here of Goebbels and Nazi propaganda, they warned, just as Bernays had done earlier) and the new computer revolution fully converged.

The critical investigation of the science behind the underhand manipulation of public opinion, as we have seen, greatly gained in momentum during the interwar period and even more so after the Second World War. The question of how such opinion is accurately gauged, or how it can be massaged, soothed or distorted by private interests or by mass political parties, had been of obvious concern during the 1920s and 30s (and after); indeed, the subject became a mainstay of social science research much before Packard's day. During the same period, polling companies were created to measure fluctuating opinions as reliably as possible.

Such work is not of course entirely concealed; some is hidden in plain sight. Yet we may well suspect now, after decades of work on the psychological impact of advertising, and the depredations of 'digital capitalism', that we live not only with 'known unknowns', and 'unthought knowns', but also the realm of the truly mysterious 'unknown unknowns', the phenomena that may entirely blindside us. We are aware, presumably, that our digital footprints are traced, our data tracked and stored, wherever it may be. We are perhaps mindful of tools, techniques and practices that make a mockery of the idea of fair and transparent elections; cognizant, in theory at least, that this process, which ideally would require millions of people to exercise judgement based on extensive knowledge of the options, is conducted with much voter misapprehension, indeed in a sea of propaganda, with campaigns designed precisely to manipulate the necessary data and news.

We might also seek to gauge, however, as best we can, where plausible, critical warnings about the corruption of democratic processes give way to the conspiracy theorists' overblown fears. All this in a context in which we now give away information daily on our personal computers on a scale that (during the 1950s and 60s) advertising agencies, or companies such as Simulmatics or for that matter Cold War spying agencies, could only have dreamt about. We sign contracts at the click of a mouse, without time or inclination to read the small print. And yet despite the alacrity with which we just press 'accept', we might also find ourselves caught up in an apprehensive internal dialogue: what if the phone in my pocket, the tablet, the Kindle or even that beautiful laptop so deftly named 'Air' gives unseen others intolerable access? What if I put time into the problem and tried to refuse? Some people tape over the aperture / camera or turn off all the most obviously invasive settings. And yet, who can be sure? Each of us has become so heavily integrated into the ecosystem of digital surveillance that mundane activities – communicating with friends, watching a show, reading an article or hailing a taxi – all come with potential consequences of privacy violation.

We live in a world where we are bound to suspect that corporations know a great deal about us; far more than we may wish, and far more, in all likelihood, than we know about them. Amid the plethora of warnings and theories, it has become harder to know where appropriate – sane – public wariness ends, and a delusional narrative about omnipotent alien powers, hidden manipulations and clandestine interferences truly begins. The world may be in many ways unrecognisable from that described by advertising's most trenchant critics post-war; and yet strikingly, many prescient accounts emerged at that time about where the industry, in its alliance with business and politics, could be taking us. And about whether a future of corporate and governmental 'people shapers' could ever be changed.

To be wary about conspiracy theories and theorists is not to deny that real nefarious plots and subterranean strategies of many kinds are pursued on behalf of commercial and political interests, domestic and foreign agencies. From the point of view of the West, the question of influencers and of advertising today is as likely to be considered in relation to hostile states, notably Russia, China and Iran. As the 2016 US election showed, a state may use multiple tools and hire many proxies to influence people in another country. A foreign power may have an obvious interest to polarise, to unsettle and to encourage scepticism in the very foundations of liberal democracy, just as the West may seek to use cyberwarfare methods against its adversaries.

In one sense all those historical warnings about a brave new world of online propaganda ring true. We require all the help we can get to see more clearly how companies, political parties and governments, not to mention foreign intelligence agencies, exploit new opportunities created by companies such as Google, Meta and so on; to consider how the algorithms work, and what decisions lie behind them; to recognise how corporations create vast data sets that they then sell on to those who are able to pay, and who may have every interest in distorting elections, opening social divisions, or spreading disillusionment in the value of voting. State-sponsored disinformation is rife. For instance, there are credible reports that Russia played a role in seeking to dampen the overall African-American vote in the 2016 election, especially so in the closest-run states.[74] The scale of the digital 'information wars', authorised by Putin and others, during the 2010s, to achieve certain electoral outcomes in the UK, continental Europe and the United States, is only now becoming apparent to most of us. We have legitimate and rational grounds to suspect webs of deception at work around us. But we also need to be mindful that certain kinds of warnings about these many clandestine forces may also prove disabling, distracting and overblown, leading to cynicism or mass paranoia.

Before ending this chapter, let's bring these thoughts about surveillance together with a few further observations about continuity and change in the world of advertising.

*

Marketing of goods and services has come a long way since the 1950s. Corporations try, of course, to keep pace with the cultural times, social trends and the latest street fashions and technologies. There are so many ways for businesses to seal a pact, to try to engage with consumers, to keep their business shows on the road, to infuse and sponsor contemporary culture and captivate us. Some advertisements are made by extremely talented film directors and have eye-watering budgets; they can also be so beautifully made they inspire scenes in movies, rather than the reverse. Some remain artistic talking points for years, or decades. A case in point, the now fondly remembered black-and-white Guinness surfer commercial, directed by Jonathan Glazer, which was first broadcast on St Patrick's Day, 1999. It stunningly portrayed a surfer riding the waves, amid leaping horses. 'Surfer' featured remarkable visual effects by the Computer Film Company (CFC), was skilfully edited, boasted a powerful, thumping soundtrack and stylish narration. It is now often still closely analysed, and celebrated as a classic, a work of art, as much as an advert that caught the moment.[75]

Some adverts or campaigns seem, to the delight of the companies, to transcend the genre, to leap off the screen, become part of the zeitgeist. Coca-Cola campaigns have often sought to capture the era, to reflect or even to lead social changes, 'growing' with their customers and casting them in a new light. Each series of Coca-Cola adverts provides a heavily loaded sign of its times. Either way, the endless circuit of assessing and selling remains, and is updated year on year.

Interwar, Coca-Cola notoriously got busy with Santa Claus, helping to rebrand his image. Father Christmas was then heavily used to enhance the reputation of the company and its product.[76] The 1950s approach to advertising the drink was often based around pictures of an inviting, carefree blonde American woman. In the 1960s, customers would have been familiar with a jaunty song, 'Things Go Better with Coke', and, again, with commercial film sequences heavily accenting American *whiteness*. (This was in stark contrast to recent company training seminars, urging that Coca-Cola employees think much harder about their own implicit racism or 'white fragility'; although this has caused a predictable backlash from American conservatives.)[77] In the aftermath of civil rights campaigns, the feminist movement and so many political struggles against imperialism, this approach was then replaced, or at least complicated, in the 1970s, by a new message: Coke as the drink to relish in a multicultural, multi-ethnic post-1960s world – the 'Real Thing'.

Capitalism is, evidently, and as Marx had foreseen in the nineteenth century, remarkably protean, capacious and capable of assimilating and transforming what stands in its path, even gathering up one-time sources of opposition into new sales pitches. That 1970s Coca-Cola theme song, 'I'd Like to Teach the World to Sing', became a big musical hit on its own. The advertising agency and film team behind the commercial brought together fresh-faced young people of different ethnic backgrounds and had them singing to the world from a hilltop. The commercial conveyed hope and innocence, harmony and globalisation all in one stroke. That whole aesthetic dimension of advertising has become an important part of the hall of mirrors; the social images, cool styles, quintessential looks and path-breaking campaigns, which came to be widely appreciated, ranked and prized.

Other companies also traded on an apparently inclusive, rebellious, edgy new vision, or allied their promotional activities with art – witness United Colors of Benetton, although in that case, the *cause célèbre* was the carefully contrived, ever more outrageously provocative images, pushing at the limits of the permissible, on behalf of cultural 'freedom'. This approach was at its height during the 1990s, where the campaigns were shrilly designed at all costs to draw the viewer's attention, even at the risk of scandal: scenes of people living with AIDS, 'transgressive' nuns, bloodied babies just after delivery, internal organs, Mafia murder victims on the street.[78]

These examples are part of the branding – in the case of Benetton, the courting of controversy to revive the firm's fortunes – the creation or recasting of a business with a strong identity or character, designed to inspire customer loyalty and personal recommendation. There is much discussion of late in the advertising industry of how that approach can now work, and how loyalty can be sustained, when consumers, like voters, may be more impatient, fickle, fractious, fragmented ... no longer perhaps identifying with one another as classes, communities, generations.

In a recent think piece for the business magazine *Forbes*, Thomas Dichter, the son of Ernest Dichter and a writer on finance and consumer habits, reflects upon a younger generation of internet users, and muses on changes afoot since his father's old dispute with the author of *The Hidden Persuaders*. 'The generations that live and buy online are savvy about what and how they are being pitched. If advertising is going to work for them now an even more subtle and deep reach into their hearts and emotions is called for than what worked in the Mad Men era.'[79] That is surely true: advertising often assumes consumers are cognizant of the most obvious strategies of formal, in-your-face open advertising and make more and more use of intermediaries, of information and imagery shared, transmitted and liked by 'friends' on social media. We might be sensitive in some respects, obtuse elsewhere, sophisticated in some transactions and naive in others, and the advertising industry will surely evolve yet further to try to reach people who have grown wise to old techniques. Nonetheless, in that sophisticated and critical response, we can also see how people at large, and indeed often the young, may constitute powerful agents of change, against a particular order of things.

No brand can assume that the relationship with their customers is simply settled or for life: after all, crowd outrage, even informal (albeit usually transient) boycotts, does occur in response to campaigns.[80] In 2017 Pepsi released and then withdrew a notoriously ill-judged advert, featuring Kendall Jenner, offering a can to a police officer during a protest. This naked appropriation of 'social protest' was roundly rejected by much of its intended audience. It caused a backlash and was widely decried as crass and exploitative. It resulted in a significant slump in sales and was even dubbed the 'fail of the year'.[81]

That was a single instance, but more generally, levels of trust by the public in commercial and political advertising are now in question, and regularly surveyed by pollsters; their findings commissioned and then pored over by the big agencies as they study how best to 'connect'. There is a wealth of data each year on the relative scepticism of different generational cohorts towards such messaging on each particular technology, for example on smartphones.[82] Should we be alarmed, or maybe heartened, that some are now rather more confident about the accuracy of commercials for established and dependable brands, than they are of news broadcasts or political messaging?

A 2017 US report describes such changing attitudes: it announced a poll that found that over half of millennials (those born between the early 1980s and mid-1990s) and Generation Xers (born between around 1965 and 1980) generally trusted commercial advertising, compared to less than half (44 per cent) of Baby Boomers (post-war babies, born between 1946 and 1964). Eighty-one per cent of millennials had made a purchase influenced by advertising in the thirty days before the survey was conducted. 'Baby Boomers come from a time when there were a lot fewer regulatory bodies in advertising,' declares Julie Wierzbicki, account director at a Canadian advertising agency. In short, they were more wary. 'For example, cigarettes used to be advertised as good for you, and we found out that these brands we thought were great were lying to us. Millennials feel like brands have to be honest because there's so much more information out there, and if you're doing things in a fraudulent or misleading way, it's going to eventually come out.'[83] Evidently, trust and wariness can be distributed in diverse ways and co-reside in people's minds.[84]

Many consumers since that 'golden age' of advertising post-war have grown more interested in or even hyper-aware of the psychology of advertising – not necessarily hostile to it but inclined to scrutinise campaigns and even to discuss them appreciatively as well as critically. These days much is written on how consumers' relationships to branding are far more complex, and sometimes more consciously self-fashioned than in the past. To speak of unidirectional commercial influence over us all, let alone absolute brainwashing of a population, cannot quite encompass the complex way minds and markets work, the myriad ways that people interact or, to look at it more cynically, the degree to which they are so fully incorporated into modern consumerism that peer-to-peer advertising or waves of recommendations, and style advice, instant feedback, etc., does much of the work that was previously achieved by explicit and orchestrated commercials.

Critics would now want to qualify Packard's old account and consider with more nuance how purchasers may be trusting of, and influenced by, brands, even while aware, maybe hyper-aware, that this is happening. Rather than mind-controlled puppets on one side and rational consumers on the other, we are more likely embroiled, in Miłoszian fashion, in those bargains and rationalisations inside of ourselves. Might we even be willing participant observers in such affairs, buying products, absorbing the culture of advertising, the art of the sell, imbibing a form of ideology, even as we decry it and can 'see through' it?

It is hard to know how to begin to disentangle culture and markets, advertising and art, today. There is a seamless traffic, after all, between news, spectacle, design, style, fashion and everyday purchasing and consuming. We may gain considerable visual pleasure from looking at certain images in a 'sponsored' movie, sporting event or artful TV commercial; are we then being bought? What if we may knowingly consume stories and images of ourselves in the act of consuming, swallow, say, product placements, accept and even savour them, and enjoy our own dream-like submersion in that process? Admire, as connoisseurs, the art of the ads, the brilliance of editing, the mastery of sound and image, the way that products are placed in our field of vision, envelop us with lush sounds. What if we concur, and delight in putting aside our wary attention and critical faculties? People may savour that very capacity of those little movies, such as the Guinness surfer, to sweep over us and into us, thus accepting how we are being 'called', and how we are taking part, complying, assuming, with some awareness, our designated places as consumers, while the message works its 'magic' on us.

We can be constantly torn, part-analysts, part-critics of advertising, and at the same time consumers; our minds can give licence to our own temporary passivity, or our choice to zone out, and to be surprising strangers to ourselves. For example, we might condemn a campaign on TV encouraging people to bet money on sporting outcomes; be able to see quite clearly how the dream of winning masks the much more likely pain of losing … and yet in the right company, for a big occasion, allow ourselves 'a treat', have our own flutter and use the online betting site, whose address is now firmly lodged in our memory. More seriously, many gambling regulars, and addicts, claim to have been directly influenced by such advertising. They may know they are being manipulated by the marketing, the illusory idea, for practically all, of ultimately 'winning big' but can't seem to quit. Of course, addiction to gambling has complex causes, but the onslaught of advertising is rightly a source of much public outrage.

In 2020, the UK Gambling Commission reported that six in ten consumers saw gambling adverts or sponsorships at least once a week. Just over a third of people who had gambled in the twelve-month study period claimed to have been prompted to spend money on a gambling activity by advertising they had seen in the past year. And around one in six adults followed gambling companies on social media.[85]

If there is much to encourage fatalism in the literature regarding the commercial and technological manipulation of people's lives or whole communities, there are also instances of resistance by individual campaigners, and united groups, that remind us of the powers we have to take concerted, collective action, be it through trade unions, pressure groups, legal campaigns or long-running protest movements. Sarah Milov, for example, in her recent history of the cigarette, notes substantial (albeit always only partial) victories that resulted from action in the United States, mostly by women, against the domination of the tobacco industry. One fight was for public spaces free of smoking, and for clean air. For decades Big Tobacco, supported by the state, blocked their demands with denials and smokescreens. Even long after the surgeon general warned of the health crisis smoking was causing, the industry and its powerful lobbyists fought back, although finally, under pressure, it gave up on TV advertising, and later had to accede to further restrictions. The late 1960s and early 1970s saw notable legislative achievements in US environmental protection laws, and commensurate developments in other Western societies too, suggesting that what is deemed politically unrealistic and impossible at the start of a decade may have fundamentally changed a few years later.

In the West smoking has declined, but of course that is not yet so everywhere. Anti-smoking groups became more powerful in the United States, and in other countries too; adroit, effective, witty and tough, skilfully using counter-images, mounting clever campaigns, including cartoons, inviting derision of the idea that smoking is alluring. These were large-scale grassroots endeavours that had considerable success. One important task was to expose how the tobacco industry in the 1950s and 60s had known about the harm that smoking could do and deliberately sowed doubt about the medical and scientific evidence that cigarettes were killing people, delaying action to inform and protect the entire population from the dangers.[86]

The tactics of obfuscation and spreading doubt employed by the tobacco companies have also been used effectively by fossil fuel industries to intensify scepticism about climate change. For example, lavishly funded campaigns financed by the Koch brothers, huge investors in fossil fuels, did their utmost to postpone effective legislative changes. They took a leaf out of the playbook of the tobacco lobby fifty years earlier, by finding a maverick alternative view within the very broad ranks of science to foster doubt in the minds of the public.

Advertising and campaigning may be as much about creating apathy, hopelessness or confusion as it is an injunction to buy certain products.[87] The Koch brothers used their 'outlier', 'specialist' opinion shapers to stage a kind of public health warning about bogus scientific authority. Behind the claim of making the electorate more sanely cautious and sceptical was a massive enterprise, an orchestrated endeavour, a muddying of the waters. Like the tobacco lobby before it, the campaign against climate change action seemed like a perverse exploitation of the kind of academic work that had emerged in post-war decades and that had pointed out that the truth claims of modern medicine and science did indeed need careful critique, not simply naive acceptance. We do need a better understanding of how knowledge, even in a lab, is produced, of course; not to be credulous about how science generally works. But this kind of critical thinking was then harnessed for obvious financial and ideological ultra-libertarian purposes to cast doubt on the need for urgent collective political and economic action. The cynical campaign thus invited the recipients to imagine that in heeding this call they were being more sophisticated than the gullible, increasingly mainstream 'green' view: go deeper, their 'think tanks' explained; get behind the facades, and really you would find that those great numbers of alarmed expert advisers and committees, for example at the UN, were just crying wolf, or were in the pocket of lobbies themselves.

We will look at conspiracy theories in the next chapter, and the kinds of measures that are now being proposed to counter their influence, protect societies from orchestrated misinformation, and strengthen democracies. Clearly stronger legal frameworks are required so that corporations and states that subvert liberal democracies and threaten societies and the ecosystem cannot just run riot. Efforts are also underway by legal experts to create a crime of 'ecocide', which might lead to prosecutions in the international criminal court.[88] The challenges of doing that are immense. Much of the media and business world remain intent on a politics of distraction, disavowing the scale of the climate crisis. However, the potential of such legal reforms, or even of mass public engagement with serious current endeavours to achieve them, could be great.

Packard was right to warn that a great deal of the underlying craft behind selling is at least partially *disguised*, whether it is broadcast to millions, tweaked to reach a committed target audience, or offered, as today, by an influencer online to millions of fans. Some pessimists predict that ultimately each of us will live inside our own world of commercials, games and tailored 'news', a cyber-based unreality, ever more honed to persuade us, and ever further from serious engagement with the existential threats that face us. Information technology will surely advance, but how it is most powerfully used, and whose interests it will ultimately serve, are of course a matter of constant political contention.

Each day brings us closer, so we are warned by contemporary pundits, or sometimes by neuromarketing companies, to a time when machines will be capable of reading our private thoughts via neurotransmitters in the brain. But even without the ultimate machine–brain reader, the vast bank of information held about us can be hard to comprehend. We may choose to ignore all of that, content to have such miraculous virtual spaces to store our data, photo collections, millions of emails, a lifetime of memorabilia. We should not, of course, keep our head in those clouds. The cloud image we really need to hold in mind is of corporate ownership, or more materially still, that vast array of warehouses, data centres, server farms, that are not in the 'Cloud' at all; a global apparatus consuming huge amounts of energy and other resources down on the ground; a physical infrastructure stretching from enormous desert facilities to thousands of miles of undersea cables. It is a gigantic digital storage system that enables hitherto incredible forms of mapping and analysis of individual and group behaviour, and much of it is sold, in one form or other, not simply stored.

The scale and resources of the giant data-based corporations are hard to fathom. Google and Facebook were once start-ups, the result of far-sighted innovations, often brilliant engineering, maths and technical know-how, the product of clever design ideas and entrepreneurial visions of the future. As they got bigger, the enterprises could often just buy up the competition and incorporate smaller companies into their own portfolios. These were businesses that capitalised on earlier, often publicly funded research and development, and were then able to steal a march on more lumbering rivals, sometimes gaining near monopoly powers, and now providing billions of us with the extraordinary search facilities, social media, and so many other now indispensable tools of everyday life in modern economies, that we take for granted.[89]

In her book *The Age of Surveillance Capitalism* (2018), Shoshana Zuboff explores the competitive dynamics of the market today, and the forces that have driven, as she puts it, 'surveillance capitalists to acquire ever-more-predictive sources of behavioural surplus: our voices, personalities, and emotions'. Zuboff shows how behavioural data is now used 'to nudge, coax, tune and herd behaviour towards profitable outcomes'.[90] Packard saw much of this coming, as he reviewed, with dismay, the easy acceptance in the 1960s of surveillance machines and hidden technologies – cameras, lie detectors, closed-circuit TV systems, wiretaps, and so on. Surveillance, he argued, was sold by companies to people back then as a means of enhancing individual power and protection; but it might also provide a means for others to look in and eavesdrop on people in their homes.[91]

It is companies such as Google and Meta that are now at the heart of the story of advertising and of democratic politics. The data they gather, willingly signed away by us, makes platforms such as Facebook the crucial vehicles for advertisers and hidden campaigners to reach us. The accuracy with which advertising agencies can ensure our *awareness* of products is what is most valued. TV and newspaper advertising is rapidly declining, the internet giants booming; there, the advertisers have our near-constant attention, our all-too-willing participation, or even our desperate addiction.

It's hard to forgo being part of the online world, and why should we have to? After all, the digital technology we now practically all rely upon has offered immense gains, and is indeed replete with future possibilities. But the manipulation of the digital economy to change elections, to foment confusion, to engender division and even, as noted, to block meaningful intergovernmental action to address ruinous climate change, is the darkest 'cloud'. What would it mean to face that reality, and to seek to change the terms of trade and to extricate ourselves from 'business as usual'? Even to contemplate what is happening in the environment, in politics, commerce, advertising and technology, may be to face an extreme level of anxiety. And yet, as environmental activists urge, we need to try to get our heads around the array of forces at work to resist essential change and recognise the complexity of the problem without feeling defeated; to think harder about the trade-offs we are making, the ways we are implicated, perhaps without even realising, and the degree to which we are self-ensnared in a system.

This was brought home to me powerfully when I corresponded with and then met the late Zygmunt Bauman, in 2015, to film an interview for the 'Hidden Persuaders' project at Birkbeck, which we subsequently put online. In our correspondence, Bauman insisted on retaining the word 'brainwashing' in considering the effects of this new cyber-based attention economy, with its mixture of surveillance and clickbait. As he said, with evident passion and urgency, the 'net' appears to be closing us in ever further: its effects, he said, choosing his words carefully, are 'evasive', 'clandestine', often 'unspottable' and 'unpinpointable'. We are caught now in a 'spider net' of surveillance; and yet, as he added, also 'drawn into the role of the spiders who weave it'.[92]

PART 6

THE PARANOID STYLE

On 6 January 2021, an angry crowd of Trump supporters, protesting about the 'stolen election', broke into the Capitol. Jacob Chansley stood out in the throng thanks to animal pelts, tattoos with Nordic insignia, a beard, bare chest, a chain, fur headgear topped with horns, and a face painted in the colours of the flag – red, white and blue.[1] He was soon widely known as the 'QAnon Shaman'. That his striking image was broadcast globally, through social media as well as news agencies, illustrates how, nowadays, a face, story or meme can suddenly go viral *everywhere*. Chansley became the best-known face of the riot, and a public talking point. He was viewed in the liberal press as a flamboyant proponent of conspiracy theory, an exemplar (or victim) of the paranoid style and a symptom of the breakdown of the normal political process. In fact, there were many reasons for people to be there protesting that day; no single case can characterise all. But we have something to learn from his story, its media coverage and the argument made in defence by his attorney.

QAnon is a multi-faceted online conspiracy theory, and a terrifying sign of the times; terrifying because of the claims it makes, and because of the sway it holds over huge numbers of voters, not just a maverick few. The QAnon phenomenon has aroused enormous apprehension, especially in the liberal media, generating headlines such as 'QAnon is an American invention, but it has become a global plague'.[2] Polls abound, illustrating the scale of public support for such sources of 'news'; one, from Ipsos, in December 2020, for instance, estimated that over 50 per cent of Republican voters gave QAnon 'teachings' some credence.[3]

We are all vulnerable to states of mind where we misread what is happening in ourselves and in the world; this 'difficulty' is not just born of ignorance of facts or available interpretations. It can sometimes be just that, but we may also actively reject sources of information that enable us to better understand our minds and relationships. Everybody at times, and some people all the time, is riven by narcissistic wounds and grievances, haunted by overblown fears or governed by a mood of 'suspicious discontent', as Richard Hofstadter put it in his landmark 1963 lecture and subsequent essay on the paranoid style in US politics. Moreover, paranoid attitudes can be deliberately cultivated and exploited by cynical agencies, most obviously today to target mass fury and public aggression, while avoiding analyses of other 'messy' threats and problems, in which perhaps the accusers might themselves be implicated. People may suffer paranoia, and/or seek to inflame a paranoid view in others; they might well want to provide at the same time soothing or titillating 'circuses' designed to distract or de-politicise.

Hofstadter noted how conspiracy fears may arise for a plethora of reasons, and how they came to be exploited in the United States, not least by demagogic politicians and reactionary clerics. The important questions for him, as for us now, include: what makes large numbers inclined to adopt the paranoid style; who benefits; and what might counter that style, and help redirect public concern towards real rather than chimerical dangers?

The paranoid style can serve many purposes, psychically and socially. We might buy into new claims of conspiracy because they reflect our prior, entrenched, paranoid frame of mind. In other cases, the temptation to adopt that style may be more fleeting and circumstantial. Either way, there are parties in society that use states of terror politically or strictly for business. Some entrepreneurs, for instance, sell health treatments in the same virtual space on which they peddle delusional narratives, turning a tidy profit. Hedge funds seek to make a killing by creating digital platforms on which authoritarian populists have free rein to undermine democracies. Largely unfettered social media organisations have massively cashed in; yet their major shareholders and directors may be broadly indifferent as to who spreads persecutory tales and lies, or what those lies are, so long as the lying serves well to colonise the greatest amount of public attention possible, keeping advertising revenue and data collection rolling in. They are not necessarily in favour of people believing scurrilous propaganda; just willing to bet on every possible outcome and loath to disrupt the flow of absorbing chatter and constant engagement, since their business model relies upon that uncritical engrossed attention.[4]

*

As to the motives of the millions of individual subscribers, online, each day, for sharing in conspiracy tales, there might, again, be myriad reasons for participation: an inkling that the real sources of power are bound to be hidden, a desire to clinch a larger political argument about the bankruptcy of the existing regime, an inclination to share feelings of dread, or perhaps just a pleasure in secretive conversations about *other* secretive networks. It may make the participant feel special, party to the latest gossip, 'in the know' to hear of horrific conspiracy. One might swap vicious canards, fanciful hypotheses and counter-narratives doubtfully, a little agnostically, or, alternatively, give the benefit of the doubt, and conclude 'no smoke without fire'. Many, however, have gone a great deal further on the spectrum of credulity; the most avid take proclamations by 'Q' or other such bogus sources as certain revelations and instructions, as, perhaps, did some of the Capitol rioters. Followers of conspiracy theories have been known to take the law into their own hands. In 2016 a man attacked a Washington DC pizza restaurant following preposterous internet claims that Hillary Clinton and her associates were sexually abusing children in satanic rituals in its basement.

A person need not be a paranoid conspiracy theorist, perhaps needless to say, to research political plots, complain of propaganda and dirty tricks or criticise undemocratic, back-room deals. For instance, after the 2008 crash, when certain southern European countries, especially Greece, faced complete financial meltdown, the EU was accused by hard-headed critics, as well as conspiracy theorists, of bypassing its own parliament and operating in a byzantine, oppressive fashion. Protestors may have plenty of cogent arguments as to why they deplore opaque political decision-making, be it in the EU or any other bloc or country. However, such critiques of secrecy can also switch tracks, not in the business of serious analysis of real eventualities, but rather caught up in apocalyptic warnings, fantastical terrors, omniscient assumptions that, deep down, 'everything connects'.

Chansley apparently thought that the Illuminati,[5] the Trilateral Commission and the Bilderberg Group between them 'control the world'.[6] The first of these entities was a secret society created in late-eighteenth-century Bavaria; the second, a non-governmental discussion group founded by David Rockefeller in 1973, the third, a regular gathering of financiers, media moguls and politicians who have met discreetly, if not completely in secret, since 1954. The extreme right-wing conspiracy theorist Alex Jones of the Infowars website, in similar vein, heckled one Bilderberg meeting through a megaphone: 'We know you are ruthless. We know you are evil. We respect your dark power.'[7] Like many other conspiracy theorists, Jones is notorious for peddling visions of Jewish mafias and world-wide interwoven conspiracies to his many followers.[8]

Stories about Bilderberg and other such organisations, meetings or clubs easily morph into visions of a singular, omnipotent enemy. The language of conspiracy theory today is often still replete with tropes about back-stabbing elites and, specifically, 'conspiratorial' Jews, sometimes with images redolent of the old blood libel, where Jews were supposedly involved in ritually drinking the blood of murdered children.[9] The Far Right is once again awash with tales of global Jewish 'puppet masters' orchestrating the ills of the world. Accusations may be direct or insinuated; for instance, with the invocation of the name of the billionaire financier George Soros, or with the resuscitation of stories about the untold influence of the Rothschilds. So, before we know it, allusions to a particular powerful individual or group change into signifiers of an omnipotent shadowy world government, or references to organised networks with devilish designs on white, God-fearing, Christian people. An early blueprint for such stories, concocted at the start of the twentieth century and then unleashed to terrible effect in the febrile Europe of the 1920s, was a fiction, portrayed as though a genuine document, detailing Jewish conspiracy: *The Protocols of the Elders of Zion*.[10]

Devoted followers of QAnon believe that 'Q', the mysterious source (purported to be a single former military intelligence officer, but perhaps in fact a group of misinformation spreaders), offers them real clues to the truth of the world, elements of genuine enlightenment, indeed, an antidote to the mass brainwashing conducted by a liberal elite. A user codenamed 'Q' or 'Q Clearance Patriot' first set a potent thread running online in 2017, posting a message and warning of the 'Calm Before the Storm'. Cryptic communications were designed to intrigue, and before long a story had crystallised: a governing cabal was committing obscene criminal acts, enjoying impunity from prosecution and pursuing all means to *rob* the Republicans, or rather, Donald J. Trump, of legitimate victory.

Trump was perceived, in this QAnon narrative, as a moral redeemer, the scourge of a rotten system. He was someone to rescue at all costs, so he could save 'the people'. As to the pernicious extremity and fantastical nature of the claims at the heart of this narrative, here is how *The New York Times* drily summarised the key plank of QAnon theory: a cabal made up of 'Satan-worshiping paedophiles' included politicians, financiers, leaders and media figures, among whom were top Democrats like Biden, Clinton, Obama and Soros, entertainers and Hollywood celebrities such as Oprah Winfrey, Tom Hanks and Ellen DeGeneres, and religious leaders including Pope Francis and the Dalai Lama. In addition to molesting children, the cabal supposedly committed many other crimes that would not be amiss in a horror movie … they 'kill and eat their victims to extract a life-extending chemical called adrenochrome'.[11] The image of grievous harm being inflicted on children by monstrously exploitative, selfish adults is potent, of course. And accurate news about past crimes and cover-ups may make it hard for people to be sure the more outlandish accusations don't have some merit. At any time, day or night, after all, somewhere children are indeed being terrified, beaten, abused, used, discarded. Children can also become the signifier of elite exploitation of the mass.

It is hard to know for sure to what extent followers believe parts or all of the QAnon fantasy. We should not assume all those millions are a solid, homogenous block – some, as I've noted, may swallow such stories entirely; others partially or perhaps not at all, engaging with 'Q' more searchingly or opportunistically – so when we say 'follower', it begs such questions. Clearly some people appear to follow but are really there to exploit mass interest, to express solidarity with the fanatics, seeing 'Q' as a battering ram that can be seized upon for their own purposes or immediate interests. Trump, for example, was reluctant to condemn QAnon, which is not to say he truly believed in such ridiculous claims; it was perhaps for him all part of the political game, a tactic to use to try to retain power at all costs.

It is striking that some of the more obviously self-promoting fellow travellers with QAnon, at a certain point, peeled off, publicly insisting the ideas had – finally – grown too bizarre for them, leaving the foot soldiers high and dry. Even Alex Jones eventually lost patience completely, spectacularly parting company with the 'Shaman' and his conspiracy cause live on air. Admittedly it was late in the day (in an interview in March 2021) when he told a disconcerted Chansley: 'I will not suffer your Q people after this! ... I'm sick of all these witches and warlocks and pumpkin popsums [sic] and everything ... Hahaha ... God, sorry ... Bye Q, I can't talk to you anymore.'[12]

It is worth restating here an obvious point: 'populism' is a term that can be used lazily and, worse, contemptuously. It's not populism as such that is the problem, but the nature of the political programmes that are often promoted by populists in the name of the people.[13] Various recent demagogic disrupters of liberal democracies who have gained prominence and power on the Right (in Western and Eastern Europe, the United States, Latin America, etc.) provide wrong-headed, extremely sinister, even crazed *answers*. But they may, all the same, be alert to important *questions* that we all need to consider seriously. In other words, they hijack legitimate and vital criticism about the ravages wreaked on many societies over recent decades; they cotton on to the crisis of political legitimacy that is already happening, albeit their answers drastically deepen that crisis, and serve to imperil democracies. The questions may well concern the heavy price paid by populations for neoliberal policies, for globalisation, for the unregulated flows of capital, outsourcing, voracious asset stripping. They seize on the widespread perception that systems of governance or ideals of democracy and freedom have been badly corrupted, that once-flourishing communities are dying, that good jobs have become scarcer, that a narrow band of 'winners' are disjoined from a vast array of 'losers', that corporate forces have grown so vast and entitled that they can dictate policy to governments.

Authoritarian populists may even pose, directly or implicitly, salient questions about the corruption of public speech (even as they corrupt that speech further and give their own frighteningly brutal 'solutions'): what has debased debate in the public sphere; why is the mass media not talking about what really matters; to what end has the digital economy vitiated human exchanges; how has social media alienated us from each other? How have we moved so far from the ideals, let alone the practice (when did it ever fully exist?), of 'deliberative democracy'? Even Chansley, who loved Trump greatly, had more than an inkling that something was, indeed, drastically wrong with communication in contemporary society, with the operation of technology and the mass media, and, moreover, that much about liberal democracy may be fake and illusory. However, he saw the threat in an extremely concrete sense, more akin to an 'influencing machine'.

He warned of forces that could meddle directly and control people absolutely inside their heads, telling a reporter how radio and TV operate on 'very specific frequencies that are inaudible that actually affect the brain waves of your brain'.[14]

Conspiracy theories range widely today, frequently shifting public attention from the ordinary and open to the extraordinary and closed, pointing to undiscovered machinations in the infernal depths.[15] Many hubs exist around the world where people can hear of outrageous cover-ups and explore all manner of perturbing theories about hidden conspiracies, past and present; stories that are then used ostensibly to explain the parlous state we are in. On the internet there is great scope for people to exploit search engines, especially where relevant data is limited. Media manipulators often work in concert to take advantage of these 'data voids',[16] gaming the system so that people subsequently searching then immediately stumble on misinformation, including dire, concocted warnings of terrible deeds and monstrous plots.

True, of course, some conspiracies do really exist, but conspiracy theories may lead us along pathways that zigzag between plausible, conceivable, unlikely and incredible political scenarios, as though they are all worth the same consideration: the Illuminati had a hand in the French Revolution; freemasons lay behind the case of Jack the Ripper; high-ranking Nazi scientists were allowed to escape the Allies' net and smuggled to the West; the vice president was at the heart of the plot to kill JFK; the reasons for and scale of the war in Vietnam were not as officially stated; the Apollo moon landing was faked; the Clintons conspired to assassinate dozens of opponents; 9/11 was a false flag operation; the Sandy Hook massacre in which twenty children and six educators died was all entirely staged to attack the right of Americans to bear arms; the Covid-19 vaccine programme was designed to destroy you; reptilian aliens are here in our midst, disguised as humans.

It is quite possible to operate in a virtual, parallel universe, where facts are never checked online, where fictions morph into news and where demonology shapes the 'analyses' of global problems. Here is a not uncharacteristic report, from 2021, about a conspiracy theory regarding Covid-19 that circulated widely, in Arabic, on Facebook: 'Bill Gates is dressed as the Joker. His hair is fluorescent green, his face painted white … In his hand is a large needle, filled with bright green liquid … a caption teases Gates' "horror plan".' It is just one of dozens of disinformation operations that have been viewed millions of times, promoting the case for mass vaccine resistance.[17] Other popular stories shift readers' attention seamlessly from known facts, such as CIA-funding of the Mujahadeen in Afghanistan (to provide an anti-Soviet bulwark) or the insistent claim that Hillary Clinton, as secretary of state, intentionally created Islamic State to wipe out the Arab oil states and to damage irreparably the Arab world. Some theorists declare with certainty that the United States not only reinstalled the Taliban in Afghanistan but also formed an alliance with al-Qaeda to defeat Islamic State; or contend that behind practically all the malice and discord everywhere lies Mossad (the best-known branch of the Israeli secret services).

In sum, the lines between rational critique and the paranoid style, or what might be called a 'hermeneutics of ultra-suspicion', can easily blur. In any society, some people who are not actually persecuted can suffer a sense of persecution for years, and then, by virtue of that condition, be attracted to causes that confirm some ghoulish intrigue; but today many others are also easily drawn in by conspiracy talk, seduced, albeit to varying degrees, by insidious, utterly misleading 'information'. The internet enables stories to spread faster and wider than in earlier times, thereby joining up individuals swiftly into loosely associated virtual groups. Sometimes the same untrustworthy 'dog whistle' inflammatory tales are recycled from one site or one extreme political party's Twitter stream to another abroad, thus 'off the peg' theories are translated from one country to another.

We are all sometimes prone to deny or disavow a piece of reality, to exaggerate a story, occasionally preferring to entertain the most questionable or even quite unhinged view of 'the facts'. There can be paranoid, perhaps even psychotic, streaks in neurotic people; we may 'go mad' for a time, overwhelmed with extreme suspicions, states of jealousy, hate and envy; or be smitten by 'road rage', intent on murdering, or feel as though we are being murdered, but then, hopefully, swiftly recovering, before we act on the impulse. Or we might fall into temporary, massive self-pity, assuming that problems in our lives are not – indeed could not possibly be – connected to complex causes, or even stem from chance and contingency. Instead, it can be tempting to assume a hidden, malevolent human agency *must* be pulling the strings, persecuting us personally, giving us the hope that if only we can expose and destroy that source, that plot, we will be free. Conspiracy theory, in short, can resonate for all kinds of people, not just a crazy few; its effect cumulatively, in recent times, is to weight much public inquiry heavily towards a shrill and adversary tone, and to assume, *a priori*, the prevalence of nefarious schemes. The task for the conspiracy theorist is to work back from the 'effects' to trace the *necessary*, clandestine cause in a discrete group of plotters, while perhaps ignoring the 'plot' hidden in plain sight; for example, conflicts of class, vast wealth inequalities or the bitter fruits of a particular culture, governing system or ideology.

During the Cold War, various clinicians and historians noted how conspiracy theory and the paranoid style might be especially alluring when a people are already traumatised, or feel most heavily imprisoned; when a population is wounded, aggrieved, anxious and under intense pressure, or most unmoored. Loneliness can breed paranoia, and paranoia can exacerbate loneliness and draw people towards dangerous demagogues. Arendt, let's recall, said that totalitarianism is built on 'organised loneliness'. Loneliness prepares people for totalitarian domination; and, to put it the other way around, totalitarianism, once installed, always destroys the public spaces that mitigate loneliness, leaving each person isolated in an 'iron band of terror'. She also said of totalitarianism that it creates a world where truth and lying are impossible to disentangle. Arendt worried acutely about liberal democracies that corrupted themselves and grew ever more mired in lies and deceptions. She knew where all this could lead: collective confusion, isolation, even madness, and the destruction of any remnant of deliberative politics.

As he sought to defend his client, Chansley's former attorney Albert Watkins made this point too, of the United States and its liberal democracy, observing how we need to look beyond individual cases to a whole climate of opinion and face up to how society can all too easily turn a blind eye or actively foster basic attacks upon thinking, culminating in disasters such as 6 January 2021. His client, he let it be known, was a victim of brainwashing and in the thrall of a dangerous cult.[18] The politics of hate and deception in the United States had created the trouble, he argued. January 6, when the riot took place, was 'a day on which our nation was compelled to commence bellying up to the bar to acknowledge each of our roles in permitting, fostering, tolerating, endorsing or ignoring without action an ever-increasing barrage of divisiveness, intolerance, untruths, mis-representations, and mischaracterizations through an unrelenting multi-year propaganda odyssey'.[19]

Hofstadter had already explored the problem of lying barrages and conspiratorial mischaracterisations sixty years earlier. He reflected upon politics, paranoia and conspiracy theory, which had been rife during the 1950s, and in the United States most especially focused upon putative hidden communist plots.[20] He had given his lecture on the paranoid style in Oxford on 21 November 1963. This was the year after the Cuban Missile Crisis, the time when the superpowers – the United States and the USSR – came closest to a calamitous nuclear exchange. The lecture was delivered, by chance, the day before President Kennedy was killed, an event that lent new significance to his thesis, and spawned a plethora of additional theories, some of which still have a following. Those grim events in Dallas represented, for many Americans, a disorientating turning point after which the state could never be trusted again; as though here was the real launch pad of the 'turbulent sixties', the dawn of a new 'age of fracture'.[21]

Although we can draw distinctions between mainstream political views in Western democracies after 1945 and the more outlandish conspiracy theories of those on the fringes, including such extreme conservative and overtly racist organisations in the United States as the John Birch Society, we should not forget how senior figures in the political establishment, including many in leadership roles, expressed paranoid views and/or displayed paranoid symptoms. Some psychiatrists opined freely at the time about the ultra-suspicious views of the head of the FBI, J. Edgar Hoover, and of Republican Party leading players such as Richard Nixon and Barry Goldwater, speculating if they were clinically ill. This reached a notable crescendo in the run-up to the 1964 election, where Goldwater stood (and lost) against Lyndon Johnson.

Goldwater's extreme anti-communism, and stubborn opposition to major civil rights reforms, led hundreds of mental health professionals to diagnose him as a mortal danger to the country, a 'megalomaniac', with a 'persecution complex'. Goldwater complained, after defeat, to the American Psychiatric Association (APA). No doubt his ire was intensified by the extensive mockery to which he was subjected during the campaign, such as the dismissive and widely circulated attack line: 'In your guts you know he's nuts.' The APA thereafter created the 'Goldwater rule', suggesting it was unethical for clinicians to make comments about public figures whom they had not personally examined.[22]

That debate was revived in the years of Trump's presidency; but the issue, in the 1960s, as in the 2010s and 20s, is not just whether a particular leader is mentally ill, but how and why the paranoid style resonates across constituencies and is taken up so powerfully in political movements. And the issue is also why authoritarian populists, spouting conspiracy views and operating in the paranoid style, can at times gain so much traction. For evidently the paranoid style has boomed in the West, and around the world, in the new millennium, facilitated greatly by the internet, and fallout from 9/11, the 2008 financial crash and the Covid-19 pandemic. Across continents, researchers suggest how huge numbers of people are now primed to be doubtful of the 'facts' they are offered, deeply mistrustful of government information, suspicious of the bona fides of official bodies and implicitly or explicitly critical of the various brands of liberal philosophy and liberal democratic conventions that shaped so much Western political thinking through to the end of the Cold War.[23] Consensus, such as it was, in the West, about the basic trustworthiness of state authorities has weakened, and sometimes broken down, leaving a vacuum for the most illiberal and reactionary forms of populism to fill.[24]

While it is true that the idea of 'futureless futures' or 'living in end times' is not a new experience for all, it is also the case that many citizens see themselves thrown, only of late, into a more dangerous, fraught situation, and are acutely aware of downward mobility compared with parents or grandparents. We are all, no doubt, thirsty for explanations (if not rationalisations) about the current state of our world and the shape of the future. Envisioning ever greater environmental disasters and yet further political, military and economic chaos, even many privileged people, those in the wealthiest 'one per cent', are profoundly worried and feel at a loss about what to do. There are today, in that still smaller fraction of the 'elite', after all, billionaires building supposedly disaster-proof refuges in New Zealand, preparing for the end times.[25] In the post-war decades, admittedly, end times were in fact also easily imaginable in the West, as in the East, even if, under the two old systems, jobs and livelihoods were more secure and predictable for the majority than they are now; it was nonetheless an age when nuclear fear was widespread, and it was not necessarily paranoid at all to believe an apocalyptic ending was possible.

To recap, real dangerous conspiracies may occur in *any* state, or supranational organisation. But the paranoid style serves to generate and then make use of a climate of fear, to assume a hidden enemy, often but not always peopled by stereotypical, racialised, villainous figures; it may well distract, displace and focus the attention of subscribers on a particular 'meta-explanation', decry a general imperilment of human freedom, before proposing as an answer to social ills, a draconian, fundamentalist or fascistic response. The paranoid style tends to invite us to locate the blame for real problems in some occult, shadowy force that is already the source of disquiet (or prejudice), rather than enable one to see contemporary history as a matter of thorny social problems, policy choices, open political struggles and competing ideologies. To debunk a style of rhetoric that lures us into conspiracy theory is not necessarily to deny the baleful and clandestine activities that can occur inside any party or government.

However, to say that we need to make that distinction, and appraise genuine problems and face real crises, as far as we can, without falling into this paranoid style, is easier said than done. Debates continue about the relative vulnerabilities of different constituencies, and whether those at the 'top', in the 'middle' or at the 'bottom' are more susceptible: people in 'gated communities' and other secluded cocoons, leaders who enjoy positions of great power, those protecting their middling perch in the social hierarchy, the 'just about managing', or those at the bottom, bereft of a stake in society, poor, deprived of reliable data, perhaps even of adequate literacy, without the necessary critical tools of analysis.

In deprived communities, the Rust Belt, flyover states, neglected inland or coastal towns, as a Bob Dylan line once had it, 'you don't need a weatherman to know which way the wind blows'. Polling reports on the ultra-suspicious state of opinion in continental Europe, in the United States in the 2016 and 2020 elections, during the 2016 Brexit referendum in Britain or now in the midst of a global pandemic, suggest the depth of mistrust of old sources of elite authority. The continuing appeal of media-savvy, mostly ultra-right-wing populist politicians, conspiracy theorists and outright fascists is evident in many countries. There are also notable left-wing populists, for instance in Latin America as well as in Europe, who make use of conspiracy narratives, so I do not want to suggest some right-wing monopoly. However, in the last ten years the most striking and consequential examples in the West, I contend, have come from the Right.

During the 2010s, leaders such as Trump and Bolsonaro took something important from the playbook of the Italian right-wing media tycoon turned politician Silvio Berlusconi, who first became prime minister in 1994. Even before the internet provided a supercharged mode of communication, Berlusconi was already adept at dominating media attention, exploiting his ownership of TV channels and captivating huge audiences with his own demotic style. The skill was to seem both huge and successful and yet 'like the workers', in contrast to the so-called political elite. Such politicians displayed considerable guile in setting the agenda of the daily news, always appearing larger than life, and yet salty and real by comparison with the 'robot' professional politicians. Such charismatic leaders have an army of 'people shapers' to help sustain the illusion.

Current debate about such leaders (above all Trump) and what they signify might also lead us to discuss the history of the uses made of lying in politics. Trump's direct falsehoods, while US president, would be recorded daily by various newspapers, as though to insist we were now in completely uncharted waters. The lying was indeed monumental. Some pundits have suggested that the scale of it is unprecedented, a function of a new kind of performative politics, an expression of a breath-taking novel mindset of shamelessness, a symptom of the unaccountable nature, perhaps, of so much discourse on the internet, leading politicians to care only about attention, not about probity. Some point to a post-truth era; others to something more cyclical in the prominence of political mendacity. In the last decade or two, there have been many commentaries about the brazen nature of this complete untruthfulness by such political leaders, suggesting the current abandonment of a more measured, careful and sometimes hypocritical style of liberal politics that had largely prevailed since 1945. Are we witnessing, they ask, a new kind of swaggering braggadocio, a discourse of 'open' dishonesty, a frank embrace of fraud that we have not previously seen in our lifetimes? And what should we make of the careless revelations, or perhaps sometimes more-or-less deliberate public parading, of marital infidelities by various national leaders: Berlusconi and Trump, for instance, but also in Britain, Johnson? Are we now in a world where open expressions of personal as well as political deceit are required, to create a certain look, like some inverted badge of honour, part of the anti-feminist backlash, the attack against 'political correctness', a means to show that you can conquer people's hearts at will, and then dispense with them, do not care, and are sufficiently macho to reach 'the top'?

While it is true that political mores and constraints on deception may shift, questions about corruption and degeneration of political morals, not to mention debate about who guards the guardians, who polices the police, who arbitrates truth and lies, who can protect a citizenry from poisonous stories and shameless liars that threaten the state, are in fact as old as political philosophy. In Cold War times, the issue was also revived, as it is now, with many debates about truth and falsehood in the conduct of Western politics, or conversely about how to protect the probity of public discourse in a 'healthy' democracy.

Arendt's notable 1972 essay 'Lying in Politics', for example, was prompted in part by the leaking of the 'Pentagon Papers'. This was a cache of top-secret documents handed to the press by a then US defence official, Daniel Ellsberg.[26] The Papers revealed much about the war in Vietnam, and about the vast field of political lying that accompanied US military actions, under Kennedy, Johnson and Nixon alike. Arendt noted, rightly, that falsehoods in public life are age-old, and that no political state functions without some diplomatic silence and evasion to avoid international tensions, or sometimes mass panic. Like Hofstadter, she asked readers to consider basic human propensities – for example, our shared vulnerability to be attracted to liars, to accept subterfuge or to indulge in denial – and at the same time she asked that we focus attention upon the social and institutional conditions that may promote or restrict such inclinations, and disincentivise politicians, civil services and electorates from giving way to governance based on chronic deception.[27]

Arendt reminds us that we need to approach lying in politics from several directions at once. She noted the aggressive, scheming capabilities of certain people in power to manipulate; the propensity of swathes of the public to tolerate deceit; and the role of all those legions of people who staff ministries, universities, think tanks and a host of other relevant agencies: in short, all those functionaries, advisers, analysts and technicians whom she called the 'problem-solvers'. They could be truthful, challenging, well-briefed, independent and upright officials; at best, they might serve as a crucial conscience and safeguard for democracy. However, all too often such problem-solvers turned into cynical or perhaps mentally conditioned officials and hacks, working on a kind of autopilot to get the job done and maintain their careers. She had in mind Western officials whose actions might determine the fate of peoples at home or abroad about whom they knew virtually nothing, and perhaps cared even less. She saw these problem-solvers as heirs to an early Cold War ideology that was prone to treat zones of the world as test cases, chapters in a bigger story: hence Vietnam could be regarded simply as a pawn in the larger superpower chess game. A country or people might become merely collateral damage in the global task of somehow 'containing China'. Arendt also singled out, in considering contemporary lying in politics, the influence of Madison Avenue.

In a thriving society, and certainly in a flourishing democracy, Arendt suggested, politics needs to mean more than a tale of leaders, formal parties and electorates undertaking occasional votes. She emphasised the complexity of civil society, and noted the importance of critical and scrutinising agencies – a functioning and independent legal profession, the press and a robust civil service, with the requisite skills, codes, arms-length relation to the executive and appropriate ethical guidelines, supporting but also observing and sometimes constraining government. The array of necessary counterbalancing structures is easy to damage or destroy but hard to rebuild. We seek, after all, efficient but not inhuman bureaucracies, and recourse to law (or indeed 'good law projects', to borrow from the title of an organisation currently holding the UK government to account), to help to detoxify politics, not just to enforce the will of a party or leader.

Lying politicians, Arendt noted, may be adept at understanding mass psychology, tuning into wishful thinking and exploiting public reluctance to abandon preconceptions; electorates may be open to 'being perforated by single lies or torn to shreds by the organized lying of groups, nations, or classes'.[28] The liar in politics has an obvious advantage: falsehood may sound more plausible and real, as well as more palatable than inconvenient truths. The liar may have an inkling as to what the audience already keenly wishes or expects to hear. They may be very good at crafting a story in the most 'credible' fashion, whereas 'reality has the disconcerting habit of confronting us with the unexpected for which we were not prepared'.[29] The question was, how might such propensities to self-deception, as well as to lying, be contained, resisted or actively offset?

When we refer to the word 'politics' now, or aspire to see its future renewal as a means of combatting such ills, we would do well to have in mind the form that Arendt extolled. By politics she meant a process whereby a people, in their plurality, come together to engage with each other peaceably, to look at real problems, debate and try to determine collectively what is needed; to consider matters in a properly inclusive and deliberative fashion.

Politics is an achievement, maybe even an ideal; it can almost miraculously emerge, but also may tragically disappear, even if we have, formally speaking, conditions of representative democracy. It requires proper forums for ongoing debate. We have lost half the battle in advance if we accept that politics is simply a matter of occasional voting, internet surfing or angry tweeting while an administration operates in the dark and does our supposed bidding. For Arendt, freedom *is* politics. Moreover, politics always holds out the possibility of something quite new and surprising emerging. Society needs open spaces where ideas can be born and then be subject to lively exploration and critical scrutiny; sites where substantial resources exist for voters, not just officials, to consult, to test propositions, to check facts and hold governments accountable. A society, she suggested, needs to be engaged in a common conversation across all its differences. A thriving polity is surely more than a state where a majority or perhaps not even that (due to apathy, cynicism or disenfranchisement) vote in party A or party B, every few years, and leave it at that.

In politics, evidently, our capacities to think and reflect, and step back from the paranoid style, may be supported, if we are fortunate, not only by family and friends, but by serious researchers and journalists, by colleagues or workmates, by a variety of formal and informal educators, by challenging dramatists, film-makers, stand-up comics, cartoonists, artists and other commentators willing to speak truth to power. However, a politics that holds a mirror up to us and our own foibles, that invites our 'second thoughts', easily withers away, and civil society shrinks, even without recourse to totalitarian extremes and the world of Big Brother. Politics can descend, as Arendt warned, into the massaging of public opinion, appeasement of mass emotion, the wanton channelling of 'the crowd'.[30]

She considered the ideas of John Adams (the second US president) and amplified his earlier references to the importance of peer discussion, deliberation and representation. For to succeed, she insisted, the American Revolution had to create the necessary conditions for discussion and deliberation, as well as persuasion. What the Founding Fathers had realised was that after the violence required to create the Republic, the new political entity needed ongoing support and sustenance for rational debate and argument; the provision of appropriate resources, places, conventions, enduring opportunities for people to gather, *as equals*, to review, disagree, decide, and to learn. We require, this suggested, an equal 'right to assemble', and proper means to deliberate fully upon public affairs. A key word was 'deliberate'. Adams had written of conditions conducive to 'deliberative choice', and of the original animating spirit of the American Revolution, the assumption of a right to assemble, in order to 'deliberate upon public affairs'. We need, ideally, to deliberate actively about our chosen representatives, and to understand what they wish to enact and what they stand for. Deliberation means deciding *carefully*, not just randomly, emotionally or quixotically, not plucking an idea out of the air or going along with received opinion. To spell out the requirements can sound now, as in the past, hopelessly naive, and certainly Arendt's work has been contested and debated by other political philosophers ever since. Evidently, we are so far from such an ideal that even to pose it as a goal may invite cynicism; however, it is essential to keep that vision of politics in mind, not least to note how much we fall short.[31]

The most egregious examples, today, of the exploitation of people's feelings and desires for expression, and the milking of popular rage, fears, suspicions and hopes online to create personal and corporate fortunes and devastate democracies, invite consideration of a much larger question: how capitalism has proved so vastly adaptable to changing times, pulling us into new shared forms of fantasy, and denial. Some critics on the Left insist that we should face the cruel illusion that deliberative democracy, liberal justice or any hope of radical, progressive change is impossible within the form of governance we call liberal democracy; perhaps, they argue, the goal of communist revolution should be revived once again, extricated from its bad history, and revitalised so as to address the real sources of the paranoia, fear and insecurity, the fundamental and otherwise irresolvable antagonisms at the heart of our economic and political systems.[32]

Whatever conclusion we draw about that, clearly sinister forces are always lurking to threaten that *open* space of politics and our capacity to think freely. This is widely apparent in the world that is now shaped by the digital economy and by corporate capitalism. Conspiracy theory, marshalled by unaccountable interests, notably the fossil fuel industry, can have a devastating effect, as we saw in the notorious 2009 hack of emails at the University of East Anglia, to discredit climate science, that has come to be known as 'Climategate'.[33] There are massive interest groups that seek relentlessly to cancel that space for careful deliberation, to render forums for debate null and void, by corrupting the process, whether it be for personal gain, narcissistic gratification or on behalf of corporations and states. As this book was completed, in the autumn of 2021, a whistle-blower from Mark Zuckerberg's company was making a stir, informing senators in the United States that the business model of Facebook and Instagram paid little if any heed to the harm the platforms are causing to millions of children; profit trumped care in that business every time, she said, although the CEO instantly hit back.[34]

The process of politics can be derailed for and through money, via advertising, propaganda and lobbying, as Arendt noted. She also mused on how this very insistence on the importance of the *process* could seem tiresome or even intolerable to those who claim to know best for all others. Genuine engagement let alone deliberation in an electorate is truly a problem for those who assume history entails merely the implementation of foregone conclusions and plans. Let's recall here Rosa Luxemburg's anguished realisation that the Russian Revolution was killing itself, foreclosing an open revolutionary future, creating a society where 'public life gradually goes to sleep'.[35] Or rather where public life was actively put to sleep by the Party.

Politics may affect psychology, but a particular mass psychology may also be seized, solicited and then used by parties or demagogues to produce a form of anti-politics. In other words, an attack on the due process, the necessary skein of protections that politics requires. As Arendt scholar Samantha Hill put it in 2021, we need to consider how conditions come to be fostered, in Western societies, of 'organized loneliness', 'characterized by cynicism', that lead people:

down rabbit holes of thought, always thinking the worst while convincing them that there is a true reality beyond the reality of everyday life that we share. You destroy their relationship with themselves, which isolates them and cuts them off. This makes people hungry for meaning. The regime creates the conditions for loneliness through political propaganda, while also meeting that hunger for meaning by telling people how to think and who to blame.[36]

We need to hold in mind now, as much as ever before, Arendt's notion, indeed her ideal, of politics: to ask what spaces exist for listening, witnessing, speaking, collaborating, dissenting and collectively choosing.[37] And continuously to analyse how far we are from such a model, and then seek to lessen the gap. As I have noted, some believe the gap can be closed within the prevailing system; others seek its revolutionary transformation. We need to consider today the combination of a sense of frantic hyper-connectivity, and fragmentation, a constant flow of news 'nuggets', where nothing really makes sense, or is contextualised and fully explained: a 'news cycle' where at best we oscillate between attending to the constant buzz and switching off.

The path of politics, as Arendt conceived it, must be open; people are bound to have contrasting experiences, divergent stories, opposing fears, clashing desires; but that is different from a system where the worst passions are cultivated by the parties with the most money and power, drowning out alternative voices, refusing even to allow fact checkers to have a proper hearing. The question now must surely be about the renewal of systems and structures that enable politics in Arendt's sense. In short, we need to struggle for the creation, or in some instances the restoration, of conditions that enable us better to engage with each other as people, with requisite information, and to think in company with others about our futures, to compare notes on harms and on remedies, with less role for money and the banishment of corrupt corporate lobbyists in that process, and to protect as far as we can shared forums for news – where paranoid fears and false accounts are turned around.

Politics must mean more than formal parties, stage-managed conferences, law-making chambers, with all the rest of the process reduced to shrill shouting matches on social media. Politics should not be just a means to an end; it is a value in itself. The idea of human beings as political animals can be traced back to the Greeks, especially to Aristotle; Arendt was one of the most formidable modern thinkers to retrieve this idea of our essential political identities, and what can then happen to pervert or destroy those identities.

A central implication of the material in the present book is, indeed, that we need to attend to how a society creates or hampers conditions for politics in that sense; and, I'd add, more specifically democratic politics; how it enables or disables a population from having the means to *think* and to choose, as equals, deliberatively, wisely, when it most matters. Politics is always at risk of corruption, erosion or even abolition. Yet politics can potentially also be renewed, retained as the lodestar, brought back closer to actual shared life. Politics can disappear into a barren desert, of course, but there can also be new oases, innovative spaces for thinking afresh, new public arenas for engagement and debate that we have yet to foresee.[38]

Arendt was not alone in conceiving of politics as vital to human flourishing, or in warning that the process of politics required constant vigilance and careful nurture and could all too easily be foreclosed. Other intellectuals post-war linked the idea of an open democratic political process to the healthy mind, hence pluralistic, tolerant of difference, open to challenge and doubt, capable of entertaining new possibilities, never ossified or tyrannised.[39] A generation older than Arendt was Melanie Klein, a psychoanalyst whose concern primarily was the inner world, but whose ideas also have an important bearing on politics and the paranoid style. Klein developed a model of the mind based around two central concepts: the depressive position and the paranoid-schizoid position.[40] In the former, which she regarded as a psychic achievement, there is more integration, but an integration that is also based on plurality, recognition of one's own mixed thoughts and feelings, some insight into one's own destructiveness, real concern for others, a wish to repair, a capacity to mourn.

In the paranoid-schizoid position, the one that comes earliest in life, the mind, or rather the nascent ego, that she envisaged, is fragile, porous, divided, sensitive and explosive; it feels easily bombarded; it is concerned with survival and ejects what it can't bear, constantly projecting bits of itself and what feels 'bad' onto another. The fledgling ego may be terrified of its own total disintegration, or conversely in awe of its own imagined, terrifying omnipotence. In the depressive position one has a chance to gather and think. The depressive position, for Klein, is never secure: we are never simply 'mature', integrated, cured, balanced. Rather, those of us who are sane enough, and not simply stuck, oscillate between the paranoid-schizoid and depressive positions, hopefully increasingly staying with the latter. Paranoid-schizoid mechanisms are the earliest ways the psyche finds to protect itself, but if we stay in that position always, then things never come together in our minds, to enable thoughtful reflection. In early life, we have thoughts but are not able to reflect much on those thoughts, or to contain our own most intense feelings.

The infant's capacity to think about its own mind and others' comes about through its internal struggles, and crucially through its evolving relationship with a thinking and sensitive caregiver. In Klein's wake, others, most notably Wilfred Bion, developed this idea, showing how the baby projects its feelings (for example by crying) in the hope that these projections will find a suitable 'container', a carer who not only picks up on the baby's feelings but also provides a crucial thinking function, based on sufficient loving and attentive care. Thinking is then ultimately facilitated inside the baby's mind – a kind of care within, linked ultimately with a capacity to tolerate and make sense of complexity in the self, in the other and in the world. Some people make the best of very little care, but we all need, Klein assumed, a 'good object' inside to help us to think. Hopefully we develop a capacity to recognise the conflicts in our emotions, wishes, thoughts; some ability to link them up and think about them, and to face our dependency and limitations. But the achievement is always reversible, and we move back to something more archaic, frightening and raw. Psychic integration (such as it is) remains precarious. We are all affected, and easily destabilised or humiliated, when our environments are convulsed, when relationships fray or break; and by the passions and drives, those warring others within. Thus, the need for psychological 'containment' goes on throughout life, inside, but also at an interpersonal and social level; to assist us to think without constantly resorting to the sometimes indispensable but often desperate and distorting mechanisms of splitting and projection.[41]

Circumstances in the 2020s are of course very different to those that prevailed when that important strand of psychoanalytic thought was elaborated by Klein and her followers, and when Arendt wrote of

politics and the human condition. We can still draw profitably upon
their vital ideas, even if we are also required to think afresh, as we
ask what shared cultural values, what social structures, economic
arrangements and technological facilities are most likely to support
a mode of politics that is properly ambitious, inclusive, uncertainty-
tolerant, self-critical and caring, avoiding, on the one hand, apathy,
depression and cynicism, and on the other, paranoia, mania and
crazed conviction.

Liberal democracy in its current incarnations is not best regarded,
I assume, as some satisfactory political end point, but rather the
foundation for a struggle towards more democracy and a deeper realisation of human freedom. We need to consider what the institutions
are that we already have that can support this never-ending struggle,
and to ask, what kinds of social conditions and modes of 'containment' are needed to reduce unbearable anxiety, manage passions and
conflicts, sustain debate, foster thinking and enable measured and
decisive collective actions? Post-war, the answer seemed increasingly
clear to many people who held sway in liberal democracies: greater
investment in the dignity of work; freedom from squalor, ignorance
and want; support of and greater access to schools and universities
and an entitlement to education and training; public service broadcasting; and adequate healthcare, either through insurance schemes
or general taxation, but, crucially, free at the point of use. In some
countries, where these measures were most fully realised, an integrated 'welfare state' would emerge.

Such measures were regarded by the majority post-war as important for the development of societies. In many instances those post-war
societies gradually did become more inclusive, less obviously unequal
and on the whole safer and more secure places in which to live. We
can't go back to the past, just seek to revive a post-1945 model of the
welfare state, and nor should we idealise it either. But many of those
values and goals surely remain essential. For those who value liberal
democracy or agree at least that it provides the necessary platform
for a more egalitarian future, it is important to consider why it has
proved so difficult to renew structures of social care and creaking old
electoral processes, to counter the influence of big money, to resist
cynical strategies of gerrymandering and voter suppression and to
avoid grotesque online disinformation wars. Innovations are clearly
needed in the way societies are organised, protected and supported if

we hope to get off the self-destructive and ominously anti-democratic paths that many parties and states are currently on.

We can begin by noting what neoliberalism's 'stealth revolution' (as Wendy Brown puts it) ushered in over the last forty or fifty years; and ask how we may find new ways in the future to counter this effectively, without surrender to authoritarian populism. Our current institutions are evidently in need of renewal, but we need to notice properly that they are under systematic attack. Clearly many of those institutions long established in liberal and social democratic politics that aspire to be more than just 'market operations', and to provide the settings for administering justice, or for providing education, health, communication, art, etc., have not always been as inclusive, transparent or equitably spread across nation states as they ought to be. Yet, if they require substantial reform and change, to meet different times, and to fulfil more adequately their original missions, they also need protection from the threat of decimation, or at least complete commercialisation, as for example today we can see in the threat from the Right, in the UK, to the BBC.

Legislative and constitutional frameworks need attending to, as do sources of news. A further and obvious implication to be drawn from much of the primary literature on brainwashing is that the manner in which a society treats and values critical commentators and probing journalists has immense political consequences; reporters need to be able to thrive without having to prostitute themselves and do the bidding of those with power, for example by working for organs of 'infotainment' designed to mislead and make profits for political tyrants and business tycoons. For we have, no doubt, equivalents in the capitalist world of the artists reduced to producing odes and marches to 'socialist realism' as described by Miłosz.

Education is certainly no guarantee, but it can offer much useful equipment to help people read politics better, to look in a more critical fashion at different points of view, to understand the models on which political offers are based, and to be able to see the present and future in relation to where we have been in the past. Citizens' assemblies are increasingly recognised as important experiments that might be expanded in democracies, where debate is tied to better information and to an insistence on listening as well as to arguing; they offer a good deal of promise which has yet to be fully explored or applied. And in this regard the technology available now clearly can help.

There are lots of ideas out there, beyond the scope of this book, for the deepening of e-democracy, participatory budgeting, co-operative working, international networking (and solidarity), or at the most local level, new forms of neighbourhood forums, town hall meetings, community actions, deliberative polling and greater transparency. In the borough in which I live in London, the local council embarked recently on just such a creative, participatory exercise to draw citizens, chosen at random, into detailed and sustained discussion with officials, of policy goals and practical actions on climate change.[42]

We have rational grounds to be very worried, for sure, about the way technology is organised now; about who owns and controls it, how algorithms are designed to ensnare us, how our data is used, who exploits data voids, and so on. Looking to the future some envisage the ever more complete triumph of the great tech corporations and warn that they could usher in a fully immersive and ultimately inescapable digital environment or metaverse. This may start to sound like the final realisation of certain sci fi tales of old, a fully simulated and synchronised world. It is hard to grasp the consequences of all these rapidly changing developments in 3-D modelling and block chain technology, or to know where the latest advances in 'augmented reality' headsets, implants, etc., may be taking us. Pessimists warn of our full descent into a 'place' that mimics the real world but also renders it null. In such visions, economic activity and communication might elude any meaningful government controls, let alone democratic accountability. But we do not have, I think, just grounds to despair. As Gramsci said long ago, we need 'optimism of the will, pessimism of the intellect'. There are campaigns for a new kind of charter; one, for instance, is being spearheaded by Tim Berners-Lee. We require, he notes, a fundamental rethink of the whole thing, a different system, in which we would seriously address how, as he puts it, prejudice, hate and disinformation are 'peddled online' and how 'scammers use the web to steal identities, stalkers use it to harass and intimidate their victims, and bad actors subvert democracy using clever digital tactics'.[43]

But the internet, the source of so much malice, cruelty and deception, is also, potentially, an excellent resource for education in its broadest sense, rebutting pernicious rumour mills, building new collective alliances and associations and informing us about events taking place in other areas, even in real time, on a scale that was previously unimaginable. Many commentators insist rightly on the importance of campaigning for greater equity of access to the internet, at home and abroad; working to achieve the break-up of monopoly companies, better regulation of political advertising, protocols for policing hate speech and dealing with trolling, and, above all, the provision, as Berners-Lee proposes, of 'pods', so that people retain their data, and can choose knowingly to whom they give access.

Given a real sense of community, offered solidarity, dignity in life, we are more likely to maintain a saner contact with the real world. As a bare minimum in any prescription for a survivable future, in which we can think without being spun, we need a community that is also open, not closed, that allows for difference, that recognises a need to mourn, individually and collectively, and that offers sufficient safeguards against mass denial or unchecked greed. Many books, such as *The Spirit Level*,[44] have offered metrics to show how, in grossly socially unfair systems, with vast disparities of income and unbridled private wealth, *everyone* may be, in emotional and social terms, worse off; they show why inequality and massive untaxed and hidden private fortunes ought to trouble us; they may well increase the sum of human unhappiness, not make us all more 'aspirational' and 'high achieving' or 'dynamic'. Much of the logic of 'trickle-down economics' has now been thoroughly debunked. Such studies often focus on inequalities inside nations; but global inequities resulting from centuries of exploitation internationally also cry out for urgent redress.

In the autumn of 2021, the UN secretary-general appealed to affluent states to do far more to protect workers in the world's poorest nations, who have suffered most extremely the consequences of the Covid-19 pandemic. He put a number on it, calling for an additional $1tn (£736bn) injection of funds to avoid a twin-track recovery that widens the gap between the wealthy and poorest nations in the immediate years ahead. Speaking in New York, the UN chief noted that the gravest global public health and economic crisis the world has faced in the past century was on course to worsen inequalities and threatened 'the long-term livelihoods and well-being of hundreds of millions, if not billions, of people'. We need to clarify the nature of the forces arraigned against necessary action, and debate what, in the face of climate breakdown, war, mass migrations and ever more economic dislocation ahead, best supports human security, interpersonal care and sustainable living. What would help create resilience, and what level or kind of prosperity is essential anyway, in any society, for it to 'prosper'? What illusions (not least, those of the wealthier nations) must now be mourned, what cover-ups faced, what corruption fought, what reparations made for wrongs and ills?

Are we more vulnerable to the paranoid style than in times past? Yes and no. True, these days ideas can 'go viral' online, within minutes. And, for sure, the near ubiquity of economic insecurity, massive financial and political corruption in many states, the rise in international tensions, the break-up of former communities, the privatisation or abolition of former public assets and spaces in cities, towns and rural communities, exacerbate the 'organised loneliness' that Arendt identified. Pessimistic political analysts point to how the internet is prone to keep us isolated or in illusory alliances, to hook and divide us, and how more careful and complex analyses of social problems are at a great disadvantage in such a medium: things move so fast. But the future of the internet, as of other forums for politics, is ultimately open, even if it is true that it has been corporatised and monetarised at present. It is also true that human action over centuries (in what we now call the Anthropocene) has transformed conditions of life on the planet, generating forces, irreversible changes, the loss of biodiversity, risks of extinction for many species, unviable habitats for people in many places, that cannot simply be reversed by future programmatic action or collective will in the coming century: hence mourning has an important place, and policies are needed aimed at practical mitigation, not some fantastical form of collective rebirth, or some blithe promise of endless, untrammelled 'growth'.

We must consider what changes are needed to reduce the atomised loneliness and sense of hopelessness that Arendt, long ago, was talking about; to renew social, political and legal structures that support us better, to listen, think, debate, understand the consequences of our actions, and not to resort to denial, disavowal or simplistic explanations, trying to drown out opposing views. We need, in short, society, community, culture, as well as that Arendtian vision of politics. No social order can abolish loneliness. It is a state that can be fundamental to our sense of self. Klein argued that loneliness, indeed, is part of the human condition, a consequence, at least in part, of our earliest infantile paranoid states.[45] But more integrated states of mind, and certain kinds of more integrated political states in which we can live together with others, help mitigate that loneliness and make us less porous to cynical thought manipulation or outright brainwashing.

The narcissism that Freud, Klein and others described in psychic life can also pervert our engagement in politics. The psychoanalyst and climate campaigner Sally Weintrobe has well described assumptions of Western entitlement, which she calls exceptionalism, the illusion bought into by many of us, and sanctioned as well as intensified by political creeds, including, of course, neoliberalism, of infinite growth, a natural right to a given lifestyle, unfettered individualism, without needing to be mindful of the long-term social and environmental consequences, even now in the face of climate disaster. This state of mind, or rather this ideology, fosters or exploits a narcissistic wish. It proceeds as though people in other countries, usually those outside the West, or even children in the West today, let alone unborn generations, require little or no consideration. And this ideology presents a massive danger to effective global action to mitigate current still spiralling carbon use.[46]

We keep reaching precipices, politically as well as ecologically. It is sobering to read how the most senior general in the US armed forces was convinced in January 2021 that Trump and his closest circle were actively engineering a coup.[47] What if the safeguards had failed, and the generals had gone the other way? And imagine, what if a new Trump emerges, more competent and focused, and thus able to railroad through the necessary measures to destroy entirely the checks and balances on which the Republic was founded, and to bring the death knell to any prospect of climate disaster mitigation? It is not far-fetched to envisage the sunset of democracies now.[48]

Some fear that coalitions for progressive change are largely helpless in the face of such evil and such madness. There is indeed no guarantee that democracy, hard-won civil liberties or the wish to care for each other and for the earth are certain to survive. Previous congratulatory assumptions that an 'open society' is always bound to outpace an authoritarian state, such as China, are now less sure and shrill than a few years ago; and, anyway, how 'open' a society is ours these days, other than to our own mass manipulators? Are we living, as Anne Applebaum has warned, in the 'twilight of democracy'? Her recent book compellingly describes the diverse attacks taking place in Hungary, Poland, the United States, the UK and elsewhere, on the very structures that sustain democracy and enable a flourishing society.[49]

Even as I write, the government in my own country, still a liberal democracy of sorts, albeit of a very peculiar kind (with so many votes in our 'first past the post' system counting for nothing), is led by a prime minister who lies shamelessly, adopts a clownish shtick and careers wildly from the most illiberal measures to calls and half steps towards an agenda for greater fairness and stepped-up climate action. Yet from the moment he came into office he was evidently also serious in weakening the historic forms of protection against authoritarian populism – a strong and free school system, a robust university sector, an independent judiciary, a transparent, accountable civil service distinct from the elected officialdom, a fully functioning parliament, public service broadcasting, proper systems of care for the young, the old and the frail, and decent safeguards for people fleeing to these shores. Our PM talks of 'levelling up' the most deprived and excluded but wants to do so without 'frightening the horses', i.e. the wealthy, who fund and vote (along with a portion of the working class) for his party.

We are not, of course, at the end of history. Whatever the future may hold, the prevalence of conspiracy theories and paranoid discourse in politics today makes revisiting the history of ideas about brainwashing and thought control relevant and urgent. Political identities are always shaped in part by states of fantasy.[50] The literature explored in these pages suggests that, in a democracy, fantasies shadow our choices, and differences of opinion, passions, struggles over the nature of justice, major tensions about equity, reward and the sharing of spoils will always occur, and that we will all – to differing extents – be vulnerable to illusions and schisms, and the lure of the paranoid style. The issue is how effectively we contain, recover from or work through such states; and what foundations we have in a particular polity for reasoned and sane debate, for justice and for concerted action in face of existential threats to life on earth.

A crisis is also an opportunity. Emergencies have been seized upon by ideologues for all kinds of purposes, not least to create those neoliberal 'utopian' projects. The question now is how the current crisis unfolds; and how we retain the freedom to think about it, and to respond to it in new ways. Slogans such as 'build back better' are worthless unless backed by concrete policy actions. As Greta Thunberg said, ahead of the vital but disappointing round of climate change negotiations, COP26, in 2021, 'blah blah blah'. As she implies, the question is what is done by those with the power, and what pressure we can exert, as citizens, to effect change in them.

So, if you are still wondering, 'am I brainwashed?', a good place to start is in consideration of the interlocking environmental, political and economic emergencies. Does the present-day crisis engage you, or do you just switch the channel? If so, why, and encouraged by whom? We do well to keep returning to those questions about the sorts of bargain we strike with ourselves, the rationalisations we make, and who else, apart from ourselves, the deceptions might serve. The best of the literature of the Cold War we have explored here investigated so many forerunners of such current psycho-political concerns; that literature was often as preoccupied with denial and disavowal as with how we can be brainwashed, lied to, enflamed, distracted, secretly influenced or cynically misled. It showed how a particular milieu can destroy us or give us better grounds for realistic hope.

We may be surveyed, policed, cajoled and controlled; sometimes people face impossible odds in exercising any freedom of mind or personal agency at all in the material world. But often we have room to act and make decisions, and certainly we bargain with ourselves and others. We cannot have complete mastery of our own minds or of our environments, but we can notice ways we are deceiving ourselves and fitting in. We may perhaps find new concrete ways to bolster and renew the democratic foundations of politics that we value. We might have more potential to change paths, and make choices, than we tell ourselves. As well as challenging the webs of lies and deceptions we are offered, we can notice the webs that we weave for ourselves, the ways we succumb to lies and deadly stories, even in conditions of relative freedom.

ACKNOWLEDGEMENTS

I owe a large debt of gratitude to the Wellcome Trust; a Senior Investigator Award enabled me to establish a research group at Birkbeck College and to have the necessary time to work on this book. Details of the publications, online resources, broadcasts and films produced under the auspices of this project can be found at www7.bbk.ac.uk/hiddenpersuaders/. My thanks to all those who supported the endeavour at the Trust and the College, and especially to Marcia Holmes, Katie Joice, Ian Magor, Sarah Marks, Naomi Richman and Charlie Williams for their impressive individual research and creative teamwork. Thanks also to Emily Bartlett, Simon Jarrett, Holly Lasko and Nicole Mennell for helpful editorial input and research assistance on the project. To Charlie and Simon for reading my manuscript at short notice, and significantly sharpening it. To Katy Pettit for administering 'Hidden Persuaders' with unfussy efficiency and much-needed humour.

Thanks to my patients for their candour and trust, and for enabling me to think afresh about several issues at stake in this work. I cannot name the numerous students, nor list all the academics, archivists and librarians in the UK and US who facilitated my work on this book, but I can mention at least those friends and colleagues who have contributed most directly, and generously, by sharing ideas and reading draft chapters. To Julia Lovell, Lyndal Roper, Quentin Skinner, Gareth Stedman Jones and Eli Zaretsky, for their creative suggestions and sage advice. To Elizabeth Coates Thümmel, Matt ffytche, Stephen Frosh, Simon Garfield, Rufus Olins and Matthew Reisz, for their invaluable thoughts about my work in progress. To Lisa Baraitser and Simon Bayly, for incisive comments, providing so many stimulating thoughts on politics and psychoanalysis along the way. To Chris Wellbelove, my literary agent, for his steady support, and for offering, along with Amy St Johnston, also at Aitken Alexander Associates, such pragmatic guidance when my writing got stuck. To Shan Vahidy, an outstanding editorial 'troubleshooter', who has been a pleasure to work with, and who has played a key role in refashioning this book.

To have the chance to discuss this history with the late Zygmunt Bauman and Robert Jay Lifton was truly a privilege. I also had illuminating exchanges on this topic over the years with Ana Antić, Shaul Bar-Haim, Joanna Bourke, Greg Brenman, Susan Carruthers, Ian Christie, D'Maris Coffman, Matt Cook, Bartek Dziadosz (and the group of talented film-makers who work with him at the Derek Jarman Lab), Nasheed Faruqi, David Feldman, Paul Feldwick, Lily Ford, the late John Forrester,

Stephen Grosz, Mary-Clare Hallsworth, Dagmar Herzog, Jenny Langham, Peter Mandler, Don Moss, Rebecca Reich, Priscilla Roth, Hilary Sapire, Simon Schaffer, Rory Sutherland, David Taylor, Phil Tinline and Lynne Zeavin. Thanks to Shui-Bo Wang for putting me in touch with David Hawkins. His contribution, for which I am also thankful, can be seen in Part 2. To Tim Allen, Mike Dibb, Lisa Guenther, Monica Kim, Jonathan Lear, Melissa Parker and Andrew Scull for their rich and thought-provoking presentations at Birkbeck, during the project. Conversations with Catherine Hall, with whom I co-edited a series of pieces on the question of 'denial', in *History Workshop Journal*, were also inspiring.

Kirty Topiwala, then employed at Wellcome, helped to set *Brainwashed* in motion. I am also grateful to my editor, Cecily Gayford, for her exceptional skill and patience, to Rebecca Gray, Graeme Hall and the team at Profile Books for their excellent input, and to Patrick Taylor for his careful and well-judged copy-editing, Caroline Wilding for the fine index, and Philippa Logan for painstaking proofreading.

My family have lived with this project for longer than reasonable. I am grateful to Irma Brenman Pick, for all her care, lively interest in this work and wealth of insights. To Anna and Tasha Pick for encouragement and the many vivid conversations we've had on these matters, not least during the time of pandemic. This book is dedicated to Isobel Pick. I owe her the biggest thanks, for all her generous help and unflagging support. She has exchanged ideas, commented closely on drafts and provided throughout a clear-eyed sense of the relevance of this troubling history in present, dark times.

Daniel Pick
London, 20 January 2022

NOTES

Where possible a freely accessible URL is provided below for newspaper and other material. All were accessible, online, when the book went to press in early 2022.

Preface

1. In the 1970s and 80s, the politics of news was a prominent subject of academic research. Much was written about implicit biases, with critics on the Left highlighting small 'c' conservative assumptions prevalent on the BBC. See, for instance, analyses by the Glasgow Media Group, resulting in publications such as *Bad News* (1976), *More Bad News* (1980) and *Really Bad News* (1982). Political coverage during the miners' strike of 1984 was also much criticised. More recently, right-wing critics as well as government ministers have complained of the BBC's liberal, or left-leaning, journalism, threaten to break up the corporation and advocate its complete commercialisation in a global marketplace. See, for example, Rowena Mason, 'Dominic Cummings thinktank called for "end of BBC in current form"', *Guardian*, 21 January 2020, www.theguardian.com/politics/2020/jan/21/dominic-cummings-thinktank-called-for-end-of-bbc-in-current-form. Cf. Adam Forrest, 'Government accused of attacking BBC to stop PM becoming "dead meat" as licence fee frozen', *Independent*, 17 January 2022, www.independent.co.uk/news/uk/politics/bbc-licence-fee-dorries-boris-b1994782.html.

2. George Lakoff and Mark Johnson, *Metaphors We Live By* (Chicago, 1980).

3. Bess Levin, 'White House: We're Going to Have to Let Some People Die So the Stock Market Can Live', *Vanity Fair*, 23 March 2020, www.vanityfair.com/news/2020/03/donald-trump-coronavirus-deaths-vs-economy. Cf. 'President Trump has shown a unique obsession with the financial markets, tweeting that high stock prices proved he was making America great again.' Ruchir Sharma, 'Trump's Dangerous Obsession With the Markets', *The New York Times*, 9 April 2019, www.nytimes.com/2019/04/09/opinion/trump-stock-market-results.html. Also, Heather Boushey, 'The stock market is detached from economic reality. A reckoning is coming', *Washington Post*, 9 September 2020, www.washingtonpost.com/outlook/stock-market-unemployment-disconnect/2020/09/09/087374ca-f306-11ea-bc45-e5d48ab44b9f_story.html.

4. John Steiner, *Psychic Retreats: Pathological Organizations in Psychotic, Neurotic*

and Borderline Patients (Hove, 1993); and idem, *Seeing and Being Seen: Emerging from a Psychic Retreat* (Abingdon, 2011).

5. Zygmunt Bauman, *Liquid Modernity* (Cambridge, 2000).

6. Mariana Mazzucato, *The Value of Everything: Making and Taking in the Global Economy* (London, 2018).

7. Kate Raworth, *Doughnut Economics: Seven Ways to Think Like a 21st-Century Economist* (London, 2017), p. 13.

8. Raworth suggests that rather than be fixated on charts about growth, we need to hold in mind an image of a doughnut, i.e. its two rings – the one indicating the resources required for human flourishing, the other the limitations of what the planet can sustain. Policy makers need to steer the economy within them.

9. Sigmund Freud, 'Observations on Transference-Love (Further Recommendations on the Technique of Psycho-Analysis)', 1915, *The Standard Edition of the Complete Psychological Works of Sigmund Freud* (London, 1953), vol 12, pp. 157–71.

Part 1: Brainwashing

1. Prior to Hunter's account, a French journalist, Robert Guillain, had written an article entitled 'China Under the Red Flag' in the *Manchester Guardian* on 3 January 1950 about Maoist re-education, or 'what Chinese papers graphically term "washing one's brains"'. For the origins of the term, see Marcia Holmes, 'Edward Hunter and the origins of "brainwashing"', 26 May 2017, www7.bbk.ac.uk/hiddenpersuaders/blog/hunter-origins-of-brainwashing/. See also Charlie Williams, 'Battles for the Mind: Brainwashing, Altered States and the Politics of the Nervous System (1945–1970)', (unpublished doctoral thesis, Birkbeck College, University of London, 2018); Timothy Melley, 'Brain Warfare: The Covert Sphere, Terrorism, and the Legacy of the Cold War', *Grey Room*, 45 (2011), 19–41, p. 28.

2. Edward Hunter, '"Brain-Washing" Tactics Force Chinese into Ranks of the Communist Party', *Miami News*, 24 September 1950.

3. Gordon Shepherd, *Creating Modern Neuroscience: The Revolutionary 1950s* (Oxford, 2010); Andreas Killen, *Nervous Systems: Brain Science in the Early Cold War* (New York, forthcoming), and online lecture, www7.bbk.ac.uk/hiddenpersuaders/blog/a-cultural-history-of-the-brain-in-the-1950s/.

4. Edward Hunter, *Brainwashing: The Story of Men Who Defied It* [1956] (Toronto, 2012). See also William Sargant, *Battle for the Mind: A Physiology of Conversion and Brain-washing* (London, 1957).

5. Reports in 1966 and after suggested how Mao was calculatedly unleashing collective 'madness', and 'brainwashing' hundreds of thousands or perhaps millions of Red Guards. See, for instance, this account of the Cultural Revolution which appeared in the Taiwanese media: 'Red Guards – A Calculated Madness', *Taiwan News*, 1 October 1966, taiwantoday.tw/news.php?unit=4&post=6958.

6. Hunter, *Brainwashing*, p. 3.

7. Ibid.

8. Robert Jay Lifton, *The Nazi Doctors: Medical Killing and the Psychology of Genocide* (New York, 1986); Paul Weindling, *Nazi Medicine and the Nuremberg Trials* (Basingstoke, 2004).

9. Hunter, *Brainwashing*, p. 3.

10. Ibid., p. 4.

11. Ibid., p. 16.

12. The word did not necessarily translate directly into the vernacular of other languages; so in French, for example, in the 1950s and 60s, other ways existed to convey the basic idea; furthermore, the new term if used at all was sometimes given in English rather than presented as '*lavage de cerveau*'.

13. For a set of visual essays by school students, reflecting on brainwashing, see the 'Hidden Persuaders' website, www.bbk.ac.uk/hiddenpersuaders/outreach/. For the context, Daniel Pick, Mary-Clare Hallsworth and Sarah Marks, 'Hidden Persuaders on Film: Exploring Young People's Lived Experience Through Visual Essays', *Research for All*, 5:2 (2021), 382–99, www.scienceopen.com/hosted-document?doi=10.14324/RFA.05.2.13.

14. Yuval Noah Harari, *Homo Deus: A Brief History of Tomorrow* (London, 2016); and idem, *21 Lessons for the 21st Century* (London, 2019).

15. 'The Affair of the Brains' appeared in a popular US publication, *Astounding Stories*, in 1932. It was written by H. G. Bates, a sci fi writer and editor, who had various *noms de plume*, including Anthony Gilmore. The story was also included in *Space Hawk: The Greatest of Interplanetary Adventurers* (New York, 1952).

16. *Der Fuehrer's Face* (1943) can be located on YouTube, as can *Stranger's Voice* (1949), www.youtube.com/watch?v=gzScYtmg0yY. For the context, Ülo Pikkov, 'On the Topics and Style of Soviet Animated Films', *Baltic Screen Media Review*, 4 (2016), 16–37, content.sciendo.com/view/journals/bsmr/4/1/article-p16.xml.

17. Ben Child, 'Fox host Lou Dobbs slams Arrietty and The Lorax for "liberal agenda"', *Guardian*, 23 February 2012, www.theguardian.com/film/2012/feb/23/fox-lou-dobbs-lorax-liberal-agenda.

18. 'Living My Life – Lyrics', genius.com, genius.com/Grace-jones-living-my-life-lyrics.

19. Jones remarked in an interview, 'there were ways of escaping the brainwashing but not for long'. Quoted in Grace Jones and Paul Morley, *I'll Never Write My Memoirs* (New York, 2015), p. 38.

20. Clive Stafford Smith, 'Welcome to "the disco"', *Guardian*, 19 June 2008, www.theguardian.com/world/2008/jun/19/usa.guantanamo. Cf. Morag Josephine Grant and Anna Papaeti, 'Introduction', *The World of Music*, special issue on *Music and Torture*, 2:1 (2013), 5–7.

21. In the case of James Vance vs. Judas Priest (1990), the band were accused of including subliminal messages in their 1978 cover of the song, 'Better by You, Better than Me'. It was alleged to have inspired teenagers James Vance and Ray Belknap to attempt suicide in December 1985. (The latter succeeded,

while the former was left permanently disfigured and died three years later.)
The judge concluded that the band could not be held responsible. For the
context and outcome, see Dominic Streatfeild, *Brainwash: The Secret History
of Mind Control* (London, 2007), pp. 178–218, and Kory Grow, 'Judas Priest's
Subliminal Message Trial: Rob Halford Looks Back', *Rolling Stone*, 24 August
2015, www.rollingstone.com/music/music-features/judas-priests-subliminal-
message-trial-rob-halford-looks-back-57552/. See also James Kennaway, *Bad
Vibrations: The History of the Idea of Music as a Cause of Disease* (Abingdon,
2012).

22. Randall Stephens, *The Devil's Music: How Christians Inspired, Condemned, and
Embraced Rock 'N' Roll* (Cambridge, MA, 2018), especially the Introduction
and Chapter 3. See also Ed Vulliamy, 'For young Soviets, the Beatles were a
first, mutinous rip in the iron curtain', *Observer*, 20 April 2013, www.
theguardian.com/music/2013/apr/20/beatles-soviet-union-first-rip-iron-
curtain; and Lily Ford's 2021 short film, *The Stuff that Screams are Made of*,
www7.bbk.ac.uk/hiddenpersuaders/documentaries/three-films-
about-mass-influence-by-lily-ford.

23. Frances Stonor Saunders, *Who Paid the Piper? The CIA and the Cultural Cold
War* (London, 1999).

24. Josh Ozersky, *Archie Bunker's America: TV in an Era of Change, 1968–1978*
(Carbondale, 2003), p. 60.

25. Olivia Waxman, 'The Story Behind That Famous Photograph of Elvis and
Richard Nixon', *Time*, 15 August 2017, time.com/4894301/elvis-president-
nixon-photo/. For a transcript of the letter, see www.archives.gov/exhibits/
nixon-met-elvis/assets/doc_1.1_transcript.html.

26. Martin Chulov, 'My son, Osama: the al-Qaida leader's mother speaks for the
first time', *Guardian*, 3 August 2018, www.theguardian.com/world/2018/
aug/03/osama-bin-laden-mother-speaks-out-family-interview. This interview,
Chulov noted, had been sanctioned by the Saudi authorities. 'The people at
university changed him,' Osama's mother said to him; her son 'was a very
good child until he met some people who pretty much brainwashed him …
You can call it a cult. They got money for their cause. I would always tell him
to stay away from them, and he would never admit to me what he was doing,
because he loved me so much.'

27. Some columnists urged a compassionate response be shown by the UK
authorities to Begum's situation; others approved, even celebrated the
government's refusal to allow her ever to return to the UK. See, for instance,
Allison Pearson, 'Sorry my heartless little jihadi bride, but you made your
bed and now you can lie in it', *Daily Telegraph*, 14 February 2019, www.
telegraph.co.uk/news/2019/02/14/sorry-heartless-little-jihadi-bride-made-
bed-now-can-lie/.

28. It appeared that the relevant authorities in Bangladesh had not been
consulted before some British officials assured the world that she could claim
citizenship there, although more likely she would have faced prosecution,
and perhaps even, it was said, the death penalty, 'Shamima Begum: IS bride

"would face death penalty in Bangladesh"', BBC News, 3 May 2019, www.bbc.co.uk/news/world-asia-48154781.

29. Anthony Lloyd, 'Shamima Begum: I was brainwashed. I knew nothing', *The Times*, 1 April 2019, www.thetimes.co.uk/article/isis-bride-shamima-begum-i-regret-everything-please-let-me-start-my-life-again-in-britain-9gotno8vn.

30. petition.parliament.uk/archived/petitions/259723.

31. See, for instance, Al Jazeera English, 'Dominic Ongwen ICC trial: Child victim or war criminal?', YouTube, 18 September 2018, www.youtube.com/watch?v=_Rho8MNlBX0&vl=en. Ongwen was found guilty by the ICC of crimes against humanity and war crimes in February 2021; see www.icc-cpi.int/Pages/item.aspx?name=pr1564.

32. On Jonestown, see Jennie Rothenberg Gritz, 'Drinking the Kool-Aid: A Survivor Remembers Jim Jones', *Atlantic*, 18 November 2011, www.theatlantic.com/national/archive/2011/11/drinking-the-kool-aid-a-survivor-remembers-jim-jones/248723/. The 'Unabomber', as Ted Kaczynski was known in the press, had undergone various psychological experiments from around 1959, while a student at Harvard. The experiments were designed by psychologists to explore, among other things, resistance to enemy interrogation. He and others were subjected to 'vehement, sweeping, and personally abusive' interrogations, during which members of the research team attacked the student-subjects' beliefs, as gleaned from their essays. Kaczynski later described these experiences as traumatic, and quite the worst of his life. During the 1960s, he lived in a hut in remote woodland. In the late 1970s, he began to send parcel bombs through the post, continuing until 1995, when he was arrested. Alston Chase, 'Harvard and the Making of the Unabomber', *Atlantic*, June 2000, www.theatlantic.com/magazine/archive/2000/06/harvard-and-the-making-of-the-unabomber/378239/; see also Brian Dunleavy, 'Did Ted Kaczynski's Transformation Into the Unabomber Start at Harvard?', *History*, 25 May 2018, www.history.com/news/what-happened-to-the-unabomber-at-harvard.

There are various published investigations of Manson, the 1960s 'family' that formed around him at a run-down ranch, and the murders committed by 'family' members in Los Angeles, including of Sharon Tate, the pregnant wife of the film director Roman Polanski. Public interest was recently revived after the release of Quentin Tarantino's 2019 film *Once Upon a Time in Hollywood*. For a news article recalling these crimes and referring to Manson's 'brainwashing' of his followers, see Jennifer King, 'Charles Manson, the cult mastermind who brainwashed hippie youth to kill', *ABC News*, 20 November 2017, www.abc.net.au/news/2017–11–20/charles-manson-mastermind-of-murderous-cult-dead/8163390.

33. Numerous speculations on this homegrown terrorist ensued, including prominently by Gore Vidal, about possible conspiracies, cover-ups, brainwashing and the supposed effect of a notorious book containing bomb-making instructions. Gore Vidal, 'The Meaning of Timothy McVeigh',

Vanity Fair, 10 November 2008, www.vanityfair.com/news/2001/09/mcveigh200109.

34. To protect patient confidentiality, these passing examples, drawn from clinical experiences, are not individual portraits, but camouflaged, illustrative composites. The purpose here is to discuss general features, not individual cases.

35. For a critical review of such approaches, see, for instance, Stephen Mitchell, 'The Psychoanalytic Treatment of Homosexuality: Some Technical Considerations', *Studies in Gender and Sexuality*, 3:1 (2002), 23–59; see also Dagmar Herzog, *Cold War Freud: Psychoanalysis in an Age of Catastrophes* (Cambridge, 2016). Cf. Naomi Richman, 'Homosexuality, Created Bodies, and Queer Fantasies in a Nigerian Deliverance Church', *Journal of Religion in Africa*, 50:2/3 (2021), 249–77.

36. Victor Tausk, 'On the Origin of the "Influencing Machine" in Schizophrenia' [1919], *Psychoanalytic Quarterly*, 133:2 (1933), 519–56, pp. 521–2.

37. Ibid.

38. For instance, A. M. Kasper, 'The Narcissistic Self in a Masochistic Character', *International Journal of Psychoanalysis*, 46 (1965), 474–86. The author described how a patient, Mr B., 'said I [the analyst] only wanted to brainwash him into mediocrity'. See also D. S. Jaffe, 'The Role of Ego Modification and the Task of Structural Change in the Analysis of a Case of Hysteria', *International Journal of Psychoanalysis*, 52 (1971), 375–93. This author describes how a patient tells her analyst how her mother was a 'dangerous person who "can get to you, brainwash you, have a power over you"'. The use of the words 'brainwash' and 'brainwashing' in these psychoanalytical papers and in other examples from the 1960s and 70s can be found by using the search facility at www.pep-web.org/.

39. Claudia Roth Pierpont, *Roth Unbound: A Writer and His Books* (London, 2014), p. 80. Cf. Robert Hinshelwood, *Therapy or Coercion: Does Psychoanalysis Differ from Brainwashing?* (London, 1997).

40. Weller Embler, 'Metaphor in Everyday Speech', *ETC: A Review of General Semantics*, 16:3 (1959), 323–42, pp. 341–2.

41. See Emma Graham-Harrison and Juliette Garside, 'Complete Control', *Guardian Weekly*, 29 November 2019, 10–14, p. 13; and the series of articles filed by these reporters in the *Guardian* online, for example, '"Allow no escapes": leak exposes reality of China's vast prison camp network', 24 November 2019, www.theguardian.com/world/2019/nov/24/china-cables-leak-no-escapes-reality-china-uighur-prison-camp. See also Raffi Khatchadourian's harrowing account in the *New Yorker*, 'Surviving the Crackdown in Xinjiang', 5 April 2021, www.newyorker.com/magazine/2021/04/12/surviving-the-crackdown-in-xinjiang.

42. Daniel Kahneman, *Thinking, Fast and Slow* (London, 2011).

Part 2: Breaking Point

1. news.gallup.com/poll/11887/ronald-reagan-from-peoples-perspective-gallup-poll-review.aspx.

2. Newt Gingrich lauded Reagan as a trailblazer and beacon of hope, who restored the nation, at least for a time, despite 'three generations of brainwashing', he said, by 'the hard Left'. Gingrich, 'Three Generations of Brainwashing Is Paying off for the Left', *Newsweek*, 17 June 2020, www.newsweek.com/three-generations-brainwashing-paying-off-left-opinion-1511553. See also Rebecca Klar, 'Trump says Biden has been "brainwashed"; "He's been taken over by the radical left"', *The Hill*, 9 July 2020, thehill.com/homenews/campaign/506700-trump-says-biden-has-been-brainwashed-hes-been-taken-over-by-the-radical.

3. *'Every Man Has His Breaking Point': Reagan, Brainwashing and the Movies* (2017), directed by Phil Tinline, www.bbk.ac.uk/hiddenpersuaders/documentaries/every-man-breaking-point-reagan-brainwashing-movies.

4. Charles S. Young, 'Missing Action: POW Films, Brainwashing and the Korean War, 1954–1968', *Historical Journal of Film, Radio and Television*, 18:1 (1998), 49–74. Cf. Michael Strada and Harold Tropa, *Friend or Foe? Russians in American Film and Foreign Policy, 1933–1991* (Lanham, 1997), pp. 79–80. For the broader context, see David Seed, *Brainwashing: The Fictions of Mind Control: A Study of Novels and Films Since World War II* (Kent, OH, 2004).

5. The film was rushed through by MGM, initially with considerable encouragement from officials in the US defence establishment. However, signals were apparently crossed at some stage about what kind of tale this would turn out to be. Whatever the military establishment may have hoped for, it was clearly not this production; see Young, 'Missing Action'.

6. Hunter, *Brainwashing*, pp. 14, 86.

7. Ibid., p. 14.

8. Ibid., p. 268.

9. Ibid., p. 270.

10. In *The Rack* (1956), Paul Newman played a disgraced but likeable captain, Edward Hall, court-martialled for betraying fellow American soldiers in a Korean War POW camp. We are shown how the camp guards destroyed his resolve; how his identity was attacked, and his mind overwhelmed. The argument made in the film is that his fragile personality could be traced to a painful infancy and childhood, indeed a disastrous family history, with an absent mother and cold, authoritarian military father.

11. Joost A. M. Meerloo, *The Rape of the Mind: The Psychology of Thought Control, Menticide, and Brainwashing* (Cleveland, 1956).

12. Barbed-wire disease or syndrome was named by a Swiss doctor who had looked at evidence about German POWs. See Avi Ohry and Zahava Solomon, 'Dr Adolf Lukas Vischer (1884–1974) and "Barbed-Wire Disease"', *Journal of Medical Biography*, 22:1 (2013), 16–18. For the longer history from shellshock to PTSD, see Ben Shephard, *A War of Nerves: Soldiers and Psychiatry in the Twentieth Century* (Cambridge, MA, 2001).

13. Sargant, *Battle for the Mind*; Robert Jay Lifton, *Thought Reform and the Psychology of Totalism: A Study of 'Brainwashing' in Communist China* (Chapel Hill, 1961). This notion of brainwashing, as Lifton pointed out, came to be applied 'to just about anything which the communists did anywhere' (ibid., p. 3).

14. Eric Linstrum, *Ruling Minds: Psychology in the British Empire* (Cambridge, MA, 2016). On psychiatry, for and against decolonisation, see Frantz Fanon, *Black Skin, White Masks* (1952); and idem, *Alienation and Freedom*, edited by Jean Khalfa and Robert J. C. Young (London, 2018); cf. Camille Robcis, *Disalienation: Politics, Philosophy and Radical Psychiatry in Postwar France* (Chicago, 2021). See also Nasheed Faruqi's film *Re-reading Fanon* (2021), www7.bbk.ac.uk/hiddenpersuaders/documentaries/re-reading-fanon/.

15. Rebecca Reich, *State of Madness: Psychiatry, Literature and Dissent After Stalin* (DeKalb, 2018).

16. Robert Jay Lifton, 'Home by Ship: Reaction Patterns of American Prisoners of War Repatriated from North Korea', *American Journal of Psychiatry*, 110:10 (April 1954), 732–9. This article is contained, with additional notes, in Lifton's archives; see Lifton Papers, Manuscripts and Archives Division, The New York Public Library, box 57. See also Lifton's memoir, *Witness to an Extreme Century* (New York, 2011).

17. Lifton, 'Home by Ship', p. 736.

18. Quoted in Anthony Wohl, '"Dizzi-Ben-Dizzi": Disraeli as Alien', *Journal of British Studies*, 34:1 (1995), 375–411, p. 404.

19. Clara Gallini, *La sonnambula meravigliosa: magnetismo e ipnotismo nell'Ottocento italiano* (Rome, 1983); Alison Winter, *Mesmerized: Powers of Mind in Victorian Britain* (Chicago, 1998); Daniel Pick, *Svengali's Web: The Alien Enchanter in Modern Culture* (New Haven, 2000).

20. The phrase 'Free World' was used frequently in the 1940s and after by US presidents, and in stirring works of cinema, to suggest a contrast with a 'slave world' or a 'tyrannised world'. It featured notably in Frank Capra's Second World War propaganda film series *Why We Fight*. See John Fousek, *To Lead the Free World: American Nationalism and the Cultural Roots of the Cold War* (London, 2000).

21. Paul Betts, 'Religion, Science and Cold War Anti-Communism: The 1949 Cardinal Mindszenty Show Trial', in *Science, Religion and Communism in Cold War Europe*, edited by Betts and Stephen Smith (London, 2016), pp. 275–307 (p. 286).

22. Susan Carruthers, *Cold War Captives: Imprisonment, Escape, and Brainwashing* (Berkeley, 2009), Chapter 4.

23. Archive footage of Vogeler's speech, containing these phrases, can be found at www.youtube.com/watch?v=F4hmNsv1VwE&ab_channel=historycomestolife. See also Sam Licklider, 'Robert Vogeler', *Cornell Daily Sun*, 1 May 1951, cdsun.library.cornell.edu/cgi-bin/cornell?a=d&d=CDS19510501-01.2.25.

24. Quoted in Matthew Dunne, *A Cold War State of Mind: Brainwashing and Postwar American Society* (Boston, MA, 2013), p. 40.

25. John Rawlings Rees et al., *The Case of Rudolf Hess: a Problem in Diagnosis and Forensic Psychiatry, by the Physicians in the Services Who Have Been Concerned with Him from 1941–1946* (London, 1947), p. 88.

26. On the treatment of Hess, Daniel Pick, *The Pursuit of the Nazi Mind: Hitler, Hess, and the Analysts* (Oxford, 2012), Chapter 8. On the use of Evipan see ibid., p. 61. On truth drugs, Alison Winter, 'The Making of "Truth Serum"', *Bulletin of the History of Medicine*, 79:3 (2005), 500–533. For the Korean War and interrogation practices, Monica Kim, *The Interrogation Rooms of the Korean War: The Untold History* (Princeton, 2019). For experiments in prison design during the Spanish Civil War, Paul Preston, *The Spanish Holocaust: Inquisition and Extermination in Twentieth-Century Spain* (London, 2012), p. 418; Carl-Henrik Bjerstrom, '"Enhanced Interrogation" in the Spanish Civil War: The Curious Case of Alfonso Laurencic', 15 July 2016, www.bbk.ac.uk/ hiddenpersuaders/blog/enhanced-interrogation-spanish-civil-war-curious-case-alfonso-laurencic/.

27. The subject has been copiously studied; see John Marks, *The Search for the 'Manchurian Candidate': The CIA and Mind Control* (London, 1979). More recently, Jane Mayer, *The Dark Side: The Inside Story of How the War on Terror Turned into a War on American Values* (London, 2008). See also Scott Selisker, *Human Programming: Brainwashing, Automatons, and American Unfreedom* (Minneapolis, 2016); Streatfeild, *Brainwash*; Rebecca M. Lemov, *The World as Laboratory: Experiments with Mice, Mazes and Men* (New York, 2005); Joel Dimsdale, *Dark Persuasion: A History of Brainwashing from Pavlov to Social Media* (New Haven, 2021). On some of the wilder intelligence-based experiments during the Cold War and after, see Jon Ronson, *The Men Who Stare at Goats* (London, 2004). On US and Canadian experiments on 'brainwashing', see Charlie Williams, 'Battles for the Mind'. For the post-war context in Eastern Europe, see Mat Savelli and Sarah Marks (eds), *Psychiatry in Communist Europe* (London, 2015); Ana Antić, *Therapeutic Fascism: Experiencing the Violence of the New Nazi Order* (Oxford, 2016); for the abuses of 'psy', East and West, also see Knuth Müller and Ana Antić's contributions to *Psychoanalysis in the Age of Totalitarianism*, edited by M. ffytche and D. Pick (London, 2016), Chapters 11 and 12.

28. Central Intelligence Agency (hereafter CIA), *Kubark Counterintelligence Interrogation*, July 1963, nsarchive2.gwu.edu/NSAEBB/NSAEBB27/docs/ doc01.pdf.

29. On the Cold War language (freedom, tyranny, totalitarianism) through which MK-Ultra and other related projects were defended and criticised, see Andreas Killen and Stefan Andriopoulos, 'Editors' Introduction' to feature, 'Brain Warfare: The Covert Sphere, Terrorism, and the Legacy of the Cold War', *Grey Room*, 45 (2011), 7–17. On Cameron's work and reputation, Rebecca Lemov, 'Brainwashing's Avatar: The Curious Career of Dr. Ewen Cameron', *Grey Room*, 45 (2011), 61–87. Timothy Melley suggests that what began as an

orientalist propaganda fiction exploited by the CIA, in the end convinced some of the staff at the agency. See his article, 'Brain Warfare'. Some commentators on 1950s Maoist brainwashing, such as Edgar Schein, returned in a new guise in the following decade as advisers on how to use solitary confinement, sensory deprivation and sedatives in the US prison system. See Lisa Guenther, *Solitary Confinement: Social Death and Its Afterlives* (Minneapolis, 2013), p. 87. As Guenther puts it, in Schein's account, 'If coercive persuasion is approached in the right way, with the proper goals, it can be good for both the individual prisoner and for society as a whole'. Ibid.

30. CIA, *Kubark Counterintelligence Interrogation*, p. 86.

31. Alfred W. McCoy, *A Question of Torture: CIA Interrogation, from the Cold War to the War on Terror* (New York, 2006), p. 7. See also McCoy, 'Mind Maze: The CIA's Pursuit of Psychological Torture', in *The United States and Torture: Interrogation, Incarceration and Abuse*, edited by Marjorie Cohn (New York, 2011), pp. 25–52 (p. 25); Timothy Melley, *The Covert Sphere: Secrecy, Fiction, and the National Security State* (Ithaca, 2012); Streatfeild, *Brainwash*.

32. Various think tanks, institutes, clinics and research centres were involved, including the Geschickter Fund for Medical Research, the Human Ecology Fund and the NIMH Addiction Research Center in Kentucky. See Melley, 'Brain Warfare'; Marks, *The Search for the 'Manchurian Candidate'*; Williams, 'Battles for the Mind'; Lemov, 'Brainwashing's Avatar'.

33. See Williams, 'Battles for the Mind'; and idem, 'On "Modified Human Agents": John Lilly and the Paranoid Style in American Neuroscience', *History of the Human Sciences*, 32:5 (2019), journals.sagepub.com/doi/full/10.1177/0952695119872094.

34. Quoted in Williams, 'Battles for the Mind', p. 97. Williams cites John Lilly, 'Special Considerations of Modified Human Agents as Reconnaissance and Intelligence Devices (Committee D, Intelligence and Reconnaissance)', [n.d.], John Cunningham Lilly Papers (1915–2001), Special Collections and University Archives, Stanford University Library, Palo Alto, CA, USA, box 54, folder 17.

35. See the conference website, www.floatconference.com/. According to a UK company, Floatworks, floating is 'scientifically proven to increase ... mental and physical wellbeing', and leaves participants 'more happy and relaxed, with fewer aches and pains', 'confident of a better night's sleep', all within an hour. 'The benefits of floating', floatworks.com/.

36. Ronson, *The Men Who Stare at Goats*; David Kaiser and W. Patrick McCray (eds), *Groovy Science: Knowledge, Innovation and American Counterculture* (London, 2016).

37. Raffi Khatchadourian, 'High Anxiety: LSD in the Cold War', *New Yorker*, 15 December 2012, www.newyorker.com/news/news-desk/high-anxiety-lsd-in-the-cold-war.

38. *Report of the International Scientific Commission for the Investigation of the Facts Concerning Bacterial Warfare in Korea and China*, www.documentcloud.org/documents/4334133-ISC-Full-Report-Pub-Copy.html.

39. Stephen Endicott and Edward Hagerman, *The United States and Biological*

Warfare (Bloomington, 1998); Judith Miller et al., *Germs: Biological Weapons and America's Secret War* (New York, 2001).

40. Robert Jay Lifton, *Death in Life: Survivors of Hiroshima* (New York, 1968); Ran Zwigenberg, *Hiroshima: The Origins of Global Memory Culture* (Cambridge, 2014); on the use of 'agent orange' in Vietnam, see Marilyn Young, *The Vietnam Wars 1945–1990* (New York, 1991), pp. 325–6; for the Korean War context, see Max Hastings, *The Korean War* (London, 1987); Bruce Cummings, *The Korean War: A History* (New York, 2010).

41. 'Dr. Mayo Calls Reds' Torture Method Subtle', *Los Angeles Times*, 27 October 1953, p. 9, www.newspapers.com/clip/22881732/the-los-angeles-times/.

42. Sam Roberts, 'Harriet Mills, Scholar Held in "Brainwashing Prison" in China, Dies at 95', obituary, *The New York Times*, 29 March 2016, www.nytimes. com/2016/03/30/world/harriet-mills-scholar-held-in-brainwashing-prison-in-china-dies-at-95.html.

43. I rely for this account on *Thought Reform*, Chapter 7; 'Jane Darrow' was the pseudonym used here by Lifton to protect his source.

44. Alexandra Stein, *Terror, Love and Brainwashing: Attachment in Cults and Totalitarian Systems* (London, 2016); see also idem, 'Attachment Theory and Post-Cult Recovery', *Therapy Today* (September 2016), 18–21; and 'Terror and Love: A Study of Brainwashing', *Anthropology Now*, 4:2 (September 2012), 32–41.

45. William Graebner, *Patty's Got a Gun: Patricia Hearst in 1970s America* (Chicago, 2008). Stockholm Syndrome is named after a robbery in the Swedish capital (23–28 August 1973) in which several employees were held hostage in a bank vault. The victims rejected assistance from government officials, became emotionally attached to their captors and even defended them after they were freed from the six-day ordeal. The term was coined by criminologist and psychiatrist Nils Bejerot and developed by the psychiatrist Frank Ochberg.

46. Interwar, various psychoanalysts, including Sándor Ferenczi and Anna Freud, had written about victims of various kinds of trauma, and of their potential 'identification with the aggressor'. Bruno Bettelheim would then explore the issue autobiographically in his influential paper about his experience in a concentration camp. See 'Individual and Mass Behavior in Extreme Situations', *Journal of Abnormal and Social Psychology*, 38 (1943), 417–52. Hannah Arendt took note of his work as she prepared *The Origins of Totalitarianism* (1951), as did Stanley Elkins as he developed a substantial account of the psychological legacies of slavery across generations. See his *Slavery: A Problem in American Institutional and Intellectual Life* (Chicago, 1959).

47. Brian Keenan, *An Evil Cradling: The Five-Year Ordeal of a Hostage* (London, 1991), p. 294.

48. Keenan, *An Evil Cradling*.

49. See Kathleen Taylor, *Brainwashing: The Science of Thought Control* (Oxford, 2004).

50. Note Allan Young's controversial and pioneering study, *The Harmony of*

Illusions: Inventing Post-Traumatic Stress Disorder (Princeton, 1996). See also the
recent volume edited by Mark Micale and Hans Pols, *Traumatic Pasts in Asia:
History, Psychiatry and Trauma from the 1930s to the Present* (New York, 2021).
For valuable contemporary clinical and theoretical reflections on trauma, see
Susan Levy and Alessandra Lemma (eds), *The Perversion of Loss: Psychoanalytic
Perspectives on Trauma* (Chichester, 2004); Joanne Stubley and Linda Young
(eds), *Complex Trauma: The Tavistock Model* (London, 2021). In the half
century after 1945, a large literature had emerged on the psychology of
survivors of concentration camps in Nazi Germany and in the Soviet Gulag.
By the 1970s PTSD diagnoses were increasingly commonplace. Symptoms
include nightmares, insomnia, rage, loneliness, acute anxieties, depression,
dissociation, numbness, skin conditions, gastrointestinal disorders, cognitive
impairments of one kind or another, in some cases psychoses, and in many
others chronic physical illnesses or general malaise. Clinicians also wrote
powerfully of the transmission and diverse impacts of 'intergenerational
trauma'. See Ilse Grubrich-Simitis, 'From Concretism to Metaphor:
Thoughts on Some Theoretical and Technical Aspects of the Psychoanalytic
Work with Children of Holocaust Survivors', *Psychoanalytic Study of the
Child*, 39:1 (1984), 301–19. In 1945 René Spitz had also written influentially
about the psychological consequences of 'institutionalisation' and employed
another term, 'hospitalism'. He sought to convey the devastating
psychological impact of a long-stay institution upon the mental development
of infants and children; see 'Hospitalism: An Inquiry into the Genesis of
Psychiatric Conditions in Early Childhood', *Psychoanalytic Study of the Child*, 1
(1945), 53–74.

51. The sociologist Albert D. Biderman challenged those who offered blanket
descriptions of the 'weak-willed' POWs. See his *March to Calumny: The Story
of American POWs in the Korean War* (New York, 1963), especially pp. 14–16.

52. William E. Mayer's lecture, 'Brainwashing: The Ultimate Weapon', was
delivered at the San Francisco Naval Shipyard in the Naval Radiological
Defense Laboratory. A. W. Kramer, 'Brainwashing: The Ultimate Weapon:
William E. Mayer', Sound Recording (2016 [4 October 1956]), deepblue.lib.
umich.edu/handle/2027.42/121557. Cf. Mayer, 'Why did Many GI Captives
Cave In?', *US News and World Report*, 24 February 1956, p. 56. For the context,
Lewis H. Carlson, *Remembered Prisoners of a Forgotten War: An Oral History of
Korean War POWs* (New York, 2002), pp. 1–8. Eugene Kinkead described this
supposed weakening of moral character in a prominent *New Yorker* article in
October 1957, and at more length, two years later, in a book. See Kinkead,
'The Study of Something New in History', *New Yorker*, 26 October 1957; and
In Every War But One (New York, 1959). Such dramatic exposés of the
exceptional nature of prisoner breakdowns in Korea downplayed reports
about the many military psychiatric casualties who were treated during and
after the two world wars. See Andrew Scull, *Madness in Civilization: A Cultural
History of Insanity* (London, 2015), pp. 336–7.

53. Kim, *The Interrogation Rooms*.

54. Among POWs from the North Korean side, 75,823 chose repatriation and went back to the North, while 7,826 opted against repatriation and headed for South Korea or Taiwan; 74 chose a neutral nation such as India or Argentina. Among the Chinese POWs, 6,670 chose to repatriate; 14,342 decided not to, and 12 preferred to resettle in a neutral nation. See David Cheng Chang, *The Hijacked War: The Story of Chinese POWS in the Korean War* (Stanford, 2020), p. 4; Kim, *The Interrogation Rooms*, pp. 288–99, 357; Hastings, *The Korean War*, p. 406. Despite earlier signals to the contrary, none of these POWs were offered the option of direct transit to the United States. However, some would make the passage later, their journey facilitated by 1965 US legislation (the Hart–Celler Immigration Act) that removed de facto racial or ethnic 'quotas' for entrants. I am grateful to Monica Kim for advice on these POW figures, and on the wider context.

55. On this subject, Lewis Carlson writes: '[a]fter being exposed to extensive U.N. indoctrination sessions, at least half of the 140,000 taken prisoner insisted they did not want to return to their communist homelands'. *Remembered Prisoners*, p. 280, n. 4.

56. Kim, *The Interrogation Rooms*, pp. 288–99.

57. Ibid., p. 8.

58. Ibid., p. 271; Hastings, *The Korean War*, pp. 377–8.

59. Carlson, *Remembered Prisoners*, Chapter 9. See especially p. 205.

60. Hastings, *The Korean War*, p. 407.

61. I draw here on the archive footage, interviews and commentaries provided in a documentary film about the twenty-one POWs, *They Chose China*, directed by Shui-Bo Wang (2005). It can be found online at www.youtube.com/watch?v=sDTPhT8mZ9o&ab_channel=AaronShang. For the historical context, see Carlson, *Remembered Prisoners*; Carruthers, *Cold War Captives*; Dunne, *A Cold War State of Mind*; Charles S. Young, *Name, Rank, and Serial Number: Exploiting Korean War POWs at Home and Abroad* (Oxford, 2014).

62. See *They Chose China*.

63. Virginia Pasley, *21 Stayed: The Story of the American GIs Who Chose Communist China: Who They Were and Why They Stayed* (New York, 1955), p. 207.

64. Quoted in ibid., p. 122.

65. An excerpt from an interview with Tenneson's mother is included in *They Chose China*. See also her son's rebuttal of her claims in Pasley, *21 Stayed*, p. 153.

66. Hunter, *Brainwashing*, p. 11.

67. The camps were usually known by their number ('1', '2', etc.). See Carlson, *Remembered Prisoners*, for an account of the conditions, and for many of the soldiers' reminiscences of the life they endured in the various camps.

68. Quoted in Carson, *Remembered Prisoners*, p. 200.

69. Pasley, p. 179.

70. Ibid.

71. See *They Chose China*.

72. Julia Lovell, *Maoism: A Global History* (London, 2019).

73. Clarence Adams, *An American Dream: The Life of an African American Soldier and POW Who Spent Twelve Years in Communist China*, edited by Della Adams and Lewis H. Carlson (Amherst, 2007), p. 39.

74. Ibid., p. 44.

75. Ibid., p. 40.

76. Ibid., p. 50.

77. Ibid., p. 51.

78. Quoted in Carlson, *Remembered Prisoners*, p. 208.

79. *They Chose China*.

80. Adams, *An American Dream*, pp. 64, 66.

81. Ibid., p. 66.

82. Ibid., p. 104.

83. These recollections by Adams are included in *They Chose China*.

84. Quoted in Carlson, *Remembered Prisoners*, p. 210.

85. Quoted in ibid.

86. Carlson, *Remembered Prisoners*, and *We Were Each Other's Prisoners: An Oral History of World War II American and German Prisoners of War* (New York, 1997).

87. Carlson, *Remembered Prisoners*, p. 205. See also *The Graybeards*, 16:4 (2002), www.kwva.org/graybeards/gb_02/gb_0208_final.pdf.

88. See, for instance, B. Palmer et al., 'Aging and Trauma: Post Traumatic Stress Disorder Among Korean War Veterans', *Federal Practitioner*, 36:12 (2019), 554–62.

89. 'Ex-P.O.W. and Wife Into Seclusion at Oklahoma Home', *St. Joseph News-Press*, 6 October 1957, news.google.com/newspapers?id=tCZUAAAAIBAJ&sji d=MDoNAAAAIBAJ&pg=3511,631797&dq=korea+david-hawkins&hl=en/.

90. *David Hawkins: A Battle of the Mind* (2017), directed by Nasheed Faruqi, www. bbk.ac.uk/hiddenpersuaders/documentaries/david-hawkins-battle-mind.

91. Extracts from the interview can be heard in Faruqi's film. Hawkins can also be heard talking about his experiences in a radio documentary, 'Brainwash Culture', that the author presented on BBC Radio 3, www.bbc.co.uk/ programmes/po3m8ltq.

92. The interview can be found in the Mike Wallace Collection, Harry Ransom Centre, University of Texas at Austin, Austin, TX, USA, hrc.contentdm.oclc. org/digital/collection/p15878coll90.

93. Personal communication by David Hawkins to the author (21 October 2014).

94. Ibid.

95. Kim, *The Interrogation Rooms*.

96. Adriana Carranca, 'Absolution: A former child soldier in the Lord's Resistance Army tells his story', *Granta*, 18 March 2020, granta.com/ absolution/.

97. Eric Weiner, 'Waterboarding: A Tortured History', NPR, 3 November 2007, www.npr.org/2007/11/03/15886834/waterboarding-a-tortured-history.

98. Reuters suggested in 2019 that 1 million or even 1.5 million of the approximately 8 million Uighurs inhabiting the region had been held in

custody and subjected to a panoply of mind-control measures. Stephanie Nebehay, '1.5 million Muslims could be detained in China's Xinjiang: Academic', *Reuters*, 13 March 2019, www.reuters.com/article/us-china-xinjiang-rights/15-million-muslims-could-be-detained-in-chinas-xinjiang-academic-idUSKCN1QU2MQ. See also Amnesty International UK, 'Urgent Action update: Detained Uighur has nervous breakdown', 2019, www.amnesty.org.uk/resources/urgent-action-update-detained-uighur-has-nervous-breakdown. Later estimations raised the figure to 2 million detained, or more.

99. Emma Graham-Harrison, 'Secret memo on how to run China's prison camps – annotated', *Guardian*, 24 November 2019, www.theguardian.com/world/ng-interactive/2019/nov/24/china-cables-instructions-on-how-to-run-a-chinese-detention-centre-annotated-document. Cf. Graham-Harrison and Garside, 'Complete Control', p. 13. Emphasis added.

100. Graham-Harrison and Garside, 'Complete Control', p. 13.

101. Lily Kuo, 'China claims detained Uighurs have been freed', *Guardian*, 9 December 2019, www.theguardian.com/world/2019/dec/09/china-claims-detained-uighurs-have-been-freed.

102. 'China state TV pulls Arsenal game after Ozil Uighur comments', *Al Jazeera*, 15 December 2019, www.aljazeera.com/sports/2019/12/15/china-state-tv-pulls-arsenal-game-after-ozil-uighur-comments.

103. Austin Ramzy and Chris Buckley, 'Leaked China Files Show Internment Camps Are Ruled by Secrecy and Spying', *The New York Times*, 24 November 2019, www.nytimes.com/2019/11/24/world/asia/leak-chinas-internment-camps.html.

104. Aminda Smith, *Thought Reform and China's Dangerous Classes: Reeducation, Resistance, and the People* (Lanham, 2013), p. 2.

105. Edgar Schein, *Brainwashing* (Cambridge, MA, 1960), p. 1. Available online at dspace.mit.edu/bitstream/handle/1721.1/83028/14769178.pdf.

106. Lovell, *Maoism*.

Part 3: The Captive Mind

1. Tony Judt, 'Captive Minds, Then and Now', *New York Review*, 13 July 2010, www.nybooks.com/daily/2010/07/13/captive-minds-then-and-now/.

2. See, for instance, Sladja Blazan, 'Urban Dwellers: Women Writers Who Left Eastern Europe Never to Arrive in the United States', *Amerikastudien/American Studies*, 53:2 (2008), 189–208.

3. Eva Hoffman, *Lost in Translation: A Life in a New Language* (New York, 1989).

4. Eva Hoffman, 'Complex Histories, Contested Memories: Some Reflections on Remembering Difficult Pasts', UC Berkeley Occasional Papers, 1 September 2000, escholarship.org/content/qt25p7cov4/qt25p7cov4.pdf.

5. Hannah Arendt, *The Origins of Totalitarianism* (New York, 1951), p. 474.

6. Eli Zaretsky, 'The Big Lie', *London Review of Books*, blog, 15 February 2021, www.lrb.co.uk/blog/2021/february/the-big-lie.

7. Norman Davies, *God's Playground: A History of Poland, Vol II: 1795 to the Present*

(Oxford, 1981), pp. 578–9. On the scale of deportations in the Soviet-controlled zones of eastern Poland during the war, see ibid., pp. 447–8. See also Davies, *Heart of Europe: A Short History of Poland* (Oxford, 1986), pp. 3–9.

8. Ian Kershaw, *Hitler* (London, 2010); *Working Towards the Führer: Essays in Honour of Sir Ian Kershaw*, edited by Anthony McElligott and Tim Kirk (Manchester, 2003).

9. Edna Friedberg, 'The Truth about Poland's Role in the Holocaust', *Atlantic*, 6 February 2018, www.theatlantic.com/international/archive/2018/02/poland-holocaust-death-camps/552455/.

10. Miłosz, 'Elegy for N. N.', *Czeslaw Milosz: The Collected Poems (1931–1987)* (London, 1988), p. 240. Cf. Sven Birkets, 'Last Things First: Czeslaw Milosz's Witness of Poetry', *Agni Review*, 19 (1983), 113–29, p. 115.

11. The Soviet penal establishments came to stretch from sites of former Nazi concentration camps in East Germany to the vastly expanded former Tsarist dumping grounds for political 'undesirables' in Siberia. In 1954, around 85,000 political prisoners were still in custody in Poland, in camps closely modelled on their Soviet equivalents. Many thousands of Poles were also killed or deported much further to the east. See Anne Applebaum, *Gulag: A History of the Soviet Camps* (London, 2003), p. 41; cf. Daniel Beer, *The House of the Dead: Siberian Exile Under the Tsars* (London, 2016).

12. Orlando Figes, *The Whisperers: Private Life in Stalin's Russia* (London, 2008).

13. For the background, see Tony Judt, *Past Imperfect: French Intellectuals, 1944–1956* (Berkeley, 1992); Sunil Khilnani, *Arguing Revolution: The Intellectual Left in Post-War France* (New Haven, 1993).

14. The best-known works in the West by Aleksandr Solzhenitsyn were *One Day in the Life of Ivan Denisovich* (1962) and *The Gulag Archipelago* (1974).

15. Andrzej Franaszek, *Miłosz: A Biography* (Cambridge, MA, 2017), pp. 305–6. In this sketch of Milosz, I draw heavily on Franaszek's excellent biographical study. See also Bruce Donahue, 'Viewing the West from the East: Solzhenitsyn, Milosz, and Kundera', *Comparative Literature Studies*, 20:3 (1983), 247–60. Miłosz was warmly appreciative of Camus, the author of *The Outsider*, *The Plague* and *The Rebel*. See Miłosz, *The Captive Mind* (1953), p. vii. Camus, as Miłosz noted at the start of his book, had recognised that the Soviet Union had a system of concentration camps; and yet this was something many French intellectuals, including Sartre, were reluctant to dwell upon.

16. Some early readers of *The Captive Mind* found nothing in the book other than the anti-Stalinist message, ignoring the challenge that Miłosz posed to the West. For example, Paul Kecskemeti, a hawkish observer of communism who wrote for the RAND Corporation and various US journals, used the book as ammunition to expose the evils of communism. Having lavishly praised the writer for his 'extraordinary', 'noble', 'frightening' and 'magnificent' achievement, he commented on how it revealed the 'projects of regimentation' that ultimately led those on the other side of the Iron Curtain to accommodate themselves to a pack of state lies. Eventually,

Kecskemeti warned, the mind is 'transformed from within'; under one-party rule the subject lives on but is effectively dead; in those totalitarian societies, the citizen endures, but with a new 'master' inside their own head. Paul Kecskemeti, 'The Captive Mind, by Czeslaw Milosz: Coercion from Within', *Commentary*, 1 September 1953, www.commentarymagazine.com/articles/the-captive-mind-by-czeslaw-milosz/.

17. Gobineau made these remarks in his study *Religions and Philosophies of Central Asia* (1865).

18. Miłosz, *The Captive Mind*, pp. 56–7.

19. I refer here to the depiction of Hamlet's visceral revulsion in Zbigniew Herbert's great poem 'Elegy of Fortinbras', published in 1961, a work he dedicated to Miłosz. For the context, and discussion of the uses of Shakespeare to comment on contemporary political life in communist Poland, see Celina Wieniewska, *Polish Writing Today* (Harmondsworth, 1967), p. 133. Regarding Shakespeare and Polish poetry, note that Miłosz translated, with Peter Dale Scott, 'Hamletism', a poem of 1933 by Antoni Słonimski, and included it in *Postwar Polish Poetry*, edited and translated by Miłosz (New York, 1965). See also Jan Kott, *Shakespeare Our Contemporary* (London, 1964). Cf. Krystyna Kujawińska Courtney, 'Celebrating Shakespeare under the Communist Regime in Poland', in *Shakespeare in Cold War Europe: Conflict, Commemoration, Celebration*, edited by Erica Sheen and Isabel Karremann (London, 2016), pp. 23–35.

20. That argument, widely made in the anti-psychiatry movement, has recently been revived in Adam Curtis's BBC TV documentary series, billed as an 'emotional history of the modern world', *Can't Get You Out of My Head* (2021). Cf. Interview by David Runciman with Adam Curtis, Talking Politics podcast (April 2021) no. 314, www.talkingpoliticspodcast.com/.

21. Miłosz, *The Captive Mind*, p. 5.

22. Ibid.

23. Ibid., p. vii.

24. Marcia Holmes and Daniel Pick, 'Voices off: Stanley Milgram's Cyranoids in Historical Context', *History of the Human Sciences*, 32:5 (2019), 28–55, doi.org/10.1177/0952695119867021.

25. Joan Riviere, 'Womanliness as a Masquerade', *International Journal of Psychoanalysis*, 10 (1929), 303–13.

26. Erving Goffman, *The Presentation of Self in Everyday Life* [1959] (Harmondsworth, 1969), p. 1.

27. Suzanne Stewart-Steinberg, *Impious Fidelity: Anna Freud, Psychoanalysis, Politics* (Ithaca, 2012).

28. Jenni Marsh, 'Chinese Dissident Ai Weiwei Dismissed Tennis Star Peng as Party "Soldier"', Bloomberg, 6 January 2022, www.bloomberg.com/news/articles/2022-01-06/china-s-ai-weiwei-dismissed-tennis-star-peng-as-party-soldier.

29. Lee Edwards, 'Is China Totalitarian?', The Heritage Foundation, 26 February 2020, www.heritage.org/asia/commentary/china-totalitarian.

30. Ma Jian, 'Tiananmen Square 25 years on: 'Every person in the crowd was a victim of the massacre', *Guardian*, 1 June 2014, www.theguardian.com/world/2014/jun/01/tiananmen-square-25-years-every-person-victim-massacre.

31. James Griffith, *The Great Firewall of China: How to Build and Control an Alternative Internet* (London, 2019).

32. For instance, as Ross Andersen puts it in the *Atlantic* ('The Panopticon is Already Here', February 2020 issue): 'Even in the U.S., a democracy with constitutionally enshrined human rights, Americans are struggling mightily to prevent the emergence of a public-private surveillance state. But at least America has political structures that stand some chance of resistance. In China, AI will be restrained only according to the party's needs.' www.theatlantic.com/magazine/archive/2020/09/china-ai-surveillance/614197/. Cf. Anna Mitchell and Larry Diamond, 'China's Surveillance State Should Scare Everyone', *Atlantic*, 2 February 2018, www.theatlantic.com/international/archive/2018/02/china-surveillance/552203/.

33. This argument is well set out by Bruce J. Dickson, in *The Party and the People: Chinese Politics in the 21st Century* (Princeton, 2021).

34. Eric Schlosser, 'The Prison-Industrial Complex', *Atlantic*, December 1998, www.theatlantic.com/magazine/archive/1998/12/the-prison-industrial-complex/304669/.

35. For an account of the medical treatment and institutionalisation of Soviet dissidents, see Reich, *State of Madness*.

36. Erving Goffman, *Asylums: Essays on the Social Situation of Mental Patients and Other Inmates* (Garden City, NY, 1961), p. 14.

37. Rachel Aviv, 'The Shadow Penal System for Struggling Kids', *New Yorker*, 11 October 2021, www.newyorker.com/magazine/2021/10/18/the-shadow-penal-system-for-struggling-kids.

38. Linda Mussell, 'Intergenerational Imprisonment: Resistance and Resilience in Indigenous Communities', *Journal of Law and Social Policy*, 33 (2020), 15–37. See also the final report of the Truth and Reconciliation Commission of Canada (2015), irsi.ubc.ca/sites/default/files/inline-files/Executive_Summary_English_Web.pdf.

39. Streatfeild, *Brainwash*.

40. Another controversial film that sought to illuminate the inhumanity of the asylum and of psychiatry that might be compared with *One Flew Over the Cuckoo's Nest* was the hard-hitting *Titicut Follies*, in 1967, directed by Frederick Wiseman. For the broader context, see Glen Gabbard and Krin Gabbard, *Psychiatry and the Cinema* (Washington, DC, 1987).

41. Michel Foucault, *Folie et déraison: Histoire de la folie à l'âge classique* (Paris, 1961).

42. A powerful Hollywood example of that scenario was *Suddenly, Last Summer* (1959). The film, based on a play by Tennessee Williams and starring Elizabeth Taylor, Katharine Hepburn and Montgomery Clift, shows how a surgeon in search of research funds might be manipulated by a devious

relative to confine and then lobotomise a vulnerable young woman, to
eliminate her 'dangerous' memories.

43. Gretchen Diefenbach et al., 'Portrayal of Lobotomy in the Popular Press:
1935–1960', *Journal of the History of the Neurosciences*, 8:1 (1999), 60–69, p. 67.

44. Kate Millett, *The Loony-Bin Trip* (New York, 1990), pp. 314–15. But contrast
Millett's account with Barbara Taylor's history of the asylum, and personal
account of her time residing in a mental hospital while contemporaneously
continuing psychoanalysis, in *The Last Asylum: A Memoir of Madness in Our
Times* (London 2014). Institutions and psychiatrists varied, as did patients'
circumstances, needs, support system and treatments, as Taylor shows.

45. Reich, *State of Madness*.

46. Diego Gambetta, 'Primo Levi's Last Moments', *Boston Review*, 9 July 2012,
bostonreview.net/articles/diego-gambetta-primo-levi-last-moments/.

47. Nelson Mandela, *Long Walk to Freedom* (London, 2004), p. 751.

48. Keenan, *An Evil Cradling*, p. 294.

49. Wyatt Mordecai Johnson, 'The Faith of the American Negro' [1922], www.
blackpast.org/african-american-history/1922-wyatt-mordecai-johnson-
faith-american-negro/.

50. Frederic Douglass, speech, 5 July 1852, in *Black Political Thought: From David
Walker to the Present*, edited by Sherrow O. Pinder (Cambridge, 2020),
pp. 40–44 (p. 44).

51. James Baldwin, 'Letter from a Region in My Mind', first published in the *New
Yorker*, 9 November 1962, reprinted in *The Fire Next Time* [1963] (New York,
1993).

52. Gwendolyn Brooks, *Report from Part One* (Detroit, 1972), p. 86. Cf. Richard
Flyn, '"The Kindergarten of New Consciousness": Gwendolyn Brooks and
the Social Construction of Childhood', *African American Review*, 34:3 (2000),
483–99, p. 483.

53. Toni Morrison, *The Last Interview: And Other Conversations* (New York, 2020),
p. 57.

54. Alison Walsh, 'The criminal justice system is riddled with racial disparities',
Prison Policy Initiative, 15 August 2016, www.prisonpolicy.org/blog/2016/
08/15/. See also solitarywatch.org/2019/01/04/how-many-people-are-in-
solitary-today/.

55. George Jackson, *Soledad Brother: The Prison Letters of George Jackson* (New
York, 1970), p. 21. See also idem, *Blood in My Eye* (Baltimore, 1996).

56. For the context, see Eric Cummins, *The Rise and Fall of California's Radical
Prison Movement* (Stanford, 1994).

57. See 'New German Ghetto Show' [1960], 'Napalm and Pudding' [1967] and
'Water Cannons: Against Women, Too' [1968], in *Everybody Talks About the
Weather ... We Don't: The Writings of Ulrike Meinhof*, edited and with an
introduction by Karin Bauer (New York, 2008).

58. Davis at that time was already a prominent campaigner for the rights of
Black political prisoners. She was in correspondence with the 'Soledad
Brothers'. It came to light that she owned some weapons that were

subsequently used, on 7 August 1970, by the seventeen-year-old Jonathan Jackson, younger brother of George Jackson, in his attempt to storm a courthouse and free three Black prisoners on trial in Marin County, California. He took the judge, a prosecutor and three jurors as hostages. In the subsequent confrontation with police, the judge, Jonathan Jackson and two armed prisoners were killed. Davis went into hiding, but, once arrested, was charged with conspiracy to murder and other offences. A public campaign for her release gained momentum. After sixteen months in detention, she was released on bail, and on 4 June 1972 found not guilty by a jury, unpersuaded that her ownership of the guns was sufficient grounds to assume her culpability.

59. Angela Davis and Dylan Rodriguez, 'The Challenge of Prison Abolition: A Conversation', *Social Justice*, 27:3 (2000), 212–18, p. 213. See also Angela Davis, *Abolition: Are Prisons Obsolete?* (New York, 2003), and *Abolition Democracy: Beyond Prisons, Torture, and Empire* (New York, 2005).

60. Miłosz, *The Captive Mind*, p. 55.

61. Quoted in 'Susan Sontag Provokes Debate on Communism', *The New York Times*, 27 February 1982, movies2.nytimes.com/books/00/03/12/specials/sontag-communism.html.

62. Franaszek, *Miłosz*, p. 303. An influential elaboration of this argument about positive and negative liberty can be found in Isaiah Berlin, *Two Concepts of Liberty* (Oxford, 1958).

63. Franaszek, *Miłosz*, p. 251.

64. Keith Somerville, *Radio Propaganda and the Broadcasting of Hatred: Historical Development and Definitions* (London, 2012), p. 56.

65. Franaszek, *Miłosz*, p. 252.

66. Ibid.

67. Quoted in ibid., p. 251.

68. Young, *The Vietnam Wars*, pp. 201–2. On Miłosz's sympathies with the US civil rights movement and views about protests against the Vietnam War, see Franaszek, *Miłosz*, pp. 373–4.

69. See Gary Gerstle, *American Crucible: Race and Nation in the Twentieth Century* (Princeton, 2001), p. 243.

70. See Jeff Woods, *Black Struggle, Red Scare: Segregation and Anti-Communism in the South, 1948–1968* (Baton Rouge, 2004), pp. 26–9.

71. Tori DeAngelis, 'Unmasking "racial micro aggressions"', American Psychological Association, February 2009, www.apa.org/monitor/2009/02/microaggression. Cf. David Theo Goldberg, 'On Racial Judgment', 2018, www7.bbk.ac.uk/hiddenpersuaders/blog/on-racial-judgment/.

72. CNN, '"Plaid shirt" guy removed from Trump rally for facial expressions', YouTube, 8 September 2018, www.youtube.com/watch?v=CFnF3jAvpTw.

73. This point has been developed by recent theorists, for example, in Lacanian terms, notably in the work of Slavoj Žižek. See, for instance, *The Sublime Object of Ideology* (London, 1989).

74. See Mark Fisher, *Capitalist Realism: Is There No Alternative?* (Ropley, 2009).

Cf. Luc Boltanski and Eve Chiapello, *The New Spirit of Capitalism* [1999] (London, 2018); Wendy Brown, *Undoing the Demos: Neoliberalism's Stealth Revolution* (Cambridge, MA, 2015).

75. Judt, 'Captive Minds, Then and Now'.
76. Tony Judt, *Ill Fares the Land* (New York, 2010), p. 34.

Part 4: Groupthink

1. William H. Whyte, *The Organization Man* (New York, 1956). On his career and later writings, see *The Essential William H. Whyte*, edited by Albert LaFarge (New York, 2000); cf. Michael T. Kaufman, 'William H. Whyte, "Organization Man" Author and Urbanologist, Is Dead at 81', *The New York Times*, 13 January 1999, www.nytimes.com/1999/01/13/arts/william-h-whyte-organization-man-author-and-urbanologist-is-dead-at-81.html.

   Whyte's 1952 'groupthink' article was first published in *Fortune*. It can be found online at fortune.com/2012/07/22/groupthink-fortune-1952/. This monthly magazine had been created in 1929, with a self-consciously deluxe, glossy image, and a direct pitch to the rich and successful. As its founder, Henry Robinson Luce, declared in the first prospectus for advertisers, *Fortune*'s purpose was to be 'the Ideal Super-Class Magazine' for 'wealthy and influential people'; Joseph Epstein, 'Henry Luce & His Time', *Commentary*, 44:5 (1967), 35–47, p. 37. See also Anon, 'About Us', *Fortune*, [n.d.], fortune.com/about-us/.

   The sociologist and author of *The Power Elite* (1956), C. Wright Mills, later declared admiringly of Whyte, he 'understands that the work-and-thrift ethic of success has grievously declined – except in the rhetoric of top executives; that the entrepreneurial scramble to success has been largely replaced by the organizational crawl'. Quoted in Kaufman's obituary. Another obituarist observed of Whyte when he passed in 1999, that he 'was straight Establishment and a card-carrying, socially conservative member of the American gentleman class'. Godfrey Hodgson, William H. Whyte, obituary, *Guardian*, 15 January 1999, www.theguardian.com/news/1999/jan/15/guardianobituaries1.

2. Quoted in William Dalrymple, 'The Original Evil Corporation', *The New York Times*, 4 September 2019, www.nytimes.com/2019/09/04/opinion/east-india-company.html. See also Arthur Meier Schlesinger, 'The Uprising Against the East India Company', *Political Science Quarterly*, 32:1 (1917), 60–79. For the context, Dalrymple, *The Anarchy: The Relentless Rise of the East India Company* (London, 2019); Eric Foner, *The Story of American Freedom* (New York, 1998).

3. Dalrymple, 'The Original Evil Corporation'.

4. See Nick Joyce and David Baker, 'Husbands, rate your wives', American Psychological Association, *Monitor on Psychology*, 39:5 (2008), 18, www.apa.org/monitor/2008/05/marriage. See also Loxley Nichols, 'Keeping Up with Dr. Crane', *Flannery O'Connor Bulletin*, 20 (1991), 22–32.

5. Marilyn Loden, '100 Women: "Why I invented the glass ceiling phrase"', BBC News, 13 December 2017, www.bbc.co.uk/news/world-42026266.

6. The term 'WASP' emerged after the war and was used by a variety of writers to expose the true nature of US elites; to challenge racial or religious barriers to entry; and to protest about the lack of transparent, open competition for coveted places in prestigious institutions of education, and in well-paid, high-status employment. A notable study, in this regard, was E. Digby Baltzell's *The Protestant Establishment: Aristocracy & Caste in America* (New Haven, 1964). Cf. Isabel Wilkerson, *Caste: The Lies That Divide Us* (New York, 2020).

7. Truman's speech, to dedicate the new Washington headquarters of the American Legion, a national organisation of veterans, appreciatively noted its pledge to 'uphold and defend the Constitution of the United States ... to foster and perpetuate a one hundred percent Americanism ... to safeguard and transmit to posterity the principles of justice, freedom and democracy'. Truman insisted that Americanism meant liberty of the individual to enjoy free expression and choice of religion, to live without social discrimination and prejudice, to assume the prospect of a fair trial and to have confidence in an American system. It required work, vigilance and a struggle against dark interests. The people must keep 'working together', he urged, 'in one great community'. The United States was under attack, he warned, not only from communism, and from spies and saboteurs, but also thanks to the conspiratorial fantasies of some Americans who undermined 'Americanism', intent upon 'chipping away at our basic freedoms just as insidiously and far more effectively than the Communists have ever been able to do'. They had departed from 'the American way', he concluded. 'We have got to make a fight for a real 100 percent Americanism.' 'Address at the Dedication of the New Washington Headquarters of the American Legion', 14 August 1951, www.trumanlibrary.gov/library/public-papers/191/address-dedication-new-washington-headquarters-american-legion.

As historians have shown, the unity and homogeneity of this supposed American community conjured up in such rhetoric was misleading. Mary Caputi, for instance, in a book on myths of the 1950s, points out that tens of millions of Americans lived in poverty in the middle of that decade, and only 6 per cent of schools were racially integrated. See *A Kinder, Gentler America: Melancholia and the Mythical 1950s* (Minneapolis, 2005), pp. 141–2.

8. For an illuminating comparison of the privileged role of schools and colleges, and more generally on entry routes and barriers to advancement for applicants for senior roles in business and government, in Britain, Germany, France and the UK, see Elise S. Brezis and François Crouzet, 'Changes in the Recruitment and Education of the Power Elites in Twentieth Century Western Democracies' (2002), Bar-Ilan University Department of Economics, Working Papers, ideas.repec.org/p/biu/wpaper/2002-15.html.

9. Ed Catmull, 'How Pixar Fosters Collective Creativity', *Harvard Business*

Review, September 2008, hbr.org/2008/09/how-pixar-fosters-collective-creativity. Cf. Walter Isaacson, *Steve Jobs* (New York, 2011), pp. 362–3, 431.

10. The novel portrays the logical end point of corporate surveillance of employees at a business akin to one of the great tech enterprises in the United States. Staff enjoy extravagant perks but are bombarded with praise and rewards, or expressions of 'concern', and then punitive and sinister action if they opt out. Dave Eggers, *The Circle* (London, 2013).

11. Alex Osborn, *Your Creative Power: How to Use Imagination* (New York, 1948), p. 265. He wrote that it was in 1939 'when I first organized such group-thinking in our company'. The early participants dubbed them 'Brainstorm Sessions'.

12. The term 'critical mass' was first used by physicists to describe the minimum amount of fissile material needed to maintain a nuclear chain reaction. Writers soon adopted it, however, to suggest the sufficient level of resources required in a company, for instance, to efficiently produce certain results; too little and the task (whatever it was) did not really get going.

13. William H. Whyte, *Is Anybody Listening? How and Why US Business Fumbles When It Talks with Human Beings* (New York, 1952), pp. 88, 97, 140; Osborn, *Your Creative Power*, pp. 5, 313, 317.

14. This expansion of corporate America abroad led to considerable pushback as well, notably so in France where some right- and left-wing politicians objected strongly, by the late 1940s, to what they called the 'coca-colonization' of society. See Mark Prendergast, 'Viewpoints; A Brief History of Coca-Colonization', *The New York Times*, 15 August 1993, www.nytimes.com/1993/08/15/business/viewpoints-a-brief-history-of-coca-colonization.html; Reinhold Wagnleitner, *Coca-Colonization and the Cold War: The Cultural Mission of the United States in Austria after the Second World War* (Chapel Hill, 1994); Victoria de Grazia, *Irresistible Empire: America's Advance Through Twentieth-Century Europe* (Cambridge, MA, 2005).

15. Osborn, *Your Creative Power*, p. 274.

16. Ibid., pp. 265–7.

17. Donald W. Taylor, Paul C. Berry and Clifford H. Block, 'Does Group Participation When Using Brainstorming Facilitate or Inhibit Creative Thinking?', *Administrative Science Quarterly*, 3:1 (June 1958), 23–47.

18. In *Quiet: The Power of Introverts in a World That Can't Stop Talking* (London, 2012), Susan Cain elaborates that point; she recognises that teamwork can be effective, and collaboration vital, in many instances. But she also puts in a plea for workers to be left with more peace and quiet, allowed to get on with things separately, without the constant influence of the group (and by implication the valorisation of extroverts). See also Cain, 'The Rise of the New Groupthink', *The New York Times*, 13 January 2012, www.nytimes.com/2012/01/15/opinion/sunday/the-rise-of-the-new-groupthink.html.

19. Gary Younge, 'The view from Middletown: a typical US city that never did exist', *Guardian*, 18 October 2016, www.theguardian.com/membership/2016/oct/18/view-from-middletown-us-muncie-america.

20. Reflecting on 'Middletown', Igo notes how much was left out in such surveys, and how the very sample constituency was often skewed, reducing or leaving out portions of the local population. Furthermore, not every region or population of the United States was deemed suitable to make the same leap from the local to the supposedly national and typical. 'Southerntown' (Indianola, Mississippi), the location of John Dollard's 1937 study *Caste and Class in a Southern Town*, was not regarded as similarly quintessentially American. It remained an 'average small Southern town', while Middletown, despite being 'small, isolated, midwestern, industrial, white, native-born – required no similar list of qualifiers'. Studies of Middletown were still 'straitjacketed by the lack of early data on African Americans as well as Catholics, Jews, and immigrants', she adds. Depictions, Igo concludes, were 'less an empirically typical place than an ideologically-loaded argument about which Americans properly stood for the nation'. Her book also shows well how the surveyors of public opinion could themselves be surveyed; so we now know from such historians a good deal about how each decade had its particular polling emphases. By the mid-1960s, pollsters and other social surveyors, influenced by new rebellious social movements, more emphatically called attention to the nation's fractures than had their predecessors. Sarah Igo, *The Averaged American: Surveys, Citizens, and the Making of a Mass Public* (Cambridge, MA, 2008), p. 84. Cf. Adrian Bingham, 'The "K-Bomb": Social Surveys, the Popular Press, and British Sexual Culture in the 1940s and 1950s', *Journal of British Studies* (2011), 50:1, 156–79.

21. Sander Gilman, *Making the Body Beautiful: A Cultural History of Aesthetic Surgery* (Princeton, 2000).

22. Tom Harrison, *Bion, Rickman, Foulkes and the Northfield Experiments: Advancing on a Different Front* (London, 2000).

23. Wilfred Bion, *Experiences in Groups and Other Papers* (London, 1961), p. 56.

24. Wilhelm Reich, *The Mass Psychology of Fascism* [1933] (London, 1972). For the context, see Pick, *The Pursuit of the Nazi Mind*; ffytche and Pick (eds), *Psychoanalysis in the Age of Totalitarianism*.

25. See Lifton, *Thought Reform*.

26. There is an extensive literature on the vicissitudes of training, with significant papers on the subject by Michael Balint, Otto Kernberg and others, that I do not list here but can be consulted most easily online via PEP-Web. A notable book on this issue is Moustapha Safouan, *Jacques Lacan and the Question of Psychoanalytic Training*, translated and introduced by Jacqueline Rose (London, 2000).

27. Joyce McDougall, *Plea for a Measure of Abnormality* (New York, 1992); Christopher Bollas, *Meaning and Melancholia: Life in the Age of Bewilderment* (Abingdon, 2018); and idem, *Being a Character: Psychoanalysis and Self Experience* (New York, 2006). Cf. Harold Kelman, 'Training Analysis: Past, Present and Future', *American Journal of Psychoanalysis*, 23:2 (1963), 205–17, p. 208. This refers to increasing numbers of candidates with a 'facade of normality'.

28. Ralph Greenson, 'The Origin and Fate of New Ideas in Psychoanalysis', *International Journal of Psychoanalysis*, 50 (1969), 503–15, p. 513.

29. Lewin moved to the United States in 1933 and died in 1947. Along with his students Ronald Lippitt and Ralph K. White, he studied, from his position at the University of Iowa, the effects of different organisational structures upon behaviour and thought processes. He was interested in what he called the space of free movement of thought. In a 1939 paper for the *Harvard Educational Review* he described the boys' club project. For the context and consequences of his work, see Clem Adelman, 'Kurt Lewin and the Origins of Action Research', *Educational Action Research*, 1 (1993), 7–24, doi.org/10.1080/0965079930010102.

30. K. B. Clark and M. P. Clark, 'Racial identification and preference in Negro children', in *Readings in Social Psychology* (New York, 1947), edited by T. M. Newcomb and E. L. Hartley, Chapter 3, pp. 169–78. A later project that invites comparison with their innovative research was the 'Bobo doll experiments' at Stanford between 1961 and 1963, led by the psychologist Albert Bandura. This body of work explored behaviour of children towards a particular doll; it considered the degree to which they were influenced by first witnessing an adult model behave in a violent and cruel way towards the doll. The project was to generate, in turn, a great deal of further inquiry and debate on the shaping of infantile attitudes, the link between seeing violence and acting aggressively, and the social transmission of hate.

31. Katharina Rowold, '"If We Are to Believe the Psychologists …"': Medicine, Psychoanalysis and Breastfeeding in Britain, 1900–55', *Medical History*, 63:1 (2019), 61–81.

32. Martha Harris et al., *Your Teenager* (London, 1969), pp. 90–91.

33. Ibid., pp. 96–7, 109, 111, 117.

34. Solomon E. Asch, 'Opinions and Social Pressure', *Scientific American*, 193:5 (1955), 31–5, p. 33.

35. For the context, see Foner, *The Story of American Freedom*.

36. Richard Hofstadter, *The American Political Tradition and the Men Who Made It* (New York, 1948), p. xxxiii.

37. Herbert Marcuse, *One-Dimensional Man: Studies in the Ideology of Advanced Industrial Society* [1964] (London, 2002), p. 3.

38. Louis Althusser, *On the Reproduction of Capitalism: Ideology and Ideological State Apparatuses* [1970] (New York, 2014).

39. Marcuse, *One-Dimensional Man*, p. 22.

40. See Martin Jay, *The Dialectical Imagination: A History of the Frankfurt School and the Institute of Social Research, 1923–1950* (Berkeley, 1996).

41. Theodor W. Adorno, 'Freudian Theory and the Pattern of Fascist Propaganda' [1951], reprinted in J. M. Bernstein (ed.), *The Culture Industry: Selected Essays on Mass Culture* (London, 1991), pp. 132–57; cf. Adorno, *The Authoritarian Personality* (New York, 1950).

42. Adorno, 'On the Fetish-Character in Music and the Regression of Listening'

(1938), quoted in Robert Winston Wilkin, *Adorno on Popular Culture* (London, 2003), p. 57.

43. The United States and the USSR came close to nuclear war in 1962, after the Russians appeared determined to transfer and then retain ballistic missiles in Cuba. This moment, the 'Cuban Missile Crisis', became a test case for exploring the concept of groupthink, and was used to highlight how easily a sense of inevitability about war's 'necessity' might take hold.

44. 'House of Commons: Health and Social Care, and Science and Technology Committees – Coronavirus: Lessons Learned to Date, Sixth Report of the Health and Social Care Committee and Third Report of the Science and Technology Committee of Session 2021–22', committees.parliament.uk/publications/7497/documents/78688/default/.

45. Irving Janis, *Groupthink* (Boston, MA, 1982). Cf. Patrick Dunleavy, 'How "groupthink" in Theresa May's Downing Street delivered another round of UK political chaos', *London School of Economics*, blog, 9 June 2017, blogs.lse.ac.uk/europpblog/2017/06/09/how-groupthink-in-theresa-mays-downing-street-delivered-another-round-of-uk-political-chaos/.

46. Frank Trentmann, *Empire of Things: How We Became a World of Consumers, from the Fifteenth Century to the Twenty-First* (London, 2016), p. 523.

47. Ibid.

48. Ibid.

49. Ibid., p. 527.

50. Various influential Western social scientists made assumptions about Japanese workers' natural propensity to groupthink, and their supposedly age-old willingness to sacrifice all for the collective cause. See Elson Boles, 'Ruth Benedict's Japan: The Benedictions of Imperialism', *Dialectical Anthropology*, 30:1/2 (2006), 27–70. Cf. Peter Mandler, *Return from the Natives: How Margaret Mead Won the Second World War and Lost the Cold War* (New Haven, 2013). For an example of such stereotypes, consider the following: 'Managers in the USA seem to seek activities that require high intellectual curiosity and adventurousness'; their Japanese counterparts by contrast, shaped by a culture where individuals subsume themselves in 'group-oriented' practices, value 'a sense of harmony', share in an enthusiasm for 'brainstorming', and reflect a general propensity to 'fusion'. See Paul Herbig and Laurence Jacobs, 'Creative Problem-Solving Styles in the USA and Japan', *International Marketing Review*, 13:2 (1996), 63–71.

51. See, for instance, Correlli Barnett, *The Audit of War: The Illusion and Reality of Britain as a Great Nation* (London, 1986).

52. This was a term that combined the names of two well-known Tory and Labour figures, Butler and Gaitskell, both of whom occupied the role of Chancellor of the Exchequer, and who thought, so critics complained, broadly alike. Later some proposed 'Blatcherism' (i.e. Thatcherism merged with Blairism).

53. Jamie Cohen-Cole, *The Open Mind: Cold War Politics and the Sciences of Human Nature* (Chicago, 2014).

54. Michael Williams, *Crisis and Consensus in British Politics: From Bagehot to Blair* (London, 2000), p. 20. Cf. Martin Jacques and Stuart Hall, *The Politics of Thatcherism* (London, 1983).

55. Naomi Klein, *The Shock Doctrine: The Rise of Disaster Capitalism* (London, 2007).

56. 'From plandemic to breadcrumbs: conspiracy-theory slang', *Economist*, 17 September 2020, www.economist.com/1843/2020/09/17/from-plandemic-to-breadcrumbs-conspiracy-theory-slang.

Part 5: Hidden Persuaders

1. Joseph Schumpeter, *Capitalism, Socialism and Democracy* [1942] (London, 2003), pp. 258, 283.

2. Ernest Dichter, 'Persuasion Started with Eve', *The Strategy of Desire* [1960] (New York, 1985), Part 1.

3. See Anat Rosenberg, 'The Market Enchanters: Mind Control in the History of Advertising', 14 May 2021, www7.bbk.ac.uk/hiddenpersuaders/blog/the-market-enchanters-mind-control-in-the-history-of-advertising/.

4. Christian Potschka, 'A Changing Society (1964–1979)', in *Towards a Market in Broadcasting: Communication Policy in the UK and Germany* (London, 2012), pp. 74–85.

5. There were precedents for such media monitoring; bodies were set up previously in a bid to put curbs on the public's exposure to salacious cinema, for example, and to set standards for radio too. An array of legislation in the United States (including the Radio Act of 1927) helped in the policing of who could transmit radio and what kind of material could be decently covered, and set limits on who would be licensed to run companies.

6. Ogilvy was renowned for his panache. He made a splash by having himself driven around New York in his Rolls-Royce. After he won the contract for advertising the Rolls-Royce vehicle in the late 1950s, he developed a campaign emphasising the luxury car maker's precision engineering, as well as its effortless and timeless sense of style. He came up with the headline, 'At 60 miles an hour the loudest noise in the new Rolls-Royce comes from the electric clock'. He regarded it as one of his best lines, only to find out it had been used in an earlier campaign for the Pierce-Arrow vehicle in an ad which had appeared in 1933. See Kenneth Roman, *The King of Madison Avenue: David Ogilvy and the Making of Modern Advertising* (London, 2010), p. 99. Cf. swiped. co/file/rolls-royce-ad-by-david-ogilvy/.

7. For example, the Clio awards, created in 1959, celebrate, as the organisers explain, 'bold work that propels the advertising industry forward, inspires a competitive marketplace of ideas and fosters meaningful connections within the creative community'. clios.com/awards. Other awards include those bestowed by Clutch, for the highest-ranking 'business-to business' (or 'b2b') companies now; clutch.co/leader-awards. For the AAF awards, see www.aaf. org/.

8. By the late 1950s, Dichter's business had an annual turnover of a million

dollars. See Stefan Schwarzkopf and Rainer Gries (eds), *Ernest Dichter and Motivation Research: The Making of Post-War Consumer Culture* (New York, 2010), p. 7.

9. Ibid., p. 4.

10. Vance Packard, *The Hidden Persuaders* [1957] (Harmondsworth, 1960), p. 31.

11. Michelle R. Nelson, 'The Hidden Persuaders, Then and Now', *Journal of Advertising*, 37:1 (2008), 113–26, p. 116; Daniel Horowitz, *Vance Packard and American Social Criticism* (Chapel Hill, 1994), pp. 1–10.

12. Nelson, 'The Hidden Persuaders, Then and Now', p. 116.

13. A 1998 report on production, sales and advertising found that California accounted for 99 per cent of US and 70 per cent of the world's supply. See Julian Alston et al., 'California Prune Board's Promotion Program: An Evaluation', Research Report Series (Berkeley, 1998), escholarship.org/uc/item/8kf3z8zp. The United States remains a major global exporter of prunes, although it is now faced with far more competition and a lower market share than before. 'Prune', data for June 2019, Tridge, www.tridge.com/products/prune. Cf. Sunsweet, 'Our Story', www.sunsweet.com/sunsweet-story/. Cf. Foodnews Editor, 'Sunsweet Appoints President', 5 October 2012, iegvu.agribusinessintelligence.informa.com/CO023359/Sunsweet-appoints-president.

14. For details of the US prune market and international competition today, see Alston et al., 'California Prune Board's Promotion Program'.

15. As one newspaper reported on the 1953 'new program' for prune commercials that year, 'this will be a stepped-up version of last year's advertising, again using full color ads in Sunday magazine newspaper supplements, four-color one sheet subway posters, strong local television shows, a morning radio newscast in San Francisco, regional and national grocery trade paper advertising, and ads in nationally distributed journals in the hotel, restaurant, hospital and dietetic fields. The campaign theme, based on Industry consumer research and a psychological consumer study conducted by Dr Ernest Dichter, will continue to drive home the story that prunes, California's Wonder Fruit, are good as well as healthful. The campaign technique will continue to be aimed at the younger market by using fresh, gay and colorful ads that will stimulate the purchase of prunes on a consistent basis. The advertising will also stress the ease of preparation and the variety of uses for prunes.' *Healdsburg Tribune, Enterprise and Scimitar*, 25 June 1953, p. 15, cdnc.ucr.edu/cgi-bin/cdnc?a=d&d=HTES19530625.2.152&e=-------en--20--1--txt-txIN--------1.

16. Packard, *The Hidden Persuaders*, p. 137. Emphasis added. For the context, Lawrence R. Samuel, *Freud on Madison Avenue: Motivation Research and Subliminal Advertising in America* (Philadelphia, 2010); Sean Nixon, *Advertising Cultures: Gender, Commerce, Creativity* (London, 2003); and idem, *Hard Sell: Advertising, Affluence and Transatlantic Relations, c. 1951–69* (Manchester, 2016).

17. Dichter described the connotations of the many foodstuffs and beverages that he worked on. The products described included rice, margarine, lamb,

eggs, coffee and milk (fresh or evaporated) as well as prunes. Ernest Dichter, *Handbook of Consumer Motivations: The Psychology of the World of Objects* (New York, 1964), pp. 59–60.

18. Packard, *The Hidden Persuaders*, p. 137.

19. Packard referred fleetingly to the racial connotations of the 'black' prune and commented on how that might vitiate its appeal. He remarked upon how this was sometimes countered by placing the product in pictures alongside white products, such as cottage cheese. *The Hidden Persuaders*, p. 138.

20. 'Let's Have a Prune Party', www.reddit.com/r/vintageads/comments/4p59r5/lets_have_a_prune_party_1958_california_prune/. Prune advertisers continue to wrestle with the dilemma of how best to sell the health benefits without alienating customers with direct references to bodily functions. In 1990, a campaign was based around a twelve-week-long run of US television commercials in which a magician performed sleight-of-hand tricks, to portray prunes as highly effective, and as containing *more* vitamins and minerals than other comparable dried fruits. Reviewing the success of that campaign, researchers found what might be called a 'sleeper effect'. The television advertisements increased prune sales more in the weeks after the series had concluded than during the period when they were shown. Deals and special coupons, which reduced the effective price paid by consumers, so they found, also notably increased the sales figures. Alston et al., 'California Prune Board's Promotion Program', pp. 48–51. In 2000, a further marketing plan came to fruition: the US Food and Drug Administration approved a name change from the still troubling designation 'prune' back to the alternative descriptor – dried plums. This apparently resulted the following year in a 5.5 per cent increase in sales. Analysts continue to study the impact of the precise wording, along with special offers, television advertisements, online prompts, and so on, to see what exact degree of price elasticity producers can play with before demand falls off again. The terms still vary; the prune has not been entirely erased in marketing by the maybe more palatable dried plum label. Diane Barrett et al., *Processing Fruits: Science and Technology*, 2nd edn (Boca Raton, 2005), p. 514.

21. Sunsweet TV commercials in the 1960s featured a sceptical overweight man in a chair complaining that prunes were wrinkled and a problem to eat because of the pits. The interlocutor in the advertisement then introduces him to the marvellous pit-free product, and the man before us, while munching the prune, changes his mind. See 'Vintage 1960s Prune Commercial – Finicky Prune Eater: Hates Wringled Prunes', YouTube, 7 March 2013, www.youtube.com/watch?v=7lpytcTqaAs.

22. Robert Griffith, 'The Selling of America: The Advertising Council and American Politics, 1942–1960', *Business History Review*, 57:3 (1983), 388–412, p. 403.

23. 'Harry S. Truman: 1952–53, containing the public messages, speeches, and statements of the president, January 1, 1952, to January 20, 1953. Collection: Public Papers of the Presidents of the United States', 370–74, p. 372, University

of Michigan Digital Library, quod.lib.umich.edu/p/ppotpus/4729044.1952.00
1/421?page=root;size=100;view=image.

24. 'Report of the Medical Officer of Health for Twickenham' [1956] (London,
1957), Wellcome Collection, wellcomelibrary.org/moh/report/
b19879349/6#?c=0&m=0&s=0&cv=6.

25. Economic expansion was notable and consistent in post-war decades.
Western European democracies achieved on average around 4 per cent
growth in GDP in the 1950s, and closer to 5 per cent in the 60s, compared
with 3 per cent in the 70s, and 2 per cent in the 80s. US growth rates went
higher than that: in 1955, for example, spiking at closer to 10 per cent. During
the later 1930s, the United States had also seen quite high growth figures, as
the New Deal injected vast sums, but this followed on years during the
depression when the economy shrank severely. GDP growth had been close
to -10 per cent in 1930, and -13 per cent in 1932. See Kimberly Amadeo, 'US
GDP by Year Compared to Recessions and Events: The Strange Ups and
Downs of the US Economy since 1929', *The Balance*, 28 April 2021, www.
thebalance.com/us-gdp-by-year-3305543.

On the 1950s and 60s, growth rates and how the benefits were widely if
never fully equitably spread, see Stephen A. Marglin and Juliet B. Schor (eds),
The Golden Age of Capitalism: Reinterpreting the Postwar Experience (Oxford,
1990), p. 1. See also 'GDP growth (annual %), 1961–2020', The World Bank,
data.worldbank.org/indicator/NY.GDP.MKTP.KD.ZG?locations=US. Cf. 'US
GDP Growth Rate by Year', US Bureau of Economic Analysis, [n.d.], www.
multpl.com/us-gdp-growth-rate/table/by-year.

26. Nelson, 'The Hidden Persuaders, Then and Now', p. 114; Vaclav Smil, *Made in
the USA: The Rise and Retreat of American Manufacturing* (Cambridge, MA,
2013), p. 94.

27. Packard, *The Hidden Persuaders*, Chapter 15, 'The Psycho-Seduction of
Children'.

28. Cited by Nelson, 'The Hidden Persuaders, Then and Now', p. 126.

29. Packard, *The Hidden Persuaders*, p. 32.

30. Ibid., p. 240.

31. See Friedan on 'the sexual sell', *The Feminine Mystique* (New York, 1963),
pp. 166–89.

32. Ibid., pp. 218–19.

33. Steve Craig, 'Madison Avenue versus *The Feminine Mystique*: How the
Advertising Industry Responded to the Onset of the Modern Women's
Movement: A Paper Presented at the Popular Culture Association
Conference (1997)', online at ruby.fgcu.edu/courses/tdugas/ids3301/acrobat/
womensmovement.pdf. For some legacies of this earlier feminist activism
against the advertising industry, see Jessica Ringrose and Kaitlyn Regehr,
'Feminist Counterpublics and Public Feminisms: Advancing a Critique of
Racialized Sexualization in London's Public Advertising', *Signs*, 46:1 (2020),
229–57.

34. The transcript is in the Vance Packard Papers, Penn State, University Library, Special Collections, Box 21, Folder 15, 'TV-Radio, 1957–58'.

35. This was perhaps intended as a reference to a popular Hollywood film of 1956, *The Man in the Gray Flannel Suit*. It starred Gregory Peck, and explored in a critical light, *inter alia*, the corporate world, public relations, careerism and consumerism.

36. 'Every psychologist will tell you that "psycho-seduction" is a natural process which starts on the very first day of the child's life.' Ernest Dichter, 'Persuasion: To What End?', *Motivations*, June 1957, p. 15. Cf. Dichter, 'Buying Is an Expression of Creativeness', in *The Strategy of Desire*, p. 170.

37. On this problematic form of measure, see *Trust: The Making and Breaking of Cooperative Relations*, edited by Diego Gambetta (Oxford, 1988); cf. Joseph Hamm, Corwin Smidt and Roger C. Mayer, 'Understanding the Psychological Nature and Mechanisms of Trust', *PlosOne*, 15 May 2019, journals.plos.org/plosone/article?id=10.1371/journal.pone.0215835. See also Mike Wendling, 'The (almost) complete history of "fake news"', BBC News, 22 January 2018, www.bbc.co.uk/news/blogs-trending-42724320; and OECD, 'Trust in government, policy effectiveness and the governance agenda', in *Government at a Glance 2013* (Paris 2013), p. 25, doi.org/10.1787/gov_glance-2013-6-en.

38. adassoc.org.uk/our-work-category/trust-in-advertising/.

39. Alfonso J. Damico, M. Margaret Conway and Sandra Bowman Damico, 'Patterns of Political Trust and Mistrust: Three Moments in the Lives of Democratic Citizens', *Polity*, 32:3 (2000), 377–400, p. 384. See also Bradley Greenberg and Edwin Parker (eds), *The Kennedy Assassination and the American Public: Social Communication in Crisis* (Stanford, 1965).

40. 'Letter from Mrs Mary C. McCree', 1 December 1957, 'Samples of Reader Mail', Packard Papers, Box 21, Folder 6.

41. Letter dated August 1957, 'Samples of Reader Mail', Packard Papers, Box 21, Folder 10.

42. 'Letter from Robert Roffler', 27 October 1960, 'Samples of Reader Mail', Packard Papers, Box 21, Folder 5.

43. Letter dated 2 February 1959, 'Samples of Reader Mail', Packard Papers, Box 21, Folder 5.

44. See Packard, *The Hidden Persuaders*, Chapter 3.

45. 'Jane Mayer, New York City', undated letter, 'Samples of Reader Mail', Packard Papers, Box 21, Folder 5.

46. Rory Sutherland, vice chairman at Ogilvy, has remarked upon how he grew up on Packard's work. *The Hidden Persuaders* helped motivate him to enter the field. Paul Feldwick, another prominent British advertising executive and writer on advertising, told me the same. Personal communications to the author, respectively in June 2018 and July 2017.

47. 'Letter from R. H. Birch', 10 October 1963, 'Samples of Reader Mail', Packard Papers, Box 21, Folder 6.

48. 'The Art of Persuasion', radio transcript, Packard Papers, Box 21, Folder 15, 'TV-Radio, 1957–58'.

49. Quoted in Streatfeild, *Brainwash*, p. 193.

50. Ibid. These frightening ideas about irresistible brainwashing through the enforced viewing of rapidly changing screen images were also taken up in notable stories and movies, ranging from *A Clockwork Orange* to *The Parallax View*.

51. Streatfeild, *Brainwash*, p. 193.

52. See the account in Packard's lecture entitled 'The Picture Persuaders'; Packard Papers, Box 21, Folder 14, pp. 16–18.

53. I draw here on the discussion of this image in August Bullock, *The Secret Sales Pitch: An Overview of Subliminal Selling* (San Jose, 2004), pp. 12–14.

54. Robert Heath and Paul Feldwick, 'Fifty Years Using the Wrong Model of Advertising', *International Journal of Market Research*, 50:1 (2008), 29–59. Cf. Rory Sutherland, 'Reliable Signals in a Post-Truth World', Barb, 27 April 2017, www.barb.co.uk/viewing-report/reliable-signals-in-a-post-truth-world/.

55. Packard, *The Hidden Persuaders*, p. 32.

56. In a later edition, Packard's publishers seized on this phrase (from a *New Yorker* review of *The Hidden Persuaders*), for promotional purposes: 'A brisk, authoritative and frightening report on how manufacturers, fundraisers and politicians are attempting to turn the American mind into a kind of catatonic dough that will buy, give or vote at their command.'

57. Elihu Katz and Paul Lazarsfeld, *Personal Influence: The Part Played by People in the Flow of Mass Communications* (New York, 1955). See also Peter Simonson, 'Politics, Social Networks, and the History of Mass Communications Research: Rereading Personal Influence', *Annals of the American Academy of Political and Social Science*, 608 (November 2006), 6–24.

58. Freud, *The Interpretation of Dreams*, 1900, in *The Standard Edition of the Complete Psychological Works of Sigmund Freud* (London, 1953), vols 4 and 5.

59. Bernays' influential work *Public Relations* appeared in 1945; see also his earlier studies, *Crystallizing Public Opinion* [1923] (New York, 1926) and *Propaganda* [1928] (New York, 2004).

60. Bernays, *Propaganda*, pp. 38–9, 17–20.

61. Margaret Scammell, *Designer Politics: How Elections Are Won* (Houndmills, 1995), p. 2. See also *Election Posters Around the Globe: Political Campaigning in the Public Space* (Cham, 2017), edited by Christina Holtz-Bacha and Bengt Johansson, especially the Introduction and pp. 339–60.

62. Claude Robinson's prediction, at the American Advertising Federation in 1958, cited by Nelson, 'The Hidden Persuaders, Then and Now', p. 115.

63. Quoted in Natasha Singer, 'Making Ads That Whisper to the Brain', *The New York Times*, 13 November 2010, www.nytimes.com/2010/11/14/business/14stream.html.

64. Roger Dooley et al., 'Neuromarketing', *Neuroscience Marketing*, www.neurosciencemarketing.com/blog/companies/neurofocus.

65. Quoted in Singer, 'Making Ads That Whisper to the Brain'. Cf. A. K Pradeep, *The Buying Brain: Secrets for Selling to the Unconscious Mind* (Hoboken, 2010).

66. Baudrillard singled out Packard's notable work and cited Dichter. Jean Baudrillard, *The System of Objects* [1968] (London, 1997), p. 164.

67. Baudrillard, *The Consumer Society: Myths and Structures* (London, 1970), p. 46.

68. Baudrillard, *The System of Objects*, pp. 152–3.

69. Jill Lepore, 'How the Simulmatics Corporation Invented the Future', *New Yorker*, 27 July 2020, www.newyorker.com/magazine/2020/08/03/how-the-simulmatics-corporation-invented-the-future. See also Lepore, *If Then: How Simulmatics Invented the Future* (New York, 2020).

70. Quoted in Lepore, 'How the Simulmatics Corporation Invented the Future'. See also David Haven Blake, *Liking Ike: Eisenhower, Advertising, and the Rise of Celebrity Politics* (Oxford, 2016).

71. Ithiel de Sola Pool and Robert Abelson, 'The Simulmatics Project', *Public Opinion Quarterly*, 25:2 (1961), 167–83.

72. Thomas J. Carty, *A Catholic in the White House? Religion, Politics and John F. Kennedy's Presidential Campaign* (New York, 2004); Shaun A. Casey, *The Making of a Catholic President: Kennedy vs. Nixon, 1960* (Oxford, 2009).

73. Quoted in Lepore, 'How the Simulmatics Corporation Invented the Future'.

74. Scott Shane and Sheera Frenkel, 'Russian 2016 Influence Operation Targeted African-Americans on Social Media', *The New York Times*, 17 December 2018, www.nytimes.com/2018/12/17/us/politics/russia-2016-influence-campaign.html.

75. See, for instance, Ian Failes, '"I felt like it was a poem": the VFX oral history of Guinness "Surfer"', 18 March 2019, beforesandafters.com/2019/03/18/guinness-surfer-oral-history-vfx/.

76. See Gerry Bowler, *Santa Claus: A Biography* (Toronto, 2005).

77. Jade Bremner, 'Coca-Cola faces backlash over seminar asking staff to "be less white"', *Independent*, 24 February 2021, www.independent.co.uk/life-style/coca-cola-racism-robin-diangelo-coke-b1806122.html.

78. Eilidh Nuala Duffy, 'Benetton's Most Controversial Campaigns', *Vogue*, 8 December 2017, www.vogue.co.uk/gallery/benettons-best-advertising-campaigns.

79. Thomas Dichter, 'The Intrusiveness Of Internet Advertising: The Not So Hidden Persuaders', *Forbes*, 11 March 2019, www.forbes.com/sites/thomasdichter/2019/03/11/the-intrusiveness-of-internet-advertising-the-not-so-hidden-persuaders/#350b2b142c18.

80. For example, consider the backlash against the Swiss company Nestlé's selling of artificial milk in Africa and Latin America. A boycott campaign against Nestlé gained traction in the 1970s. Charities such as War on Want referred to the company as 'baby killers', and the very brand behind the milk was tarnished. An angry paediatrician, cited in a hard-hitting War on Want report of 1974, put it like this: 'unaffordable, high-status, processed milks have been thrust upon unprepared communities. These high-pressure advertising campaigns employ all available channels and media making use of modern

techniques of motivation and persuasion. In some places firms employ "milk nurses" to make home visits and to attend clinics to promote sales further.' War on Want, *The Baby Killer*, pamphlet, 1974, archive.babymilkaction.org/ pdfs/babykiller.pdf.

81. Peter Adams, 'Fail of the Year: Pepsi's "Jump In"', *Marketing Dive*, 4 December 2017, www.marketingdive.com/news/fail-of-the-year-pepsis-jump-in/510322/.

82. See, for instance, 'Global Trust in Advertising: Winning Strategies for an Evolving Media Landscape', Nielsen report, September 2015, www.nielsen. com/wp-content/uploads/sites/3/2019/04/global-trust-in-advertising-report-sept-2015-1.pdf and 'Millennials Are Most Trusting When it Comes to Advertising', 13 October 2015, www.nielsen.com/uk/en/insights/article/ 2015/millennials-are-most-trusting-when-it-comes-to-advertising/. Cf. Osnat Roth-Cohen, Hananel Rosenberg and Sabina Lissitsa, 'Are you talking to me? Generation X, Y, Z responses to mobile advertising', *Convergence: The International Journal of Research into New Media Technologies*, October 2021, journals.sagepub.com/doi/full/10.1177/13548565211047342.

83. Kristen Herhold, 'How Consumers View Advertising: 2017 Survey', Clutch, 7 December 2017, clutch.co/agencies/resources/how-consumers-view-advertising-survey-2017.

84. Wally Olins, *On Brand* (London, 2012), Chapter 1, 'Why brands are important to customers'.

85. www.gamblingcommission.gov.uk/statistics-and-research/publication/ understanding-how-consumers-engaged-with-gambling-advertising-in-2020.

86. Sarah Milov, *The Cigarette: A Political History* (Cambridge, MA, 2019).

87. See for instance this article, published on the website of the Heartland Institute (one of the many enterprises the Koch Brothers funded), entitled 'Pseudo Scientists Wreak Havoc on Society's Mental Stability with Fake Data'. It claimed the public are brainwashed to worry about what is happening to the glaciers, oceans, forests and deserts. All this 'hysterical news', the author declared, was the thing that was making people seriously ill: 'The excessive social media coverage and exposure to climate and weather-related natural disasters can result in any number of mental health consequences including anxiety, depression and post-traumatic stress disorder.' Ronald Stein, 'Pseudo Scientists …', 29 October 2019, Heartland Institute, www.heartland.org/news-opinion/news/pseudo-scientists-wreak-havoc-on-societys-mental-stability-with-fake-data. Cf. Jane Mayer, 'Daily Comment: "Kochland" Examines the Koch Brothers' Early, Crucial Role in Climate-Change Denial', *New Yorker*, 13 August 2019, www.newyorker.com/ news/daily-comment/kochland-examines-how-the-koch-brothers-made-their-fortune-and-the-influence-it-bought.

88. See the 'Report of the Independent Expert Drafting Panel for the Legal Definition of Ecocide', June 2021, www.stopecocide.earth/expert-drafting-panel. See also ecocidelaw.com/independent-expert-drafting-panel/.

89. Shoshana Zuboff, *The Age of Surveillance Capitalism: The Fight for a Human Future at the New Frontier of Power* (New York, 2019), pp. 6–8.

90. Ibid., p. 8.

91. 'How Safe Is Thy Castle?', Packard Papers, Box 34, Folder 7.

92. Zygmunt Bauman, personal written communication to the author, 3 April 2015. He also develops this image in a subsequent interview recorded with the author; see Lily Ford's film *Onlining*, and the filmed interview with Bauman, at www7.bbk.ac.uk/hiddenpersuaders/.

Part 6: The Paranoid Style

1. Luke Mogelson, 'Among the Insurrectionists', *New Yorker*, 15 January 2021, www.newyorker.com/magazine/2021/01/25/among-the-insurrectionists.

2. Frida Ghitis, 'QAnon is an American invention, but it has become a global plague', *Washington Post*, 10 March 2021, www.washingtonpost.com/opinions/2021/03/10/qanon-japan-germany-colombia-conspiracy-theories-disinformation/.

3. James Shanahan, 'Support for QAnon is hard to measure – and polls may overestimate it', *The Conversation*, 5 March 2021, theconversation.com/support-for-qanon-is-hard-to-measure-and-polls-may-overestimate-it-156020.

4. Tom Dreisbach, 'Alex Jones still sells supplements on Amazon despite bans from other platforms', NPR, 24 March 2021, www.npr.org/2021/03/24/979362593/alex-jones-still-sells-supplements-on-amazon-despite-bans-from-other-platforms; 'Twitter's algorithm favours right-leaning politics, research finds', BBC News, 22 October 2021, www.bbc.co.uk/news/technology-59011271; Arash Massoudi et al., 'Hedge funds make millions as shares in Trump media Spac jump', *Financial Times*, 21 October 2021, www.ft.com/content/d266e746-27af-46c8-a6d9-4081cfe3cc00.

5. Long after the organisation withered, folklore continued, suggesting how the Illuminati were intent upon the destruction of all religion and government, hell-bent on instilling a libertine philosophy, destroying property and orchestrating a global criminal underworld. Hofstadter noted how various prelates by the end of the eighteenth century were ratcheting up their language, warning that the Illuminati were hatching 'plans for making a tea that caused abortion – a secret substance that "blinds or kills when spurted in the face", and a device that sounds like a stench bomb – a "method for filling a bedchamber with pestilential vapours"'. Stories still swarm online. The secret society has been suspected of all kinds of conspiracies, from the toppling of the French monarchy to JFK's killing, from 9/11 to the orchestration of the global illegal drugs business, pandemics, and more. Richard Hofstadter, 'The Paranoid Style in American Politics' (1964), harpers.org/archive/1964/11/the-paranoid-style-in-american-politics/.

For the history of the Illuminati, see Isabel Hernández, 'Meet the Man Who Started the Illuminati', *National Geographic*, July/August 2016, www.nationalgeographic.com/history/magazine/2016/07-08/profile-adam-weishaupt-illuminati-secret-society/. Cf. Gordon Fraser, 'Conspiracy,

Pornography, Democracy: The Recurrent Aesthetics of the American Illuminati', *Journal of American Studies*, 12 November 2018, www.cambridge. org/core/journals/journal-of-american-studies/article/conspiracy-pornography-democracy-the-recurrent-aesthetics-of-the-american-illuminati /906DDB8C8B609BFC4FD7FA7233D570DC. See also Jonathan White, 'Political Eschatology: A Theology of Antigovernmental Extremism', *American Behavioral Scientist*, 44:6 (February 2001), 937–56.

6. eu.usatoday.com/story/news/nation/2021/01/09/jake-angeli-qanon-man-fur-hat-horns-capitol-riot-arrested/6609039002/.

7. Quoted in 'Bilderberg mystery: Why do people believe in cabals?', BBC News, 8 June 2011, www.bbc.co.uk/news/magazine-13682082. Cf. Josh Sanburn, 'What to Know About the Bilderberg Group's Secret Annual Meeting', *Time*, 9 June 2016, time.com/4362872/bilderberg-group-meetings-2016-conspiracy-theories/.

8. Victoria Gagliardo-Silver, 'Alex Jones: Instagram refuses to remove right-wing conspiracy theorist's anti-semitic post', *Independent*, 29 March 2019, www. independent.co.uk/news/world/americas/alex-jones-ig-antisemitism-instagram-facebook-conspiracy-theories-a8846466.html.

9. R. Po-chia Hsia, *The Myth of Ritual Murder: Jews and Magic in Reformation Germany* (New Haven, 1988).

10. Long after it was first confected in Russia, and then appeared in 1903, *The Protocols of the Elders of Zion* served in many accounts of global Jewish plots. See Norman Cohn, *Warrant for Genocide: The Myth of the Jewish World-Conspiracy and the Protocols of the Elders of Zion* (New York, 1966); and Daniel Pipes, *Conspiracy: How the Paranoid Style Flourishes and Where It Comes From* (New York, 1997). On the fictional sources of that text, and the swirl of speculation, often inaccurate, about its provenance, see Michael Hagemeister, 'The *Protocols of the Elders of Zion*: Between History and Fiction', *New German Critique*, 103 (Winter 2008), 83–95.

11. Kevin Roose, 'What Is QAnon, the Viral Pro-Trump Conspiracy Theory?', *The New York Times*, 3 September 2021, www.nytimes.com/article/what-is-qanon.html.

12. Joe Sommerlad, '"Bye Q, I can't talk to you any more": What next for Alex Jones, America's foremost conspiracy theorist?', *Independent*, 23 March 2021, www.independent.co.uk/news/world/americas/us-politics/alex-jones-trump-qanon-capitol-b1799038.html.

13. See Ernesto Laclau, *On Populist Reason* (London, 2005).

14. Fredrick Kunkle, 'Trump supporter in horns and fur is charged in Capitol riot', *Washington Post*, 9 January 2021, www.washingtonpost.com/local/jacob-chansely-horn-qanon-capitol-riot/2021/01/09/5d3c2c96-52b9-11eb-bda4-615aaefd0555_story.html.

15. The Merriam-Webster Dictionary offers 1871 as a first occasion for the term 'conspiracy theory' in the United States; the OED, 1909. 'Conspiracy theorist' evolved from a description of a person who happened to have a view about conspiracy, to a type of ultra-suspicious personality, intent upon unearthing

plots. See Andrew McKenzie-McHarg, 'Conspiracy Theory: The Nineteenth-Century Prehistory of a Twentieth-Century Concept', in Joseph Uscinski (ed.), *Conspiracy Theories and the People Who Believe Them* (Oxford, 2018), Chapter 4. On conspiracy theory, see also Timothy Melley, *Empire of Conspiracy: The Culture of Paranoia in Postwar America* (Ithaca, 2000); Michael Barkun, *A Culture of Conspiracy: Apocalyptic Visions in Contemporary America* (Berkeley, 2003); Pipes, *Conspiracy*; and David Aaronovitch, *Voodoo Histories: The Role of the Conspiracy Theory in Shaping Modern History* (London, 2009). For recent studies of Russia, Latin America and the Middle East, see the special issue on conspiracy theory, *Russian Review*, 71:4 (2012); Luis Roniger and Leonardo Senkman, *Conspiracy Theories and Latin American History: Lurking in the Shadows* (London, 2021); and Matthew Gray, 'Conspiracy Theories in the Middle East', in *Routledge Handbook of Conspiracy Theories*, edited by Michael Butter and Peter Knight (London, 2020).

16. Michael Golebiewski and danah boyd, 'Data Voids: Where Missing Data Can Easily Be Exploited' (2019), datasociety.net/wp-content/uploads/2019/11/Data-Voids-2.0-Final.pdf.

17. Matt Burgess, 'A new type of Bill Gates conspiracy theory is going viral on Facebook', *Wired*, 9 April 2021, www.wired.co.uk/article/bill-gates-conspiracy-theory-arabic.

18. ABC News reported how Albert Watkins, the St Louis lawyer representing Chansley, had 'likened the process to brainwashing or falling into the clutches of a cult'. See 'Capitol Hill rioter "QAnon Shaman" to argue he was brainwashed by online cult, as lawyer plans "dumbass" defence', 31 May 2021, www.abc.net.au/news/2021-05-31/capitol-hill-rioters-claim-to-be-brainwashed-donald-trump-fox/100177896. In November 2021 the verdict came: that argument was (predictably) not accepted by the court; Chansley was sentenced to forty-one months in prison followed by thirty-six months of supervised release.

19. Jan Wolfe, '"QAnon Shaman" lawyer says all Americans had a role in U.S. Capitol riot', Reuters, 22 June 2021, www.reuters.com/world/us/qanon-shaman-lawyer-says-all-americans-had-role-us-capitol-riot-2021-06-22/.

20. Even the 'fall' of China in 1949, Senator McCarthy insisted, was the outcome of a plot hatched ultimately in the United States; a conspiracy 'so immense', he added, 'as to dwarf any previous such venture in the history of man'. (sourcebooks.fordham.edu/mod/1951mccarthy-marshall.asp). It was an article of faith for many right-wing commentators, post-war, that the Chinese Revolution required the contribution of American traitors; it could not reflect only the toppled nationalist government's declining support, and the growing popularity of Mao. See David Brion Davis (ed.), *The Fear of Conspiracy: Images of Un-American Subversion from the Revolution to the Present* (Ithaca, 1971), p. 265. In his 'Paranoid Style' essay, Hofstadter also noted the role played by the Far-Right racist candy manufacturer and conspiracy theorist, Robert Welch, who established the John Birch Society in 1958. That organisation sought to represent aggrieved white people who felt they were

owed the restoration of former privileges, entitlements and glories, not the continuing advance of civil rights for people of colour. (Welch might well have appreciated Trump's slogan: not just 'make America great', but make it great 'again' – *for them*.)

21. Daniel Rogers, *Age of Fracture* (Cambridge, MA, 2011). What happened to Kennedy in Dallas on 22 November 1963 added a new raft of conspiracy theories that have continued to shape and intensify mass mistrust in government over the last sixty years. Was Lee Harvey Oswald 'brainwashed' in Russia, or were millions of people persuaded by forces deep in the state (or abroad) erroneously to see him as the culprit, when really he was the 'patsy', as he insisted? Was the Warren Report into the assassination not only wrong, but perversely misleading? Could even the Zapruder film of the moment of death have been manipulated by the security services? There is a vast literature on this topic. One of the best studies I've read on JFK and conspiracy is Art Simon, *Dangerous Knowledge: The JFK Assassination in Art and Film* (Philadelphia, 1996). Other notable studies that explore shifts in conspiracy theory and discuss contemporary and future social trends, and outlooks for politics, include Mark Fenster, *Conspiracy Theories: Secrecy and Power in American Culture* (Minneapolis, 1999); George Marcus (ed.), *Paranoia Within Reason: A Casebook on Conspiracy as Explanation* (Chicago, 1999); and Melley, *Empire of Conspiracy*.

22. Gerstle, *American Crucible*, p. 243. See also www.psychiatry.org/newsroom/goldwater-rule and psychnews.psychiatryonline.org/doi/full/10.1176%2Fpn.42.10.0002.

23. On liberalism, neoliberalism, social justice and anti-democratic politics, see Michael Sandel, *Liberalism and the Limits of Justice* (Cambridge, 1982); and idem, *The Tyranny of Merit: What's Become of the Common Good?* (London, 2020); Katrina Forrester, *In the Shadow of Justice: Postwar Liberalism and the Remaking of Political Philosophy* (Princeton, 2019); Wendy Brown, *Undoing the Demos: Neoliberalism's Stealth Revolution* (New York, 2015); and idem, *In the Ruins of Neoliberalism: The Rise of Antidemocratic Politics in the West* (New York, 2019).

24. See the survey (commissioned by a Cambridge University research project, on conspiracy and democracy) conducted by YouGov in 2018 on the scale of belief in conspiracy theory in the United States, the UK and various European states, www.crassh.cam.ac.uk/programmes/conspiracy-democracy. See also this summary of the report in the *Guardian*, Esther Addley, 'Study shows 60% of Britons believe in conspiracy theories', 23 November 2018, www.theguardian.com/society/2018/nov/23/study-shows-60-of-britons-believe-in-conspiracy-theories.

25. Mark O'Connell, 'Why Silicon Valley billionaires are prepping for the apocalypse in New Zealand', *Guardian*, 15 February 2018, www.theguardian.com/news/2018/feb/15/why-silicon-valley-billionaires-are-prepping-for-the-apocalypse-in-new-zealand.

26. The defence official and military analyst Daniel Ellsberg, who made this leak,

became a famous model whistle-blower for others such as Edward Snowden later to emulate. The Pentagon Papers revealed much about policy in Vietnam and laid bare the total bankruptcy of official pronouncements about the scale and consequences of the conflict during the 1960s. Prior to Arendt's account, a book had appeared providing an overview of this story; Neil Sheehan et al., *The Pentagon Papers: The Secret History of the Vietnam War* (New York, 1971).

27. Hannah Arendt, *Crises of the Republic: Lying in Politics, Civil Disobedience, On Violence, Thoughts on Politics and Revolution* (New York, 1972).

28. Ibid., p. 6.

29. Ibid., p. 7.

30. Arendt thought that while the French Revolution had long been seen as the key to revolution everywhere (even though it failed, or rather led to new kinds of dictatorship), the American Revolution had been treated as a unique case, or at least as a case that was hard to replicate. She noted the massive contradiction of a land of liberty that also was built on slavery, but she wanted to return our attention to the ideals, nonetheless, of the founding fathers. She thought it was terrible that subsequent generations of Americans, after the creation of the Republic, were not sufficiently encouraged to continue *thinking* about their revolution and adequately conceptualising the experience. See Arendt, 'The Freedom to Be Free' [1966–7], *New England Review*, 38:2 (2017), 56–69.

31. Arendt wrote in 'The Freedom to Be Free' that Adams was 'entirely right when he said that "the revolution was effected before the war commenced," not because of a specifically revolutionary or rebellious spirit, but because the inhabitants of the colonies were "formed by law into corporations, or bodies politic" with the "right to assemble … in their own town halls, there to deliberate upon public affairs," … [Adams's] point of departure is the observation that "Wherever men, women, or children are to be found, whether they be old or young, rich or poor, high or low … ignorant or learned, every individual is seen to be strongly actuated by a desire to be seen, heard, talked of, approved and respected by the people about him and within his knowledge."' Arendt added: 'This public freedom is a tangible worldly reality, created by men to enjoy together in public – to be seen, heard, known, and remembered by others. And this kind of freedom demands equality, it is possible only among peers. Institutionally speaking, it is possible only in a republic, which knows no subjects and, strictly speaking, no rulers. This is the reason why discussions of the forms of government, in sharp contrast to later ideologies, played such an enormous role in the thinking and writing of the first revolutionaries.'

32. The argument that liberal democracy can serve as a mere facade for authoritarianism and for corporate capitalism has a long history. It was powerfully portrayed in dystopian literature, including during the 1960s, in novels such as Philip K. Dick's *The Simulacra* (1964). It has always been a staple of certain Marxist analyses. And since the 1990s, a range of political

commentators on the Left have offered new critiques of liberal democracy, challenging the view that communism must now be seen as defunct, irretrievable from Stalinism and the Gulag. They point to liberal illusions about politics, the shaky assumptions of basic consensus about the rules of the game, the limitations of notions of deliberative democracy, etc.

Although there is no single school of thought on such issues, especially influential examples of such critiques include writings by Antonio Negri, Alain Badiou, Slavoj Žižek, Ernesto Laclau, Chantal Mouffe and Jodi Dean. Any analysis here, however, would need to recognise important differences between their political arguments. Dean writes about the illusions perpetrated upon us in what she calls 'communicative capitalism'. This enables a constant theatre to occur online, an arena of endless subjective expressions, viewpoints, chatter, blogs, feeds, texts; or, as she puts it, the 'now quaint term from the dot.com years, mindshare'. This present-day system, Dean adds, instead of leading to more equitable distributions of wealth and influence, or the emergence of a richer variety in modes of living and practices of freedom, creates a 'deluge of screens and spectacles [that] undermines political opportunity and efficacy for most of the world's peoples'. See Jodi Dean, 'Theorizing Conspiracy Theory', *Theory & Event*, 4:3 (2000). See also idem, *Aliens in America: Conspiracy Cultures from Outerspace to Cyberspace* (Ithaca, 1998); *Publicity's Secret: How Technoculture Capitalizes on Democracy* (Ithaca, 2002); and *Democracy and Other Neoliberal Fantasies* (Durham, NC, 2009). Cf. Mark Fisher, *Postcapitalist Desire: The Final Lectures*, edited and introduced by Matt Colquhoun (London, 2021).

Complicating any traditional Marxist account today is the challenge of green politics and the realisation that we may have to face the end of models based upon economic 'growth'. See, for instance, George Monbiot, 'Capitalism is killing the planet – it's time to stop buying into our own destruction', *Guardian*, 30 October 2021, www.theguardian.com/environment/2021/oct/30/capitalism-is-killing-the-planet-its-time-to-stop-buying-into-our-own-destruction.

33. This is well described by journalist Gordon Corera in his 2021 five-part series, 'The Hack that Changed the World', BBC Radio 4, www.bbc.co.uk/programmes/m00114h2.

34. Jane Wakefield, 'Whistleblower breaks Facebook secrecy wall, MP says', BBC News, 6 October 2021, www.bbc.co.uk/news/technology-58816118.

35. Arendt pointed out Luxemburg's great anguish about this, and cited a private letter she had written, in the late summer of 1918, that included the lines: 'With the repression of political life in the land as a whole ... life dies out in every public institution, becoming a mere semblance of life, in which only the bureaucracy remains as the active element.' Quoted in 'The Freedom to Be Free', p. 20.

36. Steve Paulson, 'How Loneliness Can Lead to Totalitarianism', WPR, 11 April 2021, www.wpr.org/how-loneliness-can-lead-totalitarianism.

37. Anon, review of *The Promise of Politics* by Hannah Arendt, *Harvard Law Review*, 119:2 (December 2005), 639–45.

38. Hannah Arendt, 'Introduction *into* Politics', in *The Promise of Politics* (New York, 2005), edited by Jerome Kohn, pp. 93–200; see the Epilogue. Cf. Anon, 'review', p. 642.

39. The point was also made by the liberal intellectual Arthur Schlesinger Jr, in his defence of an open-ended democracy in *The Vital Center: The Politics of Freedom* (Boston, MA, 1949). He took from Freud the lesson that just as psychic conflict is inevitable, so societies are bound to face interminable tensions. Nonetheless, liberal democracy was the best means of holding society and the practice of thinking together. There could be no total cure for the psyche or for the polity. 'Problems will always torment us', Schlesinger wrote in his conclusion, 'because all important problems are insoluble: that is why they are important. The good comes from the continuing struggle to try to solve them, not from the vain hope of their solution … The totalitarians regard the toleration of conflict as our central weakness. So, it may appear to be in an age of anxiety. But we know it to be basically our central strength.'

40. These were most fully set out by Melanie Klein in 'A Contribution to the Psychogenesis of Manic-Depressive States', *International Journal of Psychoanalysis*, 16 (1935), 145–74, and 'Notes on Some Schizoid Mechanisms', *International Journal of Psychoanalysis*, 27 (1946), 99–110.

41. Wilfred Bion, *Attention and Interpretation* (London, 1970).

42. Lizzie Cain and Gemma Moore, 'Evaluation of Camden Council's Citizens' Assembly on the Climate Crisis', Report, December 2019, UCL, www.camden.gov.uk/documents/20142/0/FINAL+UCL+Evaluation+of+Camden+Council%27s+Citizens%27+Assembly+on+the+Climate+Crisis.pdf/e3f39960-76ce-111d-656b-6154465fc095?t=157979908150L1.

43. Tim Berners-Lee, 'I Invented the World Wide Web. Here's How We Can Fix It', *The New York Times*, 24 November 2019, www.nytimes.com/2019/11/24/opinion/world-wide-web.html.

44. Kate Pickett and Richard Wilkinson, *The Spirit Level: Why Equality is Better for Everyone* (London, 2010).

45. In her final paper, published posthumously in 1963, Klein suggested that, in the first instance, loneliness is the result of our infantile yearning for an unattainable perfect internal state. It springs, she thought, from the (often 'paranoid') anxieties we all deal with, in, and beyond, our infancies. People often face in life a deep unconscious dilemma: greater psychic integration requires bearing guilt, coping with mixed feelings; splitting and projection, by contrast, might temporarily deal with all that is 'bad', but leaves us lonely and empty. And '[s]ince full integration is never achieved, complete understanding of one's own emotions, anxieties and phantasies is not possible, and this continues as an important factor in loneliness'. 'On the Sense of Loneliness', *Envy and Gratitude, and Other Works, 1946–1963: The Writings of Melanie Klein* (London, 1975), vol 3, Chapter 16, p. 303.

46. Sally Weintrobe, *Psychological Roots of the Climate Crisis: Neoliberal Exceptionalism and the Culture of Uncare* (London, 2021).

47. Catherine Garcia, 'New book says Joint Chiefs chairman worried Trump would attempt a coup', *The Week*, 15 July 2021, theweek.com/politics/1002626/new-book-says-joint-chiefs-chairman-worried-trump-would-attempt-a-coup.

48. David Runciman, *How Democracy Ends* (London, 2018); Anne Applebaum, *The Twilight of Democracy: The Failure of Politics and the Parting of Friends* (London, 2020).

49. Applebaum, *Twilight of Democracy*.

50. Jacqueline Rose, *States of Fantasy* (Oxford, 1996).

INDEX

Page references for notes are followed by n